MW00811632

Religion, Ethnonationalism,
and Antisemitism in the Era of the
Two World Wars

McGill-Queen's Studies in the History of Religion

Volumes in this series have been supported by the Jackman Foundation of Toronto.

SERIES ONE G.A. Rawlyk, Editor

1 Small Differences
Irish Catholics and Irish Protestants,
1815–1922
An International Perspective
Donald Harman Akenson

2 Two Worlds
The Protestant Culture of Nineteenth-
Century Ontario
William Westfall

3 An Evangelical Mind
Nathanael Burwash and the Methodist
Tradition in Canada, 1839–1918
Marguerite Van Die

4 The Dévotes
Women and Church in Seventeenth-
Century France
Elizabeth Rapley

5 The Evangelical Century
College and Creed in English Canada
from the Great Revival to the Great
Depression
Michael Gauvreau

6 The German Peasants' War and
Anabaptist Community of Goods
James M. Stayer

7 A World Mission
Canadian Protestantism and the Quest
for a New International Order, 1918–1939
Robert Wright

8 Serving the Present Age
Revivalism, Progressivism, and the
Methodist Tradition in Canada
Phyllis D. Airhart

9 A Sensitive Independence
Canadian Methodist Women Missionaries
in Canada and the Orient, 1881–1925
Rosemary R. Gagan

10 God's Peoples
Covenant and Land in South Africa,
Israel, and Ulster
Donald Harman Akenson

11 Creed and Culture
The Place of English-Speaking Catholics
in Canadian Society, 1750–1930
Edited by Terrence Murphy and
Gerald Stortz

12 Piety and Nationalism
Lay Voluntary Associations and the
Creation of an Irish-Catholic Community
in Toronto, 1850–1895
Brian P. Clarke

13 Amazing Grace
Studies in Evangelicalism in Australia,
Britain, Canada, and the United States
Edited by George Rawlyk and
Mark A. Noll

14 Children of Peace
W. John McIntyre

15 A Solitary Pillar
Montreal's Anglican Church and the
Quiet Revolution
Joan Marshall

16 Padres in No Man's Land
Canadian Chaplains and the Great War
Duff Crerar

17 Christian Ethics and Political Economy
in North America
A Critical Analysis
P. Travis Kroeker

18 Pilgrims in Lotus Land
Conservative Protestantism in British
Columbia, 1917–1981
Robert K. Burkinshaw

19 Through Sunshine and Shadow
The Woman's Christian Temperance
Union, Evangelicalism, and Reform in
Ontario, 1874–1930
Sharon Cook

20 Church, College, and Clergy
A History of Theological Education at
Knox College, Toronto, 1844–1994
Brian J. Fraser

21 The Lord's Dominion
The History of Canadian Methodism
Neil Semple

22 A Full-Orbed Christianity
The Protestant Churches and Social Wel-
fare in Canada, 1900–1940
Nancy Christie and Michael Gauvreau

23 Evangelism and Apostasy
The Evolution and Impact of Evangelicals
in Modern Mexico
Kurt Bowen

24 The Chignecto Covenanters
A Regional History of Reformed
Presbyterianism in New Brunswick
and Nova Scotia, 1827–1905
Eldon Hay

25 Methodists and Women's Education
in Ontario, 1836–1925
Johanne Selles

26 Puritanism and Historical Controversy
William Lamont

SERIES TWO In memory of
George Rawlyk
Donald Harman Akenson, Editor

1 Marguerite Bourgeoys and Montreal,
1640–1665
Patricia Simpson

2 Aspects of the Canadian Evangelical
Experience
Edited by G.A. Rawlyk

3 Infinity, Faith, and Time
Christian Humanism and Renaissance
Literature
John Spencer Hill

4 The Contribution of Presbyterianism
to the Maritime Provinces of Canada
*Edited by Charles H.H. Scobie and
G.A. Rawlyk*

5 Labour, Love, and Prayer
Female Piety in Ulster Religious
Literature, 1850–1914
Andrea Ebel Brozyna

6 The Waning of the Green
Catholics, the Irish, and Identity in
Toronto, 1887–1922
Mark G. McGowan

7 Religion and Nationality in Western
Ukraine
The Greek Catholic Church and the
Ruthenian National Movement in Galicia,
1867–1900
John-Paul Himka

8 Good Citizens
British Missionaries and Imperial States,
1870–1918
*James G. Greenlee and
Charles M. Johnston*

9 The Theology of the Oral Torah
Revealing the Justice of God
Jacob Neusner

10 Gentle Eminence
A Life of Cardinal Flahiff
P. Wallace Platt

11 Culture, Religion, and Demographic
Behaviour
Catholics and Lutherans in Alsace,
1750–1870
Kevin McQuillan

12 Between Damnation and Starvation
Priests and Merchants in Newfoundland
Politics, 1745–1855
John P. Greene

13 Martin Luther, German Saviour
German Evangelical Theological Factions
and the Interpretation of Luther,
1917–1933
James M. Stayer

14 Modernity and the Dilemma of North
American Anglican Identities, 1880–1950
William H. Katerberg

15 The Methodist Church on the Prairies,
1896–1914
George Emery

16 Christian Attitudes towards the State
of Israel
Paul Charles Merkley

17 A Social History of the Cloister
Daily Life in the Teaching Monasteries
of the Old Regime
Elizabeth Rapley

18 Households of Faith
Family, Gender, and Community in
Canada, 1760–1969
Edited by Nancy Christie

19 Blood Ground
Colonialism, Missions, and the Contest
for Christianity in the Cape Colony and
Britain, 1799–1853
Elizabeth Elbourne

20 A History of Canadian Catholics
Gallicanism, Romanism, and
Canadianism
Terence J. Fay

21 The View from Rome
Archbishop Stagni's 1915 Reports on the
Ontario Bilingual Schools Question
Edited and translated by John Zucchi

22 The Founding Moment
Church, Society, and the Construction
of Trinity College
William Westfall

23 The Holocaust, Israel, and Canadian
Protestant Churches
Haim Genizi

24 Governing Charities
Church and State in Toronto's Catholic
Archdiocese, 1850–1950
Paula Maurutto

25 Anglicans and the Atlantic World
High Churchmen, Evangelicals, and the
Quebec Connection
Richard W. Vaudry

26 Evangelicals and the Continental Divide
The Conservative Protestant Subculture
in Canada and the United States
Sam Reimer

27 Christians in a Secular World
The Canadian Experience
Kurt Bowen

28 Anatomy of a Seance
A History of Spirit Communication in
Central Canada
Stan McMullin

29 With Skilful Hand
The Story of King David
David T. Barnard

30 Faithful Intellect
Samuel S. Nelles and Victoria University
Neil Semple

31 W. Stanford Reid
An Evangelical Calvinist in the Academy
Donald MacLeod

32 A Long Eclipse
The Liberal Protestant Establishment and
the Canadian University, 1920–1970
Catherine Gidney

33 Forkhill Protestants and Forkhill
Catholics, 1787–1858
Kyla Madden

34 For Canada's Sake
Public Religion, Centennial Celebrations,
and the Re-making of Canada in
the 1960s
Gary R. Miedema

35 Revival in the City
The Impact of American Evangelists in
Canada, 1884–1914
Eric R. Crouse

36 The Lord for the Body
Religion, Medicine, and Protestant Faith
Healing in Canada, 1880–1930
James Opp

37 Six Hundred Years of Reform
Bishops and the French Church,
1190–1789
*J. Michael Hayden and
Malcolm R. Greenshields*

38 The Missionary Oblate Sisters
Vision and Mission
Rosa Bruno-Jofré

39 Religion, Family, and Community
in Victorian Canada
The Colbys of Carrollcroft
Marguerite Van Die

40 Michael Power
The Struggle to Build the Catholic
Church on the Canadian Frontier
Mark G. McGowan

41 The Catholic Origins of Quebec's Quiet
Revolution, 1931–1970
Michael Gauvreau

42 Marguerite Bourgeoys and the Congregation of Notre Dame, 1665–1700
Patricia Simpson

43 To Heal a Fractured World
The Ethics of Responsibility
Jonathan Sacks

44 Revivalists
Marketing the Gospel in English Canada,
1884–1957
Kevin Kee

45 The Churches and Social Order in
Nineteenth- and Twentieth-Century
Canada
*Edited by Michael Gauvreau and
Ollivier Hubert*

46 Political Ecumenism
Catholics, Jews, and Protestants in
De Gaulle's Free France, 1940–1945
Geoffrey Adams

47 From Quaker to Upper Canadian
Faith and Community among Yonge
Street Friends, 1801–1850
Robynne Rogers Healey

48 The Congrégation de Notre-Dame,
Superiors, and the Paradox of Power,
1693–1796
Colleen Gray

49 Canadian Pentecostalism
Transition and Transformation
Edited by Michael Wilkinson

50 A War with a Silver Lining
Canadian Protestant Churches and the
South African War, 1899–1902
Gordon L. Heath

51 In the Aftermath of Catastrophe
Founding Judaism, 70 to 640
Jacob Neusner

52 Imagining Holiness
Classic Hasidic Tales in Modern Times
Justin Jaron Lewis

53 Shouting, Embracing, and Dancing
with Ecstasy
The Growth of Methodism in
Newfoundland, 1774–1874
Calvin Hollett

54 Into Deep Waters
Evangelical Spirituality and Maritime
Calvinist Baptist Ministers, 1790–1855
Daniel C. Goodwin

55 Vanguard of the New Age
The Toronto Theosophical Society,
1891–1945
Gillian McCann

56 A Commerce of Taste
Church Architecture in Canada, 1867–1914
Barry Magrill

57 The Big Picture
The Antigonish Movement of Eastern
Nova Scotia
Santo Dodaro and Leonard Pluta

58 My Heart's Best Wishes for You
A Biography of Archbishop John Walsh
John P. Comiskey

59 The Covenanters in Canada
Reformed Presbyterianism from 1820
to 2012
Eldon Hay

60 The Guardianship of Best Interests
Institutional Care for the Children of the
Poor in Halifax, 1850–1960
Renée N. Lafferty

61 In Defence of the Faith
Joaquim Marques de Araújo, a Comis-
sário in the Age of Inquisitional Decline
James E. Wadsworth

62 Contesting the Moral High Ground
Popular Moralists in Mid-Twentieth-
Century Britain
Paul T. Phillips

63 The Catholicisms of Coutances
Varieties of Religion in Early Modern
France, 1350–1789
J. Michael Hayden

64 After Evangelicalism
The Sixties and the United Church
of Canada
Kevin N. Flatt

65 The Return of Ancestral Gods
Modern Ukrainian Paganism as an
Alternative Vision for a Nation
Mariya Lesiv

66 Transatlantic Methodists
British Wesleyanism and the Formation of
an Evangelical Culture in Nineteenth-
Century Ontario and Quebec
Todd Webb

67 A Church with the Soul of a Nation
Making and Remaking the United Church
of Canada
Phyllis D. Airhart

68 Fighting over God
A Legal and Political History of Religious
Freedom in Canada
Janet Epp Buckingham

69 From India to Israel
Identity, Immigration, and the Struggle
for Religious Equality
Joseph Hodes

70 Becoming Holy in Early Canada
Timothy Pearson

71 The Cistercian Arts
From the 12th to the 21st Century
Edited by Terryl N. Kinder and
Roberto Cassanelli

72 The Canny Scot
Archbishop James Morrison of
Antigonish
Peter Ludlow

73 Religion and Greater Ireland
Christianity and Irish Global Networks,
1750–1950
Edited by Colin Barr and Hilary M. Carey

74 The Invisible Irish
Finding Protestants in the Nineteenth-
Century Migrations to America
Rankin Sherling

75 Beating against the Wind
Popular Opposition to Bishop Feild and
Tractarianism in Newfoundland and
Labrador, 1844–1876
Calvin Hollett

76 The Body or the Soul?
   Religion and Culture in a Quebec Parish,
   1736–1901
   Frank A. Abbott

77 Saving Germany
   North American Protestants and
   Christian Mission to West Germany,
   1945–1974
   James C. Enns

78 The Imperial Irish
   Canada's Irish Catholics Fight the Great
   War, 1914–1918
   Mark G. McGowan

79 Into Silence and Servitude
   How American Girls Became Nuns,
   1945–1965
   Brian Titley

80 Boundless Dominion
   Providence, Politics, and the Early
   Canadian Presbyterian Worldview
   Denis McKim

81 Faithful Encounters
   Authorities and American Missionaries
   in the Ottoman Empire
   Emrah Şahin

82 Beyond the Noise of Solemn Assemblies
   The Protestant Ethic and the Quest for
   Social Justice in Canada
   Richard Allen

83 Not Quite Us
   Anti-Catholic Thought in English Canada
   since 1900
   Kevin P. Anderson

84 Scandal in the Parish
   Priests and Parishioners Behaving Badly
   in Eighteenth-Century France
   Karen E. Carter

85 Ordinary Saints
   Women, Work, and Faith in
   Newfoundland
   Bonnie Morgan

86 Patriot and Priest
   Jean-Baptiste Volfius and the Constitu-
   tional Church in the Côte-d'Or
   Annette Chapman-Adisho

87 A.B. Simpson and the Making of Modern
   Evangelicalism
   Daryn Henry

88 The Uncomfortable Pew
   Christianity and the New Left in Toronto
   Bruce Douville

89 Berruyer's Bible
   Public Opinion and the Politics of
   Enlightenment Catholicism in France
   Daniel J. Watkins

90 Communities of the Soul
   A Short History of Religion in
   Puerto Rico
   José E. Igartua

91 Callings and Consequences
   The Making of Catholic Vocational
   Culture in Early Modern France
   Christopher J. Lane

92 Religion, Ethnonationalism, and
   Antisemitism in the Era of the
   Two World Wars
   *Edited by Kevin P. Spicer and
   Rebecca Carter-Chand*

RELIGION, ETHNONATIONALISM, AND ANTISEMITISM

IN THE ERA OF THE TWO WORLD WARS

Edited by
Kevin P. Spicer and Rebecca Carter-Chand

Published in association with the
United States Holocaust Memorial Museum
by
McGill-Queen's University Press
Montreal & Kingston • London • Chicago

ISBN 978-0-2280-0890-3 (cloth)
ISBN 978-0-2280-1020-3 (ePDF)
ISBN 978-0-2280-1021-0 (ePUB)

Legal deposit first quarter 2022
Bibliothèque nationale du Québec

Printed in Canada on acid-free paper that is 100% ancient forest free
(100% post-consumer recycled), processed chlorine free

Published in association with the United States Holocaust Memorial
Museum. The US Holocaust Memorial Museum's Jack, Joseph, and
Morton Mandel Center's mission is to ensure the long-term growth and
vitality of Holocaust studies. To do that, it is essential to provide opportunities for new generations of scholars. The vitality and the integrity of
Holocaust studies requires openness, independence, and free inquiry so
that new ideas are generated and tested through peer review and public
debate. The opinions of scholars expressed before, during the course of,
or after their activities with the Mandel Center do not represent and are
not endorsed by the museum or its Mandel Center.

Funded by the Government of Canada   Financé par le gouvernement du Canada   Canada   Canada Council for the Arts   Conseil des arts du Canada

We acknowledge the support of the Canada Council for the Arts.

Nous remercions le Conseil des arts du Canada de son soutien.

Library and Archives Canada Cataloguing in Publication

Title: Religion, ethnonationalism, and antisemitism in the era of the two
    world wars / edited by Kevin P. Spicer and Rebecca Carter-Chand.
Names: Spicer, Kevin P., 1965- editor. | Carter-Chand, Rebecca, editor.
Series: McGill-Queen's studies in ethnic history. Series two ; 92.
Description: Series statement: McGill-Queen's studies in ethnic history.
    Series two ; 92 | Includes bibliographical references and index.
Identifiers: Canadiana (print) 20210312416 | Canadiana (ebook)
    20210312475 | ISBN 9780228008903 (cloth) | ISBN 9780228010203 (ePDF)
    | ISBN 9780228010210 (ePUB)
Subjects: LCSH: Antisemitism—Europe—History—20th century. | LCSH:
    Nationalism—Europe—History—20th century. | LCSH: Ethnicity—
    Europe—History—20th century. | LCSH: Religion and politics—
    Europe—History—20th century. | LCSH: Europe—Ethnic relations—
    History—20th century.

Classification: LCC DS146.E85 R45 2022 | DDC 305.892/404—dc23

Contents

Figures xi
Acknowledgments xiii

Introduction 3
Kevin P. Spicer, CSC, and Rebecca Carter-Chand

PART ONE
Theorizing Religion, Ethnonationalism, and Antisemitism

1 Adopting the Swastika: George E. Deatherage and the American
Nationalist Confederation, 1937–1942 23
Charles R. Gallagher, SJ

2 Transnational Antisemitic Networks and Political Christianity:
The Catholic Participation in *The Protocols of the Elders of Zion* 48
Nina Valbousquet

3 Julius Evola and the "Jewish Problem" in Axis Europe: Race, Religion,
and Antisemitism 72
Peter Staudenmaier

PART TWO
Supporting Ethnonationalist Efforts

4 German Catholicism's Lost Opportunity to Confront Antisemitism
before the Machtergreifung 95
Kevin P. Spicer, CSC

5 The Fate of John's Gospel during the Third Reich 121
Susannah Heschel and Shannon Quigley

6 Nationalism and Religious Bonds: Transatlantic Religious
   Communities in Nazi Germany and the United States 151
   Rebecca Carter-Chand

7 "Often you end up asking yourself, could there be a great secret
   group of Jews behind it all." – Antisemitism in the Finnish Lutheran
   Church after the First World War 174
   Paavo Ahonen and Kirsi Stjerna

8 "The Converts Were Just Delighted": Dynamics of Religious Conversion as a Tool of Genocide in the Independent State of Croatia 209
   Danijel Matijević

PART THREE
Critiquing Ethnonationalism and Antisemitism

9 Learning as a Space of Protection: The Hochschule für die
   Wissenschaft des Judentums in Nazi Berlin 245
   Sara Han

10 Ethnonationalism as a Theological Crisis: Metropolitan Andrey
   Sheptytsky and the Greek Catholic Church in Western Ukraine,
   1923–1944 274
   Kateryna Budz and Andrew Kloes

11 To Murder or Save Thy Neighbour? Romanian Orthodox Clergymen
   and Jews during the Holocaust (1941–1945) 305
   Ionuţ Biliuţă

12 Racist, Brutal, and Ethnotheist: A Conservative Christian View of
   Nazism in the Korntal Brethren 331
   Samuel Koehne

13 Ecumenical Protestant Responses to the Rise of Nazism, Fascism,
   and Antisemitism during the 1920s and 1930s 356
   Victoria J. Barnett

   Afterword 379
   Doris L. Bergen

   Contributors 387
   Index 393

Figures

0.1 Convention of the German Christians in the Berlin Sport Palace, November 13, 1933. Alamy Stock Photo. Used with permission. 5

1.1 George Deatherage at the Dies hearing in Washington, DC, May 24, 1939. Courtesy of Library of Congress Prints and Photographs Division, hec-26738. 24

1.2 ANC News Bulletin. Author's photo of copy in CSUN's archives. 31

3.1 Julius Evola, early 1940s. The Picture Art Collection / Alamy Stock Photo. Used with permission. 73

4.1 Vicar General Philipp Jakob Mayer. DDAMZ Fotosammlung, Mayer Philipp Jakob. 98

4.2 Cardinal Michael von Faulhaber, the archbishop of Munich and Freising, and Father Josef Weißthanner, 22 November 1931. EAM NL Faulhaber, Fotosammlung, Signatur 236. 103

6.1 Front page of the German Salvation Army newspaper, *Der Kriegsruf*, 12 September 1936. 164

7.1 The cover of *The Significance of the Jews in the Scope of World History, as the People of God in the Past and as Flock of Satan Today* by J.W. Wartiainen. Photo by Markus Schulte. National Library of Finland / WSOY. 186

8.1 Father Silvestar Zubić with his class. *Report for School Years 1941–42, 1942–43, and 1943–44* (Vukovar: Državna realna gimnazija u Vukovaru, 1944), 92. Original report held at the National and University Library in Zagreb, Croatia, call number 155.075. 215

9.1 Students on the steps of the Lehranstalt für die Wissenschaft des Judentums (1935). Leo Baeck Institute, Jüdische Lehrerbildungsanstalt AR 3107, LBI Photograph: F 1960a. 254

9.2 Ernst Ludwig Ehrlich, student ID of the Hochschule. Archiv für
     Zeitgeschichte ETH Zürich: NL Ernst Ludwig Ehrlich / 25. 257
9.3 Ismar Elbogen with students, Lehranstalt für die Wissenschaft des
     Judentums (1938) 83. Leo Baeck Institute, Ismar Elbogen Collection
     AR 64, LBI Photos: F 19600. 261
10.1 Archbishop Andrey Sheptytsky in Philadelphia in October 1910.
     Philadelphia Record, October 3, 1910. Public domain. 279

Acknowledgments

The present volume evolved from two scholarly gatherings. The first, a summer research workshop convened by Victoria Barnett and Kevin Spicer, focused on "Religion, Fascism, Antisemitism, and Ethnonationalism in Europe, 1918–1945." For two weeks in early August 2015, nine scholars from Australia, Eastern and Western Europe, and North America met daily at the United States Holocaust Memorial Museum's Jack, Joseph and Morton Mandel Center for Advanced Holocaust Studies in Washington, DC, which also sponsored the gathering. At the public presentation on the workshop's final day, the participants shared their findings and recommended a second gathering to further explore the topics. Subsequently, Doris Bergen joined Barnett and Spicer to convoke a second event, a symposium on "Religion and Ethnonationalism in the Era of the Two World Wars," which Rebecca Carter-Chand coordinated. For several days in May 2017 at the University of Toronto, thirty scholars from Eastern and Western Europe, the Middle East, and North America met at the University of Toronto under the sponsorship of the University of Toronto's Chancellor Rose and Ray Wolfe Chair of Holocaust Studies and the USHMM's Mandel Center. The symposium culminated in a public event featuring Victoria Barnett, Doris Bergen, and Susannah Heschel.

Following this in-depth, multi-year exchange of ideas, the conveners invited Carter-Chand and Spicer to edit the present volume, bringing together the work of scholars who attended either or both gatherings above and additionally commissioning several new contributions to bring into conversation a broad range of geographical, political, and religious perspectives. We are pleased that each of these scholars who were instrumental in shaping the two convenings has contributed to the volume.

Both as a convener and in her role as the previous director of the Programs on Ethics, Religion, and the Holocaust at the USHMM, Victoria Barnett was instrumental in envisioning the gatherings and proposing the methodological lens of ethnonationalism through which the participants historically analyzed religion and nationalism during the era of the two world wars. We are grateful for her vision and leadership. Likewise, we wish to thank Wendy Lower, the Mandel Center's previous interim director, Lisa Leff, the Mandel Center's current director, and Robert M. Ehrenreich, the Mandel Center's Director of National Academic Programs, for their support and encouragement. We are also thankful to Claire Rosenson, Stephen Feldman, and Laura Foster in the Mandel Center's Academic Publications division, who have guided and supported the publication process. For assistance with photos, we thank Caroline Waddell, photo archivist, at the USHMM. It has been a joy to work with our editor at McGill-Queen's University Press, Richard Ratzlaff, who has been enthusiastic about this project from the beginning.

At Stonehill College, we would like to thank Rev. John Denning, CSC, president, and DeBrenna LaFa Agbényiga, provost and academic vice president, for their support for this volume. Additionally, Heather B. Perry was exceptional and continued to meet our interlibrary loan requests even during the recent pandemic challenges.

Religion, Ethnonationalism, and Antisemitism in the Era of the Two World Wars

Introduction

Kevin P. Spicer, CSC, and Rebecca Carter-Chand

On 13 November 1933, enthusiastic supporters of the German Christian Faith Movement, a German Protestant group advocating the unity of Christianity and National Socialism, gathered in the cavernous Berlin Sports Palace to promote a radical course for a united Reich Church.[1] The rally followed months of conflict within the German Protestant Church over the direction it should take under the new Nazi regime.[2] The event also took place one day after the national Reichstag election, in which all of the candidates were National Socialists running unopposed. The Nazis garnered slightly over 92 per cent of the vote.[3]

According to reports, a crowd of more than 20,000 filled "every last seat." Individuals even sat in the rafters behind the upper rows.[4] Speaking first, Joachim Hossenfelder, bishop of Brandenburg and national leader of the German Christians, set the tone when he declared his support for the Church to implement an "Aryan Paragraph" that would bar Christians of Jewish heritage from its ranks. When he finished, the crowd broke out in cheers while bellowing Luther's "A Mighty Fortress Is Our God," to the accompaniment of SA bands.[5]

Next up was the featured speaker, Dr Reinhold Krause, a teacher and secondary school director as well as the leader of the German Christians in Greater Berlin.[6] Known for his outspoken antisemitism and "natural talent for public speaking," Krause seemed a logical choice to lead the German Christians as they advanced their cause of mixing Christianity and National Socialist ideology.[7] Repeating a slogan from the previous day's Reichstag election, "One *Volk*, One Führer," Krause encouraged his audience to add "One God and One Church" as he began a two-hour diatribe that repeatedly attacked the Old Testament while also promoting a baptism litmus test based upon Aryan blood.[8]

A few days after the Sports Palace rally, German Protestants celebrated the 450th anniversary of Martin Luther's birth.[9] Throughout 1933, this anniversary and Luther's significance as a catalyst to the Reformation had been at the forefront of German Protestant thinking. National Socialist supporters, such as Krause, made every effort to appropriate Luther for their cause.[10] Krause portrayed Luther in heroic terms and implored his followers to complete the work of the German Reformation by uniting as one *Volk* (ethnically German people bound by blood) to live out the "Reformer's ethnonational [*völkische*] mission."[11] He continued, "The German fighter Luther was always on the side of the values of German ethnonational identity [*deutsche Volkstum*] in language and customs, in home and family, in poetry and music."[12] If the church fully embraced ethnonational identity, it would become a "new church," indeed, "a powerful, new, all-encompassing German people's church [*Volkskirche*]."[13]

Krause's words eventually betrayed what he truly meant by an ethnonational *Volkskirche*. It would be a church that rejected the Old Testament "with its Jewish reward-and-punishment morality, with its stories of cattle-dealers and pimps." In this church, Jews would no longer be "God's people." Nor would the church accept people of "Jewish blood" into its "ranks." He added, "We have not only fought against the mission to the Jews, but have also emphasized repeatedly that people of Jewish blood do not belong in the German people's church, either in the pulpit or in front of it."[14] As David A.R. Clark has argued, Krause and the German Christians "adopted a distinctly racialist ecclesiology" that theologized National Socialist ideology to refashion Christianity into a religion wholly divorced from its Jewish roots.[15]

Krause's speech received extensive media coverage both within and outside Germany.[16] Though many German Christians praised him afterward,[17] it soon served as a wake-up call for Protestants who favoured Adolf Hitler

Figure 0.1 Convention of the German Christians in the Berlin Sport Palace.

and National Socialism but were unprepared to embrace the more extreme tenets of the German Christian movement.[18] While most of these individuals maintained their antisemitism and support for National Socialism, Krause had simply gone too far when he rejected the Old Testament. Within a few days, even Ludwig Müller, the Reich bishop and an avid National Socialist, had begun to distance himself from Krause publicly and backtracked on thoroughly implementing the Aryan Clause in the Protestant Church.[19] Nevertheless, the struggle among German Protestants on how to define their faith tradition under National Socialism would continue throughout Hitler's years in power.[20]

In the wake of the First World War, similar struggles developed throughout Europe as postwar treaties altered borders. Religion quickly became enmeshed with new expressions of ethnonationalism, as political and religious movements sought to define national identity through ethnicity. A number of states used religion as a proxy for the malleable categories of ethnicity and race, thus making religion a marker of inclusion and exclusion. Some religious institutions or individuals proactively supported ethnonationalist projects, either out of ideological commitment or for pragmatic, political reasons. Those dismayed by the post-Versailles liberal order and the perceived threat of communism often turned to a transnational vision of political Christianity, leading some religious actors to support right-wing and fascist causes. Those who did not embrace ethnonationalist visions themselves were compelled to confront it or temper it in their own communities or networks. Those excluded from such worldviews, such as Jews, experienced ostracization and persecution as they faced new forms of antisemitism and hatred that so often manifested themselves in the nexus of Christianity and ethnonationalism.

This volume charts each of these trajectories during the 1920s, '30s, and '40s. Reaching from Finland to Romania to the United States, the chapters explore the connections between religion, ethnonationalism, and antisemitism.[21] The authors address Catholic, Protestant, and Orthodox Christianity, as well as Jewish communities and more esoteric spiritualities. Rather than focus solely on enthusiastic promoters of ethnonationalism within religious communities, this volume also considers the complex and varied responses of religious institutions, individuals, and networks to ethnonationalist policies. In doing so, we gain insight into some of the contemporary critiques of ethnonationalism and efforts of minorities to negotiate their place within such societies.

RETHINKING ETHNONATIONALISM

Ethnonationalism is a difficult concept to render in the German language. Under National Socialism, the 1940 edition of the *Volks-Brockhaus* dictionary defined *völkisch* as "national with an emphasis on the values of race and ethnicity."[22] In *Mein Kampf*, Hitler described the term using similar language, tying it directly to the superiority of German culture as the antithesis of Marxism. He bemoaned the word's misuse, especially its inaccurate linkage to religion, yet he never defined it succinctly.[23] The complexity of the adjective *völkisch* makes it challenging for anyone writing in the English language to capture its nuances solely with one word. At the beginning of *Catholicism and the Roots of Nazism: Religious Identity and National Socialism*, Derek Hastings alerted his readers to this fact by writing, "The term *völkisch*, which connotes a radical nationalist and racist orientation[,] has no effective equivalent in English and has been left in the German original."[24]

Like Hastings, many writers deem it more fitting to leave *völkisch* untranslated to avoid misinterpreting the original German. Historians regularly use the original German for related words such as *Volksdeutsche* (ethnic Germans living outside the Reich) and *Volksgemeinschaft* (ethnonationalist community) to convey the specificity of Nazi vocabulary and its emphasis on race as a determinant of insider/outsider status in the national community.[25] Yet Mark Roseman reminds us of the complexity of such terms, especially *völkisch*, which "was defined as much in competition with other groups within Germany – the competition between Germans and *true* Germans – as it was distinguishing between what was German and what was foreign." For Roseman, race was not always *the* determining factor in defining *völkisch*.[26]

Interestingly, in her English rendition of Reinhold Krause's Sports Palace speech excerpted above, Mary M. Solberg translated *völkisch* as "ethnonational." She is not alone. In recent years, authors have begun to adopt this translation.[27] While the terms ethnonational and ethnonationalism appear in historical works, the fields of sociology and political science more commonly employ them. In his classic work on ethnonationalism, Walker Connor asked: "What is it and how does it differ from just plain *nationalism*?" He answered that for him, there was no difference between the two, with the caveat that one must use nationalism "in its pristine sense." Nationalism, he stressed, "does *not* refer to loyalty to one's country." Instead, it implies "identification with and loyalty to one's nation," which he defined as "a group of people who believe they are ancestrally related."[28] Derek Hastings concurs by identifying nationalism as "a powerful sense of belonging, a sense so compelling that, when fully articulated, it overrides all (or almost all) individual attachments and markers of identification."[29]

At times in history, nationalism has emboldened individuals who believe they are "ancestrally related" to embrace an exclusionary worldview that rejects anyone outside of their self-identified nation. Atalia Omer and Jason Springs point to mid-sixteenth-century Spain, whose rulers used the Inquisition "to consolidate power and gain popular legitimacy." The Inquisition's language of "purity of blood" reinforced the idea of common ancestry within a nation while allowing for the persecution of those outside the nation.[30]

Historian of genocide Mark Levene identifies the mentality behind such actions as "ethnocentricity," which he argues is "historically universal" among all peoples. He continues that when members of one group "refer to themselves in their own tongue as 'the people' but often give derogatory names to those around them, they are doing no more nor less than human groups since time immemorial have done when confronted with outsiders."[31]

Ethnonationalism is a useful term to signal a particular articulation of nationalism that is based on an imagined ethnic community.[32] But the value in using the term ethnonationalism is that the English term can be applied more broadly beyond German *völkisch* ideology. For example, we are interested in the ways that individuals might read new approaches to understanding nationalism in other national and transnational historiographies.[33]

RELIGION, ETHNONATIONALISM, AND ANTISEMITISM IN ERA OF THE WORLD WARS

The chapters in this volume illustrate how religion was a crucial element in giving shape to ethnonationalism because of the way the Christian religion (the dominant religion in Europe) functioned as an identifying marker to define inclusion and exclusion.[34] For example, Nazi ideologues seeking to transform eastern Europe into *Lebensraum* (living space) for Germans found a desirable prototype in the Mennonite communities already living in these regions.[35] The inclusion of Mennonites as *Volksdeutsche* stood in sharp contrast to the attitude toward Jews, who were excluded from the *Volk* regardless of citizenship. The tendency of religious identity to form boundaries permeating regional, political, and socio-economic spheres is by no means unique to the period under investigation in this volume. It helps explain many so-called "religious" conflicts throughout history in which religious, ethnic, and national categories became so blurred that they were impossible to separate.

After the First World War, the conflation of religious, political, and ethnic aims became particularly acute in central and eastern Europe as the multinational empires collapsed. Millions of people now found themselves forced to recognize themselves as part of new nation-states with redrawn borders and newly constructed ethnonational identities.[36] Some regions experienced multiple regime changes, and in multiethnic regions of central and eastern

Europe, several national independence movements gained and lost territory, experienced regime change, and pushed for national independence. For example, as Andrew Kloes and Kateryna Budz show in this volume, in postwar Galicia the Greek Catholic Church served as a powerful symbol of Ukrainian nationhood in the absence of an independent state. In another part of the dismantled Austro-Hungarian Empire, the Catholic priest turned right-wing politician Andrej Hlinka strove for Slovak independence, mixing religious, linguistic, and cultural categories and becoming more radical throughout the 1920s.[37]

Religious leaders who embraced fascism, such as Hlinka, continue to draw attention from historians of religion and politics. An ever-growing number of studies examine the religious dimensions of populism and far-right political movements, often viewing them through the influential interpretive lens of political religions and the sacralization of politics, as well as the politicization of religion.[38] For example, in their volume on clerical fascism, Matthew Feldman, Marius Turda, and Tudor Georgescu demonstrate how clergy who were politically active in various fascist movements across Europe sought syncretic ways of reconciling their religious tradition with fascist politics.[39] The present volume contributes to this body of scholarship by placing particular emphasis on antisemitism as a manifestation of ethnonationalism within Christian communities and by examining some who critiqued it or sought to place limits on it based on their religious convictions.

Many of the chapters in this volume emphasize antisemitism as a factor because in the era of the two world wars, persecution of Jews was a common form of ethnonationalism across states, one that proved to be long-lasting as well as more extreme than others. Marginalized, ostracized, persecuted, and murdered in pogroms, mass shootings, and gas chambers, Jews suffered the worst. No longer did individuals of a nation simply give "derogatory names" to "outsiders." Instead, they abused, tortured, and exterminated them. John Coakley reminds us that in this process, religion played "a major role in the creation and maintenance of ethnonational boundaries." He continues, "Religion may acquire considerable ethnic significance, and it may act as an effective ethnonational marker by coinciding with some other defining characteristic – whether this is more visible, as in the case of language, or, more importantly, less visible, as in the case of descent or region of origin."[40] For example, under National Socialism, the majority of German

Catholic bishops saw Jews as "outsiders." By then, centuries of anti-Jewish teaching propagated and promoted by the Church had enabled the bishops to view Jews with suspicion and as enemies of Christianity long before the National Socialists came to power. The bishops generally did not publicly sanction the National Socialist racial ideology, but neither did they identify Jews as Germans. Their Christian outlook had instilled in them the belief that Jews were "others," outside their sphere of concern. In their pastoral letters and public statements, they professed this fact by speaking about Germans and Jews as if they were two distinct categories: Jews were not Germans. Only religious conversion could alter this "fact." By contrast, the National Socialists rejected religious conversion as a marker for entrance into the *Volksgemeinschaft*. Nevertheless, by accepting such distinctions, the bishops indirectly supported the "blood" divide between Germans and Jews propagated by National Socialist ideology, despite initially criticizing such racial teaching.[41] The biblical command to "Love thy neighbour" did little to sway their outlook or compel them to intercede for those who fell outside their ethnonational group.[42] Similar dynamics played out across confessional lines all over Europe.

Such antisemitism drew on the centuries-long legacy of Christian aversion toward Jews, with its ready-made symbols and tropes, as well as nineteenth-century political antisemitism, the myth of Judeo-Bolshevism (the pernicious idea that Jews had created and supported Bolshevism), and a reactionary interpretation of the post–First World War context that sought the supposed restoration of Western Christian civilization at nearly any cost.[43] Because these different manifestations of antisemitism overlapped with and reinforced one another, they became all the more powerful. As Paul Hanebrink explains in his influential book on Judeo-Bolshevism, ethnonationalists believed that Judeo-Bolshevism posed a threat to national sovereignty as well as to Western civilization more broadly, which they imagined as a hegemonic community of Christian nations.[44] For many Christian leaders, Judeo-Bolshevism "breathed new life into older versions of anti-Jewish hatred," which historically had relied on fears of Jewish power and manipulation.[45] The contributors to this volume are particularly attuned to the fibres connecting older forms of Christian antisemitism with the national and transnational political discourses of the 1920s, '30s, and '40s.

CASE STUDIES OF ANTISEMITISM IN
RELIGIOUS ETHNONATIONALISM

The chapters in this volume are arranged not along geographical or confessional lines but rather by how the subjects relate to the themes of ethnonationalism and antisemitism: as theorists, supporters, or responders. In part 1, Charles R. Gallagher, Nina Valbousquet, and Peter Staudenmaier consider theorists who articulated and disseminated ethnonationalist and antisemitic ideas, each contributing to transnational discourses. In the United States, the heretofore understudied George E. Deatherage's efforts to form a Christian defence against global Bolshevism hinged on the belief that Jews were behind Bolshevism. Saving America, according to Deatherage's reasoning, meant asserting Protestant Christianity and pushing back against supposed Jewish influences in American public life. As Gallagher asserts, "Deatherage's nationalism, and his antisemitism, saw Christianity as the primary bulwark against the Jewish existential threat." Gallagher argues that Deatherage's extremism was born not from isolation but from his own international experience; he first encountered anti-Bolshevism and fascism in India and was profoundly influenced by the German theorist Alfred Rosenberg.

Tracing the transnational circulation of reactionary antisemitism within Catholicism in the interwar years, Nina Valbousquet asserts that antisemitism was the vital ideological link among many right-wing – but otherwise heterogeneous – groups across Europe, including "French Catholics, Italian Fascists, White Russian émigrés, Spanish monarchists, British ultra-Tories, and German National Socialists." The Catholics who disseminated the *Protocols of the Elders of Zion* and other antisemitic ideas embraced what Valbousquet calls a "religious-political interpretation of the postwar context." Like Deatherage, they believed that a political Christianity was the only answer to the upheavals of the early twentieth century.

Another person in this period who fused together different forms of antisemitism was the Italian far-right theorist Julius Evola, whom Peter Staudenmaier evocatively describes as "reworking longstanding antisemitic clichés in a religious register." Operating squarely outside established Christianity, Evola drew on Christian teachings and practices against Judaism and Jews, eastern religions, modern race theory, and contemporary conspiracy theories to promote his "spiritual racism." Italian fascists were often bewildered by his abstract theories; he found favour instead with German National Socialists, which highlights how ethnonationalist ideas paradoxically transcended the national by appealing to the idea of a common European civilization that was under threat by outsiders.

In part 2, the chapters by Kevin Spicer, Susannah Heschel and Shannon Quigley, Rebecca Carter-Chand, Paavo Ahonen and Kirsi Stjerna, and Danijel Matijević examine Protestant and Catholic church leaders in Germany, Finland, and Croatia who supported and reinforced their country's ethnonationalist policies in one form or another. Kevin Spicer's investigation of German Catholic priests and bishops on the eve of the National Socialist ascension to power considers intra-church debates about antisemitism and the Church's role vis-à-vis the state. Spicer argues that although some Catholic clergy initially expressed opposition to National Socialism on account of its hatred of Jews, the German Catholic Church's hierarchy chose to critique Nazi ideology only when it challenged Church teachings. The inherent antisemitism within Catholicism reinforced the bishops' view of Jews as "others" who were outside the Church's sphere of concern.

In the case of the German Christian movement, church leaders and theologians acquiesced to ethnonationalist and antisemitic policies; indeed, they bolstered those policies. The Protestant theologians who developed altered versions of the New Testament did so not only to repaint Jesus as non-Jewish and remove "Jewish influences" from the text, but also to produce texts that would reflect and support the German *Volk* and make the Bible more compatible with Nazi ideology. Susannah Heschel and Shannon Quigley refer to these efforts to make Christianity relevant for the Nazi era as "theo-political." Radicalizing long-standing trends in German liberal Protestantism, these theologians removed supernatural elements such as miracles and downplayed doctrinal concepts like sin and repentance, instead stressing Jesus's strength and triumph.

Rebecca Carter-Chand considers how religious minority communities in Germany responded to Nazism, but rather than comparing them to their fellow Germans, she situates them in their international relationships with co-religionists in the Anglo-American world. Carter-Chand argues that the smaller Christian denominations in Germany, such as Baptists, Methodists, Seventh-day Adventists, Jehovah's Witnesses, Mormons, and the Salvation

Army, found ethnonationalism attractive despite sharing spiritual and institutional bonds with their co-religionists abroad. In navigating their national and international commitments, they wrestled with difficult questions about where the limits of nationalism ought to lie for Christians.

Paavo Ahonen and Kirsi Stjerna address the lesser-known topic of antisemitism within the Finnish Lutheran church. They demonstrate that the antisemitism articulated by certain influential church leaders in Finland during the 1920s and '30s was based on ethnonationalist ideas, such as the premise that Jews were disloyal to the nation-state because they were a separate race. By framing Jews as both a political and religious threat, these pastors, bishops, and theologians drew on long traditions of Christian antisemitism, particularly the legacy of Martin Luther, as well as on contemporary societal anxieties in Finland. Ahonen and Stjerna also show how some clergy were influenced by international discourse, especially by German Protestant theologians at Tübingen University and Orthodox priests from Ingria in the Soviet Union.

Danijel Matijević's chapter demonstrates how the Catholic Church in Croatia, propelled by nationalism, a spiritual impulse to make converts, and a fear of alternative political possibilities, played a key role in the Ustaša's anti-Serbian campaign. Religious identities and ethnic identity were tightly bound together, with the consequence that the regime used religious conversion from Eastern Orthodoxy to Catholicism to change Serbs into Croats. The use of religious conversion to achieve ethnic conversion for Serbs stood in contrast to the regime's policy toward Jews, for whom conversion did not provide an escape from persecution and death. Matijević describes the Church as an "obedient tool" and a "crucial accomplice in a genocidal campaign that went against both canon law and Christian morality." In the Croatian case, religion, ethnonationalism, and antisemitism were all intertwined with mass violence.

Part 3 presents several cases of religious leaders and communities critiquing ethnonationalism and antisemitism in various ways. The chapters by Sara Han, Kateryna Budz and Andrew Kloes, Ionut Biliuta, Samuel Koehne, and Victoria Barnett show how religious actors debated, tempered, or pushed back against the ethnonationalism they observed around them. In many contexts, religious institutions, practices, and symbols gave meaning to communal identity in ways that fuelled conflict and division. But Sara

Han's discussion of the Hochschule für die Wissenschaft des Judentums (Higher Institute for Jewish Studies) in Berlin shows how religious and cultural communal identity could be a force for good by becoming a space of protection and an act of resistance against the Nazis. Increasingly shut out of civic and cultural life, these German Jews recreated a sense of normalcy, hope for the future, and intellectual community. Han traces the threads of continuity and discontinuity for the institute's curriculum, its pedagogy, and its community of teachers and students until its forced closure in 1942.

Metropolitan archbishop Andrey Sheptytsky of the Ukrainian Greek Catholic Church was a staunch Ukrainian nationalist but sought alternatives to violent and antisemitic expressions of ethnonationalism. Kateryna Budz and Andrew Kloes tease out these nuances by examining Sheptytsky's consistent condemnation of violence as anathema to Christian values, his commitment to Christian ecumenism, his long-standing ties to the Jewish community in Lviv, and his efforts to help individual Jews during the German occupation.

In Romania, the Orthodox church generally supported the government's anti-Jewish measures in the 1930s and '40s, and some clergy participated in violence against Jews during the Holocaust. But a few engaged in wartime actions that ran counter to the ethnonationalism they espoused, such as the small numbers of Romanian Orthodox priests who assisted Jews, as discussed by Ionuț Biliuță. Although motivations were multifaceted and the lack of sources makes this topic challenging to analyze, Biliuță argues that, for a minority of priests, antisemitism and ethnonationalism could exist alongside a practical response to the Christian command to love one's neighbour, at least during the extreme conditions of total war and genocide.

Samuel Koehne demonstrates how two German communities with vastly different theological perspectives both recognized the critical elements of the Nazi Party's values and vision in 1933 – namely its ethnonationalist character, its antisemitism, and the way it functioned as a "replacement faith" or political religion. Koehne brings nuance to his examination of the Korntal Brethren and others living in Württemberg by analyzing how, despite their critiques of some aspects of the Nazi platform, they were attracted to the national and religious revival the Nazis promised to bring.

One of the most explicit critiques of ethnonationalism by religious leaders came from ecumenical voices. Victoria Barnett's analysis of the international

Protestant ecumenical movement charts how some mainline Protestants
loudly rejected the fusion of religion and nationalism. Ecumenists were
alarmed about the rise of nationalist movements and theological nationalism on both political and theological grounds. Having emerged from the
First World War with strong internationalist and pacifist convictions, they
viewed the rising nationalism of the late 1920s and early 1930s as politically
destabilizing for Europe. Theologically, they believed ethnonationalism to
be a distortion of the universality of the Christian message. But Barnett also
stresses that ecumenists in this period did not acknowledge the theological
antisemitism inherent in Christianity, instead viewing antisemitism as part
of a broader trend of religious persecution.

As the chapters in this volume show, the individuals and institutions
under study have often understood their religious identity through the lens
of their ethnicity. This fusion of religious, ethnic, and national identities
overlapped with a distrust and hatred of Jews. While the roots of such antisemitic discourse rest deep in Christianity's origins and history, more modern forms of racialized, socio-economic, and nationalist antisemitism gained
steam in many parts of Europe between the late nineteenth century and the
1940s. The result was the murder of more than six million Jews in the Holocaust. Though peoples and societies have progressed in many ways since the
era of the world wars, religious ethnonationalist conflict has persisted over
the post–Second World War decades and sadly continues to exist in our current world.[46] Likewise, antisemitism is on the rise in North America, Europe,
and other parts of the world.[47] Hopefully, this volume will provide its readers
with the historical contextualization to understand, confront, and combat
religious ethnonationalism and antisemitism today.

NOTES

The views expressed here are those of the authors and do not represent
those of the United States Holocaust Memorial Museum.

1 Doris L. Bergen, *Twisted Cross: The German Christian Movement in the
   Third Reich* (Chapel Hill: University of North Carolina Press, 1996), 17.

2 Victoria Barnett, *For the Soul of the People: Protestant Protest against Hitler*
   (New York: Oxford University Press, 1992), 30–46.

3 Ian Kershaw, *Hitler 1889–1936: Hubris* (New York: W.W. Norton, 1988), 495.

4 Reinhold Krause, *Ein Volk–ein Reich–ein Glaube. Die Lebenserinnerungen des DC-Sportspalastredners Dr. Reinhold Krause*, ed. Olaf Kühl-Freudenstein (Nordhausen: Traugott Bautz, 2006), 78.

5 Klaus Scholder, *The Churches and the Third Reich*, vol. 1: *1918–1934*, trans. John Bowden (Philadelphia: Fortress Press, 1988), 551–2.

6 Krause was a *Studienrat* and director of the Elisebeth-Christinen-Lzyeums in Berlin-Niederschönhausen. Beginning in mid-1933, he held the title of the German Christians' *Gauobermann* for Groß-Berlin. See Ernst Klee, *Das Personenlexikon zum Dritten Reich. Were war was vor und nach 1945*, 2nd rev. ed. (Frankfurt am Main: S. Fischer, 2003), 336.

7 Olaf Kühl-Freudenstein, "Kommentar," in Krause, *Ein Volk–ein Reich–ein Glaube*, 119.

8 On Krause's self-description of the length of his speech, see *Ein Volk–ein Reich–ein Glaube*, 78.

9 The event was scheduled for 10 November but was pushed back by Hitler's sudden announcement of Reichstag elections and plebiscite for the German withdrawal from the League of Nations, to be held on 12 November. The originally planned event was to be preceded by weeks of smaller celebrations in the Luther cities of Eisenach, Eisleben, and Wittenberg. The celebration, a combined state and church affair, took place on 19 November. On the history of the celebration, see Hartmut Lehmann, "Fatal Coincidiences in 1933: Nazism's Triumph and Martin Luther's 450th Birthday," *Svensk Teologisk Kvartalskrift* 93, nos. 1–2 (2017): 3–17.

10 On this point, see Christopher Probst, *Demonizing the Jews: Luther and the Protestant Church in Nazi Germany* (Bloomington: Indiana University Press in association with the United States Holocaust Memorial Museum, 2012).

11 Reinhold Krause, "Speech at the Sports Palace in Berlin," in *A Church Undone: Documents from the German Christian Faith Movement 1932–1940*, ed. and trans. Mary M. Solberg (Minneapolis: Fortress Press, 2015), 251–62, here 251–2. Solberg's translation was compared to the original, Reinhold Krause, *Rede des Gauobmannes der Glaubensbewegung "Deutsche Christen" in Groß-Berlin Dr. Krause gehalten im Sportpalast am 13. November 1933* (Berlin-Pankow: self-published, n.d.).

12 Krause, "Speech at the Sports Palace in Berlin," 252.

13 Ibid., 253.

14 Ibid., 258.

15 David A.R. Clark, "Antisemitism, Violence, and Invective against the Old Testament: Reinhold Krause's *Sportpalast* Speech," *Canadian–American Theological Review* 7 (2018), 124–37, here 126.

16 For example, see "Revision of scripture is urged on Germans: Return to heroic conception of Jesus and segregation of non-Aryans proposed," *New York Times*, 14 November 1933.

17 Krause, *Ein Volk–ein Reich–ein Glaube*, 79–83.

18 See Joachim Hossenfelder, "The Original Guidelines of the German Christian Movement (1932)," in *A Church Undone*, 48–51.

19 On the backlash, see Richard Gutteridge, *Open Thy Mouth for the Dumb! The German Evangelical Church and the Jews 1879–1950* (Oxford: Basil Blackwell, 1976), 120–38.

20 For an excellent example of this struggle locally, see Kyle Jantzen, *Faith and Fatherland: Parish Politics in Hitler's Germany* (Minneapolis: Fortress Press, 2008).

21 In recent years several edited volumes have brought together national case studies on religion across Europe in the 1930s and 1940s, including Lieve Gevers and Jan Bank's two volumes: *Religion under Siege I: The Roman Catholic Church in Occupied Europe (1939–1950)* and *II: Protestant, Orthodox, and Muslim Communities in Occupied Europe (1939–1950)*. Bank and Gevers continued their investigation of the European churches in *Churches and Religion in the Second World War* (New York: Bloomsbury Academic, 2016), a translation of their 2015 study written in the Dutch language. Karl-Joseph Hummel and Christoph Kösters's *Kirchen im Krieg: Europa 1939–1945* (Paderborn: F. Schöningh, 2007), is similarly focused on churches in various European countries and their wartime actions, ranging from collaboration to resistance. Omer Bartov and Phyllis Mack were among the first Holocaust scholars to expand the scope even further to consider intersections between religion and state-sponsored genocide around the world. Omer Bartov and Phyllis Mack, eds., *In God's Name: Religion and Genocide in the Twentieth Century* (New York: Berghahn Books, 2001).

22 *Der Volks-Brockhaus. Deutsches Sach- und Sprachwörterbuch für Schule und Haus*, 9th rev. ed. (Leipzig: F.A. Brockhaus, 1940), cited in Cornelia Schmitz-Berning, *Vokabular des Nationalsozialismus* (Berlin: Walter de Gruyter, 1998), 645.

23 On Hitler's understanding of the term, see Schmitz-Berning, *Vokabular des*

Nationalsozialismus, 646–7. See also Adolf Hitler, *Mein Kampf* [1924], trans. Ralph Manheim (Boston: Houghton Mifflin, 1971), 378–85.

24 Derek Hastings, *Catholicism and the Roots of Nazism: Religious Identity and National Socialism* (New York: Oxford University Press, 2010), xv. In *Hitler's Priests: Catholic Clergy and National Socialism* (DeKalb: Northern Illinois University Press, 2008), Kevin Spicer defines the term as "racial-nationalist," without subsequently translating it (31).

25 Schmitz-Berning, *Vokabular des Nationalsozialismus*, particularly the entries for "*Volk*" and related terms, 642–79.

26 Mark Roseman, "The Limits of the Racial State Model," in *Beyond the Racial State: Rethinking Nazi Germany*, eds. Devin O. Pendas, Mark Roseman, and Richard F. Wetzell (Cambridge, UK, and Washington, DC: Cambridge University Press and German Historical Institute, 2017), 31–57, here 41.

27 For example, see Christiane Tietz, *Theologian of Resistance: The Life and Thought of Dietrich Bonhoeffer*, trans. Victoria Barnett (Minneapolis: Fortress, 2016), 64; and Rogers Brubaker, *Citizenship and Nationhood in France and Germany* (Cambridge, MA: Harvard University Press, 1992), 125.

28 Walker Connor, *Ethnonationalism: The Quest for Understanding* (Princeton: Princeton University Press, 1994), xi.

29 Derek Hastings, *Nationalism in Modern Europe: Politics, Identity, and Belonging since the French Revolution*, reprint (London: Bloomsbury Academic, 2019), 2–3. There exists extensive literature on nationalism. For example, see Carlton J.H. Hayes, *Nationalism: A Religion* (New York: Macmillan, 1960); Adrian Hastings, *The Construction of Nationhood: Ethnicity, Religion, and Nationalism* (Cambridge: Cambridge University Press, 2007); and Anthony D. Smith, *Nationalism: Theory, Ideology, History*, 2nd rev. ed. (Malden: Polity, 2010).

30 Atalia Omer and Jason Springs, *Religious Nationalism: A Reference Handbook* (Santa Barbara: ABC-CLIO, 2013), 28.

31 Mark Levene, *Genocide in the Age of the Nation-State*, vol. 2: *The Rise of the West and the Coming of Genocide* (London: I.B. Tauris, 2005), 15.

32 Benedict Anderson, *Imagined Communities: Reflections on the Origin and Spread of Nationalism*, rev. ed. (London: Verso, 1991).

33 Norbert Frei, "German Zeitgeschichte and Generation, or How to Explain the Belated Career of the Nazi Volksgemeinschaft," *Social Research: An International Quarterly* 81, no. 3 (2014): 571–84.

34 Omer and Springs, *Religious Nationalism*, 29.

35 Mark Jantzen and John D. Thiesen, eds., *European Mennonites and the Holo-caust* (Toronto: University of Toronto Press, in association with the United States Holocaust Memorial Museum, 2022), 21–2. See also see Benjamin Goossen, *Chosen Nation: Mennonites and Germany in a Global Age* (Princeton: Princeton University Press, 2017).

36 Some of the significant scholarship on twentieth-century nationalism in central and eastern Europe includes Helmut Walser Smith, *Germany: A Nation in Its Time; Before, During, and After Nationalism, 1500–2000* (New York: Liveright, 2020); Brian Porter, *When Nationalism Began to Hate: Imagining Modern Politics in Nineteenth-Century Poland* (Oxford: Oxford University Press, 2000); Jeremy King, *Budweisers into Czechs and Germans: A Local History of Bohemian Politics, 1848–1948* (Princeton: Princeton University Press, 2002); Francine Hirsch, *Ethnographic Knowledge and the Making of the Soviet Union* (Ithaca: Cornell University Press, 2005), and Maria Todorova, "The Balkans: From Discovery to Invention," *Slavic Review* 53, no. 2 (1994): 453–82.

37 James Mace Ward, *Priest, Politician, Collaborator: Jozef Tiso and the Making of Fascist Slovakia* (Ithaca: Cornell University Press, 2013). See also Jörg Hoensch, "One God, One People, One Party," in *Catholics, the State, and the European Radical Right, 1919–1945* (New York: Columbia University Press, 1987), 158–81.

38 Jean-Yves Camus and Nicolas Lebourg, *Far-Right Politics in Europe* (Cambridge, MA: Harvard University Press, 2017), 13. The first to use the term *political religion* was Eric Voegelin, *Die politischen Religionen* [1993] (Munich: Peter J. Opitz, 1996). See also Neil Gregor, "Nazism – A Political Religion? Rethinking the Voluntarist Turn," in *Nazism, War and Genocide*, ed. Neil Gregor (Exeter: University of Exeter Press, 2005); and a special issue of the *Journal of Contemporary History* 42, no. 1 (2007), especially the essays by Richard Evans, "Nazism, Christianity, and Political Religion: A Debate," 5–7, and Stanley Stowers, "The Concepts of 'Religion,' 'Political Religion' and the Study of Nazism," 9–24.

39 Matthew Feldman, Marius Turda, and Tudor Georgescu, eds. *Clerical Fascism in Interwar Europe* (New York: Routledge, 2008).

40 John Coakley, "Religion and Nationalism in the First World," in *Ethnonationalism in the Contemporary World: Walter Connor and the Study of Nationalism*, ed. Daniele Conversi (London: Routledge, 2002), 206–25, here 220.

41 On this point, see Antonia Leugers, *Gegen eine Mauer bischöflichen*

Schweigens: Der Ausschuß für Ordensangelegenheiten und seine Widerstand-skonzeption 1941 bis 1945 (Frankfurt am Main: Josef Knecht, 1996); and Kevin P. Spicer, "Catholic Life under Hitler," in *Life and Times in Nazi Germany*, ed. Lisa Pine (London: Bloomsbury Academic, 2016), 239–62, here 245–6.

42 John T. Pawlikowski and Kevin P. Spicer, "Introduction," in *Antisemitism, Christian Ambivalence, and the Holocaust*, ed. Kevin P. Spicer (Bloomington: Indiana University Press in association with the United States Holocaust Memorial Museum, 2017), xiii–xxi, here xiii–xv.

43 On Judeo-Bolshevism, see Paul Hanebrink, *A Specter Haunting Europe: The Myth of Judeo-Bolshevism* (Cambridge, MA: Harvard University Press, 2020); and Lorna Waddington, *Hitler's Crusade: Bolshevism, the Jews, and the Myth of Conspiracy* (London: I.B. Tauris, 2012). On reactionary Catholicism, see James Chappel, *Catholic Modern: The Challenge of Totalitarianism and the Remaking of the Church* (Cambridge, MA: Harvard University Press, 2018); and Giuliana Chamedes, *A Twentieth-Century Crusade* (Cambridge, MA: Harvard University Press, 2019).

44 Hanebrink, *A Specter Haunting Europe*, 8–9.

45 Ibid., 27.

46 For example, see Karl Cordell and Stefan Wolff, eds, *The Routledge Handbook of Ethnic Conflict*, 2nd ed. (London: Routledge, 2019); and Omer and Springs, *Religious Nationalism*.

47 On this point, see Jonathan G. Campbell and Lesley D. Klaff, eds., *Unity and Diversity in Modern Antisemitism* (Brookline: Academic Studies Press, 2019); and Deborah E. Lipstadt, *Antisemitism: Here and Now* (New York: Schocken, 2019).

PART ONE

Theorizing Religion,
Ethnonationalism, and Antisemitism

1

Adopting the Swastika: George E. Deatherage and the American Nationalist Confederation, 1937–1942

Charles R. Gallagher, SJ

"The swastika has come to the United States to stay," announced the *News Bulletin*, the organ of an obscure, recently formed organization known as the American Nationalist Confederation (ANC) on 23 April 1938. The ANC informed its members that the swastika was now "our newly selected emblem."[1] A thick black swastika superimposed over vibrant stripes of red, white, and blue adorned the banner of the small publication, published in St Albans, West Virginia. In its layout, the *News Bulletin* looked like something halfway between a newsletter and a four-colour brochure. "The swastika is one of more than 700 types of the Christian Cross," it declared, and "is now used in the U.S. Army as the emblem of the Forty-Fifth Division of the National Guard."[2] "The swastika," the editorial noted parenthetically, "being a real Christian Cross, served as the emblem of the Russian Imperial Family massacred by the Jews."[3] Rather than a symbol of German National Socialism, the swastika was a stylized form of the Christian Cross that Jews in America and around the world had been taught "to hate and destroy."[4]

Unfortunately for the ANC, many readers of the *News Bulletin* were hesitant to adopt the Nazi symbol as a Christian signifier in 1938. Redoubling their efforts, the ANC published a second editorial on the swastika in its May

Figure 1.1 George Deatherage at the Dies hearing in Washington, DC,
24 May 1939.

1938 issue. The swastika, it stated, was the "happy token" of the American
Nationalist Confederation. Moreover, "many thousand Americans" would
find in the ANC "an outlet for the work that needs to be done to save a Christian people."[5] This second attempt to integrate the swastika encountered
further resistance. Many of West Virginia's deeply religious Protestants remained squeamish about the symbol. They could not understand how the
symbol of the Nazi regime, which was persecuting Christians in Germany,
could be adopted in America as a benign and unifying symbol. Many readers
questioned their own membership in the ANC. "The swastika is the emblem
of Christians banded together for Christian purpose," ANC editors pointed
out. Any other meaning was simply "Jewish propaganda." But ANC members
continued to be hesitant. Specifically, they wanted to know if they had to accept the swastika in order to remain members. In response, ANC leaders
wrote a long editorial titled "Nationalism Will Save America," which spelled

out the sole requirement for membership: "this is plain – to the point – and needs no further explanation – it is necessary only that all applicants proclaim their belief in the <u>Divinity of Christ</u>."[6] In adopting the swastika, Christology was key.[7]

The exchanges about adopting the swastika in the pages of the ANC's *News Bulletin* are important because they touch upon three main impulses that were present at the creation of the American Nationalist Confederation in 1937: antisemitism, nationalism, and, most importantly, "Aryan" Christianity. The founder of the ANC, George E. Deatherage, proffered a nationalist vision for the United States tied to these three main elements. In Deatherage's view, the swastika was to be the symbol that would lift America from its bondage to the Jews. For him, the swastika was not a secular symbol. To his mind, the catalyst for overcoming Jewish hegemony would be a reinvigorated American Christianity.

Deatherage's nationalist project is significant because it marks a real attempt on the part of an American citizen to wrap American Protestant Christianity in the ideology of German National Socialism.[8] Deatherage was particularly beholden to Nazi theorist Alfred Rosenberg, and he tacked toward an incipient form of antisemitic Christian nationalism to rouse his target audience. He formed an authentically American organization that religiously synchronized with Rosenberg's admittedly nationalistic principles of "Germanic Christianity."[9]

Deatherage's Nazi handlers believed that Christianity might offer the camouflage needed to make inroads in American culture. Deatherage never realized that Christianity was being used as a Nazi political stratagem. He was a deeply religious Christian. He was able to adapt to what the Nazis were selling because his inchoate American Christian nationalism harmonized neatly with Rosenberg's style of antisemitism and, more importantly, his nazified Christology.

THE EDUCATION OF AN ANTISEMITE: GEORGE E. DEATHERAGE AND THE RUSSIAN CIVIL WAR

Scholarly literature on George E. Deatherage and his American Nationalist Confederation is virtually non-existent. So far, there has been no scholarly examination of the philosophy and impact of the ANC. Serious discussion

of Deatherage and his organization is largely from press reports that date to
the period.[10] Laura B. Rosenzweig is the only modern scholar to mention
Deatherage and the ANC. In her book *Hollywood's Spies*, Rosenzweig sees
Deatherage as instrumental in the early organizational activities of Nazis on
the American west coast as well as in the "Moseley plot" that was exposed
in the summer of 1939.[11] But a thorough examination of Deatherage and his
movement fell outside the scope of Rosenzweig's research. This dearth of
material on Deatherage is surprising, since he was a common name on the
right during the 1930s and into the 1940s. Philip Jenkins, for example, considers Deatherage to have been a "widely active national leader."[12] Writing
in 1940, Harold Lavine of the Institute for Propaganda Analysis viewed
Deatherage as the one fascist leader in America whom "most of the patriots
will flock to again" if conditions permitted.[13] With greater financial backing,
Lavine averred, "a nationwide Fascist party will get underway."[14]

One of the main reasons Deatherage and the ANC have been neglected
may be connected to the arguments advanced by historian of conservatism
Rick Perlstein in 2017. As Perlstein points out, scientific study of the right
wing often has been considered "an orphan of historical scholarship."[15] In
the decades after the Second World War, historians grounded in the "liberal
consensus" shied away from detailed examinations of the right wing. Likewise, conservatives found in the history of the right a "political surrealism
of the paranoid fringe," and after the liberation of the death camps of the
Second World War, they quickly eschewed the antisemitism of their right-
wing progenitors.[16]

Conservatives preferred not to look backward. Postwar liberals, following
Lionel Trilling and Richard Hofstadter, saw the extreme right wing as filled
with "conspiracy theories and bizarre panaceas."[17] On top of this, and more
important still, liberals at the time deduced that the extreme right defied
scientific rationality. "A raving pro-Fascist" is how liberal foreign affairs journalist Dorothy Thompson once described Deatherage.[18] "Deatherage is so
completely a nut," liberal and New Deal insider Gardner Jackson wrote in
1939, "that I hesitate to dignify him by serious consideration."[19] Jackson's
stance seems to personify the position of many liberals after the Second
World War. Since 1939, historians have neglected Deatherage, perhaps for
fear of dignifying his project. Such squeamishness has meant that his project
has gone unexamined.

George Edward Deatherage was born in Duluth, Minnesota, in 1892. At the age of eighteen, he was working as a clerk in a hardware store in Duluth. By his own account, he became an engineer after taking a correspondence course.[20] Professionally, he emphasized exactitude, organization, and cost control.[21] Due to his competence and emphasis on the bottom line, he was in demand as a young construction engineer. One of his first engineering jobs was in Cleveland, Ohio, where he took an apartment in the Rockefeller Building, one of Cleveland's first skyscrapers and a socialite's address. It was most likely during this period that he adopted his urbane style, with an emphasis on culture and sartorial splendour. He was styled by newshawks as simultaneously a fascist and a "dynamo businessman," and these tags would follow him during his public phase in the 1930s and 1940s. Deatherage became more enterprising and sophisticated in his twenties, yet nothing could have prepared him for the world of international travel, culture, and politics that he would encounter over the next decade.

Taking cues from Hofstadter, most American historians view far-right extremism as born of isolated American constructions such as agrarianism, fundamentalism, and evangelicalism.[22] For most, right-wing extremism has nothing to do with cosmopolitanism, pluralism, and internationalism.[23] What makes Deatherage so eerily fascinating as a right-wing figure is that his extremism was born precisely of world travel and professional international experience.

On 23 July 1919, the young engineer left the United States and headed to India.[24] In what must be a testament to his entrepreneurialism, adventurism, and risk-taking, he took a position as a mechanical and construction engineer for the Indian Iron and Steel Company in Calcutta. At that time, Indian Iron and Steel was a new company, vying for market dominance with Tata Steelworks. During the years of Deatherage's employment there from 1919 to 1922, world market prices for steel were at their highest.[25] In the wake of the First World War, the entire iron industry in India began competing for worldwide talent through an incentive system.[26] The lure of a big paycheque inspired Deatherage to pack his bags, leave Ohio, and travel halfway around the world to India. Managers like Deatherage stood to receive not only high salaries but also huge bonuses for tasks completed on time and under budget. All of this suited Deatherage's way of doing things and his financially ambitious spirit. Deatherage also mastered Hindi, which made him even

more valuable as an employee. Global capitalism was good to the young, au-
todidactic engineer.

At the same time, it was in India that Deatherage made his first contact
with anti-Bolshevism and incipient fascism. In the early 1920s, more than
100,000 White Russians immigrated to China for safety. From there, they
fanned out into Japan, the Philippines, and India.[27] In his testimony to the
House Un-American Activities Committee (HUAC) in 1939, Deatherage indicated that he had had contact with "an outfit," presumably anti-Bolshevik,
with "contacts inside the Soviet Union."[28] "They get information that is
very good, and put it out," he said.[29] "I am associated ... with organizations
in India, China, Siberia, and even inside Russia."[30] In October 1937, Deatherage welcomed Vladimir Kositsin, whom Rosenzweig has labelled "the national leader of the fascist White Russian group in the United States," to St
Albans to help him set up his office and lay out the first editions of the
News Bulletin.[31]

Most impactful in Deatherage's metamorphosis, or metaphysical conversion, from mild-mannered engineer to truculent antisemite was his direct
experience of living in Russia during the Russian Civil War. During his time
in India, Deatherage visited Russia, presumably on business for Indian Iron
and Steel. "I lived in Russia, you see," he told HUAC in 1939. "I was in the Asi-
atic Coast in 1919, 1920, and 1921."[32] It was in Russia that Deatherage witnessed the general brutality of the Red Army. This was anti-capitalism at the
tip of a bayonet. In addition, Deatherage's American nationalism heightened
because the Red Army was killing not only White Russians but American
soldiers as well.[33]

Deatherage's sojourns in Russia impressed upon him that the Russian
Civil War was, among other things, a religious war.[34] In what may be the
first instance of "ecumenical anti-Communism," he suggested in February
1938 that "in the Soviet Union today ... Orthodox, Evangelical Protestant,
and Roman Catholics testify to their belief in Christ by suffering the severest
deprivations."[35] Deatherage wanted his American audience to know about
the "Silent Russians," those who were "persistently exterminated under the
yoke of Marxism, with their land transformed into a gigantic kingdom of
starvation, misery, and cannibalism."[36] On the brink of adopting the swastika, Deatherage was applying exterminationist language not to Jews, but
to Christians.

Deatherage was terrified of a communist global revolution, and he linked the Jews to the world's unrest. "I have hatred for the Jewish leadership and finance that is directing this movement," he told to HUAC in 1939. "They have directed it in every country in Europe."[37] Although members of Congress did not grasp it, Deatherage was expressing to them his firm belief in the myth of Judeo-Bolshevism. Judeo-Bolshevism – the idea that Jews had created Bolshevism, now supported it, and were therefore responsible for its crimes – was an obscure and little-known late-nineteenth-century concept that gained momentum during the period of the Russian Revolution and Civil War.[38] Consequently, in his public life, when Deatherage self-identified as an anti-communist, he was cryptically and simultaneously identifying as an antisemite. Given that "hatred" for "Jewish leadership" was his foundational organizing principle, keeping Christians peaceful would prove difficult for Deatherage. "Jesus Christ has been trying to do that for 2000 years," he remarked to HUAC chairman Dies.[39]

Christ was central to Deatherage when he moved to St Albans in 1936 and took a job as the head construction foreman at Carbon and Carbide Company (later Union Carbide) in South Charleston, West Virginia. Deatherage, a long-time member of the Ku Klux Klan, came to his Judeo-Bolshevism from the religious side. Historian of religion Kelly J. Baker has argued that the high level of Protestant piety among KKK members has been overlooked by historians. Ordinary members of the second KKK viewed themselves primarily as American Protestants, and they struggled to reconcile biblical theology and Christology with the paramilitary undertones of KKK ideology.[40] In addition, and perhaps more importantly, Baker argues that the staunch Protestantism of KKK members became a conduit to a greater sense of American nationalism. Deatherage's religious convictions, and his aspiration to form an umbrella organization of American pro-fascists as a "new national Christian organization," sprang in part from this impulse.[41]

For Deatherage, the Russian Revolution had implications for Christians. Lenin's coup had been a predominantly Jewish event intended to achieve Jewish domination of the world. Because Lenin's revolution espoused violence and was expansionist, Christians around the globe from Russia to Mexico to Spain were under threat of extermination. Deatherage's founding of the Knights of the White Camellia in 1934 was an effort to come up with a Christian bulwark against global Judeo-Bolshevist expansion. This project later expanded into the ANC, which allowed Deatherage to shed the KKK stigma and dial up his nationalism, while retaining Christian orthopraxis.

In 1934, the Knights of the White Camellia was a dormant Reconstruction-era organization founded for the members of the officer corps of the former Army of the Confederate States of America (the KKK was for enlisted men). Resurrected by Deatherage, the group gave him immediate prestige and instant leadership power. Membership numbers are difficult to measure. During his testimony to HUAC in the spring of 1939, Deatherage was mute on this. He indicated to Congress that to divulge any information about membership would "violate his oath" as Commander of the Knights.[42] Congress dared not push back. The *World Almanac* of 1941 listed membership at 100,000 – a number that was self-reported and wildly exaggerated.[43] From 1937 to 1940, Deatherage simultaneously held the posts of leader of the ANC and Grand Commander of the Knights of the White Camellia. Both organizations were Christian to the core.

Deatherage had always referred to Klan leaders as "Christian leaders," and he viewed himself in such terms.[44] A *Look* magazine article in March 1939 had Deatherage describing the ANC as a new "national Christian organization that we can all back."[45] It is unclear whether Deatherage was trying to position himself as a Protestant Father Coughlin. Father Charles E. Coughlin was a wildly popular Catholic radio orator in the 1930s who co-founded a political party in 1936 called the Union Party. By 1938, his radio speeches, which attracted up to 30 million listeners each week, had become openly antisemitic. Coughlin's newspaper, *Social Justice*, was aware of Deatherage, and reported on his testimony to HUAC in the spring of 1939. In that testimony, Deatherage spelled out that his groups were distinct, as well as separate from Father Coughlin's. "This is the way I size up Father Coughlin," he told HUAC. "He's got 21 million Catholics in the United States … He doesn't need George Deatherage or anyone else."[46] In an era prior to Christian ecumenism in America, Deatherage was insinuating that Coughlin held sway on the Catholic side of the street. He was hoping to take charge of the Protestant side. In fact, Deatherage had harboured Christian pastoral leadership ambitions since 1936.

In early August of 1936, Deatherage joined more than two hundred Protestant ministers as they met in Asheville, North Carolina. A conservative evangelical group called the America Forward Movement for Religion

THE AMERICAN NATIONALIST CONFEDERATION
THE NEWS BULLETIN

Vol. 1. No. 14 April 23, 1938 Ten Cents

E D I T O R I A L

THE MEANING OF THE EMBLEM - THE SWASTIKA

This issue carries at the mast head our newly selected emblem - the swastika.

According to A. E. du Bois, chief American military expert on such matters as emblems for the U.S. Army - the swastika is one of more than 700 types of the Christian Cross that he has been able to identify. It is now used in the U.S. Army as the emblem of the Forty-Fifth Division of the National Guard. They took the idea from the Indians and from the coat of arms of Francisco Vasquez Coronado, Spanish explorer.

Both Finland and Latvia use it as a marking for their aircraft, and, of course, it is best known for its use by the German Government, the Canadian Nationalist Party, the British Union of Fascists, the South African Greyshirts and, in addition, practically by all the anti-communist groups throughout the world. (The swastika, being a real Christian Cross, served as an emblem of the Russian Imperial Family massacred by the Jews).

Jewish propaganda in America, where they control the press, has done its best to cast odium on the emblem. The fact that it is one form of the Christian Cross, which their synagogue teaches them to hate and destroy, is self evidence of the source of the lying campaign.

Official organ of the Fascist Party in America—the American Nationalist Confederation—printing the "News Behind the News"—without fear or favor—upholding the principles of America for Americans. Published weekly by The American Nationalist Confederation at St. Albans, W. Va., P. O. Box 467 Subscription $2.50 for six months. Special bundle prices on application.

Figure 1.2 In the spring of 1938, the ANC began to add colour to the News Bulletin as well as the swastika. Later that year, Deatherage spoke to Nazi dignitaries in Erfurt, Germany, and announced that his organization had adopted the swastika as its primary emblem.

and Americanism sponsored the conference. The Asheville conference was to be a forum for Protestant ministers from across the nation to address an emerging problem: creeping communism within their congregations. "They were arming the faithful with spiritual weapons," historian Jonathan P. Herzog has written of the Asheville conference, "and the soldiers of righteousness prepared to fight for their country and its culture."[47] Deatherage attended the conference with high hopes of creating a united Christian front against communism.

But as the conference unfolded, Deatherage became more and more distressed by the ministers' seeming blindness to the violent threat posed by atheistic communism. Deatherage became apoplectic when the conference's organizer, Methodist minister Ralph Nollner of Houston, Texas, invited an Orthodox rabbi to speak. For Deatherage, and for all others who believed in Judeo-Bolshevism, this was like escorting the enemy inside the gates.

Rabbi Abraham L. Feinberg of Mount Neboh Synagogue in New York City delivered a speech that was well-received by liberal and moderate pastors; however, many others noticed that the rabbi never specifically condemned communism. Instead, he addressed the conference about the "challenge thundered by poverty, injustice, tyranny, and social chaos."[48] In addition, Feinberg admonished the ministers to eschew "clergymen who stir up racial prejudices, class hatreds, and sectional intolerance."[49] Deatherage and others considered this a direct swipe at the Klan. Compounding matters, when the ministers were trying to come up with a new name for their group, they deliberately dropped the descriptor "Christian."[50] Deatherage believed this created a wedge for the future participation of Jews in what should be an exclusively Christian organization. As a Judeo-Bolshevist, Deatherage believed that the concept of "Jewish anti-communism" was laughable. Rabbi Feinberg's speech did nothing to disabuse him of that notion; in fact, it emboldened Deatherage.

On 12 August 1936, as the opening session of the Asheville conference concluded, Deatherage, along with the Reverend Gerald Winrod and Ernest F. Elmhurst, secretary of the short-lived "Pan-Aryan Alliance," bolted from the conference and held their own deliberations at the First Christian Church of Asheville.[51] "Anti-Communist Conference Splits," read a headline out of Asheville; "Group of Delegates Withdraw."[52] The split among the ministers transpired because of the way Christian anti-communism was altering its assessment of Judeo-Bolshevism. Nollner and his mainstream Protestants were committed to religious pluralism; Deatherage saw inter-religious co-operation as specious, since Judaism and Bolshevism were intertwined. An astonishing forty-five religious leaders joined Deatherage and the "Asheville secessionists" at the First Christian Church in Asheville. This group would form the nucleus of an anti-communist, pro-fascist, Judeo-Bolshevist (antisemitic) Christian rump that would create a legacy far beyond its obscure origins. "The plan" of the Communists, according to the Asheville secessionists, was nothing more than "a plot to recrucify Christ."[53]

Deatherage and the dissenters accused Nollner's group of being "paid," presumably by the Jews, to "deliberately demoralize, weaken, and divide the ranks of Christian patriots" who were trying to ward off "the kind of bloody revolution that has come upon Russia ... Spain, and other countries."[54] To the Asheville secessionists, America Forward was exhibiting characteristics "typical of those forces which are endeavoring to poison and destroy the very foundations of true Christian America" – the Jews.[55] The *New Republic*'s associate editor, the novelist Hamilton Basso, covered the Asheville Conference for his liberal magazine. For Basso, two things were certain: "The Gospel of Christ is not to be found in *Mein Kampf.* And Christ, were he alive, would not be on Hitler's side."[56] It was Deatherage's aim to upend Basso on both points.

Only historian Steven J. Ross has noticed that the founding of the American Nationalist Confederation was religious in nature rather than political. After the Asheville conference, Deatherage believed that a new organization needed to be established – one that could coordinate all the Christian organizations represented by the Asheville secessionists. As Deatherage envisioned it, the ANC was to be "a coalition of several militant Christian groups."[57]

In Mrs Leslie Fry he found a trusting ally. Fry, whom Rosenzweig has characterized as "a paid Nazi propaganda agent," met with Deatherage at the Philips Hotel in Kansas City on 20 August 1937.[58] It was at this meeting that the American Nationalist Confederation was formed. Organizations bearing such names as the Militant Christian Patriots (founded by Fry), the American League of Christian Women, the Christian Constitutionalists, and the Defenders of Christian Civilization all gathered to join forces.[59] Fry's *Christian Free Press* was a newspaper and company designed to expose

Judeo-Bolshevism in the United States. Real-time commentators, and scholars since the 1940s, have persistently characterized the ANC as extra-theological. This was far from the case. Christ was central to its construction.

One of the main relationships supporting Deatherage in this goal of constructing the ANC was the one he developed in 1937 with Johannes Klapproth, a German-American chemist for Shell Oil who was an early member of the Nazi Party. Through his connections in the Nazi Party and the German Foreign Ministry, by the mid-1930s Klapproth had risen to become head of the American section of *World Service* (*Welt Dienst*). *Welt Dienst* was published in nine languages and distributed globally. Historian Hanno Plass has called it "the prime interface between anti-Semitic journalism and activism."[60]

In many ways, Klapproth viewed Deatherage as a Christian activist. He hosted Deatherage on a West Coast tour, where he met again with Mrs Fry and interviewed many pro-Nazis.[61] As a sign of their friendship, Klapproth accepted induction into the Knights of the White Camellia.[62] In early 1938, *Welt Dienst*'s English editions began running advertisements for pro-Nazi literature indicating that any books bought in North America could be purchased, for reasonable prices, through the ANC.[63] In return, Deatherage began advertising subscriptions for *Welt Dienst* in the ANC's *News Bulletin*.[64] It was Klapproth who encouraged Deatherage to write his essays on the meaning of "Nationalism" in the *News Bulletin*.

In a front-page editorial titled "Nationalism – The Solution," Deatherage argued that President Roosevelt was permitting "Communistic Control of his administration."[65] Of course, "Communistic Control" was coming about only because "International Jewry" had been so successful at government infiltration. There was only one way America could overcome the crisis: "The return of America to Americans through a reawakened Nationalism."[66]

The entire country needed to be returned to the people: "The present control of the Federal Government, press, radio, movies, and business in general must be taken from the hands of international Jews." Concomitant with the Jewish takeover of America was an equal effort to "reestablish the Christian religion." In this sense, pro-Christianity became a code word for antisemitism. "The entire Jew-ridden administration have and are now engaged in building up popular opinion against Nationalism. Nationalism will destroy their racket."[67] For those who believe in these principles, "the platform of the American Nationalist Confederation is your platform."[68] Deatherage made it clear: Christ was the central plank of his platform.

In his second editorial on nationalism, titled "Nationalism Will Save America," Deatherage warned Americans of the "planned Sovietization of America," which was taking place under the New Deal's agrarian policies.[69] Crop control plans for farmers, as set out by Secretary of Agriculture Henry Wallace, were similar to Stalin's agrarian reforms in the Soviet Union – reforms that had resulted in "the starvation of eight million people, punitive expeditions, and liquidation squads."[70] "Christian Russian people died by the millions, as they will probably die here, because they said 'It could not happen here.'"[71]

Fascism, Deatherage averred, was permissible because it "sets out to do all it can to defend and encourage the institution of private property, especially in the form of small ownership ... and small agricultural proprietors."[72] In America, private property was guaranteed "under a Christian government, and not an anti-Christian dictatorship of alien Jewry."[73] For Deatherage, neither fascism nor Nazism represented a true dictatorial threat; rather, it was global Judaism that would force dictatorship on the American people. On the home front, it was the Roosevelt administration that was the problem. While the New Deal advocated "many ... good things," it was "the planned aim of ultimate destruction of Christian people" that was wrong with the New Deal. "Nationalism is offered not because it is perfect, but because it is your only salvation from becoming a sweated laborer under the Jewish lash."[74] Combating "the Jews" was tied to the defence of American Christianity. Nationalism and salvation were linked.

Certainly, Johannes Klapproth was delighted with Deatherage's latest editorial. Nationalism, grounded in an American Christianity that saw Jews as an existential threat, seemed to open a door for American acceptance of German National Socialism. Deatherage's complete co-option by Klapproth prompted the next big move in his life. In the summer of 1938, Deatherage was invited to Germany as one of three American delegates to the World Conference of Anti-Semites. The conference, an attempt to organize antisemitic groups on an international basis, was scheduled to meet in Erfurt, Germany. Deatherage would be the only American to address the Nazi audience.

Antisemites from China (White Russians in diaspora from Harbin), Canada, South Africa, South America, and eighteen other countries gathered in Erfurt at the behest of Alfred Rosenberg, then head of the Nazi Party's Foreign Political Office. Rosenberg was arguably the foremost anti-Bolshevik among the Nazi leaders. Through his writings, he supplied Hitler with many false philosophical concepts to buttress the early racist and quasi-scientific doctrines of National Socialism. For Rosenberg, the swastika was of prime importance. Mirroring what Deatherage was printing in his *News Bulletin*, Rosenberg believed that "the myth of blood, which under the sign of the Swastika, released the world revolution ... [would awaken] ... the soul of the race."[75] The aim of the conference was to create an antisemitic international, or network.[76] This antisemitic international was to combat the "red international" of Jewish origin.[77]

Rosenberg had been told about Deatherage by Klapproth and his American agent, Ernest F. Elmhurst.[78] One author has indicated that Elmhurst may even have accompanied Deatherage to Erfurt.[79] Deatherage and Elmhurst had known each other since the Asheville Conference in 1936. Deatherage's selling point, from Rosenberg's perspective, was his near-obsession with Judeo-Bolshevism. Rosenberg viewed himself as Hitler's personal expert on Judeo-Bolshevism. Moreover, Rosenberg was working out a Christology that jibed with Deatherage's Judeo-Bolshevist Christian evangelism.

AN AMERICAN CHRISTIAN NAZISM

In what must rank as one of the most bizarre untold stories of the history of the American right, George Deatherage, the stylish mechanical engineer from St Albans, West Virginia, was invited to address the third meeting of the World Confederation of Antisemites in Erfurt, Germany. Furthermore, his speech was selected for publication in *Welt Dienst*. With his Erfurt speech, Deatherage became the first American since Charles Lindbergh to deliver a full-throated speech in front of Nazi officials.[80] The speech was saturated with Christological equations. So it was not entirely contrary to how Alfred Rosenberg viewed religion.

Many historians have argued that Rosenberg was not simply "anti-Church"; that he also believed "Christianity was incompatible with German nationalism because its central teachings were Jewish."[81] While this is true, what can be missed is that such belief did not make Rosenberg non-Christological. In his best-known work, *The Myth of the Twentieth Century*,

Rosenberg ultimately argued not that Christianity needed to be eradicated, but rather that it needed to be "reformed and saved from the 'Judeo-Roman' infections of its clerical representatives."[82] As historian Richard Steigmann-Gall points out, Rosenberg never once attacked Jesus Christ.[83] "If we were to get rid of Christianity," Rosenberg penned in his political diary, "other peoples may feel free to keep the Christian religion."[84] Rosenberg even believed in Jesus's message of love. After all, the concept of universal love allowed citizens to accept love of race and nation as an in-dwelling of the heart.[85]

The "corruptor" of Jesus's message was Saint Paul, who Rosenberg believed had affected a fake conversion to Christianity because he could not subdue it from without. According to Rosenberg, Paul never abandoned his Judaizing tendencies. Instead, he implanted a "Jewishness" in the nascent Christian church through the sheer force of his will. Saint Paul was still Saul the Jew, a plotter, a subversive – so much like the "political Jews" and Communists who had wormed their way into numerous governments around the world since 1917.[86]

It is no wonder, then, that Rosenberg and Deatherage held the same systematic and Christological views, particularly the central tenet that Jesus Christ was not Jewish. According to Rosenberg, Jesus Christ "was a descendent from the tribe of Nordic peoples expelled at the time of the Exodus ... [and] ... isolated in Galilee by the Jews."[87] "Those who say, 'it makes no difference from what race Christ came,'" Deatherage wrote in his ANC *News Bulletin*, "<u>are</u> <u>wrong</u>." "Christ was not a Jew," he argued.[88] Having publicized such views in the spring of 1938, he was even more welcome at Erfurt later that fall.

Reviewed here for the first time, Deatherage's Erfurt speech, delivered in English, was titled "Will America Be Jewry's Waterloo?"[89] The speech is important because during the height of government scrutiny of Deatherage in 1939, neither Congressional investigators, nor the FBI, nor Jewish organizations, could get their hands on a copy.[90] The speech shows a thoroughly nazified Deatherage still clinging to his Christian roots while arguing for the violent imposition of National Socialism in the United States.

"It is with great and much anticipated pleasure," Deatherage began, "to be able to extend to the patriots of Germany and the many other nations represented here today ... the greetings and good wishes of your American brothers."[91] Deatherage chose the theme of brotherhood because "after all, we are all brothers in race and culture, devoting our lives to a common cause."[92] That cause was "the salvation of the world for Christian and Aryan people."[93] Having been spurned by church leaders in Asheville two years earlier, Deatherage would use the podium in Erfurt to construct his vision of American nationalism not only in connection to the Nazi ideals of Aryan power, but also in terms of Christianity.

"The greatest crisis since the Dark Ages," Deatherage bellowed, was that of "Jewish Communism."[94] "All of us – from every nation on earth, [must] cooperate and coordinate our efforts towards destroying the power of Jewish Communism – forever [!] … That is our primary reason for our being assembled here together."[95] Deatherage implored his fellow antisemites to lend whatever help they could to the United States. "Ours is the greatest Jew-ridden nation on earth."[96] For Deatherage, Christians were the *victims* (author's emphasis) of Jewish social gains. "The United States today is in the death grip of forces alien to our past history, our aims, and our Christian ideals."[97] Deatherage's nationalism, and his antisemitism, saw Christianity as the strongest bulwark against the Jewish existential threat. "Either we rid ourselves of alien (utterly anti-American) Jewish Internationalism," Deatherage wrote elsewhere, "or suffer ourselves to be wiped out as a free Christian people."[98] Rosenberg admired Deatherage's speech so much that he had it republished four years later in the March 1942 edition of *Gelbe Hefte: Historische und politische Zeitschrift für das katholische Deutschland,* an influential Roman Catholic journal that "sympathized with selected aspects of the Nazi Party program."[99]

Before he left the podium, there was a final feature of the ANC that Deatherage did not want his Nazi sponsors to forget: the ANC had adopted the swastika. "As it brought Germany out of the depths of despair," Deatherage argued, "so it will bring the United States."[100] Deatherage expressed "faith and confidence" in the American people, but he also warned that "America will not be Sovietized without a battle."[101] The swastika, which integrated Christianity, nationalism, and antisemitism, would be the banner of the American Nationalist Confederation. The swastika was not merely the sign of a foreign country's political ideology; it promised to be the symbol of a new "Christian Nazism" which could easily be adapted to America.[102]

With America's entry into the war, however, the swastika took on a different meaning. Deatherage addressed this new state of affairs in a prominent three-column interview with a staff writer from the *Washington Post* in February 1942. When it was founded, "we were organized to prevent something [the Judeo-Bolshevist revolution]," Deatherage said of the ANC, "but [now] something has happened that has taken it out of our hands."[103] Nearly admitting to being crushed by the waves of history, Deatherage surmised: "There's nothing to do about it. Why theorize?"[104]

Deatherage's *Washington Post* interview was inconsequential, except for a snippet of information at the very end of the article that stunned many members of Congress. Since before the outbreak of war, George E. Deatherage had been working as a chief construction engineer at the Norfolk, Virginia, US Naval Base. He was privy to classified Navy blueprints, besides overseeing around $25 million of taxpayer money.

New York Democratic congressman Samuel Dickstein, who had long been scrutinizing pro-Nazi Americans, pushed Navy Secretary Frank Knox to expel Deatherage from Norfolk. The Naval Affairs Committee chair, Carl Vinson, who was a fellow Democrat, defended Deatherage, indicating that the former ANC leader was being railroaded by the press.[105] Deatherage ultimately was fired by Knox, but he remained unrepentant, calling the entire affair "a damned bunch of crap from beginning to end."[106] In reporting his dismissal from the US Navy, *Time* magazine tagged Deatherage "a swastika-lover."[107]

Adopting the swastika had profound consequences for Deatherage and his American Nationalist Confederation. Anchored in "the political surrealism of the paranoid fringe," as Rick Perlstein has put it, Deatherage melded American nationalism, antisemitism, and a mangled form of Christianity with German National Socialism. The ANC's symbol was the swastika, a symbol that represented several complex and conflicting streams of religious and political thought that coalesced somewhere on the far-right end of the American political spectrum from 1937 to 1942. Of course, the administrative form of the ANC was ephemeral, and its membership data have eluded assessment. Its political impact was negligible.

But the ANC's philosophical and religious exegeses have continued to appear in various forms and with varying fervency over the ensuing decades.

Deatherage's short-lived attempt at an antisemitic-based Christian Nationalism gave way to the Christian Nationalism movement of Gerald L.K. Smith in the postwar years. Many have viewed Smith's Christian Nationalist movement as harbouring a subdued antisemitism. In the 1960s, George Lincoln Rockwell founded the American Nazi Party. Most view Rockwell as the first American to adopt the swastika. Rockwell also maintained amorphous comparisons between Jesus Christ and Hitler. A recrudescence of "British-Israelism" and Christian Identity in 1990s America exposed some of the same philosophical sinews that would have been recognizable to George E. Deatherage in 1937 and 1938. Deatherage's April 1938 assertion about the staying power of the swastika in America continues to play out.

NOTES

The author would like to thank Allan Figueroa Deck, SJ, rector of the Jesuit community at Loyola Marymount University, for the community's support and hospitality during my research at archives in Los Angeles.

1 George Deatherage, "The Meaning of the Emblem – the Swastika," American Nationalist Confederation *News Bulletin*, 23 April 1938, CRC 2, box 47, file 5, American Nationalist Confederation: publications; The News Bulletin, April 1938, Community Relations Committee Papers, Jewish Federation Council of Greater Los Angeles, Special Collections and Archives, Oviatt Library, California State University, Northridge, CA (hereafter CSUN).

2 Deatherage, "The Meaning of the Emblem – the Swastika."

3 Ibid.

4 Ibid.

5 "The Swastika," American Nationalist Confederation News Bulletin, 14 May 1938, CRC 2, box 47, file 6, American Nationalist Confederation: publications, *News Bulletin*, May–June 1938, CSUN.

6 "Confederation Christian Membership," American Nationalist Confederation *News Bulletin*, May, [n.d.], 1938, 7, CRC 2, box 47, file 6, American Nationalist Confederation: publications, *News Bulletin*, May–June 1938, CSUN.

7 By Christology I mean the accepted area of theological hermeneutics concerning the attributes of Christ, his relational divinity, human nature, and monotheism.

8 Walker Connor makes the distinction between ethnonationalism and patriotism in "Nationalism and Political Illegitimacy," in *Ethnonationalism in the Contemporary World: Walker Connor and the Study of Nationalism*, ed. Daniele Conversi (London: Routledge, 2002), 24–49, here 25.

9 Dean G. Stroud, ed., *Preaching in Hitler's Shadow: Sermons of Resistance in the Third Reich* (Grand Rapids: William B. Eerdmans, 2013), 8.

10 *The Nation* and *The New Republic* followed Deatherage most closely, while *Harper's*, *Time*, *The American Mercury*, and the *Saturday Evening Post* all wrote major investigative articles on Deatherage. Deatherage also garnered major newspaper coverage.

11 Laura B. Rosenzweig, *Hollywood's Spies: The Undercover Surveillance of Nazis in Los Angeles* (New York: NYU Press, 2017), 123–7.

12 Philip Jenkins, *Hoods and Shirts: The Extreme Right in Pennsylvania, 1925–1950* (Chapel Hill: University of North Carolina Press, 1997), 8; on Hitler's views of Jesus, see Fritz Redlich, *Hitler: Diagnosis of a Destructive Prophet* (New York: Oxford University Press, 1999), 331–2.

13 Harold Lavine, *Fifth Column in America* (New York: Doubleday, 1940), 57.

14 Ibid.

15 Rick Perlstein, "I Thought I Understood the American Right – Trump Proved Me Wrong," *New York Times Magazine*, 11 April 2017.

16 Ibid.

17 Ibid.

18 Dorothy Thompson, "On the Record: More about the Fifth Column," *New York Post*, 27 February 1942, 4. On Thompson's devotion to liberalism, see Dorothy Thompson, *Dorothy Thompson's Political Guide: A Study of American Liberalism and Its Relationship to Modern Totalitarian States* (New York: Stackpole Sons, 1938), 64.

19 Gardner Jackson to Jerry Voorhis, 24 May 1939, H.MSS.0922, Jerry Voorhis papers, box 1, folder 20, Honnold/Mudd Special Collections Library, the Claremont Colleges, Claremont, CA.

20 1910 Census, Duluth Ward 8, Saint Louis, Minnesota; Roll: T624_725; Page: 23A; Enumeration District: 0193; FHL microfilm: 1374738, Ancestry.com 1910 United States Federal Census; "Fascist Organizer Deatherage Would Kiss Hitler – for Money," *New York Post*, 24 May 1939, Nahum Greenberg clippings collection, RG 486, vol. 26, George Deatherage file, YIVO Institute for Jewish Research, New York.

21 These traits are evident in the many books Deatherage authored for the McGraw-Hill publishing company from 1945 to 1965.

22 David S. Brown, *Richard Hofstadter: An Intellectual Biography* (Chicago: University of Chicago Press, 2007), 94.

23 Ibid.

24 US Passport Applications, 1795–1925, National Archives and Records Administration (hereafter NARA), Washington, D.C., vol. 006: Calcutta, India. Ancestry.com, US Passport Applications, 1795–1925.

25 Daniel R. Bergsmark, *Economic Geography of Asia* (New York: Prentice-Hall, 1935), 237.

26 Dietmar Rothermund, *An Economic History of India: From Pre-Colonial Times to 1991*, 2nd ed. (London: Routledge, 1993), 63.

27 Vitit Muntarbhorn, *The Status of Refugees in Asia* (Oxford: Oxford University, 1992), 59.

28 Hearings Cong. 76 sess. 1 Special Committee on Un-American Activities v. 1 1939, 3535.

29 Ibid.

30 Ibid., 3487.

31 Rosenzweig, *Hollywood's Spies*, 127; on Kositsin travelling to St. Albans, West Virginia, see George E. Deatherage to Henry Allen, 12 October 1937, [copy], John W. Jackson papers, MS 95-18, box 1, folder 6, Special Collections and University Archives, Wichita State University (hereafter WSU).

32 Hearings Cong. 76 sess. 1 Special Committee on Un-American Activities v. 1 1939, 3464.

33 About 13,000 US soldiers were deployed in Russia in 1919–20, suffering about 500 battle deaths.

34 In this respect, Deatherage was like other right-wing fundamentalists such as William Dudley Pelley and Elizabeth Dilling, both of whom spent significant time in Russia and the Soviet Union between 1919 and 1931. Both of them viewed the Russian Civil War as an anti-Christian persecution. The impact of the Russian Civil War on the American right is understudied.

35 Book review of *The White Sepulchre: An Authentic Account of Church Persecution in Russia* by Carlo von Kügelgen (London: Lutterworth Press, 1935), American Nationalist Confederation News Bulletin, 8 February 1938, CRC 2, box 47, file 3, American Nationalist Confederation: publications, The News Bulletin, January–February 1938, CSUN. Richard Hofstadter first used the

term "ecumenical anti-Communism" in relation to Senator Joseph Mc-Carthy's impact on postwar American Protestants. McCarthy pushed them to abandon their traditional anti-Catholic biases and coalesce around the issue of anti-Communism. See Richard Hofstadter, *The Paranoid Style in American Politics and Other Essays* (New York: A.A. Knopf, 1965), 70.

36 Book review of *The White Sepulchre.*

37 Hearings Cong. 76 sess. 1 Special Committee on Un-American Activities v. 1 1939, 3464.

38 Paul Hanebrink, *A Specter Haunting Europe: The Myth of Judeo-Bolshevism* (Cambridge, MA: Harvard University Press, 2018), 14.

39 Hearings Cong. 76 sess. 1 Special Committee on Un-American Activities v. 1 1939, 3510.

40 Kelly J. Baker, *Gospel According to the Klan: The KKK's Appeal to Protestant America, 1915–1930* (Lawrence: University Press of Kansas, 2011), 18. See also Juan O. Sanchez, *Religion and the Ku Klux Klan: Biblical Appropriation in Their Literature and Songs* (Jefferson: McFarland, 2016).

41 Deatherage quoted in Robert E. Herzstein, *Roosevelt and Hitler: Prelude to War* (New York: John Wiley and Sons, 1994), 263.

42 "Mr. Dies and Mr. Deatherage," *The New Masses*, 21 May 1940, 17.

43 *The World Almanac and Book of Facts* (New York: New York World Telegraph, 1941), 568.

44 Stetson Kennedy, *Southern Exposure: Making the South Safe for Democracy* (Tuscaloosa: University of Alabama Press, 2010), 185.

45 "Hitlerism in America," *Look*, 28 March 1939, 21.

46 "Dies Committee Turns Guns on Plot against World Jews," *Social Justice*, 5 June 1939, 17.

47 Jonathan P. Herzog, *The Spiritual-Industrial Complex: America's Religious Battle against Communism in the Early Cold War* (New York: Oxford University Press, 2011), 60.

48 "Anti-Communist Conference Was Asked to Fight Bigotry," *The Jewish Floridian* 9, no. 35 (1936): 5.

49 Ibid.

50 Nollner's group would call themselves the National Conference of Clergy and Laymen.

51 Ralph Lord Roy, *Apostles of Discord: A Study of Organized Bigotry and Disruption on the Fringes of Protestantism* (Boston: Beacon Press, 1953), 30.

52 Headline quoted in John LaFarge, "Christian Front to Combat Commu-
    nism," *America* 55, no. 22 (1936): 508–10, here 508.

53 LaFarge, "Christian Front to Combat Communism," 508.

54 Deatherage to Nollner, cited in Morris Schonbach, *American Fascism During
    the 1930s and 1940s* (New York: Garland, 1985), 340.

55 Ibid.

56 Hamilton Basso, "The Little Hitlers at Asheville," *The New Republic,* 2
    September 1936, 101.

57 Steven J. Ross, *Hitler in Los Angeles: How Jews Foiled Nazi Plots against
    Hollywood and America* (New York: Bloomsbury, 2017), 230.

58 Rosenzweig, *Hollywood's Spies,* 136.

59 "Information on the American Nationalist Confederation," 13 July 1938
    [copy], 1, Jewish Federation Council of Greater Los Angeles, Community
    Relations Committee Collection, Part 2 (CRC/2), box 47, folder 1, American
    Nationalist Confederation, 1938, CSUN.

60 Hanno Plass and Bill Templer, "*Der Welt Dienst:* International Anti-Semitic
    Propaganda," *Jewish Quarterly Review* 103, no. 4 (2013): 503–522, here 503.

61 *House Reports,* US Congressional Serial Set, Issue 10296 (Washington, DC:
    US GPO, 1939), 107.

62 Handwritten notes, Jerry Voorhis papers, box 1, folder 20, George Deather-
    age file, Claremont.

63 See the *Welt Dienst* collection at the YIVO Institute for Jewish Research.

64 ANC, *News Bulletin,* 23 July 1938, vol. 1, no. 27, CRC 2, box 47, file 2, American
    Nationalist Confederation: publications, *The News Bulletin,* CSUN.

65 George E. Deatherage, "Nationalism – The Solution," *American Nationalist
    Confederation News Bulletin,* 12 March 1938, vol. 1, no. 8, CRC 2, box 47, file
    4, American Nationalist Confederation: publications, *The News Bulletin,*
    March 1938, CSUN.

66 Deatherage, "Nationalism – The Solution." Underscore is Deatherage's.

67 Ibid.

68 Ibid.

69 George Deatherage, "Nationalism Will Save America," ANC *News Bulletin,*
    May 1938, CRC 2, box 47, file 6, American Nationalist Confederation: publi-
    cations, *News Bulletin,* May–June 1938, CSUN.

70 Ibid.

71 Ibid.

72 Ibid.

73 Ibid.

74 Ibid.

75 Rosenberg, quoted in Eric Kurlander, *Hitler's Monsters: A Supernatural History of the Third Reich* (New Haven: Yale University Press, 2017), 52.

76 The first International Anti-Semitic Conference was held in Budapest in 1924 and the second in Copenhagen during August 1926. The 1937 and 1938 meetings in Erfurt, Germany, were the first sponsored by the Nazi party.

77 Jan C. Behrends, "Back from the USSR: The Anti-Comintern's Publications on Soviet Russia in Nazi Germany (1935–41)," *Kritika: Exploration in Russian and Eurasian History* 10, no. 3 (2009): 527–56, here 531.

78 George J. Mintzer, *The International Anti-Semitic Conspiracy* (New York, NY: American Jewish Committee, 1946), 10.

79 Henry Reed Hoke, *It's a Secret* (New York: Reynal and Hitchcock, 1946), 206.

80 On 23 July 1936, Lindbergh delivered a lengthy speech on changes in aviation warfare at the Berlin Aero Club. In October 1938, Lindbergh was awarded the Commander Cross of the Order of the German Eagle by Hermann Göring on behalf of Hitler. It does not seem that an acceptance speech was given when Lindbergh received the award. Lindbergh gave several pro-German speeches in 1941, but all were delivered in the United States.

81 Susannah Heschel, *The Aryan Jesus: Christian Theologians and the Bible in Nazi Germany* (Princeton: Princeton University Press, 2008), 191.

82 Richard Steigmann-Gall, *The Holy Reich: Nazi Conceptions of Christianity, 1919–1945* (New York: Cambridge University Press, 2003), 95.

83 Ibid.

84 Diary entry of 14 December 1941 (Rosenberg paraphrasing a conversation with Hitler), *The Political Diary of Alfred Rosenberg and the Onset of the Holocaust*, eds. and trans. Jürgen Matthäus and Frank Bajohr (Lanham: Rowman and Littlefield in association with the United States Holocaust Memorial Museum, 2015), 269.

85 James B. Whisker, *The Social, Political, and Religious Thought of Alfred Rosenberg: An Interpretive Essay* (Washington, DC: University Press of America, 1982), 68.

86 Robert K. Wittman and David Kinney, *The Devil's Diary: Alfred Rosenberg and the Stolen Secrets of the Third Reich* (New York: Harper, 2016), 175. The authors conflate Rosenberg's attacks on Paul as attacks on Jesus Christ.

87 Ibid., 78.

88 ANC *News Bulletin*, 2 April 1938, vol. 1, no. 11, CRC 2, box 47, file 5, American Nationalist Confederation: publications, The News Bulletin, April 1938, CSUN.

89 I am grateful to Anne Kenny, interlibrary loan manager of the O'Neill Library at Boston College, for securing a copy of Deatherage's speech. I am especially grateful to the librarians at Universitätsbibliothek Johann Christian at Goethe University in Frankfurt, Germany, for searching their collection and sending me a copy of the Deatherage speech. See George E. Deatherage, "Will America Be Jewry's Waterloo?," *Welt Dienst Internationale Korrespondenz zur Aufklärung über die Judenfrage*, vol. 5, 1–15 September 1938, 8.

90 At Deatherage's HUAC hearing, he denied giving the speech.

91 Deatherage, "Waterloo," 8.

92 Ibid.

93 Ibid.

94 Ibid.

95 Ibid.

96 Ibid.

97 Ibid.

98 ANC, "News Bulletin," 26 February 1938, vol. 1, no. 6, CRC 2, box 47, file 3, American Nationalist Confederation: publications, The News Bulletin, January–February 1938, CSUN.

99 Seth D. Armus, *French Anti-Americanism (1930–1948): Critical Moments in a Complex History* (Lanham: Lexington Books, 2007), 125n100.

100 Deatherage, "Waterloo," 9.

101 Ibid.

102 Lavine, *Fifth Column in America*, 76. James True, president of James True Associates, published and distributed a newsletter like Deatherage's titled *Industrial Control Reports*. True believed that an "international alliance of Jews planned to wreck Christianity and the world," and began to lean toward the concept of "Christian Nazism" in the United States as early as 1936. See "Jew-Baiter Attempts to Hide Terror Plot," *Daily Worker*, 21 August 1936, 4.

103 Alfred Friendly, "U.S. Will Win – By Nazi Plan, Says Deatherage," *Washington Post*, 18 February 1942, 2.

104 Ibid.

105 "Memo from Washington," *New York Post*, 24 February 1942, in Nahum
     Greenberg clippings collection, RG 486, box 7, vol. 26, George Deatherage
     file, YIVO Institute for Jewish Research.

     Kenneth G. Crawford, "'Knightshirt Unrepentant," PM Magazine, in Nahum
     Greenberg clippings collection, George Deatherage file, YIVO Institute for
     Jewish Research.

107 "In & Out," *Time*, March 2, 1942, 57.

2

Transnational Antisemitic Networks and Political Christianity: The Catholic Participation in *The Protocols of the Elders of Zion*

Nina Valbousquet

Linkages between Christian and modern antisemitism did not go unnoticed in the aftermath of the First World War. On behalf of the American Jewish Committee, the New York–based journalist Herman Bernstein denounced to the Vatican secretary of state, Cardinal Pietro Gasparri, a Catholic version of the notorious forgery *The Protocols of the Elders of Zion*:

> I note a letter of yours dated June 20, 1919, on the cover of a volume by Monsignor Jouin entitled "*Les 'Protocols' des Sages de Sion*," published in Paris, which has just reached me. The impression thus given by the publication of your letter is that His Holiness the Pope and you sanction the latest work by Monsignor Jouin based upon documents which I know to be a forgery. I have made an investigation of the so-called "Protocols of the Wise Men of Zion" and have found indisputable evidence that they have been fabricated. ... I see that your letter refers to another work by Monsignor Jouin entitled *La Guerre Maçonnique* [The Masonic War], which undoubtedly has no bearing on the subject dis-

cussed in this volume on the *Protocols*, but the impression is conveyed
that the antisemitic campaign has the approval of the Vatican.[1]

Bernstein was referring to one of the first French translations of the *Protocols* in 1920, the work of Monsignor Ernest Jouin, an honorary prelate of
His Holiness. Bernstein did more than lament the ruse used by the French
cleric (who proudly displayed on the cover of the *Protocols* a Vatican letter
approving of his previous book, *The Masonic War*); he also warned Pope
Benedict XV against the damaging impression that Church officials condoned the antisemitic myth of the *Protocols*. To be sure, the Holy See never
officially endorsed the *Protocols*. Yet the postwar era saw a multitude of
Catholic articles sympathetic to the *Protocols*, in tandem with a renewal of
pervasive anti-Jewish prejudices within the Church. These factors helped
foster an environment in which hardcore antisemites felt empowered to
spread their vitriol, as exemplified by Jouin's bold subterfuge. By the time
that Herman Bernstein wrote to the Vatican (January 1921), positive comments by authoritative Church journals, as well as Catholic versions of the
Protocols, had already been published. How did the fictitious antisemitic text
gain visibility and even credibility so quickly in significant sectors of the
Catholic Church?

This chapter examines why antisemitic conspiracy theories appealed
to reactionary Catholics in the post–First World War era. The participation of some Catholics in the global dissemination of the *Protocols* raises
questions about its broader repercussions in the interwar context of ethnonationalism and fascism. In his classic study of the diffusion of the *Protocols*, historian Norman Cohn mentioned an "antisemitic international"
during the 1930s centred entirely around Nazism.[2] By focusing on Nazi
influence, Cohn overlooked the role played by Christianity in the interwar
diffusion of antisemitic propaganda. I argue that in fact, Catholic networks
were crucial vectors of transnational antisemitism and played a vital role
in the early dissemination of the *Protocols*. Delving deeper into the formation of the first international of the *Protocols* after the First World War,
this chapter reassesses the intersection between two aspects, usually neglected in the scholarship: the transnational and the Catholic dimensions
of interwar antisemitism.

While Catholic antisemites capitalized on widespread acceptance of antisemitic myths within Church circles, they also expanded their networks
beyond the Catholic world thanks precisely to the *Protocols*. The circulation
of the text led at times to political collaborations between Catholic and right-
wing activists, thus paving the way for clerical fascism.[3] The first Catholic
promoters of the *Protocols* embraced a religious-political interpretation of
the postwar context as a means to alleviate their acute sense of Western civilization's unprecedented crisis. In various countries, they shaped and propagated a vision of political Christianity as an alternative to both liberalism
and communism and the only solution to the cataclysms of war and revolution.[4] This reactionary worldview idealized medieval Christendom. The
legacy of a mythical golden age had to be defended against the quintessential
other, the Jew, whom Catholic antisemites perceived as the driving force
behind all secular and revolutionary change. Not limited to a mere religious
form of anti-Judaism, modern Christian antisemitism took a central place
in a political culture of Catholic counter-revolution.

The political context of the aftermath of the First World War provides a
good starting point for examining the circulation of the *Protocols* within the
Catholic Church. The trauma of the war, the collapse of empires, the rise of
ethnonationalism, and the Bolshevik Revolution contributed to increased
politicization of traditionalist Catholics. Against this backdrop, the perception of new threats against the Church reactivated the counter-revolutionary
and anti-modern functions of Catholic antisemitism. Because liberal revolutions had granted civil rights to Jews to the disadvantage of the Church in
countries like Italy and France, traditionalist Catholics tended to conflate
Jews with secular modernity. Nineteenth-century Catholic antisemitism had
its version of conspiracy theories that echoed the post-1789 order, namely
the idea of a generalized Jewish-Masonic plot.[5] But compared to its prede-
cessor, the twentieth-century myth of the *Protocols* raised antisemitic con-
spiration to an unprecedented scale of ubiquity and lethality.

The *Protocols of the Elders of Zion* is an antisemitic forgery that purports
to document a Jewish conspiracy to achieve world domination. It consists
of a series of twenty-four or twenty-seven meetings held at Basel, Switzerland, in 1897, at the time of the first Zionist congress, during which Jewish
leaders allegedly plotted a global scheme to subvert Christian civilization by

means of socialism and capitalism. The document was likely forged in Russia in 1905 by tsarists agents for the purpose of blaming Jews for revolutionary movements.[6] The text began to circulate outside of Russia only after the Bolshevik Revolution, having been carried by White Russian exiles to Germany and the United States.[7]

The *Protocols* allowed Catholic antisemites to combine their pre-existing opposition to liberalism and capitalism with two new and timely ingredients: anti-communism and anti-Zionism. The conspiracy theory contained in the *Protocols* provided them with a single explanatory factor for all the dramatic mutations suffered by the post-1918 world. This myth-making relied on the recurrent unmasking of the archetypal enemy of Christianity who had been already demonized by centuries of Christian hostility: the Jew.[8] After the Russian Revolution, the Christian obsession with denouncing Jews' nefarious influence and uncovering a Jewish plot took on a new dimension shaped by the fear of communist contamination, especially during the short-lived but traumatic Bolshevik republics in Central Europe.

Most Catholic leaders interpreted the events following 1917 in apocalyptic terms.[9] Catholic versions of the *Protocols* in 1920–21 translated this vision of a cosmic war between good and evil into antisemitic language. The myth of Judeo-Bolshevism quickly became pervasive among both Church leaders and antisemitic propagandists. According to that myth, Jews were the chief instigators and beneficiaries of Bolshevism. Some variants portrayed Judaism as the philosophical bedrock of communist atheism. Speculating on the actual participation of some Jews in revolutionary movements, the myth of Judeo-Bolshevism went so far in its generalization as to accuse Jews of being collectively responsible for communist violence; this served as a morbid rationale for pogroms during the Russian Civil War.

Historian Paul Hanebrink recently examined the widespread diffusion of the myth of Judeo-Bolshevism in Christian Europe. While responding to the urgency of a new political situation, the myth remained embedded in Christianity and its "set of much older anti-Jewish prejudices," such as the fear of Jewish fanaticism and messianism. Crucial to explaining its global success was its cross-referentiality in that it zealously unmasked revolutionary leaders as Jews. As Hanebrink convincingly argues, "the circulation and mimetic reproduction [of the myth] had a 'reality effect.'"[10] Recent scholarship has shed light on the pervasiveness of the Judeo-Bolshevism myth within the Catholic hierarchy and Vatican diplomacy, especially among those leaders who were at the forefront of communist revolutions, such as Eugenio Pacelli – the future Pius XII, who served as nuncio in Munich during the Soviet Republic of spring 1920.[11]

On 2 October 1920, the Jesuit journal in Rome, *Civiltà Cattolica*, published a letter dated July 1920 that the bishops of Poland had addressed to their peers in the West to defend the Church against Bolshevism, "[the] living incarnation and manifestation on earth of the spirit of the Antichrist." According to the Polish bishops, the Bolshevik front in Eastern Europe was only the visible face of a larger plan for "the conquest of the world." The letter opened with a veiled reference to the myth of Judeo-Bolshevism, stating that "we are not fighting against the Russian nation, but against those who have trampled Russia and sucked their blood." The Polish hierarchy called to action all Christians who "know the psychology of the people who direct this entire network of conspiracy."[12]

The authoritative voice of *Civiltà Cattolica* increasingly supported the belief in a Judeo-Bolshevik peril.[13] Its international news section of August 1921 depicted "Red" Vienna "under the tyrannical dictatorship of the Jews." The Jesuit journal pointed out Jews' "specific cruelty against the elderly" and the "ruin of the bourgeoisie and the deceit of the proletariat subdued to Jewish capitalism."[14] Furthermore, in October 1922, *Civiltà Cattolica* dedicated a lengthy article to "World Revolution and the Jews." Drawing upon White Russian propaganda, the article asserted that of 545 Soviet Russian officials, 447 were of Jewish origins. By looking carefully at the "faces" and "Kabbalistic names of those rabble-rousers," the Jesuit writer (likely Father Enrico Rosa, the main editor of the journal) could claim that the majority of Soviet leaders were "not Russian natives, but rather Jewish intruders, who are careful enough to hide their original names behind the mask of a Slavic pseudonym." In contrast to the "good sense of the Aryan race," a wicked "Judaic race" had generated communism: "Only the depravity of a Semitic fantasy was able to overturn all the traditions of humankind." Significantly, the Jesuit editor chose to introduce this detailed account of Jewish influence in Soviet Russia with an allusion to the *Protocols* – albeit not by name – and to the discovery of "secrets which bear the mark of the ghetto." The question of the *Protocols'* authenticity was quickly dismissed as a secondary concern compared to the actuality of Jewish dominion: "Documents or forgery? It would be difficult, as usual, to shed light on the darkness that thoroughly envelops Israel."[15]

Beyond Rome, similar arguments and tone could be found one year earlier in the French semi-official journal *Documentation Catholique* (Catholic Documentation). A monthly published by "La Bonne Presse," the Parisian press of French Assumptionists (Congregation of the Augustinians of the Assumption), which also published the well-known daily *La Croix* (The Cross), *Documentation Catholique* featured official documents of the Holy See and the French episcopate. Alongside these Church statements, one would be surprised to discover political articles selected by the main editor of the journal, Father Salvien, who injected a reactionary political tone to the publication from 1919 until his dismissal in 1923.[16] On the front page of the March 1920 issue, *Documentation Catholique* did not hesitate to promote a document from the "official American services" that had uncovered that "Jews are the main champions of global Bolshevism." The editor's comments consisted of a series of rhetorical questions, such as: "Are the 'pogroms' in Russia the result of a conscious hatred from antisemites or instead a reaction of peasants against the tyranny of ruthless usurers?" Like *Civiltà Cattolica* and *La Croix*, *Documentation Catholique* eschewed the question of its engagement with the forgery by relying on White Russian documents; the editor called for a "public discussion to shed some light on this bloody darkness." The article gave credence to a report uncovering a "secret Zionist Protocol, number 8, 1897." The main argument of the document was that American and British Jewish financiers had funded the Bolshevik Revolution to achieve "Jewish imperialism and the shaking of the Goy rule over Europe." Displaying a list of allegedly Jewish communists, the report gave as evidence of the Jewish plot the 1917 Balfour Declaration and the "Jewish republics" of Germany and Austria. The goal of the document was to mobilize Christian leaders: "Christianity remains silent, inactive, passive and inert. Who among Christian statemen will dare pay attention to these prophetic words of Jewry?"[17] The report did not emanate from the American secret services but was the creation of a White Russian propagandist, Boris Brasol. In the United States since 1916, Brasol worked for the War Trade Board, and he used his connections in the military to spread the report under the title *Bolshevism and Judaism*.[18] Brasol also edited one of the first American versions of the *Protocols*, published in Boston in the summer of 1920.[19]

The *Documentation Catholique* article of March 1920 was cited to explain the revolutionary turmoil in Bavaria in April 1920. Taking advantage of the cross-referentiality of the Catholic press, the Munich archdiocesan bulletin *Münchner katholische Kirchenzeitung* – published under the auspices of Archbishop Cardinal Michael von Faulhaber – referred to the article of the "very respected Paris journal" of the Assumptionists to launch a campaign against "Jewish imperialism" based on the *Protocols*.[20] The article in *Documentation Catholique* had a legacy into the 1930s; it was quoted at length by the Irish priest Dennis Fahey in his *The Mystical Body of Christ in the Modern World* (1935). Both Fahey and *Documentation Catholique* were cited in August 1938 as authoritative references in *Social Justice*, the Detroit-based weekly of Father Charles Coughlin, who republished the *Protocols* between July and November 1938.[21] The popular "radio-priest" was deeply involved in a nativist campaign against Jewish refugees in the United States, stirring fears of a "Jewish-Communist" world conspiracy.

The *Protocols* continued to gain legitimacy in the Catholic press, reaching a peak of visibility in October 1920 with an article titled "A Peril," published in *L'Osservatore Romano*, the Vatican's semi-official daily. Discussing the *Protocols* explicitly, that article stated that even though "a very small number" of Jews were still capable of doing good, the facts were undeniable: the "Jewish peril exists and needs to be understood as hatred against Christ and Christian peoples." The Vatican journal directly quoted the *Protocols*, praising them for their timeliness: "some sentences seem as if they had been written just yesterday for their predictions are so precise and fit with recent events." *L'Osservatore Romano* drew the same conclusion as *La Croix* and *Documentation Catholique*: although the authenticity of the *Protocols* remained questionable, the Jewish origins of the "subversive ideas" and the existence of the plot exposed in the document were "beyond doubt."[22] The Vatican daily not only endorsed previous *La Croix* articles that had given full credence to the myth of Judeo-Bolshevism but also quoted more extremist right-wing journals such as *Action Française* and *The Hidden Hand* to prove that Jews had masterminded revolutionary movements in Hungary and workers' strikes in England. *Action Française*, a daily, was published by a French monarchist league of the same name founded by Charles Maurras in 1905;[23] *The Hidden Hand*, the weekly of an ultra-Tory splinter group called the Britons, was founded in 1919 in London by Charles Beamish. Antisemitic and xenophobic, both political groups openly promoted the *Protocols*, the Britons having published their version in September 1920.[24]

Besides the contents and tone of the *L'Osservatore Romano* article, what is most striking is its position on the front page of the journal alongside another article titled "Zionism and Palestine." The latter article endorsed the critiques uttered by the Archbishop of Westminster, Cardinal Francis Alphonsus Bourne, who warned of the dangers of Jewish immigration to the Holy Land. Bourne declared that "Russian, Polish and Romanian Jews are obsessed with Bolshevik ideas" and that among them were many "extreme agitators who intend to destroy the sacred vestiges of the Holy Places."[25] This juxtaposition is not surprising, given that the Vatican newspaper had already expressed its opposition to a Jewish homeland in Palestine in three front-page articles published in June 1920.

To explain the dissemination of the *Protocols* within Catholic networks in 1920–21, one needs to consider one more ingredient: Zionism. The Balfour Declaration of 2 November 1917 deeply concerned the Vatican, and not only regarding the prospect of a Jewish homeland; it also feared British Protestant proselytism in the Holy Land. Pope Benedict XV and Cardinal Gasparri advocated for international sovereignty over the Holy Places, a request that was rebuked during the San Remo Conference of April 1920. That conference, which made official the British mandate in Palestine (although it was not ratified until 1922), was a setback for Vatican diplomacy and fuelled fierce opposition to Zionism among conservative Catholics, especially in France and Italy. After the appointment of Sir Herbert Samuel, an Anglo-Jewish official, to High Commissioner of Palestine, Benedict XV uttered a harsher condemnation of Zionism, fearing that Jewish colonizers would destroy and replace Christian order.[26]

L'Osservatore Romano referred to this turn of events in the issues of 9, 16, and 23 June 1920. Denouncing the "systematic invasion" of Palestine planned by Zionist organizations, the three articles argued that the declarations of Sir Samuel did not provide enough guarantees that Muslims and Christians in Palestine would be treated on an equal footing with Jewish immigrants. According to *L'Osservatore Romano*, the British High Commissioner's positions reflected the ambition to turn Jerusalem into a spiritual and cultural centre for all Jews with the ultimate aim of "reinstituting in the Holy City their hegemony, which repulses the entire civilized world."[27] The Holy See's semi-official newspaper drew in large part upon the antisemitic writings of French monarchist Roger Lambelin, especially his article published in *Le Correspondant* on 25 May 1920. According to historian Sergio Minerbi, Cardinal Gasparri deemed Lambelin's point of view convincing enough to be published on the front page of the Vatican paper and to be mentioned during his meeting with Sir Samuel in Rome on 25 June 1925.[28] The article of 16 June indeed praised the French antisemite as a "brilliant writer" whose "interesting article … deserves to be known." Among other arguments, *L'Osservatore Romano* endorsed the belief that Zionism and British imperialism had worked hand in hand since the second half of the nineteenth century, when "Jews attempted to force the pace in the political field" with the nomination of Benjamin Disraeli as prime minister, a real "triumph of the race." The article then accused Jews of having taken advantage of the Great War to advance their Zionist ambitions thanks to "the ability of Jewish politicians and Israelite big bankers." As such, Jews had formed in the Holy land a "threatening nation … a race, which with a proportion of one to six [inhabitants], claims to rule and annihilate the other races." Calling for the union of Muslims and Christians "against the common peril, for the common salvation," the article of 16 June concluded with a direct quotation of Lambelin, who referred to Zionism the "mastermind of Bolshevism and anarchy."[29] The French antisemite was quoted once more in the issue of 15 October, on Zionism and the *Protocols*.

Who was Roger Lambelin that he merited so much publicity in *L'Osservatore Romano*? A monarchist activist, Lambelin had started his career in the military before engaging in local politics in *fin de siècle* Paris. Presiding over the youth committee in support of the duc d'Orleans, he naturally found his place within the ranks of the Catholic and nationalistic league of Action Française. He wrote several articles for the league's journal, notably a series on the *Protocols* in 1920–21.[30] In 1921, he edited a version of the *Protocols* for a prestigious Parisian publisher, Grasset. A popular success, this version went through no fewer than twenty-five editions between 1921 and 1925. In his introduction, the French antisemite raised a rhetorical question: "Should Jews be held responsible, in large part, for the global unrest resulting from the war?" Lambelin concluded that the authenticity of the text was irrelevant, for its predictions fit perfectly in the postwar crisis: "The downfall of Russia, the abnormal clauses of the peace [treaty], the creation of a super-government called League of Nations, the establishment of Judaism in Jerusalem constitute the most striking demonstration of the reality of the plan of conquest decided upon by the Elders of Zion."[31]

For the same publisher, Lambelin released a series of three books dedicated to the "Jewish Peril: The Rule of Israel among the Anglo-Saxons" (1921), "Jewish Imperialism" (1924), and "The Victories of Israel" (1928).[32] While the latter called for a specific "statute of the Jews" in France – foreshadowing by twelve years Vichy's antisemitic laws – the two first volumes claimed to uncover pernicious Jewish influence in Great Britain and the United States. Lambelin considered both countries symptomatic of the "Jewish conquest" of gentile governments, a fate that threatened Catholic Latin countries as well. The French monarchist asserted that David Lloyd George and Woodrow Wilson were only puppets through whom the "representatives of a race of thirteen to fourteen million individuals, scattered in all the countries of the globe, have succeeded in imposing on the world a specific peace that is a *pax Judaica* and a super-government named League of Nations of which they are masters."[33] Despite his anti-American and anti-British populist claims, Lambelin was well-connected to antisemitic networks in both countries, and he praised the anti-Jewish "resistance" of the Britons in London and Henry Ford in the United States.

To show that his arguments were credible, Lambelin quoted the authoritative voices of *Documentation Catholique* and *L'Osservatore Romano* (the same article that he had himself inspired!), without forgetting to remind readers that the latter was the "semi-official organ of the Holy See."[34] The French writer was not an isolated case; he had close ties with another Catholic promoter of the *Protocols* previously mentioned, Monsignor Jouin. He collaborated with *Revue Internationale des Sociétés Secrètes* (RISS, International Journal of Secret Societies), the antisemitic journal led by Jouin (for example, writing on antisemitic movements in Romania in 1923). Lambelin even became the first president of the journal's right-wing league, Ligue Franc-Catholique, in 1928.[35] Both Lambelin and Jouin quoted a French translation of a Polish abbreviated version of the *Protocols* by Assumptionist Father Joseph Evrard, who also happened to be an editor at *Documentation Catholique*. Excerpts from this brochure cited by Jouin stated that the

Protocols were invaluable because they offered the "key that allows us to solve a full series of current issues" by explaining that Jews were the "mysterious hand that directs the destinies of the world."[36]

There were, however, meaningful differences between Lambelin and Jouin. With his ecclesiastical status, Monsignor Jouin lent a clerical legitimacy to the *Protocols*. He published the forgery in the fall of 1920, first in his *RISS* and then as a separate and first volume in a series of five books dedicated to the "Jewish-Masonic Peril" (each of them reproducing Cardinal Gasparri's letter of 1919). Lambelin called for the safeguarding of "Christian civilization" – a loose conception of political Christianity – whereas Jouin had a precise confessional agenda.[37] According to the Parisian prelate, the Roman Apostolic Church was the last bulwark against the Jewish conquest of the world, and this specific position explained why Catholicism was the first target and victim of Jewish malevolence. In this way, Jouin used the conspiracy theory presented in the *Protocols* to explain the origin of every single attack (real or perceived) against the Catholic Church. For example, Jouin blamed Jews for the 1905 French law of separation between state and church: Judeo-Masonry was the "Anti-Church" par excellence.

When he published the *Protocols*, Jouin was already the well-respected pastor of the Parisian church of Saint-Augustin, a wealthy parish of military officers. He was acclaimed for his perennial activism in defence of the Church in France. In 1918, Benedict XV honoured him with the title of prelate. Similarly, in 1924, Pope Pius XI conferred on him the honorary title of prothonotary apostolic, the highest distinction for non-episcopal prelates. By this time, Jouin had published five volumes of his "Jewish-Masonic Peril." To be sure, he had received pontifical approval not *for* his antisemitism but *despite* it. The point here is that his rabid anti-Jewish propaganda did not prevent the hierarchy in France and Rome from bestowing on him honorific ecclesiastical titles. Unsurprisingly, the Munich archdiocesan journal praised Jouin's works at the end of 1920.[38]

Jouin's version of the *Protocols* directly inspired one of the first two Italian translations of the forgery, published from March to December 1921 in *Fede e Ragione* (Faith and Reason), a confessional bi-weekly of the diocese of Fiesole, in the province of Florence. The journal benefited from the support of the traditionalist bishop, Giovanni Fossà, and Cardinal Tommaso Pio Boggiani, the Archbishop of Genoa from 1919 to 1921. Titled "Documents of the Jewish Conquest of the World," the Italian version featured an introduction, the *Protocols* themselves, the same report published one year earlier in *Documentation Catholique* (which *Fede e Ragione* had already quoted in May 1920[39]), and the appendix "Bolshevik documents of the Russian Jew," which conflated Zionism and Judeo-Bolshevism.

The Italian version was the work of a rather infamous and shadowy figure, Monsignor Umberto Benigni. A priest and journalist from Perugia, professor of Church history at various pontifical universities, and prothonotary apostolic, he held key positions within the Vatican Secretariat of State under the pontificate of Pius X (1903–14) and was the leader of an informal anti-modernist secret network (*Sodalitium Pianum*, also called Sapinière). Benigni was emblematic of integralist Catholicism, the most reactionary Catholic trend, which was dedicated to combating the alleged "infiltration" of modernist and liberal ideas within the Church.[40] He fell into disgrace under the more moderate pontificates of Benedict XV (1914–22) and Pius XI (1922–39). Frustrated by the democratization of Catholic politics after the First World War, integralist Catholics like Benigni turned more politicized in a rightward direction, supporting Action Française and clerical fascism.[41] Benigni became a paid informer for Mussolini's regime, first at the service of the Ministry of Foreign Affairs from 1923 to 1928, and then, from 1928 to 1934, at the Political Police of the Ministry of the Interior.

Integralist Catholics interpreted the Great War and the Bolshevik Revolution through a providential and conspiratorial lens as a divine punishment against modern society's apostasy. In this pessimistic view, the restoration of Christendom in Europe was presented as the only possible remedy for postwar unrest. Commenting Pius XI's first encyclical (*Ubi arcano Dei consilio*), Benigni wrote in 1923 in *Fede e Ragione*:

The peace expected by humankind – afflicted by so many hardships – is still absent ... We need peace, the true, sincere, and honest peace of nations and classes. It is impossible to reach it without the Christian spirit. Society and individuals must imperatively come back to God and our Redeemer. Hence, the primary practical duty of the good Catholics is to brandish the Cross in the face of the de-Christianized, Masonic, and Judaized world.[42]

From this perspective, all means were reasonable to re-catholicize Western civilization, including ethnonationalism and fascism if they curbed all the forces of the "anti-Church." Both prelates and close collaborators, Jouin and Benigni, need today to be understood as part of the transnational networks of traditionalist Catholicism and right-wing politics of the 1920s. The global diffusion of the *Protocols* acquainted Catholics with circles of fascists and nationalists and induced them to collaborate *de facto* with non-Catholics, Protestants, Orthodox Christians, and even atheists. At the end of 1920, while exchanging documents on the *Protocols* with Jouin, Benigni spearheaded a counter-revolutionary network of "Social Defense." This network took off in the spring of 1923 (after Benigni secretly joined the ranks of Mussolini's regime) under the name of the Roman Entente of Social Defense (*Intesa romana di difesa sociale*).[43] The five groups constituting the core of the Entente had all published the *Protocols* as proudly advertised by the 1923 program: the *Veritas* Committee in Rome (Benigni's bulletin), *Fede e Ragione* in Fiesole, the Britons in London, and RISS and *La Vieille France* (The Old France) in Paris (a weekly directed by Jean Drault and Urbain Gohier, two antisemitic nationalists). Informal and secret, the organization aimed at the underground diffusion of antisemitic materials on behalf of a transnational common cause: the defence of the Christian order against Judaism and communism. The network relied on the circulation of a dedicated press and frequent correspondence with collaborators in various countries such as Switzerland, Great Britain, Romania, Hungary, Spain, Germany, Austria, Denmark, Egypt, Canada, and the United States.

Once the network had been launched, antisemitism proved to be the vital ideological link between political groups as disparate as French Catholics, Italian Fascists, White Russian émigrés, Spanish monarchists, British ultra-Tories, and German National Socialists. Speaking for Benigni's Entente, French abbot Paul Boulin advocated for "an anti-Jewish, European, and Christian alliance" in a 1923 article published in Jouin's RISS.[44] Ironically, Benigni and his collaborators promoted a right-wing nationalistic international precisely to curb an anti-Christian, communist, and allegedly Jewish international. The group organized four "international antisemitic conferences" between 1923 and 1926, in Rome, Paris, Salzburg, and Budapest.

In June 1924, the Paris conference adopted a program of political Christianity based "upon the three fundamental principles of Christian civilization: religion, motherland, family." The goal of the international was to protect national and religious traditions against the "common enemy," the Jew.[45] Organized under the auspices of Jouin, Boulin, and Benigni, the Paris conference gathered, among others, Roger Lambelin, Georg de Pottere (a monarchist activist in postwar Vienna and later co-founder of the pro-Nazi news agency World Service, *Welt-Dienst*, in Erfurt in 1933 with First Lieutenant Ulrich Fleischhauer), Kurt Lüdecke (from the Munich-based Nazi organization Aufbau[46]), Hungarian deputy Tibor d'Eckhardt (from the right-wing EME Association of Awakening Magyars[47]), and the White Russians Eugene Brandt (a Tsarist officer exiled in Copenhagen and author of pamphlets on the blood libel) and General Aleksandr Dmitrievich Netchvolodow (exiled in France and author in 1924 of the conspiratorial book, *Tsar Nicholas II and the Jews: Essays on the Russian Revolution Regarding the Universal Activity of Modern Judaism*).

The Roman Entente developed a transatlantic dimension, in part via the role of White Russians who collaborated with Benigni and Jouin, three of them based in the United States: Boris Brasol, Major-General Arthur Cherep-Spiridovich (founder of the anti-Bolshevist publishing company in New York), and Leslie Fry; and one in London, Thaddée de Wiltchinsky, an official representative of the Grand Duke Kirill Vladimirovich (pretender to the Romanov throne). In 1920–21, all four White émigrés had contacts with Henry Ford, the Detroit auto magnate. Ford infamously launched a mass dissemination of the *Protocols* in the United States via his weekly *Dearborn Independent* (June–September 1920). In November 1920, the wealthy industrialist published *The International Jew: The World's Foremost Problem*, which became a Nazi bestseller.[48]

In these transatlantic antisemitic networks, the little-known trajectory of Leslie Fry merits further investigation.[49] Born as Louise Chandor in Paris from American parents, she married an officer of Russia's imperial army, Fedor Ivanovic Shishmareff, and lived in St Petersburg before the First World

War. Fleeing the Bolshevik Revolution and the ensuing civil war, and carrying with her a version of the *Protocols*, she reached California via the Bering Strait. She travelled to the midwest, where she met with Ford's secretary Ernest G. Liebold in the summer of 1920, and then to the northeast, where she settled down in Scranton, Pennsylvania, and launched an obscure weekly called *The Gentile Tribune*. During a trip to Western Europe in the winter of 1920–21, she met with Monsignor Jouin, Urbain Gohier, Ludwig Müller (author of the first German translation of the *Protocols*), and Fedor Winberg (a White Russian officer, who had handed over the *Protocols* to Müller in Berlin). In the wake of this antisemitic tour, Fry published articles in the spring of 1921 in RISS and *La Vieille France* on the American diffusion of the *Protocols*. In the latter, she defended the hypothesis that the *Protocols* had a Zionist origin, attributing them to the Ukrainian thinker Asher Ginsberg (under his Hebrew name Ahad Ha'am, the founder of cultural Zionism). Fry's hypothesis impressed Benigni, Jouin, and Lambelin, who made note of it in their respective publications.[50]

Between 1920 and 1922, Fry corresponded regularly with Benigni, defending the "cause of Christ" while lamenting that American Catholics were "being paid by Jews."[51] She started writing for the *Dearborn Independent* in September 1920 and collaborated with Ford until 1922. But she expressed to Benigni her disappointment over Ford's lack of sensitivity to the perspectives of French and Italian Catholics. The Roman prelate replied that antisemites had a duty to get along despite national, social, and religious differences: "[Ford] should not let himself [be] deceived by religious and social prejudices and should not be wary of individuals like you and me who are not of the same confession nor social program. The huge struggle that we are leading obliges us to a general entente of all the counter-revolutionary forces."[52]

The antisemitic program of the Roman Entente provided a shared language, a "cultural code,"[53] and a common cause that could encompass a right-wing nebula of various political and religious groups who were otherwise clearly divergent. Even so, efforts to organize an actual international fell apart after 1925 because of internal conflicts. For example, Fry shared with French Catholics Jouin and Boulin a deep aversion to pan-Germanist activists. In 1921, she released a pamphlet titled *Panjudaism versus Pangermanism* in which she argued that Jewish and German imperialisms were twins. Supporting similar views, Jouin reminded readers of his "Jewish-Masonic Peril" – that "nationalist and fascist groups are unable alone to destroy the evil who invades us." He added that the supreme authority of the pope should always guide the counter-revolutionary movement: "outside the Papacy, it is likely that [peoples] would know only a 'Jewish peace' in this world, the peace of the *Protocols*."[54] Benigni expressed concern about the proselytism of some White Russians and feared that they would attempt to reinstitute the despotic power of the Orthodox Church in Russia to the disadvantage of Catholicism. From London, Thaddée de Wiltchinsky tried to reassure him in August and November 1922 by reaffirming their common fight for the salvation of Christianity:

> In this last effort of the great struggle with Bolshevism, a sinister menace to the world's culture and Christian civilisation, we trust that we shall receive the support of all patriotic forces of Europe who can see the approaching danger of the downfall of this centuries-old culture
> …
> We are bound together by the same idea and by the same problems of fighting the International Menace of Communism … The final aim of our movement – the restoration of Monarchy in Russia – is in the interests of the whole Civilised World.[55]

Although unsuccessful, the Romain Entente, born out of the first diffusion of the *Protocols*, had a significant legacy in the 1930s. For example, the same names gravitated toward the antisemitic network formed around the *Protocols'* Bern trial of 1934–35 – recently studied by Michael Hagemeister[56] – such as Georg de Pottere, Leslie Fry, Eugene Brandt, and Henry Beamish; belonging to an older generation, Jouin and Benign had died by then, in 1932 and 1934 respectively. Following the trajectory of Leslie Fry in the 1930s, we find her editor of the *Christian Free Press* and in the ranks of the Militant Christian Patriots (based in Glendale, California), for which she continued to publish anti-communist and antisemitic pamphlets after the Second World War.[57] In this vein, in March 1938 she wrote a letter to American Jewish leaders Cyrus Adler and Stephen Wise, which recycled the myth of Judeo-Bolshevism in the context of the refugee crisis: "Jewry has decreed to impose upon the population of the United States a fate similar to that of the Russians whom you enslaved and ruined." The letter bore witness to a broad conception of political Christianity: "Kahal leaders will be held responsible and shown to the people as culprits in the vast scheme of the destruction of Christian America ... If, through your machinations, civil war is going to break out between Christians and Jews, Christians are ready, and they will not wait until the Jew-planned revolution has opened in this country, as was done by the peoples of Russia, Hungary, Spain, and Mexico."[58]

Fry also published an extensive interpretation of the *Protocols, Le retour des flots vers l'Orient. Le Juif notre maître* (Waters flowing Eastward: The Jew, Our Master) for the press of Jouin's RISS in 1931. The resurrected Britons Publishing Company translated the book into English and published it in New York (1933) and in London (1953). Titled *Waters Flowing Eastward: The War against the Kingship of Christ*, this extended version included a section on the "Sovietization of the British Empire and the United States" as well as appendixes covering the "multitude of Jews who are in control behind the Iron Curtain" and "the Jews who hold leading positions in Russia and the Satellite Countries, as well as in UNO and USA, and about the persecution of Catholics in these countries and Palestine."[59] This 1953 version updated the myth of Judeo-Bolshevism to the Cold War context.

Indeed, the legacy of the Christian antisemitic networks formed during the first wave of the *Protocols* extends beyond the interwar period and the Western sphere. Latin America became a fertile ground for the importation of Catholic versions of the *Protocols*. Roger Lambelin largely inspired the first Brazilian version (1936), edited by Gustavo Barroso, a right-wing politician.[60] In 1927, an antisemitic publisher from Leipzig printed the first Spanish translation, which included Lambelin's introduction. But Jouin's version remained the most widespread in the Spanish-speaking world. The first translation of his "Jewish-Masonic Peril" was published in Spain in 1927 and reprinted during the civil war there.[61] This translation circulated in Colombia and Argentina in 1931 (featuring Leslie Fry's 1931 article for RISS), in Chile in 1935, and in Mexico between 1952 and 1980. From 1975 through the 1980s, Cedade, a neo-Nazi press in Barcelona, produced numerous editions, featuring assorted excerpts from the translations by Jouin and Lambelin. The most recent version appeared in 2004, in Bogota, Colombia;

Jouin's name and ecclesiastical title appear on the front page, lending authority to the publication.

The aftermath of the First World War triggered a revival of the Catholic counter-revolutionary tradition. Easily grafted onto the already pervasive myth of Jewish-Masonic conspiracy, the *Protocols* received benevolent attention from traditionalist Catholics. Frequently, Church publications blended the myth of Judeo-Bolshevism with a rabid opposition to Zionism. The *Protocols* provided the ideal vehicle for this lethal fusion of antisemitic prejudices. It came to serve as a monolithic key for interpreting contemporary events, thus channelling anxieties about the decline of Christian civilization. To be sure, Catholic clerics and laymen like Benigni, Jouin, and Lambelin published their own antisemitic forgeries without the official sanction of Rome. During the interwar period, Catholics displayed a variety of responses to antisemitism. These were tied to other Catholic concerns, such as communism, liberalism, atheism, and Protestant proselytism. By contrast, antisemitism remained *the* focus for a small but dedicated group of reactionary Catholics, who capitalized on affirmative acceptance in mainstream Church journals (*L'Osservatore Romano, Civiltà Cattolica, Documentation Catholique, La Croix*) to disseminate *ad nauseam* their versions of the *Protocols*. Catholic antisemites felt compelled to act as authoritative champions for the defence of Christianity in the face of the Jewish "enemy."

Furthermore, the transnational diffusion of the *Protocols* enabled Catholic antisemites to partake in broader networks of nationalists and fascists and to advance right-wing visions for political Christianity. Antisemitism was the connecting link in these encounters between Christianity, ethnonationalism, and fascism. Such collaborations brought about tensions between divergent religious and political agendas; even so, they had a lasting impact during the interwar and postwar years, in Europe and North and South America. Ultimately, the warnings given by the *Protocols* turned antisemites into prophets, especially those Catholics who had already been involved in antisemitic propaganda since the turn of the century. In her 1931 pamphlet, Leslie Fry praised the clairvoyance of the *Protocols*: "Their importance lies in the fact that published at a definite date, they foretold historical events."[62] For Monsignor Jouin, the events of 1920–21 had been foreseen in the 1897 protocols, and that was sufficient: "We do not need any other evidence."[63] The "prophetic" dimension of the *Protocols* and their viral character as "fake news" explain their enduring and global contemporary legacy.

NOTES

1   Bernstein to Gasparri, 28 January 1921, Archivio della Congregazione per gli Affari Ecclesiastici Straordinari, Vatican (AES), Francia, pos. 1337, f. 92301.

2   Norman Cohn, *Warrant for Genocide: The Myth of the Jewish World Conspiracy and the Protocols of the Elders of Zion* [1966] (London: Serif, 1996), 256.

3   John Pollard, "Clerical Fascism: Context, Overview, and Conclusion," *Totalitarian Movements and Political Religions* 8, no. 2 (2007): 433–46.

4   Giovanni Miccoli, *Fra mito della cristianità e secolarizzazione. Studi sul rapporto Chiesa-società nell'età contemporanea* (Casale Monferrato: Marietti, 1985); Tom Buchanan and Martin Conway, eds., *Political Catholicism in Europe, 1918–1965* (Oxford: Oxford University Press, 1996).

5   Jacob Katz, *Jews and Freemasons in Europe 1723-1939* (Cambridge: Harvard University Press, 1970); and Emmanuel Kreis, "*Quis ut Deus*"? *Antijudéo-maçonnisme et occultisme en France sous la IIIème République* (Paris: Les Belles lettres, 2017).

6   Pierre-André Taguieff, ed., *Les Protocoles des Sages de Sion, faux et usages d'un faux*, [1992] (Paris: Berg International, 2004); and Cesare De Michelis, *Il manoscritto inesistente. I Protocolli dei savi di Sion, un apocrifo del XX secolo* (Venezia: Marsillio, 1998).

7   Michael Kellogg, *The Russian Roots of Nazism: White Émigrés and the Making of National Socialism, 1917–1945* (Cambridge: Cambridge University Press, 2005), 3, defined White émigrés as "right-wing exiles from the former Russian Empire who opposed the 'Red' Bolsheviks, or Majority Social Democrats."

8   David Kertzer, *The Popes against the Jews: The Vatican's Role in the Rise of Modern Antisemitism* (New York: A.A. Knopf, 2001); John Connelly, *From Enemy to Brother: The Revolution in Catholic Teaching on the Jews, 1933–1965* (Cambridge, MA: Harvard University Press, 2012); and Daniele Menozzi, "*Giudaica perfidia.*" *Uno stereotipo antisemita fra liturgia e storia* (Bologna: Il Mulino, 2014).

9   Philippe Chenaux, *L'Eglise catholique et le communisme en Europe (1917–*

1989): de Lenine à Jean-Paul II (Paris: Cerf, 2009); Patrick Houlihan, "Global Catholicism's Crusade against Communism, 1917–1963," in *Revolutions and Counter-Revolutions: 1917 and Its Aftermath from a Global Perspective*, eds. Stefan Rinke and Michael Wildt (Frankfurt am Main: Campus, 2017), 103–18; and Giuliana Chamedes, *A Twentieth-Century Crusade: The Vatican's Battle to Remake Christian Europe* (Cambridge, MA: Harvard University Press, 2019).

10   Paul Hanebrink, *A Specter Haunting Europe: The Myth of Judeo-Bolshevism* (Cambridge: Cambridge University Press, 2018), 26, 32.

11   Giovanni Miccoli, *I dilemmi e i silenzi di Pio XII* (Milano: Rizzoli, 2000); Emma Fattorini, *Germania e Santa Sede. Le Nunziature di Pacelli tra la Grande Guerra e la Repubblica di Weimar* (Bologna: Il Mulino, 1992).

12   "Le cause della Guerra russo-polacca," *Civiltà Cattolica* 71, no. 4 (2 October 1920), 86–96.

13   Ruggero Taradel and Barbara Raggi, *La segregazione amichevole. "La Civiltà Cattolica" e la questione ebraica 1850–1945* (Rome: Editori Riuniti, 2000).

14   "Austria: Nostre corrispondenze," *Civiltà Cattolica* 72, no. 3 (13 August 1921): 379–84, here 379.

15   "La rivoluzione mondiale e gli ebrei," *Civiltà Cattolica* 73, no. 4 (12 October 1922): 111–21.

16   Father Salvien, who used the penname Père Ricard, was forced by Gasparri and the *nuncio* to relocate to Locarno in February 1923 because of allegations of political ties with Msgr Benigni's network; see Archivio Apostolico Vaticano (AAV), Vatican, Nunziatura Francia, Nunz. Parigi, b. 487, fasc. 950 "Intrighi Salvian Benigni."

17   "Les Juifs sont les principaux fauteurs du bolchevisme universel. Note établie par les Services officiels américains," *Documentation Catholique* 57 (6 March 1920): 326–8.

18   The report, *Bolshevism and Judaism*, was dated 30 November 1918.

19   [Boris Brasol], *The Protocols and World Revolution. Including a translation and analysis of the Protocols of the Meetings of the Zionist Men of Wisdom* (Boston: Small, Maynard & Company, 1920); Robert Singerman, "The American Career of the Protocols of the Elders of Zion," *American Jewish History* 71 (1981): 48–78; Kellogg, *The Russian Roots of Nazism*, 130–1.

20   "Der jüdische Imperialismus," *Münchner katholische Kirchenzeitung* 15 (11 April 1920), 107.

21 "Protocols of the Wise Men of Zion," *Social Justice* (8 August 1938), 5. See
    also Christine Athans, *The Coughlin–Fahey Connection: Father Charles E.
    Coughlin, Father Denis Fahey, C.S.Sp., and Religious Anti-Semitism in the
    United States, 1938–1954* (New York: Peter Lang, 1991).

22 "Un Pericolo," *L'Osservatore Romano* (15 October 1920).

23 On Action française, see Jacques Prévotat, *Les catholiques et l'Action fran-
    çaise. Histoire d'une condamnation, 1899–1939* (Paris: Fayard, 2001); and Lau-
    rent Joly, "D'une guerre à l'autre. L'Action française et les Juifs, de l'Union
    sacrée à la Révolution nationale (1914–1944)," *Revue d'histoire moderne et
    contemporaine* 59, no. 4 (2012): 97–124.

24 Gisela Lebzelter, *Political Anti-Semitism in England, 1918–1939* (London:
    Macmillan, 1978).

25 "Il Sionismo e la Palestina. Gravi critiche e proteste," *L'Osservatore Romano*,
    15 October 1920.

26 Elena Caviglia, "Il sionismo e la Palestina negli articoli dell'*Osservatore ro-
    mano* e della *Civiltà cattolica* (1919–1923)," *Clio* 27 (1981): 79–90; Renato
    Moro, "Le premesse dell'atteggiamento cattolico di fronte alla legislazione
    razziale fascista. Cattolici ed ebrei nell'Italia degli anni venti (1919–1932),"
    Storia Contemporanea 19, no. 6 (1988): 1013–19; Agathe Mayeres-Rebernik,
    *Le Saint-Siège face à la question de Palestine. De la déclaration Balfour à la
    création de l'État d'Israël* (Paris: Champion, 2015).

27 "Sionismo e antisionismo in Palestina," *L'Osservatore Romano*, 9 June 1920;
    "La Palestina ed il Sionismo," *L'Osservatore Romano*, 16 June 1920; "La Pale-
    stina ed il Sionismo: Il programma del nuovo governatore," *L'Osservatore
    Romano*, 23 June 1920.

28 Sergio Minerbi, *The Vatican and Zionism: Conflict in the Holy Land, 1895–
    1925* (New York: Oxford University Press 1990). Minerbi based his conclu-
    sions on reports sent to the Foreign Office by the British ambassador
    to the Holy See.

29 "La Palestina ed il Sionismo," *L'Osservatore Romano*, 16 June 1920.

30 Bertrand Joly, ed., *Dictionnaire biographique et géographique du nationa-
    lisme (1880–1900). Boulangisme, ligue des patriotes, mouvements antidreyfu-
    sards, comités antisémites* (Paris: Honoré Champion, 1998), 222.

31 Roger Lambelin, *"Protocols" des Sages de Sion* (Paris: Grasset, 1921), 5, 35.

32 Roger Lambelin, *Le péril juif. Le règne d'Israël chez les Anglo-Saxons* (Paris:
    Grasset, 1921). The Boswell printing and publishing company, a notoriously

antisemitic publisher in London, translated excerpts of the 1928 volume by Roger Lambelin, *The Victories of Israel* (London: Boswell, 1928).

33 Lambelin, *Le péril juif*, 6,

34 Ibid., 193, 213–14.

35 Roger Lambelin, "La Roumanie et les Juifs," *Revue Internationale des Sociétés Secrètes* 37 (2 December 1923), 903–19.

36 Brochure quoted as "Bacznosc !! Attention !! Lis et fais-lire. 1897-1920," in Ernest Jouin, *Le Péril judéo-maçonnique*, vol. 1 (Paris: RISS, 1920), 190.

37 Lambelin, *Le péril juif*, 10.

38 "Die Französische Freimaurerei," *Münchner katholische Kirchenzeitung* 50 (12 December 1920), 313–14.

39 "Sinedrio e Triangolo, o sia la grande congiura ebraico massonica internazionale," *Fede e Ragione*, May 1920; and "I Documenti della conquista del mondo," *Fede e Ragione* March–December 1921.

40 Emile Poulat, *Intégrisme et catholicisme intégral. Un réseau international antimoderniste: la "Sapinière" (1909–1912)* (Paris: Casterman 1969); Guido Verucci, *L'eresia del Novecento. La Chiesa e la repressione del modernismo in Italia* (Turin: Einaudi, 2010).

41 On Benigni's transnational network, see Nina Valbousquet, *Catholique et antisémite: Le réseau de Mgr Benigni, Rome, Europe, Etats-Unis, 1918–1934* (Paris: CNRS Éditions, 2020).

42 H. Brand [Benigni], "Notes Internationales: L'Encyclique," *Fede e Ragione*, 4 February 1923.

43 "Pour la défense sociale, simples constatations," January 1921, fondo Benigni, b. 28; *Veritas*, 23 April 1923, fondo Benigni, b. 17, Archivio Storico diplomatico, Ministero degli Affari Esteri, Rome (ASMAE).

44 Pierre Colmet [Boulin], "Une ligue de Défense sociale," *Revue Internationale des Sociétés Secrètes* 37 (17 June 1923): 338–40.

45 Memorandum and program of the Paris Conference, June 1924, Bibliothèque Nationale de France, Département des manuscrits, Paris (BNF): fonds maçonnique, RISS, b. 66.

46 Kellogg, *The Russian Roots of Nazism*, 109.

47 Paul Hanebrink, *In Defense of Christian Hungary: Religion, Nationalism, and Antisemitism, 1890–1944* (Ithaca: Cornell University Press, 2006), 69–70, 84–98.

48 Victoria Saker Woeste, *Henry Ford's War on Jews and the Legal Battle against*

Hate Speech (Stanford: Stanford University Press, 2012); Neil Baldwin, *Henry Ford and the Jews: The Mass Production of Hate* (New York: Public Affairs 2001); Leo Ribuffo, "Henry Ford and *The International Jew*," *American Jewish History* 69 (1979–80): 437–77.

49 Michael Hagemeister, "The American Connection: Leslie Fry and the Protocols of the Elders of Zion," in *Kesarevo Kesarju, Scritti in onore di Cesare G. De Michelis*, eds. Marina Ciccarini, Nicoletta Marcialis, and Giorgio Ziffer (Florence: Firenze University Press, 2014), 217–28.

50 Leslie Fry, "Les Juifs et les Protocols. Les Protocols et l'indépendance américaine," *Revue Internationale des Sociétés Secrètes* 35 (April 1921): 293–360; Leslie Fry, "Sur l'authenticité des Protocols. Achad ha-Ham et le Sionisme," *La Vieille France*, 31 March and 6 April 1921.

51 Fry to Benigni, 15 April 1922, ASMAE, Fondo Benigni, b. 11.

52 Benigni to Fry, 1 August 1922, ASMAE, Fondo Benigni, b. 11.

53 Shulamit Volkov, "Antisemitism as a Cultural Code: Reflections on the History and Historiography of Antisemitism in Imperial Germany," *Leo Baeck Institute Year Book* 23 (1978): 25–46.

54 Jouin, *Le Péril judéo-maçonnique*, vol. 3 (Paris: RISS, 1921), 153, 161.

55 De Wiltchinsky to Benigni, August 1922, ASMAE, Fondo Benigni, b. 11; de Wiltchinsky to Benigni, 11 November 1922, AAV, Fondo Benigni, b. 60.

56 Michael Hagemeister, *Die "Protokolle der Weisen von Zion" vor Gericht. Der Berner Prozess 1933–1937 und die "antisemitische Internationale"* (Zurich: Chronos, 2017).

57 See Leslie Fry, *The Jews and the British Empire* (Glendale: Militant Christian Patriots, 1945); Leslie Fry, *California Betrayed! California Betrayed! The Factual Story about Communist Spies and How to Free Them* (Glendale: Militant Christian Patriot: 1951).

58 Fry to Adler and Wise, 28 March 28, 1938, Center for Jewish History, YIVO Archives, New York (CJH), Morris Waldman Papers, b. 29, f. 511.

59 Leslie Fry, *Waters Flowing Eastward: The War against the Kingship of Christ*, 4th rev. ed. (London: Britons, 1953), 9–10.

60 *Os Protocolos dos Sábios de Sião, texto completo e apostilado por Gustavo Barroso* (São Paulo: Agencia Minerva, 1936).

61 *Los peligros judío-masónicos Los enemigos de la Civilización. los Protocolos de los sabios de Sion, edición completa con estudios y comentarios críticos de E. Jouin*, trans. Duque de la Victoria ([Spain], 1927). Victoria also translated

Lambelin's introduction. On this point, see Thomas Williford, "Political
Dissemination of the Judeo-Masonic Conspiracy Theory and the Outbreak
of *La Violencia* in Colombia 1920–1946," in *The Global Impact of the
"Protocols of the Elders of Zion": A Century-Old myth*, ed. Esther Webman
(London: Routledge, 2011), 112–29, here 113.

62 Fry, *Waters Flowing Eastward*, 77.

63 Ernest Jouin, *Le Péril Judéo-Maçonnique*, vol. 2 (Paris: RISS, 1921): 21.

3

Julius Evola and the "Jewish Problem" in Axis Europe: Race, Religion, and Antisemitism

Peter Staudenmaier

Julius Evola was one of the outstanding personalities on the European far right in the twentieth century. An iconic figure spanning the decades from classical fascism to today's "alt-right," Evola left a multifaceted legacy. He was a charismatic teacher of esoteric doctrines and alternative spiritual worldviews, an early herald of New Age beliefs and Eastern traditions. He was also an influential theorist of aggressive antisemitism and an inspiration for generations of neo-fascists and radical right thinkers. His present-day admirers include committed political militants as well as reclusive esoteric practitioners, extending from Evola's native Italy to Germany, France, Britain, Russia, North America, and beyond.

Despite his prominence, the aura of mystery that surrounds Evola has hindered adequate historical assessment. His activities during the Fascist era remain especially obscure, as myths promoted by his followers compete with relatively sparse scholarly research. This chapter examines Evola's activities during the antisemitic campaign in Fascist Italy, perhaps the most controversial aspect of his career, placing them in the context of wider developments in Axis Europe in the 1930s and 1940s. A closer look at Evola's teachings on

Figure 3.1 Julius Evola, early 1940s.

"spiritual racism" can serve as a case study in the intersection of racial, ethnic, and religious themes in the interwar period.

Even as he sought to influence Fascist and Nazi policy, Evola's racial views remained highly idiosyncratic. He distrusted nationalism as incompatible with Aryan racial unity and drew on South Asian sources to construct a modern European myth of race founded on ostensibly ancient origins. His invocations of religion were contradictory, combining occult and pagan strands with elements borrowed from Hinduism and Buddhism, while his attitude toward biological forms of racism was conspicuously ambivalent. Evola's outlook reflected an incongruous mixture of discordant components, revealing an intellectual profile common to many interwar racial ideologies.

Born in Rome in 1898, Evola embraced the unconventional life of an artist, poet, and philosopher in the wake of the First World War. The public persona he cultivated was based on a series of affectations, from the archaic spelling of his first name (adopted as an adult in honour of his namesake Julius Caesar) to the widespread legend of his supposedly aristocratic origins. Though his disciples routinely referred to him as "Baron," an appellation that has persisted to this day, there is no evidence of noble family background.[1] A bombing raid in the final months of the Second World War left him paralyzed for the last decades of his life. At his death in 1974, the *New York Times* described Evola as "a friend of Mussolini" who was "considered the top ideologist of Italy's extreme right."[2]

In the political maelstrom of the Fascist era, however, Evola's stature was much less certain. While Mussolini privately praised "my friend Julius Evola" as "a man of profound esoteric culture," other factions within the Fascist movement took a dimmer view.[3] Religious questions were a primary point of contention, as Evola's unorthodox spiritual beliefs collided with the popular Catholicism permeating Italian culture. He spent much of the first decade of Fascist rule railing against the regime's willingness to compromise with the Church. By the early 1930s Evola was known as the "leading theorist" of a "small group of neopagan elitists who sought to re-create the aristocratic culture of ancient Rome, propounding extreme elitism, revived Roman imperialism, and a mystical ethos that borrowed from the pagan occult."[4]

Evola's abstruse ideas and high-handed manner earned him enemies within the Fascist bureaucracy. Anonymous informants decried his occult involvements, some denouncing him as an agent of German imperialism, others as an eccentric "devotee of mythology."[5] His repeated efforts to join the Fascist Party were denied by antagonistic officials who accused the aloof thinker of trying to "surpass Fascism."[6] But Evola readily found allies in the higher ranks of both the Fascist and Nazi regimes, and he used his influence to promote an elaborate racial cosmology centred on the "Jewish problem."

The cornerstone of Evola's extremism was a sweeping rejection of the modern world. In place of modern degeneracy, he proposed a revival of ancient initiatic traditions, envisioning a society based on "authority, hierarchy, order, discipline and obedience."[7]

In Evola's eyes, the full destructive force of modernity was personified by the Jews. From plutocracy to Bolshevism, from rationalism to democracy to materialism, Jews represented the negation of primeval Aryan values. He propounded these teachings in a long series of publications from the 1920s onward. Evola adapted his basic tenets from myriad contrary sources, borrowing from pagan traditions as well as Christian anti-Judaism, and from scientific racism, ancient myths, and modern conspiracy theories, to shape a potent image of the Jewish threat. When Mussolini encouraged increasingly open antisemitic rhetoric beginning in 1936, Evola brought together themes he had cultivated for a decade into a succession of book-length treatments: *Three Faces of the Jewish Problem* (1936); *The Myth of Blood* (1937); *Guide to Racial Education* (1941); and *Summary of the Doctrine of Race* (1941).[8] These books were accompanied by substantial articles in the Fascist press.[9]

He did not mince words. Evola called for "absolute intransigence" in defence of "racial purity."[10] "The Jew," he declared, had inflicted a "spiritual circumcision" on humankind. Jewry had "thrust its way" into European culture, spreading "chaos and decay," corrupting the Aryan peoples with "racial detritus." The "Semitic element" represented the very antithesis of Aryan civilization.[11] Reworking long-standing antisemitic clichés in a religious register, Evola contrasted the "Jewish spirit" with its "crass materialism" to the "sacral, Olympic, supernatural" character of the Aryan race. The Jews, "secularized and intellectualized," had brought only "decadence" and "contamination" by "inferior races," whereas the Aryans constituted the true "race of the spirit," the embodiment of "supreme biological purity" whose "primordial traditions" were destined for "re-awakening."[12] Antisemitism, for Evola, was "an essential requirement for the defense of the race."[13]

With the passage of the racial laws in late 1938, Mussolini's regime unleashed a campaign against Italian Jews.[14] Evola saw himself as the vanguard of Fascism's antisemitic turn, and he demanded severe measures to counter "the Jewish menace" through racial "discrimination and selection." This task extended well beyond Italy's borders, since the Jews were the "common enemy" of the "entire civilization of white humankind."[15] To combat such a formidable enemy, Evola advocated a "supreme Aryan elite of spiritual leaders," who would provide "a truly totalitarian formulation of racist doctrine."[16] Ending the malignant reign of the Jews was the only way to solve "the crisis of the Western world."[17]

Evola had little patience for "scientistic" approaches to the "Jewish problem" that tried to "limit racism to the material plane." Race was a matter of "heredity that is not solely biological" but eminently spiritual; it was not bound to "this earthly world" with its petty physical concerns; it partook of the "sacred" rather than the "profane."[18] He insisted on the crucial importance of "the spiritual plane" to an effective racist policy. While others concentrated on biology, Evola warned that a "totalitarian racism" must reach past the bodily level to encompass the soul and the spirit. He attributed an excessively narrow focus on physical traits to the influence of the Jews: "A vision of life that is spiritual, Fascist, and heroic will always rebuff the Jewish materialist view." In stark contrast to the crude methods of the Jews, "the noble and dominating Aryan race" stood as a "force of light" against the "Ahrimanic powers" of darkness.[19]

These lofty precepts provoked considerable controversy among other Fascists. "Racial scientists" responded indignantly to Evola's charges.[20] Pragmatic party functionaries found his grand claims bewildering. What outraged his Italian rivals even more was Evola's success in bringing his message to Nazi audiences. His long-standing ties to German right-wing circles, cultivated since the 1920s, became particularly advantageous once Hitler came to power: "Of all the Italian antisemites and racial theorists, the only one who maintained a media presence in the Third Reich from the beginning was Julius Evola."[21] He spoke German fluently and used repeated lecture tours in Nazi Germany to advance his spiritual variant of racism. In a 1937 speech in Berlin on the "authentic Aryan spirit," for example, Evola dismissed the "rationalist idols of modern biology" and proclaimed that "race is above all a spiritual power."[22] Writing for Italian readers, he praised Heinrich Himmler's SS as the prototype of an "ancient order" of warriors and a "biological elite."[23]

For many observers at the time and since, Evola's so-called "spiritual racism" remained perplexingly nebulous. Scholars have noted that the phrase served Evola and his followers primarily as an exculpatory device after 1945, when "spiritual racism" seemed to offer a convenient contrast to conventional forms of biological racism; the term is thus rightly regarded as "historiographically inadequate."[24] There were nonetheless significant reasons for Evola's emphasis on the racial "spirit," "soul," and "body" as an integrated whole. He took this tripartite model to be an inheritance of ancient wisdom traditions, but it also accorded with the contemporary work of Nazi racial theorist Ludwig Ferdinand Clauss, an important influence on and interlocutor for Evola.[25] In Evola's view, Aryan racial superiority was anchored in eternal spiritual truths, whereas physical forms were simply material manifestations of this higher order of being. A final factor had to do with Evola's deeply misogynist worldview, in which the biological realm was associated with the feminine while pure spirituality was masculine.[26]

If the elevated domain of the spirit was the foundation of his racial theory, Evola consistently tied the spiritual dimension to the lowly level of the body. Stressing the pivotal connection between "blood and spirit," he held that the "Nordic-Germanic races" were the leading force in Europe, represented by the Rome/Berlin Axis. The bond between Fascist Italy and Nazi Germany was built on both a shared "Aryan-Roman spiritual legacy" and a common "genetic inheritance."[27] Spiritual and physical qualities were similarly linked in his antisemitic pronouncements. Employing a decidedly biological metaphor with implications of extermination, on multiple occasions Evola referred to Jews as a "virus."[28] But destruction of the Jewish enemy was only a means toward a higher goal. Through the final defeat of the Jews by Fascism and Nazism, Evola affirmed, humankind would at last be able to overcome "the spiritual decadence of the West" and "re-establish genuine contact between man and a transcendent, supersensible reality."[29]

From an Italian point of view, Evola's pan-Aryan ambitions could appear troubling.[30] His abiding commitment to Nazism and his allegiance to the Axis war effort helped shape his skeptical attitude toward nationalism. He criticized patriotic sentiment as "plebeian" and essentially feminine, unsuited to virile Aryan values. Those who put homeland above race had fallen for "the modern concept of the nation" and betrayed the "primordial Nordic-Aryan tradition."[31] At the same time, however, he acknowledged that "spiritual and aristocratic" forms of nationalism, as opposed to "collectivist" nationalism, could lead to the restoration of true hierarchy.[32] Evola argued that racism constituted a more potent and higher form of nationalism.[33]

Rather than rejected, nationalism needed to be expanded, enhanced, and ennobled. The new European order under Axis auspices was to be "supernational" instead of "anti-national or international."[34]

Although competing factions in both the Fascist and Nazi regimes looked askance at Evola's convoluted theories, he continued to receive support from Italian and German officials alike. In 1938 Himmler's SS provided funds "for Baron Evola's stay in Germany."[35] Staff from the Italian Ministry of Popular Culture took favourable note of Evola's "competence regarding racial problems and the sciences of subversion (Jewry and Masonry)."[36] When his book *Summary of the Doctrine of Race* was published in 1941, the ministry ordered all Italian newspapers to review it.[37] An expanded German edition appeared the following year.[38]

It was this book that brought Evola his greatest influence within Fascist quarters. Mussolini read it in August 1941 and was impressed by its combination of spiritual and hereditarian themes.[39] The book expounded Evola's comprehensive racial worldview and his vision of a spiritually dignified Fascism. Denouncing the "egalitarian myth," he declared the notion of a common humanity an "abstract fantasy." He ridiculed Darwinism, which could not comprehend that superior racial groups descended from "divine or celestial races." His antisemitic invective reached a crescendo here; he compared Jews to "vipers" who "poison" all of society. Evola cast the Jews as the negation of everything the "heroic Aryan race" stood for: "The Jew represents the anti-race par excellence."[40] Drawing on philology, archaeology, mythology, prehistory, anthropology, and more, the book assembled an all-embracing tale of racial struggle, rise, and fall.

Persuaded by this story, Mussolini decided to make Evola's racial doctrine the quasi-official Fascist line. One of Evola's protégés, Alberto Luchini, was appointed head of the "Race Office" in the Ministry of Popular Culture from 1941 to 1943, and Mussolini directed that "Evola's racist thought" guide the work of that office.[41] Articles by Evola's disciples and allies were featured prominently in the Fascist press.[42] His new-found influence extended to Nazi Germany as well. At an audience with Mussolini in September 1941, Evola proposed a bilingual journal on racial questions to be published in Italian and German. Mussolini approved the project, and discussions began with high-level Nazi representatives over the planned journal, which was to be titled "Blood and Spirit." Though negotiations reached an advanced stage,

the project was eventually scuttled due to the vicissitudes of wartime cooperation and internal divisions on both the Italian and German sides.[43] Evola's
hopes for uniting the Axis powers through a higher racial consciousness
went unfulfilled.

Among the stumbling blocks to broader acceptance of Evola's ideas was
his distinctive conception of the Aryan myth. The notion of an "Aryan race"
served as much more than just a counterpart to the "anti-race" of the Jews.
It signified an august racial lineage and an exalted spiritual birthright. For
Evola, the Aryans were the present-day heirs of a vastly older race, the Hyperboreans, whose long-ago grandeur was now lost to the mediocrity of the
modern world. The Hyperboreans came from the far north, the "cradle of
the Aryan race," and were the original "race of the spirit." A "union of ice
and fire," they were "the possessor of divine sciences."[44] Their racial inheritance was reflected in the glory of ancient Rome. In Evola's cosmology, the
Hyperboreans and the Aryans formed part of an immense tableau of racial
evolution stretching across millennia, along with lesser races such as the
Lemurians and Atlanteans. Most of the modern human population belonged to inferior groups; the "Negroid and Mongoloid races," for example,
were "Lemurian residues."[45] Only the Aryan race retained its links to the sacred past.

Though Evola's version of the Aryan myth displayed unusual features, it
was by no means his unique invention. The historical contours of the myth
can invite misunderstanding. In spite of the popular image of "Aryans" as
blonde and blue-eyed, an image that excludes many Italians, the Aryan myth
was in fact based on the assumption of a common racial bond joining peoples from South Asia to northern Europe. Many variants of the myth carried
spiritual overtones and were built around Europeans' fascination with India
as an ostensible source of timeless wisdom.[46] In Evola's work, the Aryan
myth centred on two main inspirations: Western esoteric lore and selective
appropriation of Eastern spiritual traditions. Both were customary elements
in occult racial thought at the time.

Evola freely mixed together disparate sources with little regard for internal
consistency. Apart from the racist uses to which he put them, his reliance on
Hindu and Buddhist texts was problematic in several ways. He often cited
such works via European secondary sources, and his contemporaries criticized his lack of Sanskrit.[47] Like others of his era, Evola's writings sometimes

exemplified an "exoticist" attitude toward South Asian intellectual traditions: "Western approaches to India have encouraged a disposition to focus particularly on the religious and spiritual elements in Indian culture."[48] This tendency all too often reflected "a Western obsession with poorly understood Eastern philosophies and religions."[49] Evola followed this pattern while invoking Asian creeds in the service of emphatically racist ends.

His adoption of esoteric teachings raised similar problems. Evola's account of racial evolution was borrowed wholesale from Theosophy, a nineteenth-century amalgam of occult worldviews synthesized by European and North American authors. The scheme of Polarian, Hyperborean, Lemurian, Atlantean, and Aryan races originated with Helena Blavatsky, founder of the Theosophical Society. Her seminal tome *The Secret Doctrine*, published in London in 1888, provided material for subsequent generations of esoteric instruction.[50] Blavatsky devoted ample attention to the contrast between "Aryan" and "Semitic" traditions, systematically denigrating Jews for having "falsified" and "mutilated" ancient religious wisdom.[51] Evola recapitulated Blavatsky's racial ideas even as he disparaged Theosophy as an Anglo-Saxon debasement of legitimate spirituality.[52] He took a comparable stance toward Dutch-German occultist Herman Wirth, another proponent of the Aryan myth in esoteric form, citing his work frequently while criticizing various "errors."[53]

Themes like these ran throughout Evola's racial writings, in a medley of scriptural allusions from across the "Aryan" world. Undeterred by chronology or coherence, he sprinkled his texts with references to the Zend-Avesta and the Bhagavad Gita, the Vedas and Puranas, the Corpus Hermeticum and the Eddas, Tibetan teachings and Celtic myths. From Vishnu to Zarathustra, from yoga to the swastika, from Thule to Avalon to Asgard, from the Druids to the Templars to the Rosicrucians, all were incorporated into Evola's oeuvre. There they mingled with more mundane antisemitic tropes: the Jews as carriers of "intellectualism" and "scientism," Jews as the evil force behind the "decadent, plebeian, democratic and mercantile" modern world, Jews as manipulators of "international finance," and so forth.[54] A robustly conspiracist strand marked Evola's publications on the "Jewish problem" from the beginning. He wrote a lengthy introduction to the Italian edition of the "Protocols of the Elders of Zion" in 1937, endorsing the notorious antisemitic forgery.[55]

An intense and enduring hostility toward all he associated with Judaism underlay Evola's acrimonious outlook on Christianity. His attacks on the Catholic Church, and on Christian religion more generally, were especially acerbic during the 1920s. The young Evola preached a "pagan imperialism" against Christianity's "Hebraic servility," insisting that the true spirit of Fascism must be resolutely "anti-Christian" if it was to "re-awaken the sacred science" of old.[56] After Mussolini concluded the Lateran Accords with the Vatican in 1929, Evola continued to denounce Fascism's compromises, though his pagan principles eventually moderated somewhat.[57] Despite occasional nods to the medieval Church as a haven for traditional values before the onset of modernity, scathing assessments of Christianity were a regular feature of his work, consistently linked to antisemitic motifs. Evola considered Christianity a deformed offshoot of Judaism and its "demonic" spirit, whose historical impact had been fatal; the established churches, whether Catholic or Protestant, had exacerbated the "demise of the West" through their "Semitic-Christian doctrine"; the majestic traditions of Imperial Rome had been "crushed by the Semitic and Oriental wave with the rise of Christianity."[58]

Between these sharply drawn lines lay noteworthy albeit unacknowledged parallels. The tripartite division of body, soul, and spirit, integral to Evola's racial teachings, was echoed in classical Christian theology. Some of his antisemitic imagery resembled the familiar prejudices of traditional Christian antipathy toward Jews and Judaism. At times Evola honoured Christian symbols while objecting to their "Christianized" forms and asserting they were derived from pagan sources. His 1937 book *The Mystery of the Holy Grail* interpreted the Grail myth not as Christian but as Hyperborean in origin, bequeathed by the "primordial race, herald of transcendent spirituality." Withstanding Christian attempts to "supplant" it, the myth had preserved its "esoteric background" and its "Aryan" character. But the precious message of the Grail was now threatened by the "darkest forces of modern times," above all "Jewry," which was responsible for the "subversion and disintegration of the remaining forms of traditional European order."[59]

Antisemitic obsessions ran deep within Evola's thought during the Fascist era. There were many other facets to his work, just as there were many other sides to Fascist racism, which targeted Slavs, Arabs, Africans, and more. But Jews were crucial to the Fascist racial imaginary, and Evola was one of its most prolific if peculiar expositors. His arcane teachings present a challenge to scholars hoping to make sense of the tangled histories of esotericism, antisemitism, and the interwar far right. Faced with these difficult topics, several studies offer perceptive critical analysis whereas others have fallen short.[60] Some treatments focus primarily on Evola's esoteric interests while downplaying his aggressive antisemitism and affinities with Nazism.[61] Others flatly deny that Evola was "any kind of fascist at all."[62]

For all his exhortations about combating the Jewish enemy and for all his active collaboration with Fascist as well as Nazi agencies, Evola was not directly involved in the genocide of European Jews. Under the right conditions, however, "spiritual racism" could turn deadly.[63] His mission to save the world from Jewish iniquity offered ideological absolution for the program of extermination pursued by the Nazi regime and its Fascist accomplices. Well after the war, Evola dismissed talk of "gas chambers" as little more than "Allied propaganda."[64] Enigmatic as they seemed, Evola's racial postulates shared key points of contact with more typical varieties of antisemitism in Axis contexts[65] and were a core component of his broader antagonism toward modern society.

Evola's adversarial relationship with modernity poses further challenges. As a recent study observes, "by now it is widely held that fascism was not some revolt against modernity but the quest for an alternative modernity."[66] In this respect Evola can be seen as emblematic of the "paradoxes of fascist modernism."[67] His quixotic revolt against the modern world appears in retrospect as a failed attempt to reconcile the ancient with the modern. Evola's efforts formed part of "the regime's romance with antiquity": "Fascism's intent was that antiquity and modernity should be perceived, if not as one organic whole, then at least as distinctly interconnected."[68] Summoning primal values in a volatile time, he simultaneously demanded a radically new future and restoration of a lost past. He touted Fascism as a "spiritual avant-garde" while calling for a return to the "hierarchical and organic" days of yore.[69]

The particulars of this incongruous worldview can seem as confounding now as they did a century ago. From Hyperborea to the Holy Grail, Evola enlisted a remarkable range of antecedents in his search for ancestral knowledge. A worldly figure whose work crossed national boundaries and breached established conventions, he unsettled his peers at home and abroad through vehement confrontation with religious beliefs and patriotic pieties. His disdain for Christianity, his oracular style, and his blatant disregard for political

or ideological propriety limited his appeal. Throughout the disputes that en-
circled him, Evola maintained an unwavering standpoint. He advocated a
racism that would rise above mere physical attributes and recover its noble
roots, which were to be found not in the transitory material world but in the
everlasting realm of the spirit. Self-styled emissary of bygone eons, he availed
himself of the contemporary opportunities that Fascism and Nazism offered.

Evola insisted that his Traditionalism was based on ancient principles.
But the ideas he espoused were thoroughly modern products of the late
nineteenth and early twentieth centuries. The same ideas have found renewed resonance in our own century, during which seemingly vanquished
strains of the far right are making a concerted effort to return to the historical stage.[70] Evola's singular vision of the "Jewish problem" as a quintessen-
tially modern affliction complicates standard interpretations of religion,
nationalism, and antisemitism in the interwar era and beyond. Racial myths
in spiritual guise did not disappear in 1945; they retain their latent potential
today. Critical attention to such beliefs, in their numerous unpredictable
forms, will be a necessary part of comprehending the current historical moment and coming to terms with a past that appears ever more relevant to
the troubled present.

NOTES

1 For basic biographical information, see Luca Lo Bianco, "Evola, Giulio Cesare Andrea," in *Dizionario biografico degli Italiani*, vol. 43 (Rome: Treccani,
   1993), 575–80. There is still no scholarly biography of Evola. His autobiography is Julius Evola, *Il cammino del cinabro* (Milan: Scheiwiller, 1963); for
   standard hagiography from his followers, see Adriano Romualdi, *Julius
   Evola: l'uomo e l'opera* (Rome: Volpe, 1971); Gianfranco De Turris, *Elogio e
   difesa di Julius Evola* (Rome: Mediterranee, 1997); and Troy Southgate, ed.,
   Evola (London: Black Front, 2011).

2 "Julius Evola," *New York Times*, 14 June 1974, 36. On Evola's enormous influence on the postwar neo-fascist milieu, see Leonard Weinberg, *After Mussolini: Italian Neo-Fascism and the Nature of Fascism* (Washington, DC:
   University Press of America, 1979), 23–5, 46–9, and 77–8; Thomas Sheehan,
   "Myth and Violence: The Fascism of Julius Evola and Alain de Benoist," *Social Research* 48 (1981): 45–73; Richard Drake, "Julius Evola and the Ideologi-

cal Origins of the Radical Right in Contemporary Italy," in *Political Violence and Terror*, ed. Peter Merkl (Berkeley: University of California Press, 1986), 61–89; Franco Ferraresi, *Threats to Democracy: The Radical Right in Italy after the War* (Princeton: Princeton University Press 1996), 43–50, 57–59, 191–200; and Elisabetta Cassina Wolff, *L'inchiostro dei vinti: Stampa e ideologia neofascista 1945–1953* (Milan: Mursia, 2012), 221–67.

3 Yvon De Begnac, *Taccuini mussoliniani* (Bologna: Mulino, 1990), 391, 408.

4 Stanley Payne, *A History of Fascism 1914–1945* (Madison: University of Wisconsin Press 1995), 113. Emilio Gentile, "Impending Modernity: Fascism and the Ambivalent Image of the United States," *Journal of Contemporary History* 28 (1993): 7–29, here 13, similarly described Evola as "a neo-Pagan philosopher who preached revolt against the modern world and the restoration of a mythical civilization of superior castes of 'Ascetics' and 'Warriors.'"

5 See his political police file: Archivio Centrale dello Stato, Rome (ACS), Polizia Politica fasc. pers. 467 Evola Giulio.

6 "Relazione alla Corte Centrale di Disciplina," ACS Ministero della Cultura Popolare b. 121, f. 759 Evola Julius.

7 Paul Furlong, *Social and Political Thought of Julius Evola* (London: Routledge, 2011), 9; see also Marco Fraquelli, *Il Filosofo proibito: Tradizione e reazione nell'opera di Julius Evola* (Milan: Terziaria, 1994); Francesco Cassata, *A destra del fascismo: Profilo politico di Julius Evola* (Turin: Bollati Boringhieri, 2003); and Elisabetta Cassina Wolff, "Evola's Interpretation of Fascism and Moral Responsibility," *Patterns of Prejudice* 50 (2016): 478–94. For his antimodern magnum opus see Julius Evola, *Rivolta contro il mondo moderno* (Milan: Hoepli, 1934); as well as the revised and expanded German edition, Evola, *Erhebung wider die moderne Welt* (Stuttgart: Deutsche Verlags-Anstalt, 1935).

8 Julius Evola, *Tre aspetti del problema ebraico* (Rome: Mediterranee, 1936); Evola, *Il mito del sangue* (Milan: Hoepli, 1937); Evola, *Indirizzi per una educazione razziale* (Naples: Conte, 1941); Evola, *Sintesi di dottrina della razza* (Milan: Hoepli, 1941).

9 Examples include Julius Evola, "Ebraismo distruttivo: Scienza, letteratura, musica," *Vita Italiana* (April 1938): 440–52; Evola, "Una vittima d'Israele," *Vita Italiana* (January 1939): 27–35; Evola, "Dottrina della razza: Idee base, orientamenti, sviluppi," *Bibliografia fascista* (June 1939): 483–93; Evola,

"Roma e l'ebraismo," *Vita Italiana* (September 1939): 313–19; Evola, "La mistica della razza in Roma antica," *Difesa della Razza* (20 May 1940): 6–10; Evola, "Le selezioni razziali," *Difesa della Razza* (20 April 1941): 28–30; Evola, "Roma aria: Le origini," *Difesa della razza* (5 July 1941): 22–4; and Evola, "La civiltà occidentale e l'intelligenza ebraica," in *Gli ebrei hanno voluto la guerra*, ed. Alberto Luchini (Rome: n.p., 1942), 13–20.

10 Evola, *Sintesi di dottrina della razza*, 239.

11 Ibid., 119, 172.

12 Julius Evola, "Sulla visione aria del mondo," *Rassegna Italiana* (March 1939): 167-175.

13 Julius Evola, "Inquadramento del problema ebraico," *Bibliografia Fascista* (August 1939): 717–28. On Evola's racial teachings, compare Fraquelli, *Il Filosofo proibito*, 268–73; Furlong, *Social and Political Thought of Julius Evola*, 113–33; Francesco Germinario, *Razza del sangue, razza dello spirito: Julius Evola, l'antisemitismo e il nazionalsocialismo, 1930–43* (Turin: Bollati Boringhieri, 2001); Aaron Gillette, *Racial Theories in Fascist Italy* (New York: Routledge 2002), 154–75; and Marie-Anne Matard-Bonucci, *L'Italia fascista e la persecuzione degli ebrei* (Bologna: Mulino, 2015), 85–90.

14 Enzo Collotti, *Il fascismo e gli ebrei: Le leggi razziali in Italia* (Rome: Laterza, 2006); Michele Sarfatti, *The Jews in Mussolini's Italy: From Equality to Persecution* (Madison: University of Wisconsin Press, 2006), 95–177; Valeria Galimi, *Sotto gli occhi di tutti: La società italiana e le persecuzioni contro gli ebrei* (Florence: Le Monnier, 2018); Claudio Natoli, "Der italienische Faschismus und die Judenverfolgung: Zwischen Geschichte und Geschichtsschreibung," *Zeitschrift für Geschichtswissenschaft* 66 (2018): 1016–28.

15 Julius Evola, "Razzismo totalitario," *Rassegna Italiana* (December 1938): 847–53.

16 Evola, *Sintesi di dottrina della razza*, 5.

17 Giulio Evola, "Sulle origini remote della crisi italiana ed europea," *Dottrina Fascista* (January 1941): 9–17.

18 Julius Evola, "Sul problema della 'razza dello spirito,'" *Vita Italiana* (February 1942): 153–9.

19 Evola, "Razzismo totalitario," 850, 852. See also Evola, "L'equivoco del 'razzismo scientifico,'" *Vita Italiana* (September 1942): 232–9; Evola, "Scienza, razza e scientismo," *Vita Italiana* (December 1942): 556–63.

20 Guido Landra, "Scienza, razza, scientismo," *Vita Italiana* (February 1943):

151–3. For context, see Francesco Cassata, *Building the New Man: Eugenics, Racial Sciences, and Genetics in Twentieth-Century Italy* (Budapest: Central European University Press, 2010), 263–8; Salvatore Garau, "Between 'Spirit' and 'Science': The Emergence of Italian Fascist Antisemitism through the 1920s and 1930s," in *Fascism and the Jews*, ed. Daniel Tilles (London: Vallentine Mitchell, 2011), 41–65; and Peter Staudenmaier, "Antisemitic Intellectuals in Fascist Italy: Promoting 'Spiritual Racism,' 1938–1945," in *Intellectual Antisemitism*, ed. Sarah Danielsson (Würzburg: Königshausen & Neumann, 2018), 95–116.

21 Andrea Hoffend, *Zwischen Kultur-Achse und Kulturkampf: Die Beziehungen zwischen "Drittem Reich" und faschistischem Italien in den Bereichen Medien, Kunst, Wissenschaft und Rassenfragen* (Frankfurt am Main: Peter Lang, 1998), 375. For examples of his German publications, see Julius Evola, "Das Hakenkreuz als polares Symbol," *Hochschule und Ausland* (April 1934): 37–46; Evola, "Die Waffen des geheimen Krieges," *Die Tat* (February 1939): 745–53; Evola, "Gralsmysterium und Kaisergedanke," *Geist der Zeit* (March 1939): 145–54; Evola, "Die Juden und die Mathematik," *Nationalsozialistische Monatshefte* (February 1940): and 81–7; Evola, *Die arische Lehre von Kampf und Sieg* (Vienna: Schroll, 1941).

22 Julius Evola, "Abendländischer Aufbau aus urarischem Geist," December 1937, Bundesarchiv Berlin, BArch B, NS 19/1848: 9–19. On Evola's activities and publications in Germany, see Alberto Luchini to Celso Luciano, 28 August 1941, ACS Ministero della Cultura Popolare b. 121, f. 759.

23 Julius Evola, "Le SS., guardia e ordine della rivoluzione crociuncinata," *Vita Italiana* (August 1938): 164–73; Evola, "L'animatore delle 'SS' e il problema delle nuove elette," *Regime Fascista* (17 December 1940): 5.

24 Cassata, *A destra del fascismo*, 13. Cassata warns that uncritical reliance on the term "spiritual racism" can play into the hands of Evola's latter-day apologists. For a salient example, see Marco Rossi, *Esoterismo e razzismo spirituale: Julius Evola e l'ambiente esoterico nel conflitto ideologico del Novecento* (Genoa: Name, 2007).

25 See the repeated references to Clauss throughout Evola, *Sintesi di dottrina della razza*; Clauss is by far the most frequently cited author in the book. For background on Clauss, see the problematic but informative study by Hans-Jürgen Lutzhöft, *Der Nordische Gedanke in Deutschland 1920-1940* (Stuttgart: Klett, 1971), 47–50, 94–9. On the distinction between the "race of

the spirit" and the "race of the soul," see Evola, "Sul problema della 'razza dello spirito.'"

26 Julius Evola, *Metafisica del sesso* (Rome: Atanor, 1958).

27 Julius Evola, "Die arisch-römische Entscheidung des faschistischen Italiens," May 1941, Politisches Archiv des Auswärtigen Amtes, Berlin (PA), Inland I Partei, R 99164, 4–17. Compare Evola, "Sulla tradizione nordico-aria," *Bibliografia Fascista* 2 (February 1939): 105–15; Evola, "La razza e la Guerra: Duo eroismi," *Difesa della razza* (20 November 1939): 14–17; Evola, "La gloria della gente aria," *Difesa della Razza* (5 June 1940): 34-37; Evola, "Il simbolismo della croce uncinata," *Augustea* (June 1942): 365–9.

28 A particularly striking instance came as early as 1936: Evola, *Tre aspetti del problema ebraico*, 63. See also Evola, *Rivolta contro il mondo moderno*, 342; and Evola, "Inquadramento del problema ebraico," 726; as well as the comparison of Jews to "bacteria" in Evola, "Sulla genesi dell'ebraismo come forza distruttrice," *Vita Italiana* (July 1941): 25–35.

29 Evola, "Sulle origini remote della crisi italiana ed europea," 17.

30 For example, see the 5 June 1942 telegram from the Italian Foreign Ministry to the Ministry of Popular Culture expressing reservations about a speech Evola gave in German on "The Mystery of the Holy Grail and the Idea of the Reich," ACS Ministero della Cultura Popolare b. 121, f. 759.

31 Evola, *Erhebung wider die moderne Welt*, 321, 360.

32 Ibid., 483. Also see Evola, "Das Doppelantlitz des Nationalismus," *Europäische Revue* 8 (1932): 618–28.

33 Evola, *Sintesi di dottrina della razza*, 15.

34 Evola, "Sulle origini remote della crisi italiana ed europea," 16.

35 Persönlicher Stab Reichsführer SS, September 1938, BArch NS 19/1848: 38. For more thorough discussion of Evola's relations with the SS, see Horst Junginger, "From Buddha to Adolf Hitler," in *The Study of Religion under the Impact of Fascism*, ed. Horst Junginger (Leiden: Brill, 2008), 107–77, here 127–40 and 166–70.

36 Memorandum for Minister Pavolini, 21 December 1940, ACS Ministero della Cultura Popolare b. 121, f. 759. For an example of Evola's joint polemics against Jews and Freemasons, see Julius Evola, "La guerra occulta: Ebrei i massoni alla conquista del mondo," *Vita Italiana* (December 1936): 645–5.

37 Press directive from Direzione Generale Stampa Italiana, 20 October 1941, ACS Ministero della Cultura Popolare b. 121, f. 759.

38 Julius Evola, *Grundrisse der faschistischen Rassenlehre* (Berlin: Runge, n.d.); the edition carries no date, but German library holdings indicate it was published in 1942 or 1943. It is a well-produced volume; the photographic appendix, for example, is of higher quality than in the Italian original. The German text diverges substantially from the Italian at several points and contains two additional chapters. According to a note printed opposite the contents page, Evola oversaw the translation himself.

39 Matard-Bonucci, *L'Italia fascista e la persecuzione degli ebrei*, 253–6; Renzo De Felice, *Storia degli ebrei italiani sotto il fascismo* (Turin: Einaudi, 1993), 244–7, 255–6.

40 Evola, *Sintesi di dottrina della razza*, 13, 25, 118, 173.

41 Alberto Luchini, Ufficio Razza, to National Fascist Party Secretariat, 13 April 1943, ACS Ministero della Cultura Popolare b. 121, f. 759.

42 Examples include Massimo Scaligero, "Sangue e spirito," *Difesa della Razza* (20 October 1941): 13–15; Scaligero, "La razza, la terra e il fuoco," *Vita Italiana* (December 1941): 626-630; Scaligero, "La razza italiana dall'Impero Carolingio al feudalesimo," *Difesa della Razza* (5 December 1941): 13–15; Roberto Pavese, "Razzismo positivo," *Regime Fascista* (15 February 1942): 3; Pavese, "Il problema ebraico in Italia," *Gerarchia* (June 1942): 256–8; Pavese, "Linee generali del problema della razza," *Tempo di Mussolini* (August 1942): 1265–9; and Alberto Luchini, "Contro l'attesismo antirazzista," *Regime Fascista* (16 June 1943): 3.

43 For a detailed account, see Peter Staudenmaier, "Racial Ideology between Fascist Italy and Nazi Germany: Julius Evola and the Aryan Myth, 1933–1943," *Journal of Contemporary History* 55 (2020): 473–91.

44 Evola, *Sintesi di dottrina della razza*, 155; Evola, "L'ipotesi iperborea: La culla della razza aria," *Difesa della Razza* (5 April 1939): 17–20; Evola, *Il mistero del Graal* (Bari: Laterza, 1937), 139.

45 Evola, *Sintesi di dottrina della razza*, 67.

46 Compare Mauro Raspanti, "Il mito ariano nella cultura italiana fra otto e novecento," in *Nel nome della razza: Il razzismo nella storia d'Italia 1870–1945*, ed. Alberto Burgio (Bologna: Mulino, 1999): 75–85; Stefan Arvidsson, "Aryan Mythology As Science and Ideology," *Journal of the American Academy of Religion* 67 (1999): 327–54; Edwin Bryant, "Myths of Origin: Europe and the Aryan Homeland Quest," in Bryant, *The Quest for the Origins of Vedic Culture* (Oxford: Oxford University Press, 2001): 13–45; Vasant Kaiwar, "The Aryan Model of History and the Oriental Renaissance" in *Anti-*

nomies of Modernity: Essays on Race, Orient, Nation, ed. Sucheta Mazumdar (Durham: Duke University Press, 2003), 13–61; and Romila Thapar, "The Historiography of the Concept of 'Aryan,'" in *India: Historical Beginnings and the Concept of the Aryan*, ed. Romila Thapar (New Delhi: National Book Trust, 2006): 1–40.

47 See the 1925 remarks from Arturo Reghini and René Guénon quoted in Christian Giudice, "Occultism and Traditionalism: Arturo Reghini and the Antimodern Reaction in Early Twentieth Century Italy" (PhD diss., University of Gothenburg, 2016), 251. Evola's 1937 book on the Holy Grail still relied heavily on Guénon's work for passages from Hindu and Buddhist sources. For his interpretation of Buddhism and its "Aryan" character, see Julius Evola, *La dottrina del risveglio* (Bari: Laterza, 1943).

48 Amartya Sen, *The Argumentative Indian: Writings on Indian History, Culture, and Identity* (New York: Picador, 2005), 139–60. Sen notes that such approaches ignore "the rationalist and humanist aspects" of Indian thought (154), aspects that were anathema to Evola.

49 Pankaj Mishra, *From the Ruins of Empire: The Revolt against the West and the Remaking of Asia* (New York: Picador, 2012), 212.

50 H.P. Blavatsky, *The Secret Doctrine: The Synthesis of Science, Religion, and Philosophy* (London: Theosophical Publishing Company, 1888). For context, see Sumathi Ramaswamy, *The Lost Land of Lemuria: Fabulous Geographies, Catastrophic Histories* (Berkeley: University of California Press, 2004); Francesco Baroni, "Occultism and Christianity in Twentieth-Century Italy" in *Occultism in a Global Perspective*, ed. Henrik Bogdan (Durham: Acumen, 2013), 101–20; Gordan Djurdjevic, *India and the Occult: The Influence of South Asian Spirituality on Modern Western Occultism* (New York: Palgrave, 2014); and Olav Hammer, "The Theosophical Current in the Twentieth Century," in *The Occult World*, ed. Christopher Partridge (London: Routledge, 2015), 348–60.

51 Blavatsky, *The Secret Doctrine*, 481–97. See also Blavatsky, *The Key to Theosophy* (London: Theosophical Publishing Company, 1889), 45: "If the root of mankind is one, then there must also be one truth which finds expression in all the various religions – except in the Jewish."

52 Evola, *Erhebung wider die moderne Welt*, 181–5, 321–2; Evola, *Il mistero del Graal*, 178–9; Evola, *Maschera e volto dello spiritualismo contemporaneo* (Turin: Bocca, 1932).

53 Evola, *Sintesi di dottrina della razza*, 75; Evola, *Erhebung wider die moderne*

Welt, 192, 442, 451, 456; Evola, *Il mito del sangue*, 68–76. On Wirth, see Luit-
gard Löw, *Herman Wirth und die völkische Symbolforschung* (Frankfurt am
Main: Peter Lang, 2016); Stefanie von Schnurbein, *Norse Revival: Transfor-
mations of Germanic Neopaganism* (Leiden: Brill, 2016), 221–2, 267–9, 273–5;
and Ingo Wiwjorra, "Herman Wirth im Kontext der völkisch-religiösen Bewegung," in *Die völkisch-religiöse Bewegung im Nationalsozialismus*, ed. Uwe
Puschner (Göttingen: Vandenhoeck & Ruprecht, 2012), 399–416.

54 Evola, "Sulle origini remote della crisi italiana ed europea," 10, 11, 15.

55 Giovanni Preziosi and Julius Evola, eds., *L'internazionale ebraica: I 'Protocolli' dei 'savi anziani' di Sion* (Rome: Vita Italiana, 1937). He cited the "Protocols" throughout his work; for example, see Julius Evola, "Inquadramento
del problema ebraico," 721–2; Evola, *Erhebung wider die moderne Welt*, 482;
and Evola, *Il mistero del Graal*, 183. Evola held that the authenticity of the
text was irrelevant; fabricated or not, the "Protocols" accurately revealed the
Jewish conspiracy against Aryan civilization.

56 Julius Evola, "Fascismo antifilosofico e tradizione mediterranea," *Critica
Fascista* (15 June 1927), 227–9; Evola, "Der Faschismus als Wille zur Welther-
rschaft und das Christentum," *Die Eiche* 16 (1928): 172–8; Evola, *Imperiali-
smo pagano: Il fascismo dinnanzi al pericolo euro-cristiano* (Rome: Atanor,
1928).

57 See the critique of misguided forms of neo-paganism in Evola, *Sintesi di
dottrina della razza*, 195–214.

58 Evola, *Erhebung wider die moderne Welt*, 230, 362; Evola, "Fascismo antifilosofico e tradizione mediterranea," *Critica Fascista* (15 June 1927): 227–9.

59 Evola, *Il mistero del Graal*, 17, 142, 182. For illuminating parallels from the
history of Catholic racism, see John Connelly, "Catholic Racism and Its Opponents," *Journal of Modern History* 79 (2007): 813–47.

60 The range of treatments includes informative accounts by esoteric sympa-
thizers; for example, see Dana Lloyd Thomas, *Julius Evola e la tentazione
razzista* (Brindisi: Giordano, 2006); Jocelyn Godwin, "*Politica Romana* Pro
and Contra Evola" in *Esotericism, Religion, and Politics*, ed. Arthur Versluis
(Minneapolis: North American Academic Press, 2012), 41–58.

61 A prime example of this tendency is the work of Austrian independent
scholar and Evola translator Hans Thomas Hakl; for example, see Hakl,
"Evola, Giulio Cesare," in *Dictionary of Gnosis and Western Esotericism*, ed.
Wouter Hanegraaff (Leiden: Brill, 2006), 345–50; Hakl, "The Symbology of

Hermeticism in the Work of Julius Evola," in *Lux in Tenebris: The Visual and the Symbolic in Western Esotericism*, ed. Peter Forshaw (Leiden: Brill, 2017): 334–62; Hakl, "Deification as a Core Theme in Julius Evola's Esoteric Works," *Correspondences* 6 (2018): 145–71; and Hakl, "Julius Evola and Tradition," in *Key Thinkers of the Radical Right*, ed. Mark Sedgwick (Oxford: Oxford University Press, 2019), 54–69. While I find much of this work highly problematic, others appreciate its virtues. I would like to thank Wouter Hanegraaff and Julian Strube for collegial discussion of Hakl's approach.

62 A. James Gregor, *The Search for Neofascism: The Use and Abuse of Social Science* (New York: Cambridge University Press 2006), 83–110. See also Gregor, *Mussolini's Intellectuals: Fascist Social and Political Thought* (Princeton: Princeton University Press 2005), 191–221.

63 For a case study, see Peter Staudenmaier, "Preparation for Genocide: The 'Center for the Study of the Jewish Problem' in Trieste, Italy, 1942–1944," *Holocaust and Genocide Studies* 31 (2017): 1–23.

64 Julius Evola, "Razzismo e altri orrori," *L'Italiano* (May 1959): 67.

65 See Stanley Payne, "Fascism and Racism," in *Cambridge History of Twentieth-Century Political Thought*, ed. Terence Ball (Cambridge: Cambridge University Press, 2003), 123–50; Fabrizio De Donno, "'La Razza Ario-Mediterranea': Ideas of Race and Citizenship in Colonial and Fascist Italy, 1885–1941," *Interventions* 8 (2006): 394–412; Johan Chapoutot, *Greeks, Romans, Germans: How the Nazis Usurped Europe's Classical Past* (Berkeley: University of California Press 2016), 51–97; Ernest Ialongo, "Nation-Building through Antisemitism: Fascism and the Jew as the Internal Enemy," *Annali d'Italianistica* 36 (2018): 327–49; and Patrick Bernhard, "The Great Divide? Notions of Racism in Fascist Italy and Nazi Germany," *Journal of Modern Italian Studies* 24 (2019): 97–114.

66 David Roberts, *Fascist Interactions: Proposals for a New Approach to Fascism and Its Era, 1919–1945* (New York: Berghahn, 2016), 7.

67 Roger Griffin, *Modernism and Fascism: The Sense of a Beginning under Mussolini and Hitler* (London: Palgrave, 2007), 15–18 and 39–42. See also Daniel Woodley, "Fascism, rationality and modernity," in Woodley, *Fascism and Political Theory: Critical Perspectives on Fascist Ideology* (London: Routledge, 2010), 21–48, and the extended discussion of Evola in Mark Sedgwick, *Against the Modern World: Traditionalism and the Secret Intellectual History of the Twentieth Century* (Oxford: Oxford University Press, 2004).

68 Jan Nelis, "Fascist Modernity, Religion, and the Myth of Rome," in *Brill's Companion to the Classics, Fascist Italy, and Nazi Germany*, ed. Helen Roche (Leiden: Brill, 2018), 133–56. See also Friedemann Scriba, "The Sacralisation of the Roman Past in Mussolini's Italy," *Storia della Storiografia* 30 (1996): 19–29.

69 Evola, "Sulle origini remote della crisi italiana ed europea," 17.

70 Nicholas Goodrick-Clarke, *Black Sun: Aryan Cults, Esoteric Nazism, and the Politics of Identity* (New York: NYU Press 2002): 52–71; Jacob Senholt, "Radical Politics and Political Esotericism: The Adaptation of Esoteric Discourse within the Radical Right," in *Contemporary Esotericism*, eds. Egil Asprem and Kennet Granholm (Sheffield: Equinox, 2013), 244–64; Elisabetta Cassina Wolff, "*Apolitìa* and Tradition in Julius Evola as Reaction to Nihilism," *European Review* 22 (2014): 258–73; Joshua Green, *Devil's Bargain: Steve Bannon, Donald Trump, and the Storming of the Presidency* (New York: Penguin, 2017); Giovanni Savino, "From Evola to Dugin," in *Eurasianism and the European Far Right*, ed. Marlene Laruelle (Lanham: Lexington, 2017), 97–124; George Hawley, *The Alt-Right* (Oxford: Oxford University Press, 2019), 78–80; and Alexandra Minna Stern, *How the Alt-Right Is Warping the American Imagination* (Boston: Beacon Press, 2019), 38–46.

PART TWO

Supporting Ethnonationalist Efforts

4

German Catholicism's Lost Opportunity to Confront Antisemitism before the Machtergreifung

Kevin P. Spicer, CSC

On the morning of Monday, 17 June 1929, three members of the National Socialist German Workers' Party (NSDAP) approached Father Johannes Rachor, pastor of St Lambert Parish in Bechtheim in the Mainz diocese, and asked him to preside at the funeral of Leonard Gundersdorff, a twenty-three-year-old party member. Rachor had been the pastor at St Lambert since 1907 and had plenty of experience dealing with challenging pastoral issues. Nevertheless, the question the party members placed before him touched upon a sensitive political issue: whether membership in a certain political party limited an individual's participation in the liturgical rites of the Church. Statements made publicly by National Socialists and reported in local newspapers had already led Rachor to conclude that the Hitler Movement was "hostile to the Church." He reasoned that a statement against the NSDAP by "individual pastors or an individual pastor was worthless" and therefore asked his diocesan superiors to offer him instructions on how he should proceed.[1]

Such initial encounters on the local level between National Socialists and parish priests have been little considered in the existing literature.[2] If these studies allude to them at all, they usually discuss them in connection with broad generalizations about the German bishops' initial resistance to National Socialism. Historians have exerted little or no effort to examine the divergent views of the German Catholic Church leadership to National Socialism and its racist ideology immediately prior to Hitler's appointment as chancellor in late January 1933.[3] Often the views of Catholic clergymen differed significantly, and at times they were contradictory. As this chapter will show, the nature of the initial opposition raised by clergymen in Mainz contrasted significantly with the official statements on National Socialism eventually made by individual bishops and church provinces. In the diocese of Mainz, early Catholic opposition to National Socialism concentrated selectively if not exclusively on the incompatibility of the Nazi Party's hatred of Jews with Catholic moral teaching on the inherent dignity of all human beings. As discussion on how best to respond to National Socialism progressed, the German bishops dropped their specific condemnation of the National Socialist "hatred of Jews" and adopted a more generic condemnation of National Socialist ideology so as to delete any reference to "Jews." This latter approach focused primarily on those issues that directly affected the Church and its pastoral ministry.

According to my research, Father Rachor's June 1929 inquiry about how pastorally to respond to someone requesting a funeral for a member of the National Socialist Party is one of the earliest recorded. At that time, the National Socialists were still a minority party in the German national parliament (Reichstag) and state parliaments (Landtage). In the 20 May 1928 election, the Social Democratic Party (SPD) had maintained its parliamentary majority, earning 29.8 per cent of the national vote, followed by a combined 15.2 per cent for the Catholic Center Party and its southern equivalent, the Bavarian People's Party (BVP). Support for the right-wing parties appeared to be diminishing. For example, in May 1928 the ultra-conservative, nationalist German National People's Party (DNVP), earned only 14.2 per cent of the vote, 6.3 per cent less than it had received in the December 1924 Reichstag election. In 1928, the NSDAP received just 2.6 per cent of the vote. With such a tiny fraction of the national vote, the Nazis were not yet a major concern for German Catholic leaders. Causing greater worry was the German Communist Party (KPD), whose support had risen steadily over the years until in the 1928 Reichstag election it earned 10.6 per cent of the vote.[4] The persecution of the Catholic Church in Mexico and Spain, and of religion in general, most notably in the Soviet Union, reinforced among German Catholic Church leaders a fear of the rise of communism in Germany.[5]

Despite their lack of success in national elections, Nazi agitators were causing serious disruption in local politics and communal life. Inevitably, these conflicts crept into parish life, where they impacted pastoral care. Many NSDAP speakers questioned the loyalty of Catholics to the German nation. These speakers were promoting an ideology that placed race above religion, thus contradicting the Church's teaching on the efficacy of baptism.[6] Likewise, National Socialists promoted a comprehensive worldview that suggested a desire on their part to displace Christianity. Yet contradictions and dissension among NSDAP proponents regarding the position of Catholicism on several issues abounded, making it a challenge for Church leaders to respond in a uniform manner. Increasingly, these incongruities caused unease among the Catholic parish clergy as they found themselves having to deal first-hand with political realities.[7]

For help with these pastoral challenges, pastors in the Mainz diocese regularly consulted the staff of the Mainz chancery (Bischöfliches Ordinariat), whose clergy personnel administered the diocese's day-to-day operations. Ludwig Maria Hugo, bishop of Mainz (1921–1935), exercised executive oversight in the diocese, but it was Monsignor Dr Philipp Jakob Mayer, the vicar general, who handled routine diocesan affairs.[8] Born in 1870 in Albig, a small town less than twenty miles from the city of Mainz, into a farming family, Mayer was a highly intelligent and diligent individual who had received a special dispensation from the Holy See to be ordained at the age of twenty-two. In between his assignments as a parochial vicar, first at St Stephen in Mainz and then at St Martin in Ober-Olm, he earned a doctorate in theology in just over a year. In 1897, he began teaching religion at the Bensheim Altes Kurfürstliches Gymnasium; in 1906, he transferred to the prestigious Mainz Ostergymnasium, where in April 1909 he received the title of professor. In August 1917, amid the First World War, he left teaching and began an administrative career in the Mainz chancery. On 19 March 1922, Bishop Hugo appointed him vicar general.[9]

As vicar general, Mayer received Father Rachor's inquiry. Because of its politically sensitive nature, Mayer consulted with Bishop Hugo before replying.[10] Both agreed that the National Socialist Movement was problematic for the Church; yet they were also unprepared to take a strong stance against

Figure 4.1 Vicar General Philipp Jakob Mayer.

it. Instead, Mayer informed Father Rachor that having received the last rites of the Church – Father Adam Ihm, pastor of Our Lady's parish in Worms, had earlier administered the sacraments – Gundersdorff had "a right to a Church funeral."[11] Still, Mayer stressed that this fact did not give National Socialists the prerogative to attend the funeral or burial wearing party uniforms or to process with flags in closed rank. He informed Rachor that if they refused to abide by this decision, he could refuse a Church burial.[12]

Father Rachor was not the only pastor facing such issues. Other priests besides were writing to the Mainz chancery seeking counsel on how to deal with National Socialists.[13] Such questioning came to a head in early August 1929 when the mother of Otto Erich Jost requested a Church burial for her son, who had died of an injury following an altercation during the Nazi Party's annual Nuremberg Rally. Like Gundersdorff, Jost had received the last rites shortly before his death. However, unlike Gundersdorff, Jost had only been informally active in the Hitler Movement and had never officially joined the NSDAP or any of its related organizations.[14] Still, local NSDAP members hoped to wear their party uniforms and walk in closed formation at his funeral. When Jost's pastor, Father Heinrich Johannes Heinstadt, the pastor of St Nazarius in Lorsch, learned about these plans, he immediately intervened, informing Jost's mother, "The Church funeral is a religious ceremony. I cannot tolerate a funeral being misused for a political demonstration, which is to be feared under the present circumstances. I demand that the National Socialists not take part in it in uniform or closed formation." In the end, she conceded to Father Heinstadt's demands. However, the local NSDAP protested by sending two NSDAP representatives to question Father Heinstadt's reasoning. Heinstadt stood by his decision, telling them bluntly, "National Socialism is unchristian because it preaches racial hatred and fights against the Jews and because it is also a national religion that promotes ancient pagan German religion." The funeral eventually took place at 11 a.m. on 9 August without uniformed National Socialist members present. Later that evening, between 220 and 250 uniformed National Socialists gathered around Jost's grave and listened to Adolf Hitler personally commemorate the deceased.[15]

News of the controversy surrounding Jost's funeral spread quickly in local newspapers supportive of National Socialism, primarily due to the *Völkischer Beobachter*'s extensive coverage of it.[16] The situation especially alarmed Catholics who supported Hitler. One such supporter, Joseph Franz Arnet, an engineer from Eberstadt near Darmstadt, who described himself as a Catholic and "dedicated National Socialist," even travelled sixty miles to attend the funeral. Having arrived late, he was only able to be present for the evening National Socialist commemoration ceremony. Still, he was upset to learn about the restrictions that had been put in place when the funeral was held earlier that day, and he wrote to Bishop Hugo seeking an explanation. At the core of his surprisingly respectful inquiry was the question, "Can a Catholic be a National Socialist?"[17]

Before anyone from the diocese answered Arnet's inquiry, Vicar General Mayer wrote to Father Heinstadt to learn more about why he was opposed to the Hitler Movement.[18] In his reply, Heinstadt cited four reasons:

1. Church funerals should not be abused for political demonstrations.
2. The hostile character of National Socialism towards Catholics. In a recent article, the K[ölnische] V[olkszeitung] reported on the conflict of the National Socialists in Saxony: The hostility of the National Socialists toward Catholics is well-known. 3. The article about National Socialism in the state lexicon also points this out. 4. I do not tolerate a Social Democrat association with red wreaths at any funeral, and I cannot permit the National Socialists turning a funeral into a political demonstration and putting red ribbons on wreaths. If I did this, then the Social Democrats would be right if they accused me of partiality, etc.

Father Heinstadt also included several books to inform the chancery about the National Socialist Party, including Alfred Rosenberg's Wesen, Grundsätze und Ziele der Nationalsozialistischen Deutschen Arbeitpartei (Essence, Principles, and Aims of the NSDAP, 1923); Gottfried Feder's Das Programm der NSDAP und seine weltanschaulichen Grundgedanken (The Program of the NSDAP and Its Fundamental Worldview, 1927); and Heinrich Czeloth, Klarheit und Wahrheit. Warum wir Katholiken die vaterländischen Verbände ablehnen müssen! (Clarity and Truth. Why We Catholics must Reject the Nationalist Associations, 1924).[19]

After reading extensively about the ideology of National Socialism and consulting with Bishop Hugo, Vicar General Mayer replied to Arnet. He recounted the events at Lorsch and then restated Father Heinstadt's reasons for prohibiting corporative attendance at the funeral by NSDAP members, namely "that National Socialism was unchristian, that it preached racial hatred and struggle against the Jews, and that it also aspired to a national religion, the old-pagan German religion." Mayer also confirmed that he agreed with Heinstadt's critique, underscoring the entire sentence in his letter. Furthermore, he reasoned, National Socialism's primary incompatibility with Christian principles was its "position regarding the Jews." Mayer pointed out,

> Number 4 of the [NSDAP] program states, citizens can only be national comrades (*Volksgenosse*); national comrades can only be those with German blood, regardless of religious denomination; therefore, no Jew can be a national comrade. Number 5 dictates that whoever is not a citizen can only live in Germany as a guest and must be subject to laws for foreigners. Number 7 demands that if it is not possible to feed the entire population of the state, then members of foreign nations are to be expelled from the Reich. Number 8 demands that all further immigration of non-Germans is to be prevented and all non-Germans who have immigrated to Germany since 2 August 1914, should immediately be forced to leave the Reich.

Mayer found that "this surge of nationalism leads to disdain and hatred of foreign peoples, especially of Jewish people, and eventually also to contempt for and persecution of Catholics, whose religion, as National Socialist writers claim, contains Jewish elements." Quoting Rudolf Jung, a National Socialist author, Mayer added: "The rigid centralism and the international character of all Christian churches, but above all the Roman churches ... are the pronounced Jewish traits in church-related Christianity. Hence the word repeatedly uttered by Hitlerites: 'Our struggle is against Judah and Rome.'"[20]

Mayer's critique of National Socialism's hatred of Jews revealed that he was not thoroughly altruistic but that his criticism was tied directly to his fear that this loathing could also lead to persecution of the Church owing to its historical roots in Judaism. Furthermore, in the letter, he emphasized this point again when he critiqued point 24 of the NSDAP platform, which professed "positive Christianity." Mayer argued that such "positive Christianity" meant understanding "Christianity only in contradiction to Judaism" without any genuine appreciation or understanding of the Christian faith. However, what is more problematic in his response is how Mayer characterized "Jewish people" as "foreign peoples," and in doing so appears to have embraced the outlook of the German right, including the NSDAP, toward Jews. Still, even in its imperfection, Mayer's overall stance was unique and significantly differed from the outlook of most Catholic clergy of the time, as evidenced by the events that followed.

By late summer 1929, the events at Lorsch had become major news and of great concern to National Socialists. In the Munich archdiocese, Otto Trojan, a Catholic and National Socialist, took it upon himself to write directly to Pope Pius XI seeking a clarification of the Holy See's position on the Hitler Movement.[21] The letter was of sufficient concern to the Vatican that an official in the Sacred Congregation of the Council wrote to Trojan's ordinary, Cardinal Michael von Faulhaber, Archbishop of Munich and Freising, for further information. Unfamiliar with the specific events in Mainz, Faulhaber had his chancery forward the Vatican inquiry to its counterpart in Mainz. The above interchange took significant time, so that the inquiry only reached Vicar General Mayer's desk a few days before Christmas. [22] By this point, Mayer had become quite adept at articulating his concerns about the NSDAP.[23] Most of his replies to inquiries followed the wording of his response to Arnet, and Mayer's reply to Munich would not be an exception. Mayer singled out the NSDAP's "position on the Jews" as the number one issue that made National Socialism problematic for Catholics. At the same time, he repeated the phrase, "disdain and hatred of foreign peoples, especially of Jewish people," in his critique of extreme nationalism, thus reinforcing the idea that Jews were not Germans.[24]

On 25 January 1930, Cardinal Faulhaber offered his opinion on National Socialism to the Sacred Congregation of the Council in a one-page letter written in Latin. In the first paragraph, he briefly described the events at Lorsch and compared the Mainz restrictions against uniformed Nazis with the "customary" practice of forbidding communists from wearing red insignias to Church liturgies. In the second paragraph, Faulhaber spent only one brief sentence acknowledging that Nazis "cultivate a particular hatred of the Jews." The rest of his paragraph focused on how National Socialism jeopardized the faith of lay Catholics by favouring Protestantism over Catholicism and thus promoting viewpoints on issues such as education, concordats, and morality that contradicted Church teaching. Likewise, he questioned National Socialism's overemphasis on "pan-Germanism," which encouraged "Catholics to mix with Protestants." In his third paragraph, Faulhaber focused on whether it was important to reply to Trojan. On this question, he did not take a specific position.[25]

Figure 4.2 Cardinal Michael von Faulhaber, the Archbishop of Munich and Freising, and Father Josef Weißthanner, Faulhaber's secretary, greeting parishioners of St Augustine's Church on 22 November 1931.

Historians have surprisingly neglected Faulhaber's letter. In 2005, Heinz Hürten emphasized this fact in a brief article; yet his analysis misrepresented the letter's content by exaggerating Faulhaber's critique of National Socialism's hatred of Jews. Faulhaber only in passing acknowledged the NSDAP's "particular hatred of Jews" before dedicating the rest of his letter to other concerns. Faulhaber's subsequent statements on National Socialism support this interpretation. However, Hürten did correctly acknowledge that Faulhaber deviated from the Mainz position by broadening the scope of his critique to include critical points on Catholic schools and family life "that directly affected him in his capacity as bishop."[26]

Tensions between the Church and the NSDAP continued to rise as Nazi speakers increasingly ranted against "Jewry and Rome," giving the impression that the party had placed its anti-Catholicism on equal footing with its antisemitism. Various stances on National Socialism that churchmen took led to significant confusion among Catholics.[27] To address this issue in the

Mainz diocese, Vicar General Mayer wrote "Catholics and National Socialism," under the byline "by a Catholic priest," for the 25 August 1930 edition
of the *Mainzer Journal*, a Catholic newspaper associated with the Center
Party. Mayer reminded the reader, "Christian moral law is based on the love
of neighbour. By contrast, the entire literature of the National Socialists
abundantly reveals that the greatest commandment of love of mankind as
Christ taught it has no place in the thinking of the Hitler Party. Instead, the
National Socialists preach an almost blind adoration of their race and a glorification of the struggle and hatred against all foreign races. This hatred is
unchristian and un-Catholic ... Christ, the founder of our Catholic Church,
is the saviour of all people, the heathens and the Jews."[28]

On the same day that the *Mainzer Journal* published Mayer's editorial,
Father Heinrich Weber, the pastor of St Bartholomew parish in Kirsch-
hausen, wrote to the Mainz chancery complaining that the "agitation" of the
National Socialists in his town had reached unacceptable levels and asking
for clarity regarding how he should deal with it.[29] A day later, utterly separate
from Weber, Father Rachor of Bechtheim, who had made an initial inquiry
about the burial of National Socialists in June 1929, wrote a similar letter.[30]
Mayer was prepared to take a stronger stance against National Socialism. On
1 September, he replied that Catholics could no longer be members of the
Nazi Party nor could they receive the sacraments if they remained in that
party. He added that National Socialists were not allowed to attend Mass or
funerals in uniformed groups.[31] Mayer would certainly have consulted with
Bishop Hugo before taking such a definitive stance.

In mid-September, Father Weber made the Mainz diocese's decision public during Sunday High Mass by boldly informing his parishioners that the
Church forbade Catholics from joining the Hitler party.[32] He sternly warned
them that anyone who ignored this ban could neither participate in Church
liturgies nor receive the sacraments; thus they would be risking their eternal
salvation for their immortal soul. Weber's pronouncement quickly became
national news.[33] When the Gau Hessen leadership of the NSDAP inquired
whether Father Weber's declaration were true, Vicar General Mayer confirmed that it was, repeating much of what he had written in his August editorial.[34] As a result of this confirmation, on 30 September 1930, the diocese
of Mainz under Bishop Ludwig Maria Hugo's leadership became the first
German diocese to take a definitive stance against the Hitler party.

Of course, the National Socialist press fought back with numerous articles accusing Bishop Hugo of many improprieties, including taking a stance against the NSDAP to bolster support for the Catholic Center Party. The Nazi press likewise accused Mayer of being a "baptized Jew," working against all good Aryan Germans.[35] Some Catholic National Socialists took the even more drastic step of withdrawing from the Church altogether, a legal step due to Germany's intricate Church tax system, and of announcing the withdrawal publicly in newspapers.[36] However, most Catholics in Mainz appeared to heed the warnings of Bishop Hugo and Vicar General, Philipp Jakob Mayer.[37]

Even though the prohibition against Catholic membership in the NSDAP was generally successful, Vicar General Mayer remained relentless in his stance against the Hitler party. In mid-October, he submitted a new editorial to the *Mainzer Journal*, which ran in two consecutive parts under the title "Can a Catholic Be a National Socialist?" Mayer declared that as far as he knew, all his ancestors were "good Germans, and that not a droplet of Israelite blood flowed in his veins. However, even if I were a Jewish-Christian, my statements would not lose their authenticity; these concerns here pertain to the issues at hand and their rationale, not the person who advances the issues." Yet Mayer once again revealed that he was not free of cultural antisemitism by stating, "Jews exert influence on the German *Volk*, especially through the press, theatre, literature, etc.," even adding that "Hitler [had] strikingly described this in his book *Mein Kampf*." This antisemitic charge was ingrained in almost all Christians of this time, irrespective of class or standing. It was also part of Catholic teaching. In the 1920s and '30s, numerous European Catholic theological works distinguished between two forms of antisemitism: an unacceptable form that was "un-Christian," racist and hate-filled; and an acceptable form that monitored and offered a "healthy evaluation" of the danger to society and the Church emanating from a belief in the dominance of Jews in economic and public life.[38]

Notwithstanding this serious antisemitic remark, Vicar General Mayer revealed that he did not concur with how the National Socialists planned to solve the "Jewish Question." He continued:

I do not consider it appropriate to make exceptional laws for Jews and to declare them lesser citizens. Let Christians band together to repel

the menacing threat to faith and morality; let them insist that relevant
laws be passed in parliament to protect religion and morality; let there
be harsh legal action against anyone who violates such laws – not only
against Jews but also against those who call themselves Christians, exploiting their neighbours or destroying their souls for the sake of filthy
profit. Still, I cannot speak in favour of exceptional laws against Jews
and foreigners. Such exceptional laws in Germany would give rise to
the harshest protests in other countries, and Germany would be isolated in the end.[39]

Before the end of October 1930, Vicar General Mayer had officially condemned National Socialism and its ideology with Bishop Hugo's support.
Through his words, Mayer made it clear that the National Socialism's worldview was incompatible with Catholicism and its fundamental gospel-based
teaching of love of neighbour. Mayer also directly criticized National Socialists' hatred of Jews, even while succumbing to the cultural and economic
antisemitism that plagued most Catholics at this time. Notwithstanding his
failure to reject these forms of antisemitism, Mayer would be one of the few
Catholics who boldly and clearly critiqued National Socialism's hatred of
Jews and labelled it incompatible with Catholic teaching.

While Vicar General Mayer was pointing out the differences between National Socialism and Catholic teaching and taking his stand against the National Socialists in Mainz, German Catholic leaders elsewhere were only
beginning to grasp the sudden rise of Adolf Hitler and his NSDAP and to
draw up an adequate response to this unforeseen change. In the Reichstag
election of 14 September, the NSDAP had pulled off a surprising show of
numbers, garnering 18.3 per cent of the total vote, far surpassing its performance in the May 1928 national election, when it won only 2.6 per cent.
However, the NSDAP was not the only party to benefit from Germany's precarious economy since the arrival of the Great Depression in October 1929.
The KPD increased its numbers, winning 13.1 per cent of the vote, a notable
increase from its 10.6 per cent performance in 1928. This persistent rise of
the far left made Catholic leaders fearful of a communist takeover.[40] Only
the SPD exceeded the gains of the two radical parties, winning 24.5 per cent
of the vote.[41] The German bishops inherently distrusted the SPD despite its
past coalition with the Catholic Center Party.

The rise of the National Socialists forced the German Catholic bishops to take a stance on the NSDAP. But such a stance was easier said than done since the German bishops were far from being of one mind over how to respond to the phenomenon. Similarly, Catholic National Socialists individually were equally worried about their personal standing in the Church, at times writing to their diocesan chanceries and even to the Holy See for guidance and clarification.[42] Meanwhile, National Socialist newspapers endeavoured to counteract the negative publicity first generated by the diocese of Mainz in a concerted effort to discredit the Church and to bolster the party's Catholic support. On 25 November 1930, Vicar General Mayer released a new editorial to the German press to address the charges in the Nazi press. Reiterating his diocese's position against Catholic membership in the NSDAP, Mayer assured Catholics that they were neither excommunicated nor expelled from the Church if they remained in the NSDAP; however, they could not receive the sacraments unless they withdrew from the party. He stressed, "The imposition of excommunication and the denial of the sacraments are not the same."[43] The National Socialist press was not impressed by this distinction and continued attacking Mayer, Bishop Hugo, and the Catholic Church in general. The tactics of the press were clever. Reporters skillfully drew on the fears and anxieties of German Catholics, many of whom were still historically perplexed by the Bismarckian *Kulturkampf*. Many older Catholics, remember, had been teenagers at the time of the *Kulturkampf*, sixty years earlier. An example of this adept manoeuvre can be found in the National Socialist daily *Der Tag*, under the striking headline, "Care for a *Kulturkampf*?" Reporter Hans Götz asked, "Has the Medieval Age arisen from its grave?" He then answered the question by comparing Mainz's prohibition of NSDAP membership among faithful Catholics to the intrusive control the Church had exerted over early modern European society. According to Götz, Bishop Hugo was doing the "will of Judas," the latter word a euphemism for Jews.[44]

Gradually, the rest of the German hierarchy became caught up in the question of membership and reception of sacraments for Catholic NSDAP members. In early December, Cardinal Bertram wrote to the members of the Fulda Bishops' Conference, presenting them with a proposal for a united statement on National Socialism, which, among other things, forbade Catholics from joining the NSDAP.[45] However, nowhere in the draft statement did Bertram condemn the NSDAP's racial teaching or its hatred of Jews.

Unlike Bishop Hugo and Vicar General Mayer, who specifically mentioned Jews, Bertram did not. He addressed race only once, remarking that National Socialism's ideology "makes the feeling of a race the judge over religious truths, over the revelation of God, and over the legitimacy of the God-given moral law."[46]

As a courtesy, in early December, Bertram sent a copy of the draft statement to Cardinal Faulhaber, the head of the Bavarian (Freising) Bishops' Conference, which consisted of all the bishops of the Bavarian dioceses and the bishop of Speyer.[47] Though Cardinal Faulhaber was concerned with the situation, he deemed it pastorally "unacceptable" to bar all Catholic National Socialists from receiving the sacraments without reviewing individual cases.[48] He placed less emphasis on developing a joint statement critiquing the National Socialist ideology and more on the creating pastoral instructions for clergy.[49] By taking this stance, Faulhaber hoped to avoid confrontation between the Church and the National Socialist Party, which he believed would play out in the public forum, especially in the media. He preferred to confine the matter to the pastoral sphere by issuing instructions to his archdiocesan clergy.

In his draft of pastoral instructions, Faulhaber condemned National Socialism as "heresy because it rejects fundamental points of the doctrine of the Catholic faith and according to a statement of its leaders wants to put a new worldview in place of a Christian worldview." He added, "National Socialism places race higher than religion. It rejects the revelations of the Old Testament, including the ten commandments of Sinai." Despite these stern words, Faulhaber still advocated a case-by-case examination rather than a sweeping statement with far-reaching consequences that would specifically exclude Catholic National Socialists from receiving the sacraments.[50]

Faulhaber shared both his draft and Cardinal Bertram's version with the bishops of Bavaria. Generally, the Bavarian bishops agreed that the diocese of Mainz had been overzealous in its sweeping pronouncement against National Socialism. Several of them recommended greater emphasis on pastoral needs, which often arose when they ministered to individuals who supported the NSDAP. None of the bishops came close to reiterating the language used by Vicar General Mayer to condemn outright National Socialism's hatred of Jews. Instead, they focused almost exclusively on issues that directly affected the Church's parochial mission. Their vision was myopic, almost a rationalization of institutional self-interest and devoid of anything overtly political.[51]

By mid-December, Faulhaber had produced a revised draft of the pastoral instructions based on the suggestions made by his fellow bishops. No longer did he call National Socialism a "heresy"; now he described only "its cultural-political program" as "heretical." Still, he retained the essential elements of his first draft, including his comments on race and the Old Testament.[52] Faulhaber informed Cardinal Bertram that the majority of the Bavarian bishops could not support a joint statement on the part of the German episcopate, for three reasons: concern that German youth would leave the Church for National Socialism, coupled with the possibility of change in the Hitler Movement's attitude toward the Church; concern that such a statement would revitalize and unify the NSDAP by providing it with a new target (i.e., the Church) for its propaganda efforts; and concern that they would appear disunited and in opposition to the stance of the Mainz Vicar-General.[53] In all these discussions, the bishops did not share any repudiatory words about the Nazi Party's hate-filled antisemitism. It was as if they could find no means to condemn antisemitism except through silence.

The Bavarian bishops were not the only members of Germany's episcopate to reject a joint statement addressing Catholic concerns about National Socialism. In early January 1931, Hermann Wilhelm Berning, the bishop of Osnabrück, informed Monsignor Bernhard Dinkgrefe, Pastor *Primarius* of Hamburg, that "except for the bishop of Mainz, until now none of the German bishops have issued a regulation that Catholic members of the National Socialist Party may not receive the sacraments. Considering that the movement is still in fermentation and many Catholic followers do not comprehend the scope of the party's intentions, the bishops have so far refrained from a joint statement aimed directly against the National Socialist Party."[54]

It is noteworthy to point out that, according to the statements of Faulhaber and Berning, at least some of the bishops held out hope that the National Socialists would alter their ideological hostility toward the Catholic Church. It must also be noted that on certain points, such as anti-communism, anti-liberalism, and condemnation of vice-related immorality, the Catholics bishops and clergy concurred with National Socialists.[55] Such commonalities led Christian Schreiber, bishop of Berlin, for example, to encourage the members of the Cartel Federation of German Catholic Student Associations,

of which he was an honorary member, to rescind their prohibition against
membership in the NSDAP. Schreiber believed that a "well-informed"
Catholic might be able to work within the Nazi Party to counteract any views
that were critical of the Church.[56]

The bishops could not agree to issue a joint statement against National
Socialism; however, Cardinal Bertram did garner support from the Fulda
Conference for a joint statement on nationalism's dangers.[57] On New Year's
Eve, Bertram released "The Position of the Catholic Church Concerning
Radicalism and Nationalism: A Frank Word at a Grave Hour at the Close of
1930." In his widely distributed nine-page statement, Cardinal Bertram incorporated sections from his draft statement on the NSDAP, though he never
addressed the Hitler party by name. Instead, he indirectly attacked its ideology under the guise of "egotistical" and "false" nationalism. Bertram did
concede that it was an error "to proceed with contempt for divine revelation
and the commandments of God" by proclaiming a "one-sided glorification
of race." Still, he devoted only a few sentences to a direct critique of racial
ideology. Instead, he wrote, "We Catholic Christians recognize no race-re-
lated religion, but only Christ's world-governing revelation that has offered
to all peoples the same treasure of faith, the same commandments, and the
same means to salvation."[58]

Meanwhile, in Munich, Cardinal Faulhaber continued to press the bishops of Bavaria to respond to the National Socialists. Adhering to his initial
response to Cardinal Bertram's draft statement, Faulhaber worked to gain
support among the bishops for pastoral instructions to help priests minister
to Catholic National Socialists and to address the challenge presented by the
tenets of the movement's ideology that went against Church teaching. By 26
January, the bishops of Eichstätt, Passau, Speyer, and Augsburg had given
their consent to Faulhaber's approach.[59]

On 29 January, Michael Buchberger, bishop of Regensburg, finally agreed
to lend his support to the dissemination of the instructions, but he also
shared his concern that National Socialists had "not sufficiently clarified and
defined" their ideology "in conceptual and programmatic terms." He continued, "Indeed, leading men and newspapers have made the crudest attack
upon the Christian faith and our holy Church. However, these are always
more the errors of individuals with whom most National Socialist voters are
not likely to agree. For example, in my diocese, I have not yet had any great

difficulties in this regard, and many genuinely practising Catholic men are committed to the Hitler party for economic and political reasons."[60] Buchberger's response shows, at least in part, some sympathy toward the party and a growing concern over Catholic support of it. At the same time, it reveals how difficult a hard-line stance might become for the German bishops vis-à-vis the state if the Nazis came to power. National Socialist Catholics could turn against the bishops and their Catholic faith.

By the end of the second week of February 1931, all the Bavarian bishops had consented to release the joint pastoral instructions regarding National Socialism to their clergy.[61] The leader of the Fulda Bishops' Conference, Cardinal Bertram, welcomed the pastoral instructions of the Bavarian bishops and shared a slightly edited version of them with his archdiocesan clergy.[62] Furthermore, on 19 February, Bertram also wrote to the Fulda Conference bishops, inviting them to consider using the Bavarian bishops' instructions as a basis for a joint statement of the German episcopacy. In contradiction to his usual uncontroversial posture, Bertram cautioned the bishops even more about the danger of supporting National Socialism. He warned, "It is self-deceptive if followers think that their involvement can be limited to one part of the program; for as long as a party advances its entire program, the support of a part of it is equal to the support of the entire program."[63]

By the end of March 1931, the remaining Church provinces had heeded Cardinal Bertram's call to issue statements on National Socialism.[64] Even Ludwig Maria Hugo, the bishop of Mainz, joined his fellow bishops in the Upper Rhine Province to issue a rather bland statement on National Socialism that emphasized the bishops' "love of *Volk* and fatherland," even in the face of their earlier critique of the NSDAP.[65] In their various statements about National Socialism, the German bishops limited their responses to issues that decisively contradicted Church doctrine. In no pronouncement did their words specifically uphold the gospel command to "love neighbour" and challenge directly National Socialism's hatred of Jews. Instead, the bishops committed themselves only to challenging National Socialism's racial principle when it explicitly went against Catholicism's salvific claims. In taking such a path, most bishops were choosing to adhere to a more inwardly limited course as first articulated by Cardinal Faulhaber – that is, to bypass the broader, more universal approach that had been advocated by Vicar General Mayer. From the existing evidence, it was largely Cardinal Faulhaber who was responsible for leading the Germans bishops away from Mainz's definitive prohibition. Instead of condemning the NSDAP's hatred of Jews, Faulhaber redirected the bishops to take issue with the Nazis, if not censure them, for their glorification of race, which sanctified blood over sacramental baptism. In doing so, he left out any words that directly condemned Nazi hatred of Jews. Despite this initial adoption of Faulhaber's approach, diversity still existed among the bishops, as each individually considered the consequences of their choices in light of a possible National Socialist assumption of power. Most bishops feared that too strong a stance against National Socialism might alienate lay Catholics who were supportive of Hitler and the NSDAP. The NSDAP electoral successes in the 1930 national election must have heightened any insecurities the bishops had regarding such thinking. Inevitably, ingrained antisemitism also played a role. Church teaching condemned racial antisemitism, yet it permitted a cautious monitoring and critique of Jewish participation in public life, especially when Church leaders perceived such engagement as a danger to a Christian-based society. In practice, such nebulous dualistic teaching at best confused Catholics and led them to a greater distrust of Jews; at worst, it emboldened antisemites to hate Jews even more. In the 1930s, very few if any Catholics were completely free of antisemitism in some form, be it racial, social, cultural, economic, or religious, or some mixture of these conflictive preferences.

In the face of such hatred and uncertainty, a lone voice continued to drive home the inconsistencies of National Socialism's attack on Jews with Christianity's teachings. In early April 1931, Vicar General Mayer, in a private correspondence, reiterated the same stance he had taken earlier – that a Catholic could not be a member of the NSDAP unless the recruited individual promised to "agitate" for ideological change from within the party, thus reflecting the newly articulated position of the bishops of the Upper Rhine Province. However, Mayer still stressed that "National Socialism is a heresy that no Catholic is allowed to embrace," for it inherently contradicted Catholicism by its "rejection of the Old Testament and its support for an unchristian hatred of Jews, the so-called racial antisemitism."[66] Recent works have argued that it would have been too much to ask the 1930s German Catholic Church to embrace universal human rights rather than concentrate on milieu-specific issues, first and foremost the securing of freedom for the Church to administer the sacraments.[67] The stance of Vicar General

Mayer shows that at least one individual in the Church hierarchy understood that the two points, love of neighbour and protection of Church doctrine and teaching, could not be separated and, for all practical purposes, were theologically synonymous. Sadly, the German bishops were not yet ready to proclaim this truth in their sermons and public pronouncements.

NOTES

I would like to thank Hermann-Josef Braun, Martina Cucchiara, and Antonia Leugers for their historical insights. Likewise, I am grateful to the American Philosophical Society and the Vidal Sassoon International Center for the Study of Antisemitism for grants that supported research for this chapter.

1 Rachor to Ordinariat Mainz, 17 June 1929, Dom- und Diözesanarchiv Mainz (DDAMz) B.O., Generalia, Abt. Nr. 52/54, 9b, f. 1. In the letter, Rachor asks if he should follow the example of a pastor in Offenbach who had refused a Church burial for a member of the Socialist Party of Germany (SPD). In 1921, the Fulda and Freising Bishop Conferences jointly issued pastoral instructions to assist clergy when dealing with individuals who belonged to organizations that were hostile to the Catholic faith. The bishops gave clergy permission to withhold the sacraments and Church burial from such individuals. See "Winke betr. Aufgaben der Seelsorger gegenüber glaubensfeindlichen Vereinigungen" (1921) and "Stellung der Kirche zu sozialistischen und anderen kirchenfeindlichen Vereinigungen" (1924) in *Sammlung kirchlicher Erlasse Verordnungen und Bekanntmachungen für die Erzdiözese Köln*, ed. Wilhelm Corsten. (Cologne: J. P. Bachem, 1929), 619–25.

2 For generalizations in chronologically broad studies, see, for example, Olaf Blaschke, *Die Kirchen und der Nationalsozialismus* (Stuttgart: Philipp Reclam, 2014), 57–9; Ulrike Ehret, *Church, Nation, and Race: Catholics and Antisemitism in Germany and England, 1918–1945* (Manchester: Manchester University Press, 2012); Heinz Hürten, *Deutsche Katholiken 1918 bis 1945* (Paderborn: Ferdinand Schöningh, 1992), 163–5; Guenter Lewy, *The Catholic Church and Nazi Germany* (New York: McGraw–Hill, 1964), 8–15; and Klaus Scholder, *The Churches and the Third Reich*, vol. 1: *Preliminary History and the Time of Illusions, 1918–1934*, trans. John Bowden (Philadelphia: Fortress Press, 1988), 132–4. While informative, the focused study by Ludwig Volk,

Der Bayerische Episkopat und der Nationalsozialismus 1930–1934, 2nd ed. (Mainz: Matthias-Grünewald, 1966), in Chapter 3, only briefly summarizes the initial encounters before moving to a larger discussion of the Bavarian bishops' pastoral response to National Socialism.

3   For a recent exception, see Christoph Hübner, *Die Rechtskatholiken, die Zentrumspartei und die katholische Kirche in Deutschland bis zum Reichskonkordat von 1933. Ein Beitrag zur Geschichte des Scheiterns der Weimarer Republik* (Berlin: LIT, 2014), esp. 619–40. In this section, Hübner briefly focuses on Mayer and the bishops in the context of right-wing lay Catholics and their overtures to the Holy See.

4   Votes for the KPD gradually increased with an exception between the May 1924 Reichstag election (12.6 per cent) and the December 1924 Reichstag election (9.0 per cent). In December 1924, 78.8 per cent of the eligible voters cast a vote. Though the number of eligible voters and votes cast increased in 1928, the percentage of voters participating fell to 75.6 per cent. On these points, see Jürgen Falter, Thomas Lindenberger, and Siegfried Schumann, *Wahlen und Abstimmungen in der Weimarer Republik. Materialien zum Wahlverhalten 1919–1933* (Munich: C.H. Beck, 1986), 69–71.

5   On this point, see Horst W. Heitzer, "Deutscher Katholizismus und Bolschewismusgefahr bis 1933," *Historisches Jahrbuch* 113 (1993): 355–87; and Heribert Smolinsky, "Das katholische Rußlandbild in Deutschland nach dem Ersten Weltkrieg und im Dritten Reich," in *Das Rußlandbild im Dritten Reich*, ed. Hans-Erich Volkmann, 2nd enlarged ed. (Cologne: Böhlau, 1994), 323–55. On the failure of the Vatican–Soviet Concordat, see Winfried Becker, "Diplomats and Missionaries: The Role Played by the German Embassies in Moscow and Rome in the Relations between Russia and the Vatican from 1921 to 1929," *Catholic Historical Review* 92, no. 1 (2006): 24–45; Giuliana Chamedes, "The Vatican and the Reshaping of the European International Order after the First World War," *Historical Journal* 56, no. 4 (2013): 955–76; and Anthony Rhodes, *The Vatican in the Age of the Dictators, 1922–1945* (New York: Holt, Rinehart, and Winston, 1973), 131–40.

6   See Wolfgang Altgeld, "Racist Ideology and Völkisch Religiosity," in *Catholics and Third Reich: Controversies and Debates*, ed. Karl-Joseph Hummel and Michael Kißener, trans. Christof Morrisey (Paderborn: Ferdinand Schöningh, 2018), 63–83, here 81, which argues that the NSDAP had, in essence, become a "Protestant milieu party."

7 On the contradictory statements of National Socialists toward Roman Catholics, see Kevin P. Spicer, *Resisting the Third Reich: The Catholic Clergy in Hitler's Berlin* (DeKalb: Northern Illinois University Press, 2004), 15–17; and Richard Steigmann-Gall, *The Holy Reich: Nazi Conceptions of Christianity, 1919–1945* (Cambridge: Cambridge University Press, 2003).

8 On Hugo, see Hermann Josef-Braun, "Das Bistum von 1886 bis zum Ende des Zweiten Weltkrieges," in *Handbuch der Mainzer Kirchengeschichte*, vol. 3: *Neuzeit und Moderne*, part 2, ed. Friedhelm Jürgensmeier, (Würzburg: Echter, 2002), 1142–60, esp. 1202–15; Anton Brück, "Hugo, Ludwig Maria (1871-1935)," in *Die Bischöfe der deutschsprachigen Länder*, 335–6; Paul Schnitzer, "'Für Christus und seine Kirche bis zum letzten Atemzug!' Bischof Ludwig Maria Hugo und der Nationalsozialismus," *Glaube und Leben: Kirchenzeitung für das Bistum Mainz* 16, no. 21 (22 May 1960): 365–6.

9 G. Lenhart, "Prälat Dr. Phil. Jakob Mayer, Generalvikar und Domkapitular," and Obituary Card, DDAMz Personalakt Dr. Jakob Philipp Mayer; *Necrologium Moguntinum 1802/03-2009* (Mainz: Bischöfliche Kanzlei, 2009), 3–4. See also Anton Brück, "Mayer, Philipp Jakob (1870-1936)," in *Die Bischöfe der deutschsprachigen Länder 1785/1803 bis 1945. Ein biographisches Lexikon*, ed. Erwin Gatz (Berlin: Duncker & Humblot, 1983), 490.

10 On the consultation between Mayer and Hugo, see Ludwig Lenhart, "Dr. Ludwig Maria Hugo (1871–1935). Ein theologisch-religiös markanter, den Nationalsozialismus frühzeitig durchschauender Rheinpfälzer auf dem Mainzer Bischofsstuhl (1921–1935)," *Archiv für mittelrheinische Kirchengeschichte* 18 (1966): 119–99, here 180–3.

11 Father Ranchor confirmed reception of Last Rites. See Rachor to Ordinariat Mainz, 17 June 1929, DDAMz B.O., Generalia, Abt. Nr. 52/54, 9b, f. 1.

12 Ordinariat Mainz to Rachor, 18 June 1929, DDAMz B.O., Generalia, Abt. Nr. 52/54, 9b, f. 2.

13 See the extensive correspondence in DDAMz B.O., Generalia, Abt. Nr. 52/54, 9b.

14 Jost's mother declared to Mayer that her son had never officially joined the NSDAP. On this point, see Mayer to Ordinariat München, 24 December 1929, DDAMz B.O., Generalia, Abt. Nr. 52/54, 9a, ff. 11–12.

15 Heinstadt to Ordinariat Mainz, 18 August 1929, DDAMz B.O., Generalia, Abt. Nr. 52/54, 9a., ff. 2–3.

16 *Völkischer Beobachter*, Bavarian ed., 13 and 14 August 1929.

17 Arnet to Hugo, 10 August 1929, DDAMz B.O., Generalia, Abt. Nr. 52/54, 9a, f. 1.

18 Ordinariat Mainz to Heinstadt, 16 August 1929, DDAMz B.O., Generalia, Abt. Nr. 52/54, 9a, f. 1R.

19 Heinstadt to Ordinariat Mainz, 18 August 1929, DDAMz B.O., Generalia, Abt. Nr. 52/54, 9a., ff. 2–3. It is possible that Vicar-General Mayer also received published works on the NSDAP from the Borromaeus Verein, which provided reading material to German Catholics. On the Borromaeus Verein, see Jeffrey T. Zalar, *Reading and Rebellion in Catholic Germany, 1770–1914* (New York: Cambridge University Press, 2019).

20 Ordinariat Mainz to Arnet, 31 August 1929, DDAMz B.O., Generalia, Abt. Nr. 52/54, 9a ff. 4–6.

21 Trojan to Holy Father, 14 August 1929, DDAMz B.O., Generalia, Abt. Nr. 52/54, 9a, f. 11.

22 Ordinariat München to Ordinariat Mainz, 17 December 1929, DDAMz B.O., Generalia, Abt. Nr. 52/54, 9a, f. 8.

23 For example, see Ordinariat Mainz to Oberle, 16 September 1929, DDAMz B.O., Generalia, Abt. Nr. 52/54, 9b, ff. 5–6 and additional letters in this file.

24 Ordinariat Mainz to Ordinariat München, 24 December 1929, DDAMz B.O., Abt. Nr. 52/54, 9a, ff. 9–10. On the genesis of Mayer's letter, see Herman-Josef Braun, "Widerstand aus den Reihen der katholischen Kirche," in *Verfolgung und Widerstand in Hessen 1933–1945*, eds. Renate Knigge-Tesche and Axel Ulrich (Frankfurt am Main: Eichborn, 1996), 269–89, here 270–3.

25 Faulhaber to Konzilskongregation, 25 January 1930, original Latin text and German translation in *Akten deutscher Bischöfe über die Lage der Kirche 1918–1933*, vol. 2: *1926–1933*, ed. Heinz Hürten (Paderborn: Ferdinand Schöningh, 2007), 1002–4.

26 Heinz Hürten, "Kardinal Faulhaber und die Juden. Eine frühe Stellungnahme der katholischen Kirche zum Nationalsozialismus," *Zeitschrift für bayerische Landesgeschichte* 68 (2005): 1029–34, here 1034.

27 On this point, see Ordinariat Mainz to Stotzheim, 8 July 1930, DDAMz B.O., Generalia, Abt. Nr. 52/54, 9b, f. 8.

28 "Der Katholik und der Nationalsozialismus," *Mainzer Journal*, Nr. 195, 25 August 1930.

29 Weber to Ordinariat Mainz, 25 August 1930, DDAMz B.O., Generalia, Abt. Nr. 52/54, 9c, f. 1.

30 Rachor to Ordinariat Mainz, 26 August 1930, DDAMz B.O., Generalia, Abt.
Nr. 52/54, 9b, f. 3.

31 Ordinariat Mainz to Rachor, 1 September 1930, DDAMz B.O., Generalia, Abt.
Nr. 52/54, 9b, f. 3r and Ordinariat Mainz to Weber, 1 September 1930, DDAMz
B.O., Generalia, Abt. Nr. 52/54, 9c, f. 1r.

32 The original date of Father Weber's pronouncement was not recorded but
took place on a Sunday sometime between his reception of Ordinariat
Mainz's letter of 1 September 1930 and the letter of inquiry from the
Gauleitung Hessen to Ordinariat Mainz of 27 September 1930 (DDAMz B.O.,
Generalia, Abt. Nr. 52/54, 9c, f. 2).

33 For a list of the newspapers, see Sigrid Durchhardt-Bösken, ed., *Das Bischöfliche Ordinariat Mainz und der Nationalsozialismus* bis 1933. *Eine
Dokumentation* (Mainz: Bischöfliches Ordinariat Mainz, 1983), 30.

34 Gauleitung Hessen to Ordinariat Mainz, 27 September 1930 and Ordinariat
Mainz to Geschäftsstelle der Gauleitung der NSDAP Offenbach am Main,
30 September 1930, DDAMz B.O., Generalia, Abt. Nr. 52/54, 9c, ff. 2–3.

35 "Naziboycott gegen katholische Vereine und Kirchensteuern," *Kölnische
Volkszeitung*, 18 October 1930, Archiwum Archidiecezjalne we Wrocławiu
(AAW) IA 25p/64.

36 "Die Folgen von Mainz. Täglich neue Kirchenaustritte," unnamed newspaper clipping, 1930, Archivio Segreto Vaticano (ASV), Archivio della Congregazione deglt Affari Ecclesiastici Straordinari (AES) Germania R10 Pos. 606,
Fasc. 118, accessed from the United States Holocaust Memorial Museum Archives RG 76.0001M/R10. On *Kirchensteuer*, see Ralf Banken, *Hitlers Steuer-
staat: Die Steuerpolitik im Dritten Reich* (Berlin: Walter de Gruyter, 2018),
579–604; Friedrich Hartmannsgruber, "Die Kirchensteuer unter dem Nationalsozialismus. Reformen, Revisionen und verfehlte Ziele," in *Religiöse Prä-
gung und Politische Ordnung in der Neuzeit. Festschrift für Winfried Becker
zum 65. Geburtstag*, eds. Bernhard Löffler and Karten Ruppert (Cologne:
Böhlau, 2006), 431–9; and Heiner Marré, "Die Kirchenfinanzierung durch
Kirchensteuern," in *Geschichte des Kirchlichen Lebens in den deutschsprachigen Ländern seit dem Ende des 18. Jahrhunderts*, vol. 6: *Die Kirchenfinanzen*
(Freiburg im Breisgau: Herder, 2000), 213–27, esp. 224–7.

37 "Protestschreiben der katholischen Verbände der Diözese Mainz," *Mainzer
Journal*, Nr. 247, 24 October 1930, and "Der Dank des Bischofs von Mainz,"
Kölnische Volkszeitung, 18 November 1930, AAW IA25p/65.

38 *Civiltá Cattolica* 79 (1928): 335–44, qtd in Hubert Wolf, *Pope and Devil: The Vatican's Archives and the Third Reich*, trans. Kenneth Kronenberg (Cambridge, MA: Harvard University Press, 2010), 116–17. See also Gustav Gundlach, "Antisemitismus," in *Lexikon für Theologie und Kirche*, vol. 1, ed. Michael Buchberger (Freiburg: Herder, 1930), 504–5. For a review of this dualistic view of antisemitism, see Karl Heinz Rengstorf and Siegfried von Kortzfleisch, eds. *Kirche und Synagoge. Handbuch zur Geschichte von Christen und Juden*, vol. 2 (Stuttgart: Ernst Klett, 1970), 386–90 and 408–9.

39 "Kann ein Katholik Nationalsozialist sein?," *Mainzer Journal*, Nr. 239, 15 October, continued in Nr. 240, 16 October 1930. Reprinted in other Catholic newspapers, including the *Augsburger Postzeitung*, 16 October 1930, ASV AES Germania Pos. 606 Fasc. 117/ USHMMA RG 76.0001M/R10.

40 On the fear of the left, see Robert Gerwarth, *The Vanquished: Why the First World War Failed to End* (New York: Farrar, Straus and Giroux, 2017), 153–70.

41 Falter et al., *Wahlen und Abstimmungen in der Weimarer Republik*, 71–2.

42 For example, Mayer refers to the inquiries he received in "Nationalsozialistische Irreführung," *Kölnische Volkszeitung*, 25 November 1930, AAW IA25p-64. See also the correspondence in DDAMz B.O., Generalia, Abt. Nr. 52/54, 1a–b, and ASV AES Germania Pos. 606 Fasc. 117/USHMMA RG 76.0001M/R10.

43 "Nationalsozialistische Irreführung," *Kölnische Volkszeitung*, 25 November 1930, AAW IA25p-64.

44 "Kulturkampf gefällig?," *Der Tag. Tagblatt der Deutschen Nationalsozialistischen Arbeiterpartei*, 28 November 1930, DDAMz B.O., Generalia, Abt. Nr. 52/54, 6a.

45 Through its nuncio, Caesar Orsenigo, the Holy See closely monitored the controversy over Catholic membership in the NSDAP. On 29 December 1930, Orsenigo reported that Cardinal Bertram had "secretly" invited the German bishops to express their opinions on how to respond to National Socialism. On this point, see Orsenigo to Pacelli, 29 December 1930, ASV AES Germania Pos. 604 Fasc. 112/USHMMA RG 76.0001M/R9.

46 Entwurf, Stellungnahme der Mitglieder der Fuldaer Bischofskonferenz zur Nationalsozialistischen Deutschen Arbeiterpartei, 2 December 1930, in *Akten deutscher Bischöfe über die Lage der Kirche 1933–1945*, vol. 1: *1933–1934*, ed. Bernhard Stasiewski (Mainz: Matthias Grünewald, 1968), 787–9.

47 Bertram to Faulhaber, 3 December 1930, in *Akten deutscher Bischöfe*, vol. 1, ed. Stasiewski, 787.

48 Faulhaber to Bavarian Episcopate, 6 December 1930, in *Akten deutscher Bischöfe*, vol. 1, ed. Stasiewski, 789–91.

49 Faulhaber had originally discussed this approach in a mid-November archdiocesan synod. On this point, see Referat A. Scharnagls und Feststellungen Faulhabers, 19 November 1930, in *Akten Kardinal Michael von Faulhabers*, vol. 1: *1917-1934*, ed. Ludwig Volk (Mainz: Matthias Grünewald, 1975), 509–13.

50 Entwurf Faulhabers für Pastorale Anweisungen, 6 December 1930, in *Akten deutscher Bischöfe*, vol. 1, ed. Stasiewski, 791–4.

51 On the positions of the individual bishops, see Volk, *Der bayerische Episkopat und der Nationalsozialismus*, 25-27.

52 2. Entwurf Faulhabers für Pastorale Anweisungen, December 18, 1930, in *Akten deutscher Bischöfe*, vol. 1, ed. Stasiewski, 795–7. On 10 February 1931, Faulhaber issued the final version of the Pastoral Instructions of the Bavarian Episcopate, which essentially mirrored the content of the Faulhaber's second draft. See Stasiewski, ed., *Akten deutscher Bischöfe*, I, 806-809.

53 Faulhaber to Bertram, December 18, 1930, in *Akten deutscher Bischöfe*, vol. 1, ed. Stasiewski, 798–9.

54 Berning to Dinkgrefe, 3 January 1931, BAO 04-61-00-3. Dinkgrefe, who died shortly after making this inquiry, was *Pastor Primarius* in Hamburg. On Dinkgrefe's exemplary life, see Clemens Heitmann, "Bernhard Dinkgrefe (1858-1931), Pastor Primarius in Hamburg," in *Der katholische Klerus im Oldenburger Land: Ein Handbuch*, ed. Willi Baumann and Peter Sieve (Münster: Dialogverlag, 2006), 250–2.

55 Spicer, *Resisting the Third Reich*, 21–3.

56 Siegfried Koß, "Christian Schreiber," in *Biographisches Lexikon des KV*, vol. 1, ed. Siegfried Koß and Wolfgang Löhr (Schernfeld: SH Verlag, 1994), 93–4; Koß, "Bischof Christian Schreiber, der KV und die NSDAP," *Grotenburg-Lusaten-Echo* 26 (April 1992): 50–2.

57 For support for the statement among the Fulda bishops, see Berning to Dinkgrefe, 3 January 1931, Bistumsarchiv Osnabrück (BAO) 04-61-00-3.

58 "Die Stellung der katholischen Kirche zu Radikalismus und Nationalismus. Ein offenes Wort in ernster Stunde am Jahresschluss" 1930, BAO 04-61-00-10/11, (p. 7).

59 Faulhaber to Archbishop of Bamberg and the Bavarian Bishops of Bavaria, 26 January 1931, Erzbistumsarchiv Paderborn (EBAP) OA NSXII.A.1. In a diary entry from 19 July 1932, Faulhaber referred to the conflict of approach among the German bishops: "Bishop Buchberger passed through on his way

to Mittenwald ... No statement against the National Socialists like the German bishops from the north because nothing can be changed any longer and because the cultural-political goals of the Socialists are much worse." See Archiv des Erzbistums München und Freising, NL Faulhaber 10014. For similar outlooks, see Faulhaber to Ehrenfried in *Akten Kardinal Michael von Faulhabers*, vol. 1, 611, n. 3; Faulhaber to Bavarian Bishops, 27 July 1932, in *Akten Kardinal Michael von Faulhabers*, vol. 1, 612; and Protokoll of the Fulda Bishops' Conference, 17–19 August 1932, in *Akten deutscher Bischöfe über die Lage der Kirche 1918–1933*, vol. 2, 1204–20, here 1206.

60 Buchberger to Faulhaber, 29 January 1931, in *Akten deutscher Bischöfe*, vol. 1, ed. Stasiewski, 537–9, here 538.

61 Faulhaber to Archbishop of Bamberg and the Bishops of Bavaria, 3 February 1931, EBAP OA VII.A.1. The instructions were released on 10 February 1931. They appeared in the official diocesan bulletins for clergy in each of the Bavarian dioceses. For example, see "Nationalsozialismus und Seelsorge," *Würzburger Diözesanblatt* (Beilage), 11 February 1931, Diözesanarchiv Würzburg (DAW) Mandate: Bischöfe Bayerns and "Nationalsozialismus und Seelsorge," *Pastoralblatt des Bistums Eichstätt*, 11 February 1931.

62 Pastoral Winke betreffend Stellung zum Nationalsozialismus, *Beilage zum kirchlichen Amtsblatt der Erzdiözese Breslau*, 14 February 1931, AAW IA25p/64.

63 Bertram to Members of the Fulda Bishops' Conference, 19 February 1931, BAO 04-61-00-10/11. Bertram's biographer missed this key point. See Sascha Hinkel, *Adolf Kardinal Bertram. Kirchenpolitik in Kaiserreich und Weimarer Republik* (Paderborn: Ferdinand Schöningh, 2010), 240–9.

64 On this point, see Schulte to Berning, 1 March 1931, and Berning to Schulte, 2 March 1931, BAO 04-61-00-10/11.

65 "Gemeinsames Hirtenschreiben der Bischöfe der Oberrheinischen Kirchenprovinz zur heutigen Not," *Kirchliches Amtsblatt für die Diözese Mainz*, 15 April 1931, 17–19.

66 Klostermann to Ordinariat Mainz, 3 April 1931, and Mayer to Klostermann, 11 April 1931, DDAMz B.O., Generalia, Abt. Nr. 52/54, 9b, ff. 20–1.

67 For example, see the essays in Maria Anna Zumholz and Michael Hirschfeld, eds. *Zwischen Seelsorge und Politik: Katholische Bischöfe in der NS-Zeit* (Münster: Aschendorff, 2018).

5

The Fate of John's Gospel during the Third Reich

Susannah Heschel and Shannon Quigley

On 4 March 1936, *The Times of India* proclaimed as its headline: "Bible Acceptable to Nazis: New Translation."[1] While political developments in Germany after 1933 were reported throughout the world, it is less well-known that the international press also reported on developments within the German churches. The efforts of certain prominent theologians to reconcile Christianity with the National Socialist regime became headline news from the United States to India. The article in *The Times of India* copied a report that had appeared a month earlier in *The Times of London* about an announcement by the Protestant bishop of Bremen, Heinz Weidemann (1895–1976), to a conference of churchmen that a new translation of the Gospel of John was under way that would make Christ relevant to today.[2] Weidemann was quoted as saying that as Nazis, they were drawn to the Gospel of John because "in it the bearers of the Divine message stood in an embittered fight against the Jewish people"; he also noted that Christianity was anti-Jewish and the "ultimate source of power for the National Socialist worldview."[3] Weidemann explained that his "germanizing" of the New Testament had begun with the Gospel of John because it was "the most sharply anti-Jewish document."[4] Many of Weidemann's comrades agreed. According to the newspaper report, Weidemann's announcement was welcomed at the conference by his fellow pastors. One pastor even stood up and declared, "Galilee had not been a purely Jewish country and ... Christ's life had been nothing else than a fight of increasing intensity against the Jews." He went on to say that Paul's epistles were "passionate documents against the Jews."[5] A year later, *The Times of India* announced that the translation of the Gospel of John had been published by Weidemann with the intention of "modifying Christian teaching to bring it into harmony with the Nazi 'world outlook' based on 'blood and soil.'" Changes in the text were made, according to the newspaper account, to discredit the Old Testament (John 6:31–32) and to distinguish Galilee from "Jewland," the translation's term for Judea.[6]

A similar report also appeared in the Jerusalem newspaper, *The Palestine Post*, on 26 February 1936, making it clear that pro-Nazi developments in the German church were of interest outside Europe.[7] Once published, Weidemann's new rendition of *The Gospel of John* brought renewed attention: an article in the *New York Herald Tribune* by Ralph W. Barnes appeared on 13 January 1937 under the headline "Nazis Publish 'Antisemitic' Gospel of John: Luther Version Revamped in a Manner Picturing Author as Foe of Jews." That article was then transmitted via the Jewish Telegraphic Agency, a wire service.[8] Barnes, a distinguished American journalist stationed in Germany, editorialized that Weidemann's translation "is enough to make Luther turn over in his grave." He compared the translation, an eighty-six-page pamphlet, to Reichbishop Ludwig Müller's recent rendition of the Sermon on the Mount, published in 1936, in which "Nazi catchwords were interpolated." Barnes wrote that Weidemann's goal, like Müller's, had been to turn the Gospel "into anti-Jewish propaganda" by inserting words and deliberately mistranslating. In Weidemann's version, "Judea" was translated as "Judenland," or the land of the Jews; references to Moses, Elijah, and Isaiah were purged; and terms such as rabbi and Israelite, used in the Gospel to identify Jesus, were eliminated. For example, "Rabbi" was replaced by "Meister" (Master).[9]

A few days later came a report in *Time* magazine, "Gospel According to Saint Hitler":

> German booksellers did roaring business last week when there appeared on the market an anti-Semitic, Nazified version of The Gospel According to St. John, adapted from Martin Luther's standard German translation of the Bible. This was big news for Nordic churchgoers, be-

cause the man responsible for the metamorphosis of St. John into an up-to-date Nazi was none other than Dr. Heinz Weidemann, bishop of Bremen, who is no black sheep of the German Evangelical Church but one its prime spiritual forces.[10]

The publication of Weidemann's John translation, *Das Evangelium Johannes Deutsch*, received renewed attention in *The Times of India*, on 30 January 1937. The article discussed Weidemann's publication and noted that Hebrew words such as "manna" and "rabbi" had been eliminated, references to Moses as serpent handler and lawgiver had been omitted, the Hebrew prophets were not named, and in John 6:31–32, Jesus was said to have told the "*Volk*": "The Bible also reports that bread fell from Heaven for our fathers in the desert. Then Jesus said unto them, Verily, verily, I say unto you, these old stories to which you are always referring do not help you. My father alone gives you the true divine bread."[11]

The Gospel of John has long been regarded as the most anti-Jewish of the Gospels because of Jesus's sharp criticism of "the Jews" rather than, as in the synoptic Gospels, the Pharisees or Sadducees. The Nazi-era translations went further. What caught the attention of the international press, which ordinarily did not carry articles about German theologians, was the scandalous nature of Weidemann's efforts: altering the text of scripture in accordance with the antisemitic principles of the Nazi regime. In emphasizing the non-Jewish nature of Galilee, Weidemann's translation introduced people as "Galilean Philip" or "Jew Nathanael." (John 1:45–47): "The Galilean Philip meets the Jew Nathanael and calls to him: 'We have found the Lord of whose coming your prophets have spoken of old: Jesus, the son of Joseph, from Nazareth.' The other answered: 'From Nazareth? Since when comes salvation from the heathen?' Philip answers: 'Convince yourself with your own eyes!' When Jesus sees him coming, he addresses him: You are a true man of God in your people!"[12] Nathanael's Israelite identity was eradicated, with Jesus addressing Nathanael in John 1:47 not as "an Israelite in whom there is no guile," but "as a sincere man of God in your people."[13] In John 12:13, "Hosanna: Blessed is He who comes in the name of the Lord, even the King of Israel," "Hosanna" was replaced with "Heil," "Hail [*Heil*] to him who comes in the name of God! Hail to you, you shall be our King!," and "King of Israel" was diminished to "king."[14] Large chunks of chapters 20 and 21 of

John were missing entirely, for Protestant scholarship had, since the nineteenth century, argued that those chapters were later additions to the Gospel. The translation used words drawn from Nazi terminology; for example, whereas the Luther translation used the term "Herrlichkeit" to translate "glory," Weidemann's translation used the term "Sieg" (victory), a term with strong resonance in Nazi Germany.[15]

Small-scale efforts to revise the New Testament in the spirit of National Socialism had already been undertaken by theologians who were members of the pro-Nazi faction within the Protestant church, the German Christian Movement (*Deutsche Christen*).[16] In 1934, Hans Schöttler, later the director of the German Christian Movement's Bible school in Bremen, had published *Gottes Wort Deutsch* (God's Word in German), which included selected New Testament texts retold using Nazi language (for example, using the term "Führerpflichten," obligations to the Führer, in translating Matthew 5:13–16, and describing Jesus's "Kampf," or struggle, in Jerusalem).[17] Bishop Müller's version of the Sermon on the Mount similarly omitted references to the Old Testament and emphasized the importance of "Kameradschaft" (camaraderie). Müller also revised the Ten Commandments to read a bit more like commandments of the Nazi *Volk*: "You shall do no murder ... But whosoever tries to ruin him morally, or threatens to assault him, destroys the national fellowship and makes himself deserving of the severest punishment before God and men."[18] Likewise, Müller's translation of Matthew 7:12 highlights the teaching, "Anything you want people to do to you, you should do to them," omitting the rest of the verse: "for this is the law and the prophets." Müller attributes the teaching neither to the Hebrew Bible, nor to Jesus, but presents it as a divine truth steeped in German blood and given by German fathers.[19]

Significant in these various efforts to produce nazified versions of biblical texts was not only the anti-Judaism, pursued in nearly every verse, but also the effort to transform the Bible into a this-worldly set of teachings that would foster a strong sense of German *Volk*. The international press was already reporting in 1936 on German discussions about removing Moses, a Jew, from the Old Testament.[20] In Terplitz, a village in Saxony, children were being advised to read *Der Stürmer*, a Nazi propaganda organ, instead of the Old Testament.[21]

In Weidemann's translation, miracles were also eliminated – including in the final chapter of the Gospel of John, where Jesus rises from the dead and appears to his disciples. Removing the resurrection narrative was part of the German Christian Movement's effort to eliminate the supernatural from its version of Christianity. That was the heritage of liberal Protestantism, with its neo-Marcionism and rebellion against doctrine alongside the German Christian Movement's desire to create a manly and antisemitic church suited to the National Socialist regime.[22] In 1942, Weidemann explained his efforts as serving the needs of Nazis: "What can a National Socialist, an SA man, a German child of our day do with a gospel where [John] chapter 1:17 reads: 'For the law was given by Moses, but grace and truth come by Jesus Christ'?"[23] His translation was intended to remedy such biblical failures, and his Bible school planned a translation of the entire New Testament, though that never was achieved.

The changes of scripture were noted in the United States by a young columnist for an African American newspaper in Norfolk, Virginia, Lem Graves Jr, who wrote:[24]

In Germany, the Nazis want to remove Moses from the Bible because he was a Jew. It seems that the German children have been taught to revere Moses and yet when they leave Sunday school, they are taught to hate the Jew and everything that the Jew has contributed to civilization. If we remember correctly Jesus Christ was a Jew and the greatest of all Jews. We guess that he will be the next to go on the Nazi chopping block. When they get through with the Good Book in Germany, it will be completely revised. Without Moses in the Old Testament and Jesus in the New Testament, the Bible would be a strange book indeed.[25]

A word about bishop Weidemann. He had studied theology at Göttingen, interrupted by military service during the First World War, and served as pastor in Bremen starting in 1926. He joined the NSDAP in 1933 and was active in the German Christian Movement. In 1934, he was appointed bishop of Bremen. He sought to become the leader of the German Christian Movement but was rebuffed; he was apparently a difficult person. Ultimately, he withdrew from that movement and formed his own, equivalent group,

Kommende Kirche (The Future Church), which published a journal and sponsored a Bible institute that included as a member the theologian Emanuel Hirsch. The Nazi Party expelled Weidemann temporarily in 1938 for naming two churches in Bremen after Hindenburg and Horst Wessel, and in 1941 he was again in trouble: he was sent to the Charité Hospital in Berlin, purportedly for a psychiatric examination. In 1943, he was again expelled from the NSDAP, and in 1944 he was arrested for perjury. After the war, he was sentenced to four years in a work camp. He ended up in Thüringen, in the German Democratic Republic, where he joined the Communist Party and served as a low-level functionary.[26]

In the preface to the Gospel of John, Weidemann writes, "the decisive question confronting Christianity today is its relationship to the Jewish spirit."[27] Thus, his version renders John 4:46, when Jesus is in Cana, as follows: "For a second time he came to the city in which, through the miracle of the water jugs and the wine, he demonstrated the new age in which the Gospel conquers Jewish law."[28] Although this portion of John 4:46 is absent from Die Botschaft Gottes (The Message of God), another Nazi-era New Testament published in 1940, its writers took similar liberties with the Cana wedding story, explaining the miracle in this way: "Through Jesus, outward service of the Law comes to an end."[29]

Müller's position as Reich bishop was similarly theo-political.[30] He had been appointed Reich bishop to merge the independent state churches into a single national church that would pledge loyalty to the Reich and grant overarching authority to the Reich bishop. This effort ultimately failed. Müller was not a theologian, nor was he particularly adept as a politician, and he did not have strong support from German Protestants; he was a political lackey for the Nazi regime.[31] His 1936 publication, Deutsche Gottesworte (German Word of God), presented a Nazified summary of Christianity as a translation of the Sermon on the Mount. It opened with the words, "The eternal Christ speaks" and then offered vague moral advice about creating a loyal sense of community.[32]

In presenting the Beatitudes, Matthew 5:3–10, Müller changed "Selig" (blessed) to "Wohl" (well). Luther had translated "Blessed are they that bear grief; because they are to be comforted" (Matthew 5:4); Müller wrote "Happy is he who bears his sufferings like a man; he will find the strength never to despair without courage."[33] Müller's version of Matthew 5:38–9, which refers to the *lex talionis* of Leviticus 24, "eye for an eye," omits any reference to the Old Testament and instead states, "In the vernacular it is still said: 'As you me, so I you' or: 'An eye for an eye, a tooth for a tooth.'"[34] Müller then goes on to write that "It's better to live this with your *Volk*, that you get on well together," and he recommends that if "your comrade" hits you in the face, do not respond in kind: "It is more manly to preserve superior calm." [35] The goal is not to oppose violence but to create a sense of *Volk*. In this vein, and in display of the German Christian Movement's elevation of *Volk* above doctrine, Müller clarifies, "If every German would … act according to the Sermon on the Mount [albeit his Germanized version], all religious separation caused by church dogma and propositions would be overcome, and a truly, spiritually faithful German national community of real Christians would emerge!"[36]

To further clarify his brand of nazified Christianity, Müller writes that "mercy is an un-German conception" and that "the term 'mercy' is one of the numerous terms of the Bible with which we can have nothing to do." Müller writes in the conclusion of his pamphlet that he has translated the text into language that captures "God's Word" and eliminates extraneous elements of the Bible. Furthermore, he writes, his translation has sought to capture the understanding of the God of Nordic peoples, not the God of the Mediterranean or Roman peoples. Thus, Germans turn to God not as slaves, he writes, but in "childlike trust in God."[37]

While lauding the Luther translation, Müller writes that it needs updating after four hundred years. National Socialism, he writes, has opened the eyes of Germans to recognize that Christianity did not grow out of Judaism, "as a tree grows out of the root," running in direct terminological and theological opposition to Paul's Romans 11 allegory about the root and olive tree of Israel, onto which Gentiles are "grafted."[38] Rather, Müller's Christianity was a "fight against the Jews," with "Christ and Jew" being like fire and water: "In any case, the Jew is the oldest and most bitter enemy of Christian convictions and civilization, and he will remain so until the end of the days." Nonetheless, Müller concedes, there are numerous Hebrew words and expressions not only in church tradition but also in church music.[39] Regarding these Hebraic words and expressions, Müller goes on to predict erroneously that thanks to the "National Socialist experience" [40] and "the reshaping of our German *Volk* life, the foreign and un-German in the 'church language' will vanish and cease."[41] Müller's thoughts about "mercy" in light of the words of Jesus found in the Gospels as noted above, his fondness for the Nordic God (in opposition to the God represented in the biblical text), and his words about Jews and Judaism all give insight into the type of Christianity Müller hoped to disseminate to his fellow Germans: a radically dejudaized Christianity, and a Christianity devoid of the God of the Bible.

A radical and thorough dejudaization process was undertaken by pastors and professors of theology under the auspices of the Institut zur Erforschung und Beseitigung des jüdischen Einflusses auf das deutsche kirchliche Leben (Institute for the Study and Eradication of Jewish Influence on German Church Life), which formally opened in May 1939. The leadership of the Institute, much like Müller, praised Luther's work for the German people, feeling "an inner connection to Luther's work ... [and] his translation of the Bible, has led us to our work."[42] Its academic director was Walter Grundmann (1907–1974), Professor of New Testament and Racial Theology at the University of Jena in Thuringia, and the Institute's offices were located nearby, in the town of Eisenach. Grundmann, who had been a student of Adolf Schlatter and Gerhard Kittel at the University of Tübingen, and a member of the Nazi Party since 1930, had been teaching since 1935 at the University of Jena, itself a stronghold of National Socialism. His enthusiasm for Hitler in 1933 came with a call for the church to follow suit in his pamphlet, *Totale Kirche im totalen Staat* (*Authoritarian Church in an Authoritarian State*).[43] This meant applying the Aryan Paragraph to the church, unifying the state churches into a single national church and revising church teaching in dramatic fashion. Grundmann formulated the "Twenty-Eight Theses" for the church of Saxony (early guidelines for the German Christian Movement), leading to his rapid ascension to leadership in the German Christian movement.[44]

Grundmann was a prolific but mediocre scholar, both before and after 1945. He synthesized scholarship with Nazi ideology, and consistently sought to justify his radical claims by appealing to liberal Protestant historicism.[45] In pseudo-academic articles published by his Institute, he repeatedly argued that the text of the New Testament had been falsified by the Jewish Christians of the early church. Scholars should emend the New Testament to recover the original text, purged of Jewish alterations, he wrote. This would reveal, he claimed, that Jesus had come to eliminate Judaism, but fell instead as victim to the Jews. The Protestant Reformation had not been able to remove vestiges of Judaism from Christianity, but, Grundmann promised, he and his colleagues at the Institute – popularly known as the "Entjudungsinstitut" (Dejudaization Institute) – would carry out that task. Its central projects included a new version of the New Testament that eliminated all positive references to the Hebrew Bible and Judaism, a hymnal purged of all Hebrew words as well as hymns written by baptized Jews, and a German catechism declaring Jesus the saviour of Aryans. The Institute flourished; attracting students and pastors from the German Reich and neighbouring Scandinavian countries. It held conferences at which professors of theology delivered papers, and published numerous works for academic and popular readerships.

Weidemann's revision had been limited to the Gospel of John. The Institute's New Testament project had a more ambitious goal: to excavate the "authentic" gospel, which had been buried beneath many layers of later accretions within the text. The Institute equated the "authentic" with the original words and deeds of Jesus; the recovery of the oldest version of the text would require intense historical research by New Testament scholars. To that end, scholars, pastors, and even a German poet were engaged in the project. Its publication, titled *Die Botschaft Gottes*, was hailed in newspapers in the Reich and abroad, and thousands of copies were sold to churches throughout the Reich.

The Institute's opening ceremony, on 6 May 1939, was a festive occasion. It was held in the castle of Wartburg, in Eisenach, where Luther had translated the New Testament. The Associated Press reported on the event on 18 June 1939 with a story titled "The German Bible," which appeared in the *Baltimore Sun* and other newspapers. Two weeks later, on 2 July 1939, the *Washington Post* published a well-informed article by the noted journalist Louis Lochner, who reported on the Institute's founding and its main project – "the Bible must be nazified for Germans … Reich theologians were purging the book of all Jewish elements."

The Institute members included professors of theology, bishops, and pastors, most of them Protestant but also a few Catholics.[46] A working group would prepare the new edition of the New Testament, to be called a "Volkstestament," a gospel for the German race. The group was chaired by Grundmann and Herbert Preisker, Professor of New Testament at the University of Breslau, and included two pastors from Thuringia as well as a graduate student in theology at the University of Jena.[47] They reported on the progress of the new edition at a conference in Wittenberg in March 1940. Their work was to proceed in three stages: the synoptic Gospels; John; then the remainder of the New Testament. The synoptics were to be purged of positive Jewish references, Paul was to be downplayed so that some of his ideas were retained but autobiographical and biographical information eliminated, and the Gospel of John, with its strong anti-Jewish motifs, was to be highlighted as the most reliable source for the historical Jesus and as a theological substitute for Paul – this despite awareness among scholars since the 1820s that John was not a reliable historical source for the life of Jesus.

The Gospel of Mark provided a structural basis for the synoptic harmonization of the first part of *Die Botschaft Gottes*. The big problem for Grundmann and his colleagues was the Gospel of Matthew, recognized as the most Jewish of the gospels.[48] According to Grundmann, Matthew's image of Jesus was a distortion concocted by early Jewish Christians in order to place Jesus within the traditions of the Old Testament and did not present "the true picture of Jesus."[49] On 23 March 1940, Grundmann wrote to Hanns Kerrl, Reich Minister for Church Affairs, about the approach he was taking to the Gospels: remove all legendary material except stories related to Christmas, which are deep in the consciousness of the German *Volk*; remove reports whose historical kernel had been distorted by later formulations; and eliminate secondary sayings and obvious duplications within the text. Jesus and Christianity were European at heart and Germanic in existence and essence since the first Germanic tribes encountered the Christian message, according to Pastor Erich Fromm, an Institute member, who wrote a sixty-two page publication as a "foreword" to *Die Botschaft Gottes*.[50] The harmonization of the synoptics was intended to recreate the earliest strands of traditions about Jesus, eliminating thereby the later accretions in the text that stemmed from Jewish Christians. According to Grundmann, "The oral tradition that the Gospel authors encountered was painted over in a Jewish-Christian way and superimposed with superstition."[51] This was not simply a translation; it entailed a thorough revision and reordering. The Book of Revelation, for example, was to be almost completely omitted because, Grundmann claimed, it had been drawn from Jewish apocalyptic materials, and apart from a few liturgical pieces, it was thoroughly Jewish Christian and limited to its era; presumably, then, there was little to rescue from it.[52]

Die Botschaft Gottes is divided into four sections, each then subdivided thematically. For example, Section I, "Jesus the Saviour" (*Jesus der Heiland*), is a life of Jesus based on excerpts from each of the synoptic gospels, reorganized to present a story of triumph, its last three units describing "His Struggle, His Cross, His Victory." Section II, "Jesus the Son of God," the theological backbone of the work, is a condensed version of the Gospel of John, less about Jesus's actions than their theological significance. John's Gospel was the favorite among the Institute's theologians; for them, it presented the best image of who Jesus was, particularly the antisemitic Jew-hating Jesus they had conceived.[53] In the words of these men, the Gospel of John was "especially prized among the New Testament writings … 'For the Gospel of John, the Jews are quite clearly the representatives of the satanic counter-power.'"[54]

Section III, "Jesus the Lord," contains brief excerpts from the various epistles, organized according to religious teachings, such as those relating to hope, comfort, the community of God, and so forth. Section IV, "The Emergence of the Christian Community," presents an account, based on Acts and the Pauline epistles, of Paul's mission to the Gentiles and his break with the judaizers of Palestine. Paul is acknowledged as a Pharisee to whom God revealed Jesus and who was persecuted by Jews who hated him and sought to kill him.[55] The retention of Joseph as Jesus's father without clarifying his racial status sparked one pastor to complain to the Institute. Grundmann replied to him that Joseph's ancestry was most likely Aryan, since he stemmed from the Galilee.[56]

Die Botschaft Gottes retells Jesus's life with an emphasis on his triumph rather than his defeat through death; he is not the "lamb of God," as in the Luther translation of John 1:29, but rather "the chosen of God."[57] Luther translated John 1:1 as "In the beginning was the word"; *Die Botschaft Gottes* translated it as "From the beginning, the eternal spirit was," thus removing the allusion to Genesis 1:1.[58] References to Jewish names or places, as well as citations from the Old Testament, are retained only when they express a negative view of some aspect of Judaism. Cut from *Die Botschaft Gottes* are the genealogy in Matthew and Luke linking Jesus to Old Testament figures; the hymn of Mary; Herod's killing of the children and the flight to Egypt; Zacharias and Hannah; and the story of the wise men from the Orient. The title "King of the Jews" is only included when it casts the Jewish religious leadership in a negative light.[59] Deleted, too, is every cry for mercy and each word of exaltation to the Son of David, along with any fulfillment in Jesus of an Old Testament prophecy, although the fact that Jesus knew of Jewish ways has been preserved.

In *Die Botschaft Gottes*, Jesus is not the messiah and the word "Christus" is replaced most of the forty-eight times it appears in Luther's version of the Gospels.[60] Where the Greek text has "Christos" and Luther writes "Christus" (John 3:28 and 4:29), *Die Botschaft Gottes* writes "the promised One" or "the Revealer."[61] Jesus is presented as a master or a teacher who comes to refute the Jews, and the word "messiah" (John 1:41 and 4:25) in reference to Jesus is absent from the text.[62] The few times the term messiah is present in the text of *Die Botschaft Gottes* serve as means to demean the Jewish people or denigrate Jewish religiosity, the religiosity in which the Jesus of the New Testament participated.[63] John 1:45, rather than defining Jesus in terms of Mosaic law and the prophets, is altered to generically speak of Jesus in relationship to "the fathers."[64] The elimination of any messianic claims was intended to break any connection between Jesus and the Hebrew Bible and Judaism, and it was rooted in a theological argument put forward in the 1920s by the New Testament scholar Ernst Lohmeyer that two types of eschatology existed in first-century Palestine: messianism, found in Judea, and son of man, found in Galilee. Lohmeyer, despite being a critic of the Nazi Party who refused to endorse the antisemitic uses of scripture by the German Christian Movement and other Protestant theologians in the Nazi era, in this way inadvertently provided theological ammunition to Institute members who argued that Galilean eschatology was in fact Aryan and that messianic claims about Jesus were falsifications of the Gospels.[65]

The repudiation of Jews is made clear in *Die Botschaft Gottes*. John 8:44 is retained: "You have the devil as your father, and you want to fulfill your father's desire. He was a human murderer from the beginning." To this is added, "For he avoided staying in Judaea, because the Jews hated him to the death."[66] Additionally, when Jesus taught in the Temple and asked the people why the scribes believed that the messiah had to be the son of David, the text states, "The *Volk* listened to him gladly, as he hit the Scribes with their own weapons."[67] In this loaded imagery, we encounter the Jesus of the German Christian Movement's imagination: a violent enemy and a ridiculer rather than a man who was linking himself to the great David of Jewish history via this text.[68] This passage in *Die Botschaft Gottes* builds the antagonism between Jesus and what had come to be understood as *all Jews* in the minds of the theologians who emphatically set out to dejudaize the New Testament text and the world in which they lived.

At the same time, Jesus's own Jewishness is negated, as exemplified in John 4. *Die Bottschaft Gottes* retains the story of Jesus and the Samaritan woman, but cuts verse 9, eliminating Jesus's self-identification as a Jew.[69] Instead of the Samaritan woman saying, "You are a Jew," she tells Jesus, "You come from Judea," leaving his ethnic identity undefined.[70] *Die Botschaft Gottes* and Weidemann's version also differ on their treatment of John 4:22, "You worship what you do not know; we worship what we know, for salvation is from the Jews."[71] By contrast, Weidemann renders John 4:22, "The Jews at least know of the God from whom alone salvation comes," distancing "the Jews" from divine salvation."[72] In a 1938 article, Grundmann argued that the verse was a later interpolation since John's Gospel was otherwise anti-Jewish, identifying Jews not as the source of salvation, but as murderers of Christ, descendants of Satan, and opponents of Jesus; the church should ban sermons based on John 4:22.[73]

John 1:47 was rendered by Luther: "Jesus says, behold, an upright Israelite"; in *Die Botschaft Gottes*: "See one who seeks God with sincere earnestness."[74] The Temple is not absent from the text, but it refrains from mentioning religious offerings brought to it. Instead, "the parents came with the Jesus child, in order to bring him before God."[75] Jesus is not circumcised but is simply given a name.[76] Other linguistic changes are notable: the Sabbath becomes "holiday" (*Feiertag*), whereas Luther translates Passover/Pesach as "Easter of the Jews," in *Die Botschaft Gottes* the language varies depending on who is celebrating – it is called "*Passahfest*" when Jews are celebrating, presumably to reinforce the Jewishness that is being repudiated, and "*Ostern*" in relationship to Jesus and his disciples.[77] While the Jews celebrate Passover, Jesus and his disciples simply gather for a meal, without any connection to Passover.

In *Die Botschaft Gottes*, apocalyptic ideas have been removed, as well as doctrinal concepts such as sinner, righteous, repentance, and penance. It treats Jesus's racial identity gingerly. References to Jesus as a rabbi are eliminated. Luther calls him "Rabbi" or "Rabbuni," but he is called "Meister" in *Die Botschaft Gottes*, as in John 1:49.[78] Luther writes, "Nathanael speaks to

Jesus: Rabbi, you are the Son of God, you are the king of Israel"; *Die Botschaft Gottes* writes, "Master, you are the Son of God, bringing the seekers to life."[79]

In *Die Botschaft Gottes*, Jesus is called son of God.[80] That way he is identified as neither a Jew nor an Aryan; he is simply a resident of certain regions, though the Galilean-Aryan equation would have been understood by readers. The text identifies the warm reception of Jesus with Galilee, both in origins and activities, and associates Judea with menace. Jesus must leave Judea out of fear of the Pharisees and move to Galilee; in this way, the New Testament's tension between Galilee and Jerusalem is retained (John 1:46; 7:41–3).[81] The latter locale is identified with peril (Luke 13:33): "Only in Jerusalem do the prophets die."[82] Also reflecting this, Luke 9:53 is changed from Jesus's journey to Jerusalem to his journey to the "hated Jerusalem."[83]

In John 4:1–42, describing Jesus's encounter with the Samaritan woman, the exchange follows the text of John's Gospel, but the word "messiah" (used in the Luther Bible, John 4:25) is changed to "promised one."[84] The word synagogue is also eliminated, as in John 6:59: "He taught that in the synagogue of Capernaum," which becomes "He taught that in the community of Capernaum."[85] Obviously, reference to circumcision is also eliminated; "circumcision" is replaced with "sign of covenant" in John 7:19.[86] Depending on the context, the word "Hebrew" is either eliminated or changed to *"jüdisch"*; see John 19:20, 19:13, 19:17.[87]

In John 12:12–15, when Jesus enters Jerusalem during the feast of Passover, he is met by crowds exclaiming, "Hosanna: Blessed is He who comes in the name of the Lord, even the King of Israel," containing a direct quote from Psalm 118.[88] As noted earlier, Weidemann's version of John 12:13 replaced "Hosanna" with "Heil" and changed "King of Israel" to "our King."[89] *Die Botschaft Gottes* similarly replaces "Hosanna" with "Heil" and changes the "King of Israel" to "the King of Life."[90] *Die Botschaft Gottes* omits both the quotation of Psalm 118 and the references from Zechariah and Zephaniah found in the verses that follow. This section is titled "The King of Life comes to the City of his Death" rather than "The King of Israel comes to Jerusalem."[91]

The Sermon on the Mount appears early in *Die Botschaft Gottes* and mixes the texts from Luke's Gospel with the version in Matthew. The text is not as militarized as other nazified versions, such as Müller's, but it includes notable changes to key terms. The classic term "compassionate" (Matthew 5:7), is omitted, along with the blessings for the poor, for those in mourning, and for the meek.[92] Whereas Luke 6:20 reads, "Blessed are you who are poor, for yours is the kingdom of God," *Die Botschaft Gottes* renders, "Blessed are you who look for God! God is coming to you!"[93] Both the "poor" and "the kingdom" are replaced, perhaps suggesting that Hitler and the Nazi empire have already arrived.

The description of the arrest and crucifixion in the Gospel of John is extended considerably in *Die Botschaft Gottes*.[94] The account follows John's narrative closely, although the language is simplified relative to Luther's version. Loosely following Mark 14 and Luke 22–3, Jesus is asked by the high priests if he is a messiah, and he gives an ambiguous reply. When he is then asked, "So are you the Son of God?" he replies, "I am."[95] Most references to him as messiah (Matthew 26:68, 27:17, 22) are omitted.[96] Still, Jesus's citation of Psalm 22:1 when he is on the cross is retained, though in German only and not in Aramaic (Matthew 27:46, Mark 15:34).

The printing of *Die Botschaft Gottes* proceeded unhindered. Paper was not easily available if a project was deemed contrary to wartime propaganda, but while other publications in Germany were shut down by the Reich on the stated grounds of a paper shortage, the Institute faced no such difficulties. Its benefactor, Friedrich Werner, president of the Old Prussian Union, had hoped that *Die Botschaft Gottes* would be published before Easter 1940, in time to be distributed to all candidates for Confirmation.[97] That deadline was not met; publication came a few months later. At the same time, a very small, ninety-six-page synoptic Gospel harmony was printed. By the end of 1941, however, the Institute was pleased to announce that 200,000 copies had been sold or distributed, a sign – according to the Institute's newsletter – of how important the new "Germanization" was.[98] The volumes were sold individually, for thirty pennies for the shorter version of excerpts from the synoptic Gospels, or for 1.50 RM for the entire edition. This was not enough to recoup printing costs, which suggests that the project was subsidized by the Protestant Church.

The Institute's New Testament project was ambitious in another sense as well: its goal was to reach a popular – and not simply scholarly – audience. "The creation has to be scientifically proper, practically applicable, and linguistically without blemish,"[99] wrote Grundmann in the first issue of the Institute's quarterly newsletter.[100] Propagandistic in tone, the newsletter presented Institute "scholarship" in popularized form, with a heavy emphasis on antisemitism.

What impact did the dejudaized Bible have? The Institute certainly spared no effort to send copies wherever possible. Institute business manager Heinz Hunger, who was among those who signed the foreword, claimed to have sent a copy to all soldiers who were members of the German Christian Movement.[101] In Lübeck, Die Botschaft Gottes was introduced to religious services and Bible study,[102] while in Weimar, German Christian pastors presented a copy to young people at Confirmation, and in Altenburg it was given to wedding couples.[103] A large number of church congregations purchased copies and presumably used the so-called "Volkstestament" for their weekly scripture readings. How many regional churches altered their lectionary to accord with the new version is not known.

By the time Die Botschaft Gottes was printed and distributed, at least some Germans had lost interest in the Bible altogether. In 1939, a group of sixty students of theology from the universities of Erlangen, Göttingen, Leipzig, Marburg, and Tübingen as well as the theological seminary of Bethel travelled through rural Thuringia. Reporting on their experiences, they wrote that Christian faith could only be found among the elderly: "Otherwise, the obtuseness was huge. Sometimes we met with overt rejection, 'The Bible is a Jew book, Mein Kampf is today's Bible.' In one house, in which we were certain we would meet understanding, we were told about a new Bible that had just appeared, in which everything Jewish was expunged because otherwise the Bible was unusable."[104]

The reception of Die Botschaft Gottes among scholars who were members of the Confessing Church, the rival faction within the Protestant church that was formed in 1934 in opposition to the German Christian Movement, was mixed.[105] Hans von Soden, Professor of New Testament at the University of Marburg, published a privately printed pamphlet accusing the editors of Die Botschaft Gottes of acting like "Pharisees" by emending the biblical text and thus creating a new canon.[106] Grundmann, in response, accused anti-Christian Nazi ideologues of having been "judaized" by the eighteenth-century Jewish philosopher Moses Mendelssohn, for their claim that Jesus was a Jew. This interchurch dialogue in the most antisemitic of times revealed the inherent challenges that centuries of anti-Jewish theology presented to those who had been commanded to love their Jewish (and other) neighbours as themselves, borrowed from the Hebrew Bible, by the one they purported to defend.

In 1940, Karl Fischer, a Confessing Church pastor in Dresden, published a pamphlet against *Die Botschaft Gottes*, printed by the Confessing Church of Saxony. He noted that every positive tie of Jesus to the Old Testament was missing from *Die Botschaft Gottes*, making Jesus "no longer the fulfiller but the destroyer … the great revolutionary, who gave only a clear No to his era."[107] Missing was Jesus's affirmation, a positive message.

The New Testament scholar Ernst Haenchen, then a young professor at the University of Giessen, called the project unscholarly, its choice of texts tendentious; it was a "mißlungenen Versuch," or abortive attempt.[108] The New Testament scholar Hans Lietzmann, then Professor of Theology in Berlin, wrote a letter dated 16 June 1941, to his colleague, Hans von Soden: "the effort to distance Jesus from everything Jewish is clearly seen in all of Grundmann's publications. It is also in Hirsch's Gospel of John, though handled with a different caution. With Grundmann it seems to me dominated by a happy naivete."[109]

Indeed, Emmanuel Hirsch's commentary on the Gospel of John, published in 1936, set forth the major German Christian Movement arguments. According to Hirsch, John's Gospel made it clear that Jesus was not a Semite, and the Gospel represented Pauline Christianity, not Jewish Christianity. It was Pauline, Hirsch writes, because the author "understood the Pauline assertion that 'Christ is the end of the law' (Romans 10:4).[110] Hirsch, himself a member of the NSDAP and the German Christian Movement, also claimed that the author of John's Gospel was a poet, which gave him licence to deviate from historical evidence: "What he has written down from a free poetic perspective as Jesus' word is truly Jesus' word for him, revealed to him by the spirit. I believe that the distinction between truth and reality was thereby completely eradicated for him."[111] While Hirsch was not a member of Grundmann's Institute, his work served as a template for *Die Botschaft Gottes*, at least in its treatment of John's Gospel.

The main struggle between the Confessing Church and the German Christian Movement was whether scripture itself could be altered to mesh with Nazi principles. While the Confessing Church, affirming the sanctity of the sacrament of baptism, concerned itself with non-Aryan Christians

(Jews who had been baptized) but for the most part not with the rest of the Jewish community, the German Christians insisted that baptism did not overcome or erase racial identity, with the consequence that non-Aryans were fired from positions within the church – religion teachers, pastors, organists – once those churches fell under German Christian Movement control.

As noted, a principal source of conflict between the two groups was the text of scripture. The Confessing Church along with German Catholics insisted on preserving intact the canon of scripture, while the German Christian Movement wanted scripture to be altered, allegedly to recoup its original, pristine text, thus making it palatable for Germans in the Nazi era. Yet there was also a commonality between the German Christian Movement and Confessing Church, with regard to the theological anti-Judaism they shared and their use of racial imagery. The German Christian Movement sought to create what they considered a racially pure Bible, that is, a Bible without any Jewishness. The concern of the Confessing Church was to protect the "body" of the canon against the threat of the "Pharisaic" theological corruption of the German Christian Movement. From the perspective of the German Christian Movement, the Bible was a body that had to be purified of Jewish corruption. For the Confessing Church, the German Christian Movement's effort to dejudaize the Bible was "Pharisaic" in that it violated the integrity of scripture; the Confessing Church charged the German Christian Movement with representing the very spirit of Jewishness that was threatening Christianity. In both cases, the Nazi prohibition against sexual relations between Aryans and non-Aryans was transferred to the scriptural level.

The urge to draw a line separating Jesus from Judaism, or at least to indicate the originality and distinctiveness of his message, has haunted Christian theologians for generations. The urge received added impetus with the rise of Jewish scholarship during the nineteenth century that demonstrated the parallels between Jesus's teachings and those of rabbinic literature. Grundmann's version of the New Testament made use of earlier scholarship, such as Lohmeyer's two-site eschatological argument. Some earlier scholars had already claimed that the Galilee was a site of Aryan immigration and that Jesus most likely came from an Aryan family.

The goal was to make Christianity relevant to the new Nazi era. This was accomplished by stressing Jesus's triumph rather than defeat through death, and his destruction at the hands of Jews, who ought now to be defeated by Germans as revenge. In Grundmann's catechism, *Deutsche mit Gott: Ein deutsches Glaubensbuch* (Germans with God: A German Catechism), published in 1941, the message is clear:

> Jesus of Nazareth in Galilee shows in his message and attitude a spirit diametrically opposed to Judaism. The battle between him and the Jews became so inexorable that it led to his crucifixion. Thus, Jesus could not have been a Jew. To this day, Judaism pursues Jesus and all those who follow him with unforgiving hatred. On the other hand, in Jesus Christ, especially among Aryan people, their last and most profound questions are answered. So, he became the Savior of the Germans.[112]

Speculations about Jesus's race or his relationship to Jewish teachings took on great significance during the Nazi period. Suddenly, Aryan identity meant life, and Jew meant social exclusion, expulsion, and death. Note that the German word *Judentum* means Jews as well as Judaism. In the minds of Church leaders with nationalistic and Nazi affinities, the ideological struggle of the German *Volk* against the Jewish people demanded both a reinvented image of Jesus (as a non-Jew or an Aryan fighting the Jews) and a gospel distanced from the Jewish teachings of his ancestors, the Hebrew Bible, and any messianic conceptions. Numerous theologians, including Grundmann, Weidemann, and Hirsch, believing themselves to be reformers following in the footsteps of Luther, answered the call, inventing conceptions of Christianity and Jesus fitting the Nazi Reich.[113] The unparalleled efforts of these churchmen to dejudaize Jesus and Christianity in harmony with Nazi antisemitism by rewriting the New Testament and the Gospels culminated the efforts by Christian theologians to distance Jesus from his Jewish environs.

The Gospel of John contains plenty of passages that could easily be rendered in harsh, antisemitic denunciations. John 8:44, in which Jews are told their father is the devil, could serve as an excuse to further demonize the Jews and justify Nazi measures against them. Yet *Die Botschaft Gottes* is restrained, with changes to the New Testament text that are slight and elusive, and much less indicting than the other Institute publications, which are filled with palpable hatred and antisemitism.[114] Jesus's burial according to Jewish custom, his tears wept with his Jewish friends in mourning, and his last and most intimate talk with and prayer for his Jewish disciples (The Farewell Discourse of John 14–17), all unique to the book of John, complicated the dejudaization efforts of the authors of *Die Botschaft Gottes*.[115] In contrast to Weidemann and Müller's versions of the Gospels, *Die Botschaft Gottes* presents itself as if without explicit ideological or political claims, but rather as a work of theological scholarship.[116] The Weidemann and Grundmann renditions are not as vicious as Nazi propaganda, nor are they as crude as Ludwig Müller's rendition of the Sermon on the Mount, making them more palatable. Concealing antisemitism under the false veneer of theological "scholarship" was a finely honed technique. Still, the international press – in India, Palestine, and the United States – was aware of the scandalous nature of the effort. Immune to the ongoing antisemitic propaganda of the Reich, journalists from other countries could see through the false veneer and alert their readers to the nazified Gospel translations and their antisemitic purposes.

Within Nazi Germany, the impact of antisemitic theology was mixed. The German Christian Movement had a strong impact on the church, gaining control of many regional churches, theological faculties, and publications. Their ultimate goal, however, was winning support and respect from the Nazi regime: recognition and acknowledgment that they were important figures in the Third Reich. They did not succeed. While the regime did not hinder the publications, it had no particular need for theological antisemitism, and the positions of honour that Grundmann, Weidemann, and their colleagues longed to attain remained elusive; these men were irrelevant to the Nazi machine. Yet some of the most anti-Christian Nazi theorists appreciated their efforts. Although Grundmann had sparred with Alfred Rosenberg in 1933, he was nonetheless invited to a July 1944 conference that Rosenberg organized, an international conference on antisemitism that was supposed to be held in Krakow. Among those he invited to lecture were leading Christian antisemitic theologians and leaders of the Institute, including Karl Euler, Georg Bertram, and Gerhard Kittel. The conference ultimately did not take place due to war conditions, but the invitations make it clear that even Rosenberg, despite his hostility to Christianity, recognized the importance of including these theologians when discussing antisemitic propaganda.[117]

The fall of the Third Reich brought an end to formal, public, and explicit church-sponsored efforts to dejudaize Christianity. The German Christian Movement was defeated, although some of its attitudes concerning Judaism were transmitted in subtle ways to the next generation. The Institute was disbanded by church officials in Thüringen, despite pleas by its leaders to retain it. With news of the Nazi regime's defeat, Bishop Müller committed suicide in Berlin. Bishop Weidemann convinced a tribunal that he had been a loyal Christian who had endured persecution from Nazi authorities; he died in 1976.[118] After losing his professorship at the University of Jena due to his early Nazi Party membership (he had joined in 1930), Grundmann achieved denazification by depicting himself as a naive theologian who knew nothing of politics; he later taught at seminaries in Eisenach and Leipzig in East Germany, and his postwar Gospel commentaries were required reading for Protestant theology students throughout East and West Germany until the late 1990s. He died in 1974. Emmanuel Hirsch, who had become a member of the NSDAP in 1937, took early retirement from his professorship at the University of Göttingen in 1945, and died in 1971 without ever having withdrawn any of his *völkisch* antisemitic statements, while retaining the devotion of his students and colleagues.[119] Of the many other professors, pastors, bishops, and students who participated in dejudaization efforts, most retained their positions or transferred to other institutions. None published statements of regret or repentance for their antisemitic activities, and many went on to train the next generation of theologians.[120] Their many conference papers and pamphlets, as well as the catechism and dejudaized versions of the Bible, are scattered throughout Germany, in private homes, libraries, and archives, and are available from booksellers and even on the internet, but they are no longer used for liturgical purposes.

The Gospel of John did not simply fall victim to unscrupulous and antisemitic Nazi interpreters. Elements within the Gospel lend themselves to antisemitic interpretation: the term "the Jews" (*hoi Iudaioi*) appears more than seventy times, usually (but not always) implying something negative. At the same time, that Gospel, composed at the end of the first century or early second century, is aware of contemporary Jewish religious practice and texts. "The Jews" of John's Gospel could be understood as straw men, a literary device that is part of a theological argument or an intra-communal struggle over Jewish identity in the face of claims concerning Jesus's messianic status.

Given that the harsh statements concerning "the Jews" in the Gospel of John could so easily be mobilized for antisemitic purposes, the text requires caution. Surely its polemics that demonize "the Jews" cannot be taken at face value; Jews are not the children of the devil (John 8:44), and their religious beliefs and practices, shared by Jesus, are obviously not intrinsically immoral or degenerate. The importance of Judaism for the coherence of the Christian message, and the horrific consequences of Nazi antisemitism in the Holocaust, have given an imperative to postwar theologians to understand the Gospel of John for its potential dangers. The Gospel author's harsh language may have had polemical purposes at one historical moment in antiquity, but should carry no timeless or universal significance.[121]

NOTES

1 "An Anti-Jewish Gospel: New German Version of St. John," *The Times of India*, 30 January 1937.
2 "A Bible Acceptable to Nazis: A New Translation," *The Times* (London), 13 February 1936.
3 Heinz Weidemann to Franz Ritter von Epp, December 1936, in Doris Bergen, *Twisted Cross: The German Christian Movement in the Third Reich* (Chapel Hill: University of North Carolina Press, 1996), 161.
4 Bergen, *Twisted Cross*, 161.
5 "Bible Acceptable to Nazis: New Translation," *The Times of India* (4 March 4, 1936.
6 "An Anti-Jewish Gospel."
7 "A Bible Acceptable to Nazis," *The Palestine Post*, 26 February 1936.
8 "Nazis Publish Antisemitic Version of Gospel of St. John," *Jewish Telegraphic Agency*, 14 January 1937.
9 Heinz Weidemann, *Das Evangelium Johannes deutsch* (Bremen: Kommende Kirche, 1937), 12.
10 "Gospel According to Saint Hitler," *Time*, 25 January 1937.
11 Weidemann, *Das Evangelium Johannes deutsch*, 25–6.
12 Ibid., 5.
13 John 1:47, Revised Standard Version (RSV).

14 Weidemann, *Das Evangelium Johannes deutsch*, 55. The RSV translation of John 12:13 reads: "So they took branches of palm trees and went out to meet him, crying, 'Hosanna! Blessed is he who comes in the name of the Lord, even the King of Israel!'"

15 Weidemann, *Das Evangelium Johannes deutsch*, 73.

16 Artur Dinter, an early and avid supporter of Hitler, also published a version of the gospels, *Das Evangelium unseres Herrn und Heilandes Jesus Christus* (Langensalza: E. Kabisch, 1923). The *Deutche Christen* (German Christian) Movement came to an end in 1945 with Nazi Germany's defeat. For more on this, see Bergen, *Twisted Cross*, esp. Chapter 11.

17 Reijo E. Heinonen, *Anpassung und Identität: Theologie und Kirchenpolitik der Bremer Deutschen Christen 1933–1945* (Göttingen: Vandenhoeck & Ruprecht, 1978), 217.

18 Ludwig Müller, *Deutsche Gottesworte: Aus der Bergpredigt verdeutscht* (Weimar: Verlag Deutsche Christen, 1936). See also the English translation, *The Germanisation of the New Testament,* foreword by H.C. Robbins (London: Friends of Europe, 1938). See also Thomas Martin Schneider, *Reichsbischof Ludwig Müller: eine Untersuchung zu Leben, Werk und Persönlichkeit* (Göttingen: Vandenhoeck & Ruprecht, 1993).

19 Müller, *Deutsche Gottesworte*, 28. Note that Matthew 7 continues, "for this is the Law and the Prophets."

20 "Nazi Parents Debate Striking Moses from the Old Testament," *Chicago Daily Tribune*, 7 November 1936.

21 "Nazi Pupils Told to Read *Stürmer* instead of Bible," *Jewish Telegraphic Agency*, 20 November 1936, reprinted as "Nazi Pupils Told to Read *Stürmer*," *Jewish Advocate*, 25 December 1936.

22 Bergen, *Twisted Cross*.

23 Weidemann, "Mein Kampf um die Erneuerung des religiösen Lebens in der Kirche: Ein Rechenschaftsbericht," qtd in Doris Bergen, "One Reich, One People, One Church: The German Christian Movement and the People's Church, 1932–1945" (PhD diss., University of North Carolina, 1991), 480. In the fall of 1939, Weidemann also began work on a collection of the major texts of the New Testament, tentatively titled "Christustestament," but it never materialized. Reijo E. Heinonen, *Anpassung und Identität. Theologie und Kirchenpolitik der Bremer Deutschen Christen 1933–1945* (Göttingen: Vandenhoeck & Ruprecht, 1978), 228.

24 Lem Graves Jr (1917–2002) was a student when he wrote the column in 1936;

he subsequently was a war correspondent during the Second World War. He later became a distinguished journalist, worked for the Marshall Plan, and was appointed by President Kennedy to head the Voice of America in Latin America.

25 Lem Graves Jr, "Exit Moses from the Nazi Bible," *New Journal and Guide*, 14 November 1936, 9.

26 Heinonen, *Anpassung und Identität*, 228.

27 Weidemann, *Das Evangelium Johannes deutsch*, Foreword.

28 Ibid., 16.

29 *Die Botschaft Gottes* (Leipzig: Otto Wigand, 1940), 105.

30 Thomas Martin Schneider, *Reichsbischof Ludwig Müller: eine Untersuchung zu Leben, Werk und Persönlichkeit* (Göttingen: Vandenhoeck & Ruprecht, 1993).

31 Schneider, *Reichsbischof Ludwig Müller*. Müller was effectively stripped of his authority in 1935 when new ecclesiastical leadership was appointed after he failed to unify the German Protestant churches into one national church.

32 Müller, *Deutsche Gottesworte*, 9.

33 Ibid. "Happy is he who, in childlike simplicity, trusts in God; he has community with God (Mat 5:3); Happy is he who bears his sufferings like a man; he will find the strength never to despair without courage. (4); Happy is he who is always a good comrade; he will make his way in the world (5); Happy is he who hungers and thirsts to come to an understanding with God; he will find the peace of God. (6); Happy are they who keep peace with their fellow-countrymen; they do the will of God (9); Happy are they who live and work honestly and faithfully, but who, nevertheless, are persecuted and abused; they keep community with God (10)."

34 Müller, *Deutsche Gottesworte*, 16.

35 Ibid.

36 Ludwig Müller, "God's Word in German: The Sermon on the Mount, Germanized," in *A Church Undone: Documents from the German Christian Faith Movement 1932–1940*, trans. Mary Solberg (Minneapolis: Fortress Press, 2015), 386–94, here 392.

37 Müller, *Deutsche Gottesworte*, 37.

38 Romans 11:17–24, NASB; Müller, *Deutsche Gottesworte: Aus der Bergpredigt verdeutscht*, 38.

39 Müller, *Deutsche Gottesworte*, 38.

40 Müller, *God's Word in German*, 393.

41 Müller, *Deutsche Gottesworte*, 39.

42 *Die Botschaft Gottes*, VII–VIII.

43 "Everyone on first meeting [our Führer Adolf Hitler] shockingly recognizes: that is a completely pure man! All of us see it thus. In this man there is nothing disunited. He is in himself completely one, completely simple, clear, and true. We also know that the power of such a clear and truthful man does not derive from the earth, but rather out of that higher world that the Master, Christ, called the kingdom of heaven. We also know from men who are close to the Führer that he knows of his inner connection with God. He knows himself to be the instrument of God and has the clear, simple trust in God of a man who – as the Bible puts it – is reconciled with God. Some people have said to Adolf Hitler that a magic power radiates from him. I do not know whether one ought to put it that way. When one experiences this man for the first time, he certainly feels one thing: the deep humility of the man which is at the same time completely consistent with his higher commission. This oneness of man with his God is a symbol of what the old church teachers intended to say with the Trinity." Walter Grundmann, "Führererlebnis und Priestertum," *Glaube und Volk* 2 (1933): 147–52, here 148, in James Zabel, *Nazism and the Pastors: A Study of the Ideas of Three Deutsche Christen Groups* (Missoula: Scholars Press for the American Academy of Religion, 1976), 139. Similar tributes to Hitler as a divine saviour are expressed by Grundmann in his article "Die Neubesinnung der Theologien und der Aufbruch der Nation," *Deutsche Theologie* 1 (1934): 39–54.

44 Susannah Heschel, *The Aryan Jesus: Christian Theologians and the Bible in Nazi Germany* (Princeton: Princeton University Press, 2008), 201.

45 On Grundmann's postwar career, see Susannah Heschel, "Die zwei Karriere des Theologen Walter Grundmann: Der Neutestamentler als Nazi Propagandist und Stasi-Informant," in *Täter und Komplizen in Theologie und Kirchen 1933–1945*, ed. Manfred Gailus (Göttingen: Wallstein, 2015), 171–196; and Lukas Bormann, "Walter Grundmann und das Ministerium für Staatssicherheit – Chronik einer Zusammenarbeit aus Überzeugung (1956–1969), *Kirchliche Zeitgeschichte* 22, no. 2 (2009): 595–632. Grundmann was academic director of the Institute until 1943, when he was drafted into the German military. The Institute closed its doors in 1945, but most members

remained active in church leadership and on theological faculties. During
the denazification process, Grundmann lost his faculty position due to his
early membership in the Nazi Party but remained active in German theological circles, publishing commentaries and teaching throughout his life-
time. For more on the Institute members after the war, see Heschel, *The
Aryan Jesus*.

46 On Catholics at the Institute, see Lucia Scherzberg, *Zwischen Partei und
Kirche: Nationalsozialistische Priester in Österreich und Deutschland, 1938–
1944* (Frankfurt am Main: Campus, 2020); and Kevin P. Spicer, *Hitler's
Priests: Catholic Clergy and National Socialism* (Dekalb: Northern Illinois
University Press in association with the United States Holocaust Memorial
Museum, 2008), esp. 154–202.

47 The graduate student, Heinz Günkel, a member of the NSDAP and the SA,
completed a dissertation at the University of Jena on the origins of the Sermon on the Mount in 1939 and was awarded honours by Gerhard von Rad,
professor of Old Testament, and Grundmann.

48 Walter Grundmann, "Die Arbeit des ersten Evangelisten," in *Christentum
und Judentum*, ed. Walter Grundmann (Leipzig: Georg Wigand, 1940), 53–78.

49 Grundmann, "Die Arbeit des ersten Evangelisten," 77–8.

50 Erich Fromm, *Das Volkstestament der Deutschen, Ein Geleitwort zu der vom
"Institut zur Erforschung des jüdischen Einflußes auf das deutsche kirchliche
Leben" herausgegebenen Botschaft Gottes* (Leipzig: Verlag Georg Wigand,
1940), 6–7.

51 Walter Grundmann, "Unsere Arbeit am Neuen Testament," *Verbandsmittei-
lungen* 1 (December 1939): 6–22, here 9.

52 Walter Grundmann, "Die ewige Wahrheit des Evangeliums und seine Zeitgebundenheit," in *Die Bedeutung der Bibel für den Glauben*, ed. H.E. Eisen-
huth (Leipzig: Georg Wigand, 1941), 191–261, here 223. Also see Oliver
Arnhold, *"Entjudung": Kirche im Abgrund. Die Thüringer Kirchenbewegung
Deutsche Christen 1928-1939 und das "Institut zur Erforschung und Beseitigung des jüdischen Einflusses auf das deutsche kirchliche Leben" 1939–1945*
(Berlin: Institut Kirche und Judentum, 2010), 662.

53 Fromm, *Das Volkstestament der Deutschen*, 29, in Shannon Quigley, "Aban-
doning the Jewish Jesus and Abandoning the Jews: The Anti-Jewish
Polemic, Christian Dejudaization Efforts, and *Die Botschaft Gottes* in the
Nazi Era" (MA thesis, University of Haifa, 2018), 25.

54 Walter Grundmann, "Die ewige Wahrheit des Evangeliums und seine Zeitgebundenheit," 218; Fromm, *Das Volkstestament der Deutschen*, 29.

55 *Die Botschaft Gottes*, 253, 274–5.

56 Arnhold, *"Entjudung": Kirche im Abgrund*, 679–80.

57 *Die Botschaft Gottes*, 102.

58 *Die Botschaft Gottes*, 99.

59 *Die Botschaft Gottes*, 90, 91, 154, 156–7.

60 Matthäus 1:16, 16:20, 24:5, Markus 1:1, 8:29, 15:32, Lukas 2:11, 4:41, 22:67, Johannes 1:20, 3:28, 20:31, Luther Version 1912. Another thirty-six verses contain the term "Christus" in Luther's version of the Gospels.

61 *Die Botschaft Gottes*, 101, 103, 109, and 111.

62 Ibid., 103 and 110.

63 Ibid., 32 and 79.

64 "Wir haben den gefunden, von dem Mose im Gesetz und die Propheten geschrieben haben." (Luther) I (Susannah) would like to express my gratitude to my colleague, the Protestant theologian Siegfried Virgils, for reading and discussing with me passages from *Die Botschaft Gottes* and how they compare to Martin Luther's translations.

65 Ernst Lohmeyer, *Galiläa und Jerusalem* (Göttingen: Vandenhoeck & Ruprecht, 1936). See also James R. Edwards, *Between the Swastika and the Sickle: The Life, Disappearance, and Execution of Ernst Lohmeyer* (Grand Rapids: Eerdmans, 2019).

66 *Die Botschaft Gottes*, 117, 126.

67 Ibid., 79.

68 Refers to an exchange found in Matthew 22:41–6, Mark 12:35–7, and Luke 20:41–4 between Jesus and some scribes related to an excerpt from Psalm 110.

69 Quigley, "Abandoning the Jewish Jesus and Abandoning the Jews," 42–3 and 72.

70 Ibid., 42.

71 John 4:22, RSV.

72 Weidemann, *Das Evangelium Johannes deutsch*, 14.

73 Walter Grundmann, "Das Heil kommt von den Juden: Eine Schicksalsfrage an die Christen deutscher Nation," *Deutsche Frömmigkeit* 9 (1938): 1–8. In the Institute-sponsored version of the New Testament, verse 22 was simply omitted from the narrative of John 4. See *Die Botschaft Gottes*, 109–10.

74 John 1:47, Luther Version 1912. *Die Botschaft Gottes*, 103.

75 *Die Botschaft Gottes*, 4.

76 Ibid.

77 Ibid., 6, 84, 105, 138–9.

78 John 1:49, Luther Version 1912. *Die Botschaft Gottes*, 103.

79 John 1:49, Luther Version 1912. *Die Botschaft Gottes*, 103.

80 *Die Botschaft Gottes*, 7, 8, 18, 26, 88, 101, 103.

81 Ibid., 109

82 Ibid., 74.

83 Ibid., 45. Also see Quigley, "Abandoning the Jewish Jesus and Abandoning the Jews," 25.

84 *Die Botschaft Gottes*, 110.

85 In John 18:20, "Synagoge und Tempel" is rendered "*Gemeinde und Tempel.*" *Die Botschaft Gottes*, 116.

86 *Die Botschaft Gottes*, 119.

87 Ibid., 156.

88 John 12:13 (RSV).

89 Weidemann, *Das Evangelium Johannes deutsch*, 55.

90 *Die Botschaft Gottes*, 139.

91 Ibid., 139.

92 Ibid., 21–2.

93 Ibid., 21.

94 The account of the arrest and crucifixion extends from page 74 to 98, drawing from the synoptics, and is retold on pages 152–66, following the Gospel of John's account.

95 *Die Botschaft Gottes*, 88.

96 Ibid.

97 Werner to D. Hymmen, 22 January 1940, Zentral Archiv der Kirche in Berlin (ZAK), 7/4166.

98 *Verbandsmitteilung* 4 (1941).

99 Grundmann, "Unsere Arbeit am Neuen Testament," 9.

100 The *Verbandsmitteilung* appeared irregularly, and it is not clear how many issues were ultimately published nor how many copies were printed. The financing of the newsletter is also not clear; it contained advertisements for publications of the Deutsche Christen Verlag in Weimar, which may have subsidized printing costs; the cost of mailing the *Verbandsmitteilung* to Institute members remains unclear.

101 Birgit Jerke, "Wie wurde das Neue Testament zu einem sogennanten Volks-
    testament 'entjudet. Aus der Arbeit des Eisenacher "Instituts zur Erfor-
    schung und Beseitigung des jüdischen Einflusses auf das deutsche
    kirchliche Leben," in *Christlicher Antijudaismus und Antisemitismus*, ed.
    Leonore Siegele-Wenschkewitz (Frankfurt am Main: Haag und Herchen,
    1994), 201–34, here 228.

102 Jörg Thierfelder and Eberhard Röhm, eds., *Evangelische Kirche zwischen
    Kreuz und Hakenkreuz: Bilder und Texte einer Ausstellung* (Stuttgart: Calwer,
    1981), 43.

103 Säuberlich to Albertz, 26 July 1940, Landeskirchen Archiv Eisenach (LKA),
    DC III 2f.

104 Repertorium des Archivs der Bekennnenden Kirche Schlwswig-Hosltein,
    Alte Signatur 32; Neue Nummer 184. Nordelbisches Kirchenarchiv Kiel
    (NEK-Archiv).

105 For a more thorough look at the Confessing Church, see Shelley Bara-
    nowski, The *Confessing Church, Conservative Elites, and the Nazi State*
    (Lewiston: Edwin Mellen Press, 1986); Victoria Barnett, *For the Soul of the
    People: Protestant Protest against Hitler* (New York: Oxford University Press,
    1992); Eberhard Bethge, *Dietrich Bonhoeffer: A Biography*, rev. ed., ed. Victo-
    ria Barnett (Minneapolis: Fortress Press, 2000); and Wolfgang Gerlach, *And
    the Witnesses Were Silent: The Confessing Church and the Persecution of the
    Jews,* trans. Victoria Barnett (Lincoln: University of Nebraska Press, 2000).

106 Hans von Soden, *Die synoptische Frage und der geschichtliche Jesus* (Essen:
    Lichtweg, 1941).

107 Karl Fischer, *Das Volkstestament der Deutschen Christen* (Dresden: Beken-
    nende evangelische-lutherische Kirche Sachsen, 1940).

108 See Ernst Haenchen, "Gottes Wort Deutsch," *Deutsche Theologie* 8 (1941):
    120–31, in Heinonen, *Anpassung und Identität*, 229.

109 Arnhold, *"Entjudung": Kirche im Abgrund*, 677.

110 Emanuel Hirsch, *Studien zum vierten Evangelium* (Tübingen: Mohr, 1936),
    80, in Ernst Haenchen, "Johanneische Probleme," *Zeitschrift für Theologie
    und Kirche* 5, no. 1 (1959): 19–54, here 30.

111 Hirsch, *Studien zum vierten Evangelium*, 77, in Haenchen, "Johanneische
    Probleme," 32.

112 Wilhelm Büchner, Paul Gimpel, Walter Grundmann, Hans Pribnow, Kurt
    Thieme, Max-Adolf Wagenführer, Heinrich Weinmann, Hermann Werde-

mann, eds., *Deutsche mit Gott: Ein deutsches Glaubensbuch* (Weimar: Verlag Deutsche Christen, 1941), 46.

113 Walter Grundmann's works, *Wer ist Jesus von Nazareth?* (Weimar: Verlag Deutsche Christen, 1940); *Jesus der Galiläer und das Judentum* (Leipzig: G. Wigand, 1941), and "Das Messiasproblem," in *Germanentum, Christentum und Judentum: Studien zur Erforschung ihres gegenseitigen Verhältnisses*, vol. 2, ed. Walter Grundmann (Leipzig: G. Wigand, 1942), 381–412, as well as most of the publications of the Institut zur Erforschung und Beseitigung des jüdischen Einflusses auf das deutsche kirchliche Leben, worked towards this end.

114 Quigley, "Abandoning the Jewish Jesus and Abandoning the Jews," 33.

115 Ibid., 71.

116 The dejudaized and nazified Sermon on the Mount, the Gospel of John, and the New Testament published by Müller, Weidemann and the Institute, and Grundmann did not remain in use after the Nazi era. Some of the ideas can be found in postwar theological writings, though in very different contexts and using different language. On this point, see Susannah Heschel, "Configurations of Patriarchy, Judaism, and Nazism in German Feminist Thought," in T.M. Rudavsky, ed., *Gender and Judaism: The Transformation of Tradition* (New York: NYU Press, 1995), 135–56.

117 Max Weinreich, *Hitler's Professors* (New York: YIVO, 1946), 219–35.

118 Bergen, *Twisted Cross*, 222.

119 On Hirsch, see Robert P. Ericksen, *Theologians under Hitler* (New Haven: Yale University Press, 1985), 191–7.

120 On the failure of theologians of the Third Reich generation to discuss their own culpability, see Björn Krondorfer, Norbert Reck, and Katharina von Kellenbach, *Mit Blick auf die Täter: Fragen an die deutsche Theologie* (Gütersloh: Gütersloher Verlagshaus, 2006).

121 Susannah Heschel would like to express thanks to Pastor Siegfried Virgils, of Bonn, Germany, who kindly located some of the texts we wanted to examine, and Dr Wendel Cox, research librarian at Dartmouth College, who located some of the newspaper accounts. Shannon Quigley would like to express gratitude to David Silberklang at Yad Vashem for encouraging her on this path of research.

6

Nationalism and Religious Bonds: Transatlantic Religious Communities in Nazi Germany and the United States

Rebecca Carter-Chand

In March 1936, American Seventh-day Adventist Louise Kleuser found herself in a professional and moral predicament. Employed by the General Conference of the Seventh-day Adventists, Kleuser was tasked with accompanying a German Adventist representative named Hulda Jost on her three-month North American speaking tour. Serving as Jost's interpreter, Kleuser travelled with Jost to more than 140 public lectures for church congregations, college campuses, women's clubs, and German societies. As the head of the German Adventist welfare organization, Jost spoke about progressive German social welfare practices and how helping the poor and needy was the essence of Christianity.[1] But what became increasingly apparent to Kleuser was that Jost's talks often veered away from the devotional into the political, praising Hitler, his efforts toward peace, and his reconstruction of the economy, while dismissing reports about the mistreatment of Jews and the suppression of the German churches.[2]

As a German-American woman, born in Barmen, Germany, in 1890, and having immigrated to the United States as a child, Kleuser was deeply concerned about Jost's political messages and wrote several letters to the

Adventist leadership while on the road.[3] After the *Oregon Journal* reported
on a Portland event with the headline, "German Church Emissary Denies
Hitler Jew Hater," Kleuser wrote a candid letter – newspaper article attached
– to the President of the General Conference:

> This [newspaper] article clearly reveals that her main burden for her
> visit was to clear Germany's record. No wonder [German] consuls wel-
> come this! … I can't help wondering where we as a church might be
> if, in the near future, Germany decides to turn on Hitler. Our sister is
> positively playing with fire. Getting a perspective of Sister Jost's whole
> propaganda, I feel she may bring to us in the future far more embar-
> rassment than we can trust our brethren right close up to the problem
> in Europe, to now see."[4]

The letters reveal Kleuser wrestling between her professional duty as an interpreter, the spiritual bonds she felt toward a fellow Adventist, and her grave
concerns that the American Adventist Church was being drawn into the political agenda of Nazi Germany. Despite her warnings, Jost's tour continued
as planned.

Jost's propaganda tour fits into a wider pattern: small Christian groups
were subtly mobilized by the German government in the mid-1930s to promote Germany abroad and to assuage any doubts about religious freedom
under National Socialism.[5] The story of how the Nazi regime came to use
these religious communities as soft propaganda tools is a fascinating one
that explains much about Nazi pragmatism.[6] But the interplay between
Hulda Jost and Louise Kleuser (and the respective communities they represented) also highlights some of the challenges faced by the smaller Christian churches that had ties to the Anglo-American world – namely, how to
relate to fellow Christians when one has embraced a political regime built
on exclusionary ethnonationalism.

During the early years of the regime, Nazi policy regarding small religious
groups was arbitrary and inconsistent. Uncertain of the new government's
intentions vis-à-vis Christianity, Germany's Free Churches, religious associations, and sects sought to navigate a delicate position. Many welcomed
the rise of Nazism, sharing similar nationalistic outlooks and resentments
as other Germans.[7] They were concerned about their autonomy and often
overcompensated for their vulnerable status by emphasizing their loyalty to

the state. Despite their foreign ties and certain religious practices that appeared suspicious to the Nazis (such as the Adventists' practice of worshipping on the Sabbath, the Quakers' ties to socialism, and several groups' pacifist traditions), most of these groups proved more useful than threatening to the government throughout the 1930s, as Hitler sought to promote a positive image of Germany abroad. The Jehovah's Witnesses and a few other groups were outliers, as a result of their unwillingness to embrace Nazism's all-encompassing worldview and its demands for public demonstrations of allegiance.

It may appear counterintuitive that Germany's smaller churches would orient themselves toward Nazism, given their long-standing marginal status on the German religious landscape and their institutional and historical ties to co-religionists abroad. It goes against a common argument, largely based on the famous case of the French Huguenots of Le Chambon, that minorities are more likely to show solidarity with other persecuted groups. Indeed, the humble townspeople of Le Chambon themselves cited their collective memory of persecution as a religious minority when asked to explain why they sheltered and assisted Jews during the Second World War.[8] Recent research on the Low Countries during the Second World War by social scientist Robert Braun argues that religious minorities were more likely than the majority population to protect victims of persecution.[9] A similar dynamic appears to have been at play elsewhere in Europe, including in the borderlands of northeastern Poland, where Jews and Muslims (of Tatar heritage) lived peaceably together.[10] Although this hypothesis may help explain the minority groups' oppositional stance toward the Nazis and willingness to offer assistance to Jews in Nazi-occupied Europe, one cannot say the same of religious minorities in Germany.[11]

Perhaps even more surprising is that many of these religious groups were not only allowed to continue operating in the Nazi period but also found their place in the *Volksgemeinschaft* (ethnonational community) and participated in various aspects of Nazi society.[12] Like the larger churches, Baptists, Methodists, Adventists, Mennonites, and Mormons engaged in antisemitic measures, from excluding members of Jewish heritage to espousing antisemitic rhetoric.[13] This chapter explores how the smaller Christian churches negotiated their place in Germany and their international relationships in the Anglo-American sphere in the first five years of Nazi rule. It offers a bird's-eye view of the Anglo-American churches by considering both

the challenges and the opportunities presented by their marginal status in
Germany and their international connections. In particular, it asks how they
reconciled their religious identity – which was international in scope – with
Nazi racial ideology. It is precisely this navigation between nationalism and
internationalism that challenges our assumptions about how and why some
religious actors were attracted to ethnonationalism in this period.

Most scholarship on Germany's smaller churches examines individual religious groups. This approach takes seriously the distinctive theologies, practices, and institutional histories of the groups it examines. But it is usually
inward-focused, and its relevance for broader scholarship on Nazi Germany
is limited. A few scholars have analyzed multiple groups with shared characteristics, such as James Lichti's book on German denominations with
teachings against bearing arms (the Mennonites, Seventh-day Adventists,
and Quakers) and Daniel Heinz's volume on the Free Churches' attitudes
and actions toward Jews.[14] The groups considered here all had ties to Great
Britain and/or North America: the Baptists, Methodists, Plymouth Brethren,
and other evangelicals (who united in 1942 to form the Union of Evangelical
Free Church Congregations in Germany), as well as the Mennonites, Quakers, The Salvation Army, Seventh-day Adventists, Christian Scientists, Jehovah's Witnesses, and Latter-day Saints.[15]

FREE CHURCHES AND SECTS ON THE MARGINS
OF THE GERMAN RELIGIOUS LANDSCAPE

Unlike the main Protestant and Roman Catholic churches, which together
accounted for over 95 percent of Germans from the 1920s to the 1940s, Germany's independent churches – some recognized as "Free Churches," others
as "religious associations" or "sects" – were self-funded and remained in the
shadow of the two main confessions. The labels attached to these groups
and the status those labels denoted were fluid and evolved over the decades.
Today, the "Free Church" tent holds a greater number of churches, but in
the period considered here, "Free Church" was a specific legal category that
did not apply to all Christian groups operating in Germany.[16] "Denomination" is an Anglo-American term that does not quite fit the German context
of the Roman Catholic and Protestant state churches. The German term
"Konfession" was never used to describe these smaller groups. Therefore,

the terms "independent churches" and "Christian minority groups" are used here interchangeably as they encompass all the legal categories and are more neutral in tone than the pejorative term "sect."

The concept of "Free Churches" emerged in the mid-nineteenth century when Prussia and other German states formally recognized the small numbers of Lutheran and Reformed congregations that had refused to join the Old Prussian Union and similar united church efforts in other German states.[17] These Free Churches did not collect church taxes, but the state recognized the ministerial acts of their ministers (baptisms, marriages, and the like).[18] Other religious groups were recognized as "religious associations" (*Vereine*), including Mennonites and Moravian Brethren. Newer groups, most of them foreign imports, were usually labelled "sects," including the Baptists and Methodists in the 1830s. Another wave of foreign religious transplants developed in the second half of the nineteenth century and included the Plymouth Brethren, Adventists, Nazarenes, the Salvation Army, Christian Scientists, Mormons, and Jehovah's Witnesses. These groups faced a range of restrictions on their activities from local and state authorities but enjoyed the basic freedoms to worship and proselytize.

As a result of Anglo missionary efforts, Germans began to join these communities and they became increasingly German in character. Members of these churches still paid church taxes according to the Protestant or Catholic Church into which they had been baptized; tax exemptions were given only to the older Free Churches and Mennonites.[19] Formal withdrawals from the Catholic Church or the Protestant *Land* churches remained low, especially among the non-property-owning working classes, who did not pay property-based church taxes and therefore had little incentive to switch their church membership.[20]

The First World War foreshadowed some of the challenges faced by international religious communities during the National Socialist era. The Salvation Army, headquartered in London and at work in fifty-eight countries, was caught off guard by the outbreak of war in 1914.[21] During the war, its commitments to political neutrality and internationalism were strained but not broken. British Salvation Army leaders consistently avoided any references to "enemies" and instead spoke of solidarity among the working classes of both countries. The German branch exhibited far more nationalism, breaking off all communication with the international headquarters in London.[22] Its leadership in Berlin made a symbolic adjustment to the uniform, changing the S (for Salvation Army) into an H (for the German name of the organization, Heilsarmee). They even considered severing ties permanently with the International Salvation Army, though they never did.[23] After the war ended, in 1918, the German branch reunited with the International Salvation Army and benefited from the high reputation the British and American Salvation Army had acquired through its postwar humanitarian relief work in Germany. Even in this earlier period, international connections could be both an asset and a liability, to be emphasized or downplayed as useful.

The Weimar Republic brought new opportunities to the independent churches. Under the new federal constitution, there was no state religion and religious groups on the margins were allowed greater freedom. Now any religious association could apply for public corporation status in any state across Germany, and many did so.[24] All told, Christian minorities (the Free Churches, religious associations, and sects) accounted for around half a million people in the Weimar era, although formal membership numbers are undoubtedly conservative. These minorities varied greatly in size, status, theological teachings, governance structures, and internal culture. But they shared a common sense of inferiority, a commitment to the separation of church and state, and fierce independence from the main Protestant churches. They clung to their recent advances and hoped that their apolitical yet patriotic orientation would continue to improve their standing in German society.[25]

The Weimar Republic proved to be fertile ground for independent churches, but this did not mean that socially and politically conservative groups fully supported the secular democratic republic.[26] During the imperial era, the Baptists had figured out a way to secure their rights: through political neutrality and loyalty to the state. As historian Andrea Strübind has observed, the German Baptists preferred an authoritarian state that granted them institutional freedoms to a democratic political system that was secular.[27] And since many of these groups upheld a strict moral code on matters of health, sexuality, and material austerity, they shared the Nazi movement's criticisms of Weimar society. Christian Science, for example, did not have teachings that were inherently incompatible with Nazism – most Christian Scientists were conservative, patriotic, and engaged German citizens.[28] This

church's most distinctive feature, its alternative views on medicine and healing, was not politically subversive. Avoiding alcohol and tobacco, a practice
shared by Adventists, Salvationists, Jehovah's Witnesses, Mormons, and others, was a point of connection with Adolf Hitler, the most famous German
teetotaler of the period.

James Lichti makes a similar observation: the Free Churches' characteristics of freedom of conscience, pluralism, and separation of church and
state meshed quite well with the Nazi approach to religious freedom.[29] When
Methodist bishop John L. Nuelsen went on a lecture tour across America in
1935, he told audiences that in no European country did the Methodist
Church enjoy greater freedom than in Germany.[30]

REPOSITIONING IN 1933

After coming to power in January 1933, the Nazi government swiftly dissolved several small spiritual, esoteric, and philosophical groups, including
the Freemasons.[31] The independent churches came under investigation to
determine their political orientations and foreign connections. Previous
legal status no longer mattered as much as political reliability and the government's pragmatic concerns. As they tried to make sense of a dizzying
array of groups (many with similar-sounding names), the Gestapo and SS
did not distinguish between carefully delineated existing categories; instead,
they investigated *all* groups, writing reports with titles like "Observation on
the Activities of Non-Christian Religious Communities and Sects," which
included groups as diverse as Muslims, Mennonites, and Methodists.[32] The
Nazis did made a distinction between subversive or politically unreliable
groups and those that did not, in their view, pose a threat to the state.

The Nazis viewed the smaller religious groups with suspicion for several
interrelated reasons. First, Nazi authorities regularly referred to these groups
as "foreign sects" and questioned their loyalty to Germany and their financial
transactions in light of their relationships with religious bodies abroad.
Moreover, internationalism was associated with socialism and Jews, making
any "international" group suspect. Second, to the outside observer, these
groups' teachings and lifestyles often appeared opaque – possibly secretive
and subversive, as with the Freemasons. It was genuinely difficult to sort
out which groups had socialist or communist leanings, and which opposed

participation in political life on principle, including military service, joining political organizations, or simply giving the Hitler salute.

Church leaders had to work to convince the authorities that their followers would be loyal to the regime. "Coming into line" with Nazi *Gleichschaltung* (coordination) efforts – including disbanding their youth organizations – required compromise.[33] But many of the independent churches were able to show and explain that they were both loyal Germans and part of a spiritual family that transcended national borders. So although the Gestapo had difficulty distinguishing among them, most groups aggressively shaped their public profile between 1933 and 1939 and responded to government surveillance with a certain confidence afforded by their Aryan status. The government, in turn, proved flexible and receptive to outside pressures regarding those groups it considered harmless.

In November 1933, the Gestapo dissolved the Seventh-day Adventist Church. However, it rescinded the ban two weeks later, after the Adventist leaders wrote to the government affirming their support of "positive Christianity."[34] Only the Reform Movement of the Seventh-day Adventists was banned in 1936, over the issue of military service. That movement was a splinter group that had been founded during the First World War by a minority of Adventists who remained committed to their church's pacifist heritage.[35]

The Religious Society of Friends (the Quakers), a tiny religious community in Germany with only around 250 members, was not shut down by the Nazis, even though the Quakers did far more than any other Christian minority group to offer assistance to Jews.[36] In addition to hiding Jews, they sent packages to prisoners in concentration camps, provided community and social opportunities for isolated Jews, and maintained existing relationships with Jews (including Martin Buber). Thirteen German Quakers have received the Righteous Among the Nations award given by Yad Vashem.[37] Yet the Quakers never made a public declaration of their position on Nazism or antisemitism. It was no secret that they opposed the Nazi regime and were sympathetic to the plight of Jews, but they tried to remain discreet about their members' nonconformity or outright resistance. In 1933, the German Quakers decided that it would be left to each individual Quaker to decide how he or she would act. At a Quaker meeting on 8–9 April 1933, the members present drafted a sobering message:

We ask our members to live in the spirit which accepts "there is one God who dwells in all mankind, all men are brothers." We exhort all of our members to proclaim in word and deed the spirit of non-violence and friendship. Each of us in our own circles will find the right opportunities for action … However, we beg our members to think calmly and carefully before taking action. Actions inevitably have consequences which must be considered responsibly by each member. Do not feel that you have to bear witness as Quakers, nor that as a Quaker you should shoulder burdens that are greater than you have the strength to carry on your own.[38]

Other independent churches tried to find their footing in the new political climate by distancing themselves from their international connections and emphasizing their Germanness. For groups with a mother church or headquarters outside Germany, this was a delicate matter. In January 1933, the Salvation Army International Headquarters appointed a new leader of the German Salvation Army, replacing a German with an Englishman. The nationality of the person holding the top leadership position had long been an area of contention – most of the Territorial Commanders had been of British extraction.[39] Many German Salvationists resented the British influence on their organization, which they viewed as oppressively autocratic and incongruous with their growing national identity.[40] William Howard, the new leader, tried to keep control of the Heilsarmee by affirming the German officers' desire to be part of Hitler's national revolution.[41] He spent much of the year articulating the compatibility of the Salvation Army and the "new Germany." In December 1933, he wrote in his monthly circular letter to officers (the equivalent of clergy in the Salvation Army) that since he and his wife had been living among them "in this period of national awakening," he could appreciate their feelings. Although their main task was to be soldiers for Jesus Christ, he wrote, "we are pleased that fidelity to one does not exclude faithfulness to the other."[42] Even though this statement effectively permitted German Salvationists to support National Socialism, the German Heilsarmee soon pushed out their British leader in favour of a German.[43]

The Jehovah's Witnesses also made an early attempt to distance themselves from their international ties. The Jehovah's Witnesses were banned in

1933 and were especially targeted throughout the Nazi era. They were arrested in such high numbers that the Nazi concentration camp system assigned them a special category, denoted by the purple triangle in the concentration camp system. But the behaviours that brought them into trouble with the authorities were political in nature – refusing to give the Hitler salute, display the Nazi flag, bear arms for the state, participate in Nazi rallies and parades, join the German Labour Front, and participate in Nazi welfare and charity.

The Jehovah's Witnesses are usually portrayed as astonishingly consistent in upholding their beliefs in the face of intense persecution; even so, it is worth examining their leadership's attempts to navigate the disorienting first six months of Nazi rule. On 25 June 1933, around 7,000 Jehovah's Witnesses met at a convention in Berlin-Wilmersdorf, not realizing that the German authorities had banned their organization the day before. At this convention, a declaration was presented for approval, which was intended to clear up misinformation and convince the government to allow the Jehovah's Witnesses to continue operating (the Adventists had used much the same tactic).[44] Besides presenting the organization as oriented positively toward the state, it denied the accusation that it received funds from Jews, and it employed antisemitic language to distance itself from both Judaism and its parent organization in the United States: "The greatest and the most oppressive empire on earth is the Anglo-American empire ... It has been the commercial Jews of the British-American empire that have built up and carried on Big Business as a means of exploiting and oppressing the peoples of many nations."[45] Hindsight tells us that this manoeuvre did not work and was quite out of step with how the Jehovah's Witnesses proceeded to handle church–state relations during the Nazi era, but it is a good reminder that they too were willing to try some of the techniques used by the other independent churches.

While the Nazis were cracking down on Jehovah's Witnesses in 1933, the Seventh-day Adventists published a pamphlet clarifying that they were not the same as the Jehovah's Witnesses.[46] In a similar vein, when the Gestapo dissolved the Rhon-Brüderhof (Hutterian Brethren) in April 1937, the German Mennonites shifted from their previous support of the Brüderhof to criticism of what they now called their "communist Anabaptist cousins." When a Swiss Catholic publication reported on the dissolution of the group and referred to the Brüderhof as Mennonites, the German Mennonites quickly wrote a rebuttal, declaring that they were not Mennonites.[47]

In 1937, both the Hutterian Brethren (Brüderhof) and the Plymouth Brethren (also called Darbyists; in German: Brüderbewegung, Darbysten, or Christliche Versammlungen) were disbanded. The Hutterian Brethren were among the few in 1933 who expressed concern publicly over the Nazi movement. In December 1933, they wrote a ten-page letter to the Berlin Gestapo, explaining exactly how the Brüderhof could and could not support the state. One of their concerns was "the seemingly absolute belief in the Aryan, and especially the Nordic blood arouses fear in a Christian that the divine measure of justice and equity toward other kinds of blood will suffer."[48] But along with concerns about racial language, the Brüderhof emphasized its Germanness. Unlike some other small Christian minority groups, the Brüderhof was drawing a clear line between, on the one hand, a positive German national identity that they could embrace, and, on the other hand, a dangerous ethnonationalism built on Nazi racial ideology.

NEGOTIATING INTERNATIONAL RELATIONSHIPS

While Germany's Christian minority groups were repositioning themselves in Nazi Germany – articulating their German nationalism (and the limits thereof) and making compromises to preserve their autonomy – they were simultaneously navigating international relationships with co-religionists in the Anglo-American world. Church leaders outside Germany carefully monitored the Church Struggle as it unfolded. They were anxious about the future of the Christian churches and Christianity's ability to influence German society under National Socialism.[49] At times, British and North American churches were concerned about the optics of – and practical implications of – working too closely with Germany.

The Fifth World Congress of the Baptist World Alliance, which took place in Berlin in 1934, was one such instance. The original plans for a Berlin congress in 1933 had been cancelled. But after much debate, as well as pressure from the German government to host the event, and in spite of concerns from non-German Baptists (over antisemitism, censorship, and Nazi domestic policy), the congress did take place in Berlin in 1934. More than 10,000 international delegates attended.[50] Nils Johan Nordström, the

162

Swedish vice-president of the Baptist World Alliance, took the opportunity to make some pointed remarks on nationalism and Baptist identity in his report on the events: "We Baptists are convinced that the Church of Jesus Christ can never be a tool for nationalistic endeavours without losing her power and denying her mission to the world; that any sort of dependency on the State, which restricts her freedom to exercise love in the world, represents a real danger for the church and reduces her opportunities to carry the gospel to the end of the world."[51] Throughout the congress, there was conflict between German Baptists and the international delegates over nationalism and Nazi racial ideology. As Andrea Strübind points out, it was a significant event because it was perhaps the last time until the end of the Second World War that nationalism, racism, and militarism were publicly criticized in Germany before an international audience.[52]

The case of the Salvation Army illustrates how connections to large and respected international organizations could in fact be an asset for minority groups. In 1933, most German Salvationists supported Hitler, but in the same breath, they maintained that it was possible and desirable to sustain their status in the International Salvation Army. But there were also currents of resentment among Salvationists who thought that British influence over their national territories was too strong and autocratic.[53] In 1933, as the Protestant churches were engaged in their own battles, a small number of German Salvationists saw an opportunity to break away from the International Headquarters. The officers involved in the separatist movement were enthusiastic National Socialists and looked to the German Christian Movement for inspiration.[54] These officers saw an opportunity for patronage in the Nazis' plan for a unified Reich Church.[55] Over the summer and fall of 1933, the leader of the separatist movement, Adolph Pahlke, secretly corresponded with Reich Bishop Ludwig Müller, trying to convince him to accept the Heilsarmee into the Reich Church.[56] Despite their efforts to keep the negotiations secret, the separatist movement became known to the Heilsarmee National Headquarters. It was quickly deflated by firing the movement's leaders and reassigning other officers.[57]

It was a good thing the separatists did not succeed, for it was the Heilsarmee's international connections that led to the government's decision to "not interfere" with the organization. As a pre-emptive measure, General Evangeline Booth (the leader of the International Salvation Army in London) sent a telegram to Hitler on 19 October 1934: "Please allow me to express my deepest appreciation and sincere gratitude for your conciliatory attitude toward the Salvation Army in Germany. The only reason for our existence lies in the alleviation of grief and sorrow and in the healing of suffering. I wish that the members of the Salvation Army in Germany both individually and as a whole can participate in the efforts to create a better Germany."[58]

It seems that General Booth's telegram had its desired effect, because shortly after that, Hitler issued a personal directive, sent to Gestapo stations across Germany, that its agents should not interfere with the Heilsarmee. Hitler wrote that he did not oppose the work of the Heilsarmee, "who have never been politically active"; also, "for reasons of foreign policy," no action was to be taken against them.[59] So the Heilsarmee continued to operate in Germany throughout the Nazi period. The Heilsarmee became an approved auxiliary organization of the NSV (National Socialist People's Welfare) and was increasingly called upon to raise money and participate in NSV activities such as Winter Relief. Until the war broke out in September 1939, they continued to have contact with the International Headquarters in London.

International connections also worked to the Quakers' advantage. As mentioned earlier, most German Quakers lost their jobs on political grounds, and the Quaker community experienced hardship under the Nazis. More than twenty German Quakers were arrested and sent to prison or concentration camps. But the Religious Society of Friends was not banned, and overall, the German authorities treated the German Quakers less harshly than other groups, given the extent of their nonconformity and resistance.[60] This mild treatment happened in large part because of the Quakers' overwhelmingly favourable reputation in Germany, due to the *Quakerspeisungen* (meals for German children provided by international Quakers after the First World War).[61] The influential position of the American Friends Service Committee and the British Friends Service Council in the 1930s probably also played a role.

Yet relations between German and non-German Quakers were made difficult at times when foreign Quakers did not understand the severity of everyday life in a dictatorship. Brenda Bailey, whose parents were central figures in the German Quaker community, tells a story about a group of British Quakers who visited Bad Pyrmont, Germany, in the summer of 1939 to attend the annual meeting. After speaking out publicly against antisemitic

Figure 6.1 Front page of the German Salvation Army newspaper,
Der Kriegsruf, 12 September 1936. The photos portray a visit by
a British Salvation Army brass band to Berlin on the occasion of the
fiftieth anniversary of the Salvation Army in Germany, which
happened to coincide with the 1936 Summer Olympics.

comments they had overheard, the young British Friends suggested inviting the Gestapo guard posted at their guesthouse to lunch "to challenge his Nazi beliefs."[62] Another Quaker had to explain discreetly that to do so would ruin the "relaxed atmosphere" they had worked so hard to create and place the non-Aryans among them in danger. The fact was that German Quakers were vulnerable in ways that were difficult for their British friends to recognize.

For religious groups that existed in a nexus of fear of suppression and the exigency of winning converts, it seems that some American church leaders chose to overlook their co-religionists' embrace of National Socialism and instead focus on the opportunities for evangelism and service offered by the regime. The lead-up to the 1936 Olympics illustrates this dynamic. As a public debate unfolded in 1935–36 over whether the United States should boycott the Olympics in protest of Germany's antisemitism and racial discrimination, the issues cut close to home for the Church of Jesus Christ of Latter-day Saints. American Mormon missionaries had brought basketball to Germany, and the game was popular among German Mormons. The 1936 Olympics was the first time that basketball was included as a competitive sport, and when Germany decided to develop a team, they reached out to Mormons for help. On 25 January 1936, the *Deseret News*, an LDS-owned newspaper in Salt Lake City, printed a photo of German Mormons with the basketball team giving the Hitler salute. The accompanying text explained that "in Germany Herr Hitler has sought the services of the Elders to teach basketball to the teams he hopes will achieve a Nordic victory at the Olympic games to be held this year in Berlin."[63] The headline above the photo read, "Two Modern Methods: Sports, Radio," suggesting that the basketball on display was a positive opportunity for proselytizing.[64]

CONCLUSION

By the end of 1938, thirty-nine religious groups had been banned in the German Reich: four in 1933; three in 1934; five in 1935; seven in 1936; thirteen in 1937; and seven in 1938.[65] Most of these groups were very small and obscure; to put these numbers in perspective, the 1925 German census counted 812 religious designations, including 545 Christian groups.[66] Nearly all of the larger and established independent churches remained intact. The Jehovah's Witnesses' collective refusal to compromise on their beliefs had brought

them a different outcome. The Quakers' quiet resistance and good reputation kept them under the Nazis' radar for the most part. Nazi policy toward
religious minorities was arbitrary and flexible, but the government's
surveillance and suppression of some groups reinforced the perception
throughout the Nazi period that these groups were vulnerable. Feelings of
vulnerability and financial insecurity drove the actions of many small
Christian groups, including their efforts to distance themselves from other
groups. The Salvation Army and Religious Society of Friends turned their
international connections into an asset, and the Seventh-day Adventists,
Baptists, and Methodists all curried favour with the Nazi government by
offering pro-Nazi propaganda to their communities abroad. Each of these
Christian groups navigated these years slightly differently. What is clear
from observing them collectively is that national, international, and religious identities were not mutually exclusive.

NOTES

The views expressed here are those of the author and do not represent those
of the United States Holocaust Memorial Museum. The author wishes to
thank Joy Demoskoff and the Mandel Center writing group for their feed-
back on a draft of this essay.

1 For more detailed analysis of Hulda Jost's trip to the United States, see
   Roland Blaich, "Selling Nazi Germany Abroad: The Case of Hulda Jost,"
   Journal of Church and State 35, no. 4 (1993): 807–30.

2 "Hitler Had Enough of War, Asserts German Visitor," *Hartford Courant*,
   6 April 1936; "Meeting Hears Hitler Praised; Fraulein Jost Speaks at Battle
   Creek," *Detroit Free Press*, 11 April 1936; "Germans Want Peace Frau Jost
   Declares," *Capital Journal*, 30 April 1936; "Noted Welfare Worker to Talk at
   Loma Linda," *San Bernardino County Sun*, 5 May 1936.

3 "German Church Emissary Denies Hitler Jew Hater," *Oregon Journal*, 1 May
   1936, Correspondenc. General Conference of the Seventh-day Adventists
   Archives (hereafter, GC), RG 11, box 32, Presidential General Files, 1936 (II)
   Correspondence, Hulda Jost.

4 Kleuser to McElhany, 26 April 1936, GC, RG 11, box 3144, Presidential Files,
   1936 (II), Correspondence, Hulda Jost.

5 The co-option of certain Free Churches with international connections by

the Nazis was first observed by Nathaniel Micklem, principal of Mansfield College, Oxford, and participant in the 1937 Oxford Conference on Church, Community, and State. Nathaniel Micklem, *National Socialism and the Roman Catholic Church 1933–1938* (Oxford: Oxford University Press, 1939), 50–2. On German Methodist propaganda speaking tours in the United States, see Roland Blaich, "A Tale of Two Leaders: German Methodists and the Nazi State," *Church History* 70, no. 2 (2001): 199–225. Other types of transnational exchanges took place between Germany and the United States in the 1930s that served as powerful propaganda tools precisely because they were led by individuals with supposed objectivity and moral currency. See Stephen Norwood, *The Third Reich in the Ivory Tower: Complicity and Conflict on American Campuses* (Cambridge: Cambridge University Press, 2009).

6   Blaich, "A Tale of Two Leaders," 199–225.

7   Historians within the German Free Church traditions have begun to analyze how anti-Jewish elements in their theologies overlapped easily with contemporary racial ideology and Nazi antisemitism, taking on a new resonance after 1933. Daniel Heinz, *Freikirchen und Juden im "Dritten Reich": Instrumentalisierte Heilsgeschichte, Antisemitische Vorurteile und Verdrängte Schuld* (Göttingen: Vanderhoeck & Ruprecht, 2010); Daniel Heinz, "'… Da warst auch du wie einer von ihnen': Freikirchen und Juden im Dritten Reich. Traurige Bilanz und spätes Bekenntnis," *Kirchliche Zeitgeschichte* 30, no. 1 (2017): 175–89.

8   Pierre Sauvage, *Weapons of the Spirit: The Astonishing Story of a Unique Conspiracy of Goodness* (Los Angeles: Chambon Foundation, 2009). See also Philip Paul Hallie, *Lest Innocent Blood Be Shed: The Story of the Village of Le Chambon, and How Goodness Happened There* (New York: Harper & Row, 1979).

9   Robert Braun, *Protectors of Pluralism: Religious Minorities and the Rescue of Jews in the Low Countries during the Holocaust* (Cambridge: Cambridge University Press, 2019).

10 Holly Huffnagle, "Peaceful Coexistence? Jewish and Muslim Neighbors on the Eve of the Holocaust," *East European Jewish Affairs* 45, no. 1 (2015): 42–64.

11 Marianne Ruel Robins has argued that there were many other structural, geographical, and personal factors that explain the actions of the Trocmés and the people on the plateau. Marianne Ruel Robins, "A Grey Site of

Memory: Le Chambon-Sur-Lignon and Protestant Exceptionalism on the Plateau Vivarais-Lignon," *Church History* 82, no. 2 (2013): 317–352.

12 For recent debates about the *Volksgemeinschaft* as an interpretive lens for Nazism, see Martina Steber and Bernhard Gotto, eds. *Visions of Community in Nazi Germany: Social Engineering and Private Lives* (New York: Oxford University Press, 2014); Dietmar von Reeken and Malte Thiessen, eds. *"Volksgemeinschaft" als Soziale Praxis: Neue Forschungen zur NS-Gesellschaft vor Ort* (Paderborn: Ferdinand Schöningh, 2013); and Frank Bajohr and Michael Wildt, eds. *Volksgemeinschaft: Neue Forschungen zur Gesellschaft des Nationalsozialismus* (Frankfurt: Fischer, 2009).

13 Karl Zehrer, *Evangelische Freikirchen und das "Dritte Reich"* (Berlin: Evangelische Verlagsanstalt, 1986), 35–7.

14 James Irvin Lichti, *Houses on the Sand? Pacifist Denominations in Nazi Germany* (New York: Peter Lang, 2008); and Heinz, *Freikirchen und Juden im "Dritten Reich."*

15 Other groups that do not fit into this grouping include the German Lutheran and Reformed Free Churches, Old Catholics, the various Eastern Orthodox churches in Germany, the New Apostolic Church, the Moravian Brethren (Hernhuter or Brüdergemeine), and the Hutterian Brethren (Rhönbruderhof). See Ernst Christian Helmreich, *The German Churches under Hitler: Background, Struggle, and Epilogue* (Detroit: Wayne State University Press, 1979), 89–94; Christine King, *The Nazi State and the New Religions: Five Case Studies in Non-Conformity* (New York: Edwin Mellen Press, 1982); Klaus Schabronat, "Die Neuapostolische Kirche unter der nationalsozialistischen Herrschaft," in *Christen im Dritten Reich*, ed. Philipp Thull (Darmstadt: WBG, 2014); and Marjorie Hindley, "'Unerwünscht': One of the Lesser Known Confrontations with the National Socialist State, 1933–37," *German History* 11, no. 2 (1993): 207–21, here 215.

16 The current member churches of the *Vereinigung Evangelischer Freikirchen* can be found here: https://www.vef.de/wer-wir-sind.

17 Karl Heinz Voigt, *Freikirchen in Deutschland (19. und 20. Jahrhundert)* (Leipzig: Evangelische Verlagsanstalt, 2004).

18 Helmreich, *The German Churches under Hitler*, 25.

19 Ibid., 38. On the Mennonites, see Benjamin Goossen, *Chosen Nation: Mennonites and Germany in a Global Era* (Princeton: Princeton University Press, 2017); Mark Jantzen, *Mennonite German Soldiers: Nation, Religion, and Fam-*

ily in the Prussian East, 1772–1880 (South Bend: University of Notre Dame Press, 2010); and Mark Jantzen and John D. Thiesen, eds., *European Mennonites and the Holocaust* (Toronto: University of Toronto Press, in association with the United States Holocaust Memorial Museum, 2020).

20 Christine R. Barker, "Church and State Relationships in German 'Public Benefit' Law," *International Journal of Not-for-Profit Law* 3, no. 2 (2000), https://www.icnl.org/resources/research/ijnl/church-and-state-relationships-in-german-public-benefit-law.

21 The Salvation Army had begun in Victorian England and had been at work in Germany since 1886. It embraced internationalism yet organized itself along national lines, taking cues from the Red Cross and Protestant missionary endeavours of its day.

22 "Die Heilsarmee," *Vossische Zeitung*, 14 August 1914), Bundesarchiv Berlin (BArch B), R 901 Auswärtiges Amt, Teil: Rechtsabteilung (1885–1945), 39365.

23 Die Heilsarmee, 1905, Landesarchiv Nordrhein-Westfalen (hereafter LA-NRW), BR 0017 Landratsamt Düsseldorf, Abteilung Rheinland, Nr. 276, Überwachung der Tätigkeit der Mormonen und der Heilsarmee, Bd. 1, 1902–1927.

24 Methodists, the Evangelical Association, and the Baptists acquired corporation status by the early 1930s. *Kirchliches Jahrbuch* listed "Other Free Churches," a list that changed from year to year in the 1920s. See *Kirchliches Jahrbuch für die evangelischen Landeskirchen Deutschlands*, vol. 54 (Gütersloh: C. Bertelsmann, 1929).

25 Andrea Strübind, *Die unfreie Freikirche: Der Bund der Baptistengemeinden im "Dritten Reich"* (Neukirchen-Vluyn: Neukirchener, 1991); Karl Heinz Voigt, *Kirchliche Minderheiten im Schatten der lutherischen Reformation vor 1517 bis nach 2017* (Göttingen: Vandenhoeck & Ruprecht, 2018), 291.

26 The Quakers were an outlier in this regard, as many German Quakers had ties to the Social Democratic Party or Communist Party. A high number of them lost their jobs after the civil service laws were introduced in March and April 1933. Hans A. Schmitt, *Quakers & Nazis: Inner Light in Outer Darkness* (Columbia: University of Missouri Press, 1997), 44–7.

27 Andrea Strübind, "German Baptists and National Socialism," *Journal of European Baptist Studies* 8 (2008): 5–20.

28 King, *The Nazi State and the New Religions*, 29–31.

29 James Lichti, "Enjoying the Entitlements of German Freedom: German

Mennonites and Nazi Church–State Policy," in *European Mennonites and the Holocaust*, 108.

30 Blaich, "A Tale of Two Leaders," 201.

31 "Die Lage in der protestantische Kirche und in den verschiedenen Sekten und deren Staatsfiedliche Auswirkung (1935)," BArch B, R 58, Reichsicherheitshauptamt, 233; "Maßnahmen gegen Sekten," BArch B, R 58, 405. See also Mark Roseman, *Lives Reclaimed: A Story of Rescue and Resistance in Germany* (New York: Metropolitan Books, 2019); Peter Staudenmaier, *Between Occultism and Nazism: Anthroposophy and the Politics of Race in the Fascist Era* (Boston: Brill, 2014); King, *The Nazi State and the New Religions*; Johann Neuhäusler, *Kreuz und Hakenkreuz: der Kampf des Nationalsozialismus gegen die katholische Kirche und der kirchliche Widerstand* (Munich: Katholische Kirche Bayerns, 1946); and Wolfgang Dieker, "'Niemals Jesuiten, niemals Sektier.' Die Religionspolitik des SD gegenüber 'Sekten' und völkisch-religiösen Gruppen," in *Die völksich-religiöse Bewegung im Nationalsozialismus. Eine Beziehungs- und Konfliktgeschichte*, eds. Uwe Puschner and Clemens Vollnahs (Göttingen: Vandenhoeck & Ruprecht, 2012), 356–63.

32 Beobachtung der Tätigkeit nichtchristlicher Religionsgemeinschaften und Sekten (Islam, Mennoniten, Bahaismus, Beh'ais, Mazdazan-Bewegung, Methodisten, Buddhismus, Tao Chün (1939–1944), BArch B, R 58, 5633.

33 Andreas Liese, "Weder Baptisten noch Brüder. Die Entstehung des Bundes Evangelisch-Freikirchlicher Gemeinden," *Freikirchenforschung* 18 (2009), 102–29.

34 Johannes Hartlapp, *Siebenten-Tags-Adventisten im Nationalsozialismus: unter Berücksichtigung der geschichtlichen und theologischen Entwicklung in Deutschland von 1875 bis 1950* (Göttingen: Vandenhoeck & Ruprecht, 2008).

35 Compulsory military service was introduced in March 1935. The subsequent Adventist splinter groups that continued to pop up were dissolved and forbidden as well, in April 1937, December 1941, and January 1942. See Helmreich, *The German Churches under Hitler*, 383, 392.

36 For more on individual German Quakers who sheltered Jews, see Schmitt, *Quakers & Nazis*, 187–90.

37 The Righteous Among the Nations online database can be found at https://righteous.yadvashem.org/?/search.html?language=en.

38 Brenda Bailey, *A Quaker Couple in Nazi Germany: Leonhard Friedrich Survives Buchenwald* (York: Sessions, 1994), 41.

39 Terms and Conditions to the General from the German Salvation Army, 9 July 1915, BArch B, R 5101 Reichsministerium für die kirchlichen Angelegenheiten, Verschiedene einzelne Religionsgemeinschaften, Heilsarmee.

40 The German branch of the Salvation Army was not the only one to press for greater independence in this period. There were separatist movements in the 1920s within the Czech, Finnish, and Swiss Salvation Army branches; other national territories such as Sweden and the Netherlands experienced tensions with the London International Headquarters. Karl Ochsner, Hugo Homberger, and Paul Schiffman, *Die schweizerische Reformbewegung in der Heilsarmee 1926–1930* (St Gallen: self-published pamphlet, 1930), Evangelisches Zentralarchiv (hereafter EZA), 1 Kirchenkanzlei der Deutschen Evangelischen Kirche, 2975.

41 "Herzlich willkommen in Deutschland! Kommandeur und Frau Howard die neuen Leiter der Heilsarmee in Deutschland und Österreich," *Der Kriegsruf*, 14 January 1933, 1. He was a highly experienced leader in the Salvation Army, with more than forty-five years of experience, including leadership positions in Denmark, Sweden, Finland, the Netherlands, and Switzerland.

42 Monatsbrief des Kommandeurs (Howard), December 1933, Historisches Archiv der Heilsarmee, Internal Documents.

43 In 1933 the LDS church also appointed native Germans to leadership positions that were previously held by American Mormons. David Conley Nelson, *Moroni and the Swastika: Mormons in Nazi Germany* (Normon: University of Oklahoma Press, 2015), 100–1.

44 Detlef Garbe, *Between Resistance and Martyrdom: Jehovah's Witnesses in the Third Reich*, trans, Dagmar G. Grimm (Madison: University of Wisconsin Press, in association with the United States Holocaust Memorial Museum, 2008), 87. See also Jolene Chu, "God's Things and Caesar's: Jehovah's Witnesses and Political Neutrality," *Journal of Genocide Research* 6, no. 3 (2004): 319–42.

45 *Jahrbuch der Zeugen Jehovas* (Bern: Wachtturm Bibel- und Traktat-Gesellschaft, Volkskanzel-Vereinigung, Internationale Bibelforscher-Vereinigung, 1934), 134, cited in Garbe, *Between Resistance and Martyrdom*, 89.

46 Hartlapp, *Siebenten-Tags-Adventisten im Nationalsozialismus*, 265.

47 Lichti, *Houses on the Sand?*, 125.

48 Hindley, "'Unerwünscht,'" 215. See also Astrid von Schlachta, *From the Tyrol to North America: The Hutterite Story through the Centuries* (Kitchener: Pandora Press, 2008); and Astrid von Schlachta, *Täufergemeinschaften: Die Hutterer* (Mainz: Institut für Europäische Geschichte [IEG], 2011), http://ieg-ego.eu/de/threads/europaeische-netzwerke/christliche-netzw erke/astrid-von-schlachta-taeufergemeinschaften-die-hutterer.

49 Henry Leiper, in his 1933 pamphlet, *Personal View of the German Churches under the Revolution*, based on his travels in Germany in 1932–33, makes an effort to bring clarity and objectivity to the situation in Germany for an English-reading audience. Carl and Robert Gamer Papers, United States Holocaust Memorial Museum Archives. See also Victoria J. Barnett, "Track Two Diplomacy, 1933–1939," *Kirchliche Zeitgeschichte* 27, no. 1 (2014), 76–86.

50 For a detailed discussion of the Fifth World Congress, see Lee B. Spitzer, *Baptists, Jews, and the Holocaust: The Hand of Sincere Friendship* (Valley Forge: Judson Press, 2017), 398–411.

51 Strübind, "German Baptists and National Socialism."

52 Ibid.

53 Die schweizerische Reformbewegung in der Heilsarmee, 1926–1930, EZA/1/2975.

54 "Luther über Regierung und Volk," *Der Kriegsruf*, 18 November 1933, 2.

55 Doris Bergen, *Twisted Cross: The German Christian Movement in the Third Reich* (Chapel Hill: University of North Carolina Press, 1996).

56 This correspondence is found in the files at the EZA/1/2975.

57 Stankuweit to Pahlke, 28 September 1933, and Pahlke to Stankuweit, 29 September 1933, EZA/1/2975 "Reorganisation unseres Werkes," *Der Kriegsruf*, 14 October 1933), 3; "Reorganisation," *Der Kriegsruf*, 28 October 1933), 3; and "Die Einteilung unserer neuen Bezirke," *Der Kriegsruf*, 6 January 1934, 3.

58 Memo to the Foreign Office, Reich Ministry of the Interior and the Labour Ministry, BArch B, R 3901 Reichsarbeitsministerium, 9117 Die Heilsarmee, Berlin. This telegram is also found in files at the Reich Chancellery, BArch B, R 43 Reichskanzlei, II/179 Sonstige Bekenntnisse.

59 Memo to all Gestapo, 8 December 1934, Historisches Archiv der Heilsarmee, General Correspondence. This same memo can also be found in Gestapo records in several jurisdictions in Germany. See, for example: LA-NRW, RW 18, Nr. 2 Geheimes Staatspolizeiamt Berlin; and Kreisarchiv Göppingen

(hereafter: StA-G), C 3 Landratsamt Göppingen, Hauptverwaltung, Kultur. See also "Der Wille des Führers," *Der Lokaloffizier* (November 1934), 336.

60 Anna Sabine Halle, "The German Quakers and the Third Reich," *German History* 11, no. 2 (1993): 222–36; and University of Southern California Shoah Foundation, Visual History Archive, interview with Brenda Bailey, 21 May 1998.

61 Schmitt, *Quakers & Nazis*, 54.

62 Bailey, *A Quaker Couple in Nazi Germany*, 103.

63 As quoted in Nelson, *Moroni and the Swastika*, 116.

64 Nelson, *Moroni and the Swastika*, 146.

65 List of banned sectarian groups, BArch B, R58, 405 Maßnahmen gegen Sekten.

66 *Kirchliches Jahrbuch*, vol. 54.

7

"Often you end up asking yourself, could there be a great secret group of Jews behind it all." – Antisemitism in the Finnish Lutheran Church after the First World War

Paavo Ahonen and Kirsi Stjerna

Antisemitism in Finland during the First and Second World Wars is a sensitive and relatively unexplored topic. Historians have focused on the sacrifice of those Finns who enabled their country to rise as a free nation, against all the odds, after years of war and occupation. Over the past century, such narratives have contributed to the creation of a positive national identity and ethos among the Finnish people. Yet the heroic story of Finns defending their freedom is part of a larger narrative that involves Europe's major players and conflicts during the First and Second World Wars. During those decades, the rhetoric of antisemitism could be found in all European countries, and Finland was not immune. In particular, the Lutheran Church in Finland inadvertently propagated that hatred through the publications of some of its clergymen after the First World War.

Since the Reformation, Finland has been predominantly a Lutheran country. Over the centuries, Reformation theology derived from Martin Luther (1483–1546) has shaped Finnish legislation. This theology promotes equality of all human beings, recognizing that all of us are in similar bondage to sin and receive salvation through faith.[1] Modern-day Finland is often viewed as one of the "happy" welfare nations of the world, one whose government meets the basic needs of all its citizens and where equality and freedom are cherished. Government legislation has implemented positive Lutheran values to benefit all citizens. Politically, Finland is a neutral zone; it works to build trust and alliances between East and West, standing for the freedom of all the world's peoples.

The First and Second World Wars had a monumental impact on the Finns and their future. When the First World War broke out, Finland had been an autonomous Grand Duchy of Russia for more than a hundred years. The level of autonomy it enjoyed was dependent on the policy of the Emperor in power. At the Diet of Porvoo, after Sweden lost Finland to Russia in the Finnish War (1808–09), the Finnish Estates gave an oath of loyalty to Tsar Alexander I, and in return, he declared, "Finland has been raised to the status of a nation among nations." Russia allowed Finland to keep its own laws, official language (Swedish), and religion (Lutheranism). During the nineteenth century, the tsars also granted Finland its own currency, customs agency, and postal services.

The strengthening of the Finnish language and culture also heightened Finnish nationalism. Russia's defeat in the First World War created an opening, and the Finns seized it, declaring their independence on 6 December 1917. But a few weeks later, civil war shattered the hope that an autonomous nation would be born peacefully. With the intervention of German forces, a communist takeover was avoided. Still, an anti-communist atmosphere lingered, creating tension between Finland and Soviet Russia that would last for decades. Eventually, fear of the Soviets became a reality when tensions led to armed conflict between the Finns and the Soviets, first in the Winter War (1939–40) and then in the Continuation War (1941–44). During the latter war, the Finns fought the Soviets alongside Germans in an alliance that was broken in the Lapland War (1944–45), during which the Germans scorched the northernmost part of Finland. In the post–Second World War years, Finnish historians neglected to address the significance of the Finnish–German alliance and, consequently, the impact of antisemitism on Finnish society. More recently, a few scholars have begun to question the idea of Finland's exceptionality during the Second World War and revealed the presence of antisemitism in Finnish society and the participation of Finns in the Holocaust.[2]

Antisemitism in Finland evolved from a variety of complex but intertwined factors. Most significantly, Finland's geographic proximity to the much larger Russia instilled a culture of fear of neighbour. Russia's violent revolution of 1917 added fuel to Finns' fears of Bolshevism and a possible communist takeover. As a result, some Finns came to see Jews as villains in Bolshevik Russia. Also, during their first years of freedom, Finns found themselves having to choose ideological sides during a bloody civil war between the pro-communist Reds and the White Finns. The Whites won, thus preserving Finland's independence from Russian and particularly Bolshevik agendas. It is unclear to what extent the White Finns had embraced antisemitism; however, there is significant evidence of explicit antisemitism in anti-Bolshevist speculations of the time regarding Russians Jews' involvement in secret plots and revolutionary activities. In the religious realm, several Finnish Lutheran bishops and pastors, some of whom were also active in academia and politics (generally speaking, during those years the clergy held an esteemed position in the society), targeted Jews in their writings and sermons.[3]

While it remains unclear to what extent Finnish religious leaders and teachers conceived of Jews as both a political and religious threat, we can say that the deep roots of Christian antisemitism shaped the thinking of these individuals. Scholars have identified traces of antisemitism in political and religious discourse, but beyond these vestiges, there is little clarity on the issue. The "Jewish question" that took on so much resonance across Europe in the nineteenth century was a theoretical one in Finland, given that there were (and still are) few Jews in Finnish society. But this does not mean that Finns were free of antisemitism, which is not based on fact or experience and can be felt, transmitted, and applied in multiple ways. More research is needed to illuminate the Finnish context and to gain further clarity on the larger question of antisemitism's expression and means of transmission, be it explicit or implicit, detected or not.

This chapter examines the religious views about Jews published by Lutheran clergy after the First World War in Finland. It offers a case study in how a national identity develops and reacts to a volatile political situation, as well as how antisemitism can become a factor in drawing boundaries and naming a nation's enemies. The period is significant for Finnish history in terms of identifying the seeds of antisemitism that were sown in Finland before the Holocaust. The aim is to provide an analysis that will help us understand the phenomenon of spreading antisemitism via religious publications in a context in which explicit antisemitic ideologies could become part of political decision-making, even when not necessarily expressed or recognized in everyday discourse. The chapter first discusses the historical status of Jews in Finland and then examines the expressions of antisemitism by prominent Finnish Lutheran Church leaders in the two decades before the Second World War. It then offers some observations on the importance of mapping the tracks of antisemitism in religious discourse and how those tracks can lead to political decision-making and hate crimes, in Finland and beyond. Finally, it reflects on the significance of Martin Luther's theology in the eruption of antisemitism among the Finnish clergy and the use of the word "Lutheran" in this regard.

THE CIVIL RIGHTS STRUGGLE OF THE JEWS IN FINLAND

Compared to other Scandinavian countries, the first Jews settled in Finland relatively late, and their history is different from that of other Scandinavian Jews. Until 1809, Finland was ruled by the Kingdom of Sweden. Swedish laws were strict, mandating that Jews could live in only three cities, none of them in Finland.[4] The situation remained the same after Finland became an autonomous part of the Russian empire, which allowed the Grand Duchy of Finland to maintain its existing legal system and laws. Before the 1850s, the only Jews in Finland would have been visitors or converts to Christianity. The exception was a group of Jewish teenagers that the Imperial Russian army had drafted and sent to "canton schools." After completing their education, the Russian army compelled them to serve twenty-five years in the military, and a few of them were assigned to garrisons in Finland. In 1858, Tsar Alexander II (1818–1881) offered these soldiers, after their discharge from the army, an opportunity to settle in the cities where they had been stationed. These soldiers and their families were Finland's first Jews.[5]

By the early 1870s, the number of Jews in Finland had risen to about five hundred, an increase that alarmed several members of Parliament, who raised the question of their legal status. The debate over the civil rights of Jews in Finland began at a time when most European countries had already granted Jews emancipation.[6] By then, political antisemitism was beginning to spread across Europe, and it became a factor in the debate on the place of Jews in Finnish society. Finnish antisemites feared that giving Jews equal rights would lead to Jewish domination in business and the spread of liberal, anti-Christian ideas. From the late nineteenth century on, blatant antisemitism was present in Finnish parliamentary debates, and this hatred led the Diet of Finland to reject all proposals to grant civil rights to Jews.[7] For the next twenty years, the Diet refused to pass any legislation that would advance the status of Jews. Finally, in 1897, the Diet was ready to grant civil rights to them, but that legislation soon vanished into the Russian bureaucracy. In 1908, the new unicameral parliament of Finland attempted again to alter the situation, but the outcome was the same: the Russian bureaucracy quashed this effort. The civil rights struggle of Finnish Jews would not end until Finland declared its independence from Russia in December 1917.[8]

THE LUTHERAN CHURCH AND THE BEGINNING OF FINLAND'S INDEPENDENCE

In 1917, when Finland became independent, the Evangelical Lutheran Church of Finland was a conservative organization led by aging men, who focused on "spiritual work" in accordance with their interpretation of Luther's teaching, which distinguished between the spiritual and political realms and uses of power. The Church of Finland consisted of four dioceses, and the four bishops who led them had all held their seats for more than fifteen years. The head of the Finnish Church was Gustaf Johansson (1844–1930), archbishop for over thirty years (1899–1930), a strong leader with significant political authority.[9] Johansson had a conservative mindset, and like many Finnish churchmen of his time, he was theologically influenced by Tobias Beck, Professor of Systematic Theology at the University of Tübingen, and his so-called biblical theology. Conservative "biblicism" was the dominant theological orientation within Finnish Lutheranism toward the end of the nineteenth century. As a result, the church was slow to react to modern times and to respond positively to societal questions, such as the plight of the working class.[10]

At the beginning of the twentieth century, a new generation of Finnish priests and theologians called for the church to take a more active role in society, as the Lutheran churches in Sweden and Denmark had done. Thus, during the first years of Finland's independence, one can distinguish between two separate groups of Finnish churchmen, linked respectively to two prominent newspapers. The "Turku group" formed around Archbishop Johansson and aligned itself with the newspaper *Herättäjä* (Awakener), while the "Helsinki group," a faction of prominent university theologians and younger priests, sought ways for the church to become a folk church – that is, to participate actively in national life and treat its members with less authoritarianism. The latter group's unofficial organ was *Kotimaa* (Homeland), a Lutheran newspaper that also addressed societal questions. During the 1910s, *Kotimaa* evolved into the unofficial voice of the Lutheran Church, while *Herättäjä* embraced the role of opposition to any changes within Finnish Lutheranism.[11]

In the Diet of the Grand Duchy of Finland, Lutheran clergy played a key role in the Jews' struggle for civil rights (the clergy were an official estate within the Diet). Initially, the Clergy Estate was divided over the question of Jewish emancipation. Those who supported it incorporated Christian and universal humanitarian arguments into their views. Among these individuals was Gustaf Johansson, bishop of Kuopio at that time, who outspokenly encouraged his fellow estate clergymen to support extending legal status to Jews. He declared that the government must consider Jews as guests and legally protect them, specifically in gratitude for giving the world the Messiah. At the same time, he argued that the government must regulate Jews' legal status so that they would have no opportunity to oppress the Finnish people. Johansson's thoughts represented the opinion of many of the "pro-Jewish" members of the Clergy Estate.[12]

Not all members of the clergy supported Jewish emancipation. Since the 1880s, antisemitic ideas disseminated by German politicians and academics, such as the politician Adolf Stöcker and the historian Heinrich von Treitschke, had been making their way to Finland, where they now began to influence the parliamentary debate about Jews. The Clergy Estate's opposition was intense, escalating to the point that some individuals demanded the deportation of all Jews from Finland. One proposal advocated offering Jews a "moving aid" (bribe) to leave Finland.[13]

The parliamentary debate continued on and off for almost fifty years. Meanwhile, the Finish government permitted Jews to reside in only few cities and to engage in only a handful of commercial activities, such as trading in second-hand clothing. During this time, there were at least two mass deportations of Jews.[14] Notwithstanding these difficult realities, Jews were able to practise their religion and live relatively peaceful lives. One cannot say the same about their counterparts in Russia, who suffered through waves of pogroms between 1881 and 1906.[15]

JEWS ACCUSED OF SPECULATION

The Finnish government granted the Jews in Finland emancipation at an economically difficult time. The First World War had created a large market for Finnish goods in wartime Russia, but the economic situation quickly changed after the Russian Revolution and the Finnish Civil War. Those two conflicts led to a shortage of food and other goods. Soon, almost all the Finnish national newspapers began to accuse Jews of exploiting the economic situation by smuggling fabrics, shoes, and soap, avoiding taxes, and speculating in currency and gold. Not all of these accusations were false; in the early 1920s, the Finnish authorities deported several Jews who had lived in Finland for only a short time for illegal speculation.[16] Antisemites exploited the situation, accusing the Jews as a group of committing crimes that had been perpetrated by only a small number of people.[17] Naturally, Finland's Jews were worried by these allegations. In February 1920, Salomon Mattsoff (1883–1929) and Israel-Jacob Schur (1879–1949), representatives of the Jewish congregation of Helsinki, wrote a letter to the newspaper *Hufvud-stadsbladet* in which they agreed that every Jew found guilty by a court should be punished according to the rule of law. They also concurred that the public had the right to be informed of the names of the convicted and their corresponding crimes. But they insisted that no one should condemn all Jews living in Finland for a crime committed only by one individual.[18]

The Lutheran Church's press eagerly took up these accusations. Between 1919 and 1921, it published a series of articles on individual cases of speculation, involving a limited number of Jews. These articles covered actual cases. However, the largest circulating ecclesiastical newspaper, *Kotimaa*, published more generalized and inflammatory articles about the role of Jews in the Finnish economy. Two of the more notorious authors of these incendiary articles were Verneri Louhivuori (1884–1980), a long-time assistant editor of *Kotimaa*, and Antti J. Pietilä (1878–1932), a professor of dogmatics at the University of Helsinki.[19] Both writers were obsessed with the notion that Jews were gaining influence through the trading of goods and the acquisition of real estate.

Louhivuori contended that although it was not possible to build an economic system based on Christianity, certain Christian values such as honesty, fairness, and unselfishness were righteous principles that were also applicable to trade and commerce. Resorting to both Christian antisemitism and pro-nationalist arguments, Louhivuori had convinced himself that Jews did not share these values. For him, the future of Finland would be grim if Jews were allowed to operate unchallenged in Christian society:

> One cannot deny that if we talk about the vicious ruthlessness of capitalism or socialist-Bolshevism, the frontrunners are always the Jews. In our country, too, there have been business cases that have attracted painful attention and foreshadowed evil. We do not want to wash away the guilt of our citizens at the expense of the Jews, but in all seriousness, one must pay attention to the fact that the ruthlessness of Jewish business morals is a daunting threat to our nation. And one must stand up against it with all his might.[20]

It is not clear what Louhivuori meant by "with all his might." He did not say. In any case, it was clear to him that Finland needed to adopt some countermeasures to deal with Jews.

Antti J. Pietilä held similar views on the Jewish question. In his mind, Jews had been able to infiltrate Finnish business by both legal and illegal means. According to Pietilä, a common perception was that the desire to succeed in business was part of a natural struggle in which the more capable party would prevail. Unfortunately, in Pietilä's opinion, the situation with Jews was not as simple because they were an exception – they did not have a national home, a country of their own:

> Every nation has its homeland to which it is bound by thousands of ties, and from which individuals leave only in exceptional situations to

seek happiness elsewhere, but the international Jew is always ready to sniff-out those regions instinctively, looking for an opportunity to rise above the surface, and to flood them in an endless stream. They "force themselves to the top," regardless of consequences, collecting property, gaining influence, filling the boulevards, restaurants, and places of pleasure and bathing with their exorbitantly demanding personalities, but do not feel themselves citizens of any country; instead, they are what they are – international Jews.[21]

Pietilä held the common nationalist belief that certain groups or races belonged to particular nation-states and were linked by national feelings – in other words, by something the Jews were lacking.[22] According to him, Jews were the coldest and the most calculating people in the world, who served their country of residence only to the minimum required by law. They worked only to benefit themselves and their race, and thus their goals were not in the interest of Finland or any other country. Nevertheless, Pietilä did not demand any actions against the Jews or the withdrawal of their civil rights. Instead, Finnish society needed to teach Jews reciprocity; if the law protected them, it could also severely punish them if they broke it. Finns, for their part, required a strong and incorruptible sense of nationalism to deal with Jews. Pietilä thought that this kind of Finnish national self-awareness would prevent Jews from acquiring possessions through intermediaries and would give Jews a lesson on fairness and civic responsibility.[23]

By the mid-1920s, the negative writings about Jews and speculations had ceased as the economic situation stabilized. Still, the existing texts fortified a negative image of Jews after the First World War. Of all the ecclesiastical newspapers, *Kotimaa* was the most active in publishing antisemitic articles, and in doing so, it presented these words as the unofficial "voice of the Church." The articles it published indicate that, even though most Finnish politicians had supported Jewish emancipation for many years, antisemites were endeavouring to curtail the rights and freedoms of Finnish Jews, especially in the years following emancipation. Antisemites like Louhivuori and Pietilä were always ready to stereotype Jews as disloyal citizens ready to exploit their countrymen.

THE JUDEO-BOLSHEVIST STEREOTYPE

At the turn of the twentieth century, antisemites had connected conspiracy theories about Jews mostly to local issues. Gradually, this began to change as global theories emerged. After the Russian Revolution, rumours of a close relationship between the Bolshevist movement and Judaism spread in Russia and neighbouring countries. In the summer of 1917, months before the October Revolution, some anti-communist officers of the Russian Army and officials of the Russian Provisional Government led by Alexander Kerensky (1881–1970) began spreading these false rumours and distributing lists of revolutionaries who had Jewish or otherwise foreign-sounding names. Within a few months, the suspicion arose that the Bolshevik leaders were part of a German-Judeo conspiracy against Russia. This came to be combined with the wartime stereotype of the leftist revolutionary Jew, which had its roots in the late nineteenth century. By 1918, these rumours had developed into the prevalent view that Jews were behind the Bolshevik Revolution.[24]

The Judeo-Bolshevist conspiracy theory was both antisemitic and anti-communist in its ideological background. For many Finnish churchmen, the rise of Bolshevism in the autumn of 1917 was a horrifying development. The Bolshevists were communists, the worst kind of anti-religious socialists, and many Finnish clergymen had been opposed to them long before the Finnish working class had adopted socialism. Finnish Lutheran priests had long regarded socialism as a Jewish movement, identifying Karl Marx as a Jew and stamping socialism as an anti-Christian movement. In January 1918, when the political situation in Finland escalated into civil war, all forms of anti-communism gained unreserved support among the Whites, that is, the troops supporting the Finnish government and constitutional rule against a communist revolution and the Reds. So it is very likely that the Judeo-Bolshevist stereotype spread in Finland with the help of anti-communist voices.[25]

When discussing the battles of the First World War, the church newspapers included articles on Jewish soldiers on both sides of the front line, as well as stories on civilian suffering, persecution, and pogroms. But this unbiased reporting lasted only a brief time; soon, articles began to portray Jews as leading revolutions in Germany, Hungary, and Russia. By 1919, *Kotimaa* was reporting that the status of Jews "had become clear," for it now knew that "the majority of the current leaders and initiators of great social movements are Jews." Both theorists behind socialism, Karl Marx, the philosopher, and Ferdinand Lassalle, the founder of the General German Workers' Association, were considered Jews, as were Bolshevist leaders, including Lenin and Trotsky.[26] The church newspapers also reported on the Hungarian Revolution and the four-month reign of Béla Kun, whom they called "a Jewish Tyrant" and "the Hungarian Lenin."[27]

In the early 1920s, Bolshevism was a topic in almost every issue of the church newspapers. Though Jews appeared in only some of these articles, they were regularly portrayed negatively. The articles claimed that Jews had benefited from the Russian Revolution and blamed them for the abusive, anti-Christian Soviet policy and actions against the church. A few articles divided the Russian Jews into an arrogant Bolshevist elite and an unfortunate poor class who had to answer for the bitterness that was growing among the people. This outlook became more common when news about the growing persecution of Russian Jews spread to Finland. After 1922, ecclesiastical newspapers linked Bolshevists with Jews less often.[28]

Eyewitness testimonies of events in Bolshevist Russia, most importantly the ones reported by Lutheran priests who had worked among the Ingrian Finns, heightened Finnish anti-communism. These priests had fled from Ingria, an area around St Petersburg populated by Finno-Ugric people, whose antisemitism had been influenced by Russian anti-Jewish propaganda. Their immigration to Finland introduced new elements to the existing Finnish antisemitism.[29]

Many of these stories shared similar patterns. Even the first refugee, Nils Artur Malin (1871–1939), the vicar of the Swedish Congregation of St Petersburg, described the leaders of the Russian Revolution as Jews. In the summer of 1918, Malin fled Russia. The following year, he published *What Is Bolshevism?*, a pamphlet written for the Finnish Red prisoners.[30] Malin wrote only a few sentences about Jews, but those were negative, emphasizing that Jews had a "special ability to avoid real work, to live at the expense of others by cheating them." In his view, Bolshevist leaders resembled Finnish communists and only engaged in self-serving endeavours while in Russia.[31]

By the time Vicar Eevertti Pärnänen, the last priest to leave Ingria, came to Finland, he had been influenced by a broader spectrum of antisemitic propaganda.[32] After settling in Finland, Pärnänen gave several public presentations on Bolshevism, later compiling these into a book, *Bolsheviks: Observations and Thoughts of an Eyewitness*, published in 1922.[33]

Although he focused his book primarily on Russia and the Russians, he reserved ten of its 120 pages for a discussion about Jews. Pärnänen regarded the unwillingness to cultivate the land and to work hard as a special Jewish feature. For him, that was why Jews were always seeking opportunities to succeed in the fields of business and culture, favouring trade, industry, finance, and the professions (i.e., professor, doctor, lawyer, engineer). He argued that by acting ruthlessly in these professions, Jews had an opportunity to make substantial profits and gain power.[34]

Almost half the world's Jews lived in tsarist Russia, where they were oppressed. After the revolution, Jews took up administrative posts at various state and local levels. According to Pärnänen, international Jewry was masterminding the global Bolshevist revolutionary movement. Jewish capitalists and Jewish revolutionaries might be acting separately, but they used the same means and masked their true purposes. Pärnänen claimed that the revolutionary Jew hid behind the poor in just the same way that capitalists hid behind nationalistic ideas. Yet both had the same goal: Jewish world domination.[35]

Pärnänen's book was the most widely read antisemitic eyewitness testimony in Finland. It was also the last such book to be published without criticism.[36] In addition to Church's publicity for the book, the publisher, wsoy, worked with representatives of patriotic organizations to disseminate it as a part of the "mental work of national defence," seeing it as a tool in the fight against communism. As a result, Pärnänen's antisemitic views reached a broad audience for many years.[37]

The writings of the priests who had fled to Finland served as one avenue for antisemitism to influence the Finnish Lutheran Church and, in turn, Finnish society. The spread of antisemitism was not the main goal of these works; even so, they reinforced a negative image of Jews, portraying them as central agents in the Russian Revolution. Such images had a lasting impact on Finnish society, and this allowed the Judeo-Bolshevist stereotype to became the most persistent antisemitic view in Finland until the mid-1940s.

REJECTED AND ACCEPTED ANTISEMITISM:
THE WRITINGS OF J.W. WARTIAINEN AND
ERKKI KAILA

Erkki Kaila, the vicar of the congregation of Northern Helsinki, and Johan Wilhelm Wartiainen, the vicar of Sauvo, were two Finnish priests who had an exceptionally compelling interest in ideas related to the Jews. A comparison of their writings enables one to glean the diversity within Finnish antisemitism. These clerics represented the existing factions within the Church. Wartiainen was close to the conservative "Turku group," while Erkki Kaila was one of the most prominent priests of the more progressive "Helsinki group." In the early 1920s, each wrote a book about Jews. These two books are significant because one was praised both within and outside the Church, while the other was widely condemned as a product of antisemitic hatred.[38]

J.W. Wartiainen most likely encountered the "Jewish question" during a study visit to Germany in 1894, after which he wrote about the danger posed by Jews if they were ever emancipated. Previous Finnish studies of antisemitism have presented a one-dimensional image of Wartiainen. Although he was probably the most active and relentless Finnish antisemite, he was not simply a narrow-minded fanatic; he was also a progressive thinker who had considered views on many social issues, such as temperance.[39] Nevertheless, scholars have remembered Wartiainen largely for his 1922 book, *The Significance of the Jews in the Scope of World History, as the People of God in the Past and as Flock of Satan Today*. It is a comprehensive work that merges biblical Christian anti-Judaism with modern antisemitism.[40]

According to Wartiainen, the history of humankind was an ongoing struggle between good and evil, between the kingdom of God and the kingdom of Satan. Because humanity was unable to resist evil, one tribe had to be chosen to represent the kingdom of God and to bless the rest of humanity. This chosen tribe was the family of Abraham, a tribe whose hereditary qualities of strong faith in one God, of obedience to God's commandments, of love for one's race, and of a relentless will to seek the kingdom of God, made it an exceptional choice for the gift of salvation.[41]

Unfortunately, this tribe also inherited Abraham's poor qualities, which appeared in his grandson, Jacob, such as "guile, deceit, greed, and cunning calculation." According to Wartiainen, these bad characteristics corrupted

J. W. W.

JUUTALAISTEN

MAAILMANHISTORIALLINEN
MERKITYS ENTISAIKAAN JU-
MALAN KANSANA JA NYKYÄÄN

SAATANAN JOUKKONA

Figure 7.1 The cover of *The Significance of the Jews in the Scope of World History, as the People of God in the Past and as Flock of Satan Today* by J.W. Wartiainen, the most infamous antisemitic book written by a Finnish priest. The caricature of Josef Trotsky on the cover was drawn by Otto von Kursell (1884–1967) and was originally published in an antisemitic booklet titled *Totengräber Russlands* (Russian Gravediggers) in 1921.

everything positive left in Jews, so that they turned from a blessing for humanity into a curse. Israel could have fulfilled its world-historical mission by observing the law of Moses, but the Jews rejected it, misinterpreted the prophecy about the Messiah, and began to seek a secular kingdom and world domination. In turn, the synagogue began to teach Pharisaical self-righteousness, pride, and greed. Its spiritual leaders taught a distorted picture of the Messiah so that Jews were unable to recognize Jesus and instead chose to crucify him and to turn toward Satan. Wartiainen declared, "the Jews had been transformed from the people of God to the synagogue of Satan."[42]

He portrayed "a time of degradation," beginning with the destruction of the Temple, after which Jews were expatriated and confronted with hatred and contempt everywhere they attempted to settle. Out of this seed of hatred grew the Talmud, a collection of Jewish wisdom that cherished a vision of Jewish world domination and the idea of the Jewish people's unique position before God. "Immense national pride ... callousness and contempt for other peoples ... [and a] fierce and immutable hatred of Christ" became part of the Talmudic legacy shared by all Jews, even those who no longer believed in God.[43]

Wartiainen was convinced that Jews sought world domination, built upon the ruins of Christian states through the three Jewish ideologies of liberalism, socialism, and communism. In his view, liberalism represented false ideas spread by the Jewish press and literature, which negatively affected the economy, social order, love life, national education, and religion. Despite the greatest efforts by Jews, this negative doctrine could not reach the masses, who held hatred for the rich. Therefore, the Jews had to create socialist doctrines. Karl Marx, a Jew, took up this theoretical task. According to Wartiainen, Marx's most important idea was "hatred against Christ and all Christianity." Socialism aided the Jews, but world domination through communism demanded a violent revolution to dismantle Christians' power. Although Jews were rich, communism did not turn against them because they controlled the socialist *and* communist movements. Jews could stay behind the scenes and move Christians like chess pieces. For Wartiainen, this had already happened in Russia, where, following the bloody Revolution, Jews could implement their ultimate goal, which was to usher in the reign of the Antichrist.[44]

Wartiainen's views combined late-nineteenth- and early-twentieth-century antisemitism with his conception of Judaism and Christian eschatology. But he faced a problem: he could not demonstrate what kind of harm the Jews had caused Finland. He could only assure his readers that the threat was real; after all, domestic newspapers had been following Jewish-liberal trends for years, and literature replicated the ideas of Jews like Georg Brandes,[45] resulting in the spreading of hatred of Christ in Finnish society.[46]

Every historical study of this era has portrayed Wartiainen's book as an example of radical Finnish antisemitism. Even so, it has long been viewed as having had marginal impact, given that it was negatively reviewed in most ecclesiastical newspapers. However, with further archival research, it is now possible to trace the history of the book quite accurately. His correspondence with his publisher reveals that its publication was supported by twenty-nine Turku diocesan priests, who officially committed themselves to the dissemination of this "important" and "modern" book. There is no data on its sales, but judging from the efforts of the twenty-nine clergymen, it seems that its impact was far from marginal. For example, in the 1930s the book received repeated notices in radical right-wing magazines – an indication of its long-lasting impact.[47]

Scholars have compared Wartianinen's book to the *Protocols of the Elders of Zion* and have suspected that it was influenced by the Finnish translation of the *Protocols* two years earlier. The newspaper *Kotimaa* lumped his book together with similar antisemitic literature "as the piece of junk by some pseudonym Nilus."[48] Of course, Wartiainen must have read the *Protocols*, and there are a few similarities, especially related to claims about Jewish world domination. However, there are also significant differences. Wartiainen claims that the Jews are preparing the kingdom of the Antichrist, but there is no mention of the Antichrist in the version of the *Protocols* published in Finland. Wartiainen does not write about Freemasonry, gold, or complex structures of international finance, all of which are key elements of the *Protocols*. Instead, he limits his comments primarily to religious matters and salvation history. The main difference relates to Wartiainen's prediction that the Jews will turn to Christ before the end times.[49] Moreover, the theme of salvation is missing from the *Protocols*, though it does incorporate religious concepts such as the chosen people. Perhaps the most significant link between the *Protocols* and Wartiainen's book has to do with their reception; the general public condemned both books, and in the end, works like these may have had the opposite of their intended effect by encouraging the rejection of antisemitism in Finland.[50]

What kind of antisemitism could have *increased* anti-Jewish sentiment in Finland? To answer this question, we must turn to the writings of Erkki Kaila, the nephew of conservative archbishop Gustaf Johansson. Kaila belonged to a younger generation of theologians, who envisioned the Church taking a more active role in Finnish society. In addition to his career in the Lutheran Church, Kaila served as a member of Parliament (for the National Coalition Party) between 1917 and 1927 and was Acting Professor of Practical Theology at the University of Helsinki for several years.[51] Kaila was a well-educated priest who read widely, following international events and intellectual currents in Finnish and other Nordic journals, as well as those in German and English. Kaila held a Janus-faced attitude toward the Jews: in relation to Bolshevism or international finances, he had a negative perception of them. Yet he also sympathized with them for the persecution they faced, and he greatly respected some Jewish individuals. Scholars have described his character as "intellectually curious," and the confusing overall postwar situation in Europe offered him more than enough material to ponder.

Kaila was perhaps the first Finnish priest to notice the number of Jews among the leaders of the Russian Revolution. In his diary in the spring of 1918, less than half a year after the revolution, he wrote a list of Russian revolutionary leaders whom he believed had Jewish names. He titled this entry, "Jews, etc. in the Russian leadership," and added at the end, "Higher Nemesis!"[52] Gradually, he began to suspect that there could be a large-scale Jewish conspiracy. After hearing the news about the strikes in the Ruhr region in Germany, he shared his suspicions in his diary entry of April 1920:

> Jews now play a large role in every country. Often you end up asking yourself, could there be a large secret Jewish group behind it all. They have led, again, the coal-mining strikes in the Ruhr. *Deutsche Zeitung* writes: "The Jewish instigators basically ensure that the secret instructions of the Jewish clandestine societies and lodges are painstakingly carried out."[53]

This entry provides a good example of Kaila's approach to antisemitism: he did not invent his ideas but based them a variety of written sources. After the Russian Revolution, he incorporated many of the antisemitic writings he had collected in his book *In the Tide of Times: Thoughts on the Fate of Europe*, published in the autumn of 1921. Less religiously themed than his previous books, it offered an analysis of the post–First World War situation, focusing on the figures of Walther Rathenau (1867–1922) and Oswald Spengler (1880–1936). Kaila was particularly troubled by what he perceived as an increase in the power of Jews in postwar Europe. The book had reasonable sales and was praised both within and outside the Church.[54]

In his book, Kaila denied being "any kind of antisemite." He did not consider the "Jewish soul" strange or opposite to the Western one, and he noted that many Jews, such as the philosopher Baruch Spinoza and the politician Walther Rathenau, were talented and had contributed to the development of European civilization. Still, the "massive rise of Judaism" since the French Revolution greatly concerned him. For him, Jews had borrowed money to rise to higher positions in society and now were able to finance industries and thereby shed their "Shylock" reputation and achieve social recognition. At the same time, traditional Judaism based on law and religious faith had transformed itself into liberal Reform Judaism. According to Kaila, the modern Jewish "money-nobility" had positioned itself to take over "the economic power of the world."[55] No longer did Jews desire to return to Israel, an idea important to both Zionism and Christian eschatology; rather, they now wanted to settle elsewhere, especially in the United States. Since 1917, Palestine had been open to Jews as a British mandate, but Kaila doubted that they would wish to move to a country where their livelihood depended on agriculture. In his view, Jews wanted to be involved in trade, and he explained this by writing that for Jews "it is much more pleasant to stay where money resides and one can gain great possessions with easy labor."[56]

Kaila maintained that Jews were key players in various revolutionary movements. He thought it was inevitable that Jews would end up as revolutionary leaders because of their intelligence and superiority in trade and finance. At first, "money Jews" were willing to unite with non-Jewish revolutionaries to dismantle class societies. Jews then saw an opportunity to insert themselves into the resulting void, as a means to gain international economic domination. Yet Kaila emphasized that he did not believe in "all imageries and antisemitic claims," including conspiracies such as the one presented in *Protocols of the Elders of Zion*. Instead, his explanation was more ordinary: "But it may also be those common adversaries, common interests, and common goals have brought together separate circles of revolutionaries and Jews, when the Jews, by virtue of their ability and power, have gained leadership. This explanation is likely."[57]

Kaila underscored that he did not believe in conspiracy theories. But he firmly believed that there was danger emanating from the Jews. He regarded their influence as disproportionally large, as well as destructive. For the three European foundational pillars of religion, national spirit, and culture, the impact of Judaism was devastating:

> I am not an antisemite, but I cannot deny that the influence of Judaism on European culture seems destructive. It corrupts religion because Judaism in power is non-religious and practices agitation against the Christian churches. It weakens the national spirit because Judaism is international. In Germany, there is a general complaint about the Jewish non-national mindset. And it taints the cultural life with materialism, as it underlines material values. I will repeat what I said at the beginning of this chapter; Jews have great men of first-class status in the fields of science and the arts, such as the physicists Heinrich Hertz and Albert Einstein, or the composers Meyerbeer, Mendelssohn and Rubinstein, but the general effect of Judaism is moving towards a spiritless, material direction. Jewish erudition is not culture but civilization if we use the parlance of Spengler. If Judaism were to gain power, it would unquestionably mean the transition of Europe to an infertile old age.[58]

This extract encapsulates the nationalist side of Kaila's antisemitism. The other side was associated with anti-communism. Kaila's negative perception of Soviet Russia was similar to that of his church – the Bolsheviks ruled the country with terror and spread revolutionary propaganda elsewhere in Europe (thus fomenting failed revolutions in Hungary and Germany). Kaila had convinced himself that the Bolshevik leaders were almost entirely Jewish:

Trotsky, Zinovjev, Kamenev, Karakhan, Litvinov, Worowsky, Steklov, Rakovsky, Reinstein etc., mainly Jewish names ... The leadership of Russian Bolshevism is mainly Jewish. There are hardly any other non-Jews among the principals than Lenin-Ulyanov and Chicherin. The most important Jewish commissioners are Trotsky-Bronstein, Sinovjev-Apfelbaum, Kamenev-Rosenfeld, Lunacharsky, Karakhan, Radek. Most of the Soviet ambassadors are also Jews, like Litvinov-Finkelstein in Tallinn, Fyrstenberg-Ganetsky in Riga, Kershentiev in Stockholm, Hillerson in Prague.[59]

Kaila saw Bolshevik-led Soviet Russia as a nightmare of oppression and violence, worse than even the misery of the tsarist regime. He quoted Otto Dickel (1880–1944), who, in 1921, had written in *Die Auferstehung des Abendlandes* (The Resurrection of the Occident) that every Jew benefited from the revolution because "Bolshevism is a Jewish power."[60]

The case of Erkki Kaila reveals that antisemitism could be employed not only to discredit Jews directly but also to explain complicated world events. In addition, it also shows how hard it was at the time to distinguish clearly between reliable information and propaganda. Kaila's diaries and notes testify to this. Between 1919 and 1923, he kept copious files relating to the activities of Jews throughout the world – activities that he found troubling and that, for him, pointed to a potential world conspiracy. He also created a card index containing the names of more than 170 Jews, both in and outside of Finland, whom he deemed had worked to increase the influence of Jews in the world. The data he gathered exceeded the scope and publication date of his book. The notes he kept on these cards referenced neutral Finnish and foreign newspapers but also outright antisemitic works, such as Henry Ford's *The International Jew*.[61]

In the scope of Finnish antisemitism, Kaila's book is important for three reasons. First, it was received positively. The secular and religious press praised the book and generally embraced Kaila's ideas about Jews. Second, the author was an important figure in the Church, in academia, and in politics. Third, in his memoirs written in the 1940s, Kaila concluded that it was probably his most influential work. At the same time, he viewed his "contribution" as a reflection of the pessimistic spirit of the times, stressing that

he had been writing primarily about Spengler and not about Jews and Bolsheviks. So it is possible that Kaila later found his ideas about Jews problematic and thus focused on the book's less antisemitic sections. No matter how
Kaila portrayed his book, its positive reception revealed that antisemitism
was an integral part of the Finnish situational analysis of postwar Europe.
The spirit of the times was anti-Jewish, and Kaila's book had neatly summarized Finnish ecclesiastical antisemitism.

It is unclear why the secular and religious press praised Kaila's book but
criticized J.W. Wartiainen's, especially considering that their fundamental
ideas were not that far apart. One explanation may have to do with the characteristics of Finnish Lutheran antisemitism in its written form. Churchmen
accepted antisemitic tropes, but they were seldom the focus or main theme
of any written text. For example, Wartiainen wrote bluntly about Jews,
whereas Kaila couched his negativity toward them as a critique of Bolshevism and the downfall of the European culture. The Lutheran clergy generally abhorred works directed solely against Jews. However, when Finnish
authors presented antisemitism as one topic among many, such as Bolshevism, European decay, missionary endeavours, or Freemasonry, there was
almost no collective pressure to censure such negative writing about Jews.[62]

ANTISEMITISM AND THE BISHOPS

The bishops of the Evangelical Lutheran Church of Finland addressed current events in their books, articles, sermons, and speeches. The reports prepared by the bishop of each diocese for convocations were considered to be
of special importance.[63] In these reports, they dealt with not only the activities of their individual dioceses but also with current events and the outstanding theological issues affecting the life of the church and Christianity.
These reports had dozens of themes, which were presented briefly. For a
bishop, the report was an instrument for introducing and clarifying current
issues for his priests. In the early 1920s, Jews emerged repeatedly as an issue.[64]

Archbishop Gustaf Johansson found it surprising that the Jews had survived as a nation, even though they had no leader or temple and were repeatedly subjected to persecution and ridicule. According to Johansson's 1922
report for the convocation of the Turku diocese, there were two kinds of Jews
in the world: righteous Jews who put their trust in the Bible and sought to

bring harmony to the world, believing in God's promise to make Israel a "priestly kingdom and a holy nation" (Exodus 19:6), and non-believing Jews, the contrary opposite of believers, who negatively exemplified the accusations made against Jews after the First World War.[65]

Almost every time Archbishop Johansson wrote about Jews or related topics, world domination cropped up in his reasoning.[66] According to his report, non-believing Jews were waiting for the Messiah to bring them the keys to world domination. They had turned against Christianity, because the success of the Jews depended on the downfall of Christian nations; that, he reasoned, was how they had come to play a major role in the First World War.[67] He had convinced himself that the Jews had already subjugated the financial realm and thus already held sway over the nations, so they had means to pursue world domination.[68] So Archbishop Johansson joined a group of the churchmen who believed in a particular sort of Jewish conspiracy situated in a religious context.

Instead of preparing a report for the 1922 convocation, the bishop of Savonlinna, O.I. Colliander, wrote a book called *Current Turning Point: In Light of the History of the Kingdom of God as Announced in the Holy Bible*. In it, he wrote pessimistically about biblical prophecies and the history of humanity and interpreted current world history in light of select biblical passages.[69]

Bishop Colliander linked Judaism to the story of the beast and the whore in the seventeenth chapter of the Book of Revelation. He claimed that the beast was democracy, "great madness," where "the will of the people is the highest law" – and by people, he meant all of humankind that had forsaken God. The Bible had predicted the beast, and before the end, that beast would serve another leader, one who would also rule the kings of the earth. In the same chapter, a female figure is sitting on the beast, dressed in purple and scarlet with gold, with precious stones and pearls and "with whom the kings of the earth have committed fornication, and the inhabitants of the earth have been made drunk with the wine of her fornication." This woman also had a golden cup "full of abominations and filthiness of her fornication," and on her forehead was written "Babylon Great, the mother of harlots, and abominations of the earth."[70]

According to Colliander, the Bible testified that this whore was Judaism. If the covenant between the chosen people and God was marriage, then a nation abandoning God would commit adultery and could even be called "a whore." So, the whore was Judaism, with "an everlasting hatred of Christ" as its motif. Based on this, Colliander combined current events and movements with the following apocalyptic structure:

> Also, the precious decorations worn by the whore refer to the infinite wealth that has piled up into the hands of the Jews over the centuries and through which they control the economic life of the nations and the policies of the states. It is also well known that Judaism has always been a friend of revolution, even a leader, as in Russia, for example, and an enemy of both nationalism and the current order of society and state. And the reason is in its essential hatred of Christ, predicted by the character-type of Judas Iscariot.[71]

Bishop Colliander, who had defended Jews in the parliament in 1897, exemplified many key elements of early-1920s antisemitism and provided a biblical basis for antisemitic conspiracies.[72] His views were exceptionally strict and grim, and his biographer even questioned whether he was mentally stable (Colliander died two years later).[73] In any case, the bishop of Savonlinna viewed post–First World War antisemitism through a theological prism. He shared his analysis with the participants of the convocation and guided his clergy to use the Bible to interpret current events.

In his 1922 report, the bishop of Oulu, J.R. Koskimies, wrote about Jews and events in Russia. He saw delusional hopes behind the dire circumstances of Soviet Russia. For him, the happiness gained from decent work had been replaced by an illusion of equally shared profits and living without a need to work. If reality proved these hopes absurd, it also "revealed how cunning and wicked the nature of this race of speculators was, when it has, by making those beliefs truly comprehensible about how to gain possession of pleasures, riches and power." Quite simply and pointedly, he blamed Jews for this state of affairs: "It is Judaism, which of itself has given birth to those two monsters: capitalism and communist anarchism."[74]

These statements indicate both strong anti-communist ideas and a negative image of Jews. One should note that Bishop Koskimies described Jews a race. In his diaries, he referred to Jewish racial features and physiognomy several times, though he was the only Finnish bishop of the 1920s who expressed such racial antisemitism.[75]

But religion did not play an explicitly key role in the views of Koskimies, as it did for Johansson and Colliander. Historian Hannu Mustakallio has argued that Koskimies's antisemitism had its roots in the late-nineteenth-century nationalist Fennoman movement, which opposed Jewish civil rights.[76] While this may be true, Koskimies's report also reflected the postwar antisemitic interpretation of the position of Jews. The adaptable nature of antisemitism becomes visible in the case of Bishop Koskimies, in that his existing anti-Jewish prejudices combined with post–First World War conspiracies and modern antisemitic ideas, including racial antisemitism.

OBSERVATIONS, SUGGESTIONS, AND CONCLUSIONS VIS-À-VIS "LUTHERANISM"

The analysis presented here of the Finnish clergy's written views on Jews and Judaism in the years leading up to the Second World War suggests some clear patterns: antisemitic ideas in Finland were not a marginal matter, nor were they of interest to only a handful of nationalistic zealots or ignorant individuals. Personal and professional channels for antisemitic rhetoric can be detected within the framework of the most influential religious institution in the country, the Finnish Lutheran Church. Several leading church professionals, including bishops, have left us a written record infused with argumentation that is fundamentally antisemitic, especially in its biblical interpretations.

One could dismiss these individuals as exceptions – as not presenting the majority view, whatever that might be – in a context in which the average Finnish citizen was hardly consumed by the Jewish question or the fate of the Jews, especially in the years preceding the Holocaust. That said, there were enough religious leaders sharing anti-Jewish sentiments – and presenting biblical interpretations rooted in hoary Christian antisemitic hermeneutics – that they must be considered a significant network in the Finnish context. That network's hidden or plain, potential or actual influence must not be dismissed out of hand. How "organized" or intentional the network was, and how it was fed by and linked with similar networks in Europe –

and Nazi organizations in particular – is another matter. While not examined here, such questions are worth pursuing.

Specifically Finnish tracts are worth noting with regard to how they may have been linked to antisemitic expressions elsewhere in Europe in the interwar period, particularly because of the far-reaching channels of influence that antisemites in the Finnish church may have maintained through their ecclesiastical offices. The bishops and clergy were not only highly educated shepherds of the church; they also did much to shape Finnish culture, and they were embedded in Finnish society's upper echelons. This implicates the Lutheran Church and its theology in the matter of the spreading antisemitic sentiments. Even if the church never explicitly, publicly, or officially condoned antisemitic thought or actions, neither did it repudiate them, at least before the Holocaust. Furthermore, readers today have the benefit of hindsight and a more nuanced understanding of the inherent problems in Christian, including Lutheran, theology, and the seeds of antisemitism embedded in the regular discourse on faith. The contemporary Lutheran Church in Finland rejects antisemitism, just as the historical supersessionism has gained substantial critical attention among Christian theologians and Luther scholars. However, much ambiguity remains regarding how Lutheran communities like the Finnish church should address Luther vis-à-vis the evidence of antisemitism in his writings and its impact on the integrity of his teachings. For example, disagreement lingers regarding whether his texts should be dismissed for their explicitly anti-Jewish views and whether it is feasible to distinguish between religious, political, and national expressions of antisemitism when assessing men like Luther.

The Finnish case study provides evidence for the argument that religious proclamation and theology can serve as an insidious and far-reaching channel for inseminating antisemitic views. This reality needs to be named even in contexts where, at least so far, evidence is lacking as to which acts of violence against the Jews are a direct result of anti-Jewish proclamations. It can reasonably be said that whatever the consequences in a given situation, antisemitic proclamation generally speaking nurtures implicit biases and creates a culture of permission for antisemitic sentiments *and* acts.

This argument invites historians, theologians, and scholars of culture to reconsider the evidence unearthed so far and, through interdisciplinary study, analyze in depth how and where Christian religious proclamation has led to ethnic hatred or fuelled violence toward Jews, be it directly or indirectly. When studying ethnonationalism in relation to antisemitism, in the case of Finland one path forward is to consider the "leaking" of the Christian teachers' antisemitic convictions through their cultural and social networks so as to inject pro-Finland/anti-Russian movements with decidedly anti-Jewish arguments. In other words, the question remains, to what degree was antisemitic thinking intersecting with or an ingredient of the ideologies that supported the growing national identity?

The Christian teachers examined in this study were a small minority, but some of them had considerable spiritual authority that reached the seats of those with political authority. It is unclear whether direct links can be drawn from antisemitic sermons or tracts to explicitly ethnonationalist activities that were anti-Jewish in their impact. But it is a valid exercise to trace the clergymen's personal links to broader networks; doing so can enlighten us as to the history of violence. The roots of such networks of antisemitic ideologies are centuries deep.

In the case of the Finnish theologians, those roots, which originated in early Christian teachings, go back to Reformation theology. As has been demonstrated here, the most prominent antisemitic voices in Finland were learned Christian clergy and bishops, particularly of the Lutheran persuasion. The word "Lutheran" is thus important here, for it leads back to the man who initiated the sixteenth-century European reforms and whose name came to identify an entire religious movement and what is today a globally diverse religious tradition: Martin Luther.

A close look at the term "Lutheran" as it relates to ethnonationalism and antisemitism is relevant for some obvious reasons: (1) the Finnish Lutheran clergy drew from the Reformation theological tradition, specifically the one named after Luther; (2) Luther's own explicit antisemitic positions have drawn considerable scholarly attention and debate over time, and they still do; and (3) the word Lutheran has been associated with antisemitism, not only during the Nazi period but also more recently.

This chapter has not attended to Luther's theology per se except when interpreting Lutheran publications, in which the influence of Luther is to be expected. Our attention has remained on the pre–Second World War period. Moving forward, closer to the Second World War, we might find that Luther's most virulent anti-Jewish writings gained renewed attention from a small and extreme, pro-German nationalist constituency in Finland (a topic that has yet to be sufficiently explored and that at present draws conflicting assessments). Thus, a few words on Luther are in order before we map out the spread of antisemitism via "Lutheran" religious discourse.

Martin Luther's anti-Jewish views have gained notoriety in the context of the ongoing and manifold research on the roots of antisemitism vis-à-vis Christian theology and its most effective promulgators. Given his world stature and his massive number of publications, Luther's anti-Jewish arguments have become the centre of attention and invite perusal, purging, and a revision of Christian sources and hermeneutics.[77] Martin Luther was part of a long line of Christian theologians who passionately and sincerely believed in the superiority of the Christian religion and who could see no value in the Jewish faith.[78] When the Finnish bishops wrote of Christians as God's chosen people and of salvation, and when they argued for the "right" reading of the Scriptures, they were walking down a path prepared by Martin Luther and other Christian teachers before him. Whether or not they explicitly referred to Luther's writings in their anti-Jewish arguments, or in their theologizing in general, it is not insignificant that the Lutheran clergy was operating within a specifically Lutheran framework and applying Christian hermeneutics that had fundamentally anti-Jewish ingredients.

Taking Martin Luther – and the Finnish Lutheran clergy featured in this article – as the case study for the theological rationales for Christian antisemitism, this can be stated: at the root of the problem is Christians' exclusive and supersessionist reading of the Scriptures and their fundamental beliefs about Christ as the (only) Saviour and Messiah. This poses a larger question – beyond the scope of this chapter – about the integrity of the Christian religion and Christian hermeneutics today; it also underscores the importance of naming and rejecting supersessionist attitudes in contemporary religious discourse. Regarding the Finnish material, and specifically the Second World War era, further investigation seems in order on the details: What can be said about the explicit or implicit inspiration from Luther among Lutheran individuals and groups in their antisemitic expressions, or in rejection of those?[79] Is there any evidence from the Finnish Lutheran clergy regarding mutual debate or critical thought vis-à-vis their Lutheran biblical interpretation and the treatment of the Jews in their time? Related to this, broader consideration in each context in which antisemitism is examined – also in Finland – is its relation to expressions of racism and hate crimes involving ethnic prejudice. For instance, it would be dangerously naive to view the Lutheran bishops' and Luther's own anti-Jewish comments as "only" religious opinions and not as expressions of, or feeders of, racism and ethnic hatred.

There has been little research on these matters, expecially as they relate to Finland. As more research from the Finnish archives is made available for the larger scholarly community operating in other languages, collaborative international efforts promise important reality checks as to "what actually happened," as well as vital stimulus for truth-telling and vigilant attention to the ideologies and religious energies that continue shape our lives and values and interactions.

NOTES

1 For a comprehensive introduction to Martin Luther's impact as a reformation theologian, see Hans Hillerbrand, Kirsi Stjerna, and Timothy Wengert, eds., *The Annotated Luther*, vols. 1–6 (Minneapolis: Fortress Press, 2015–17).

2 For example, see Oula Silvennoinen, *Salaiset aseveljet: Suomen ja Saksan turvallisuuspoliisiyhteistyö 1933–1944* (Helsinki: Otava, 2008); Simo Muir and Hana Worthen, eds., *Finland's Holocaust: Silences of History* (Basingstoke: Palgrave Macmillan 2013); André Swanström, *Hakaristin ritarit* (Jyväskylä: Atena 2018); and Lars Westerlund, *The Finnish SS – Volunteers and Atrocities against Jews, Civilians, and Prisoners of War in Ukraine and the Caucasus Region 1941–1943* (Helsinki: National Archives of Finland, 2019).

3 Kirsti Kena, *Kirkon asema ja asenteiden muotoutuminen itsenäistyneessä Suomessa 1918–1922* (Helsinki: Suomen Kirkkohistoriallinen Seura, 1979), 341–50; Aila Lauha, *Suomen kirkon kansainväliset suhteet 1923–1925* (Helsinki: Suomen Kirkkohistoriallinen Seura, 1993), 36; Paavo Ahonen, *Antisemitismi Suomen evankelis – luterilaisessa kirkossa 1917–1933* (Helsinki: SKHS, 2017), 34–5. Over 98 percent of the Finns were members of the Lutheran Church in the 1920s, and at the peak, 16 out of 200 members of Parliament were priests; clearly, the position of the Lutheran Church was exceptionally strong in Finland.

4 According to the Jewish ordinance issued in 1782, Jews could reside in Stockholm, Gothenburg, and Norrköping.

5   Taimi Torvinen, *Kadimah: Suomen juutalaisten historia* (Helsinki: Otava, 1989), 21–6. On the so-called Cantonists, see Yohanan Petrovsky-Shtern, *Jews in the Russian Army, 1827–1917: Drafted into Modernity* (Cambridge: Cambridge University Press, 2009).

6   By the end of the 1870s, Jews had been granted civil rights in every European country except Spain (1910), Portugal (1911), Russia (1917), and Romania (1923).

7   The Diet of Finland was the legislative assembly during the period of autonomy. It consisted of four estates: nobility, clergy, bourgeoisie, and peasants. A law had to pass three estates to be sent to the emperor, who either accepted or rejected it.

8   Torvinen, *Kadimah*, 45–6, 65–77, 81–92, 98–103.

9   The archbishop's seat is in Turku, the former capital. In 1812, only three years after Finland became part of Russia, Tsar Alexander I moved the capital of Finland from Turku to Helsinki, farther from Sweden and closer to St Petersburg, but the centre of the archdiocese of the Church of Finland remained in the old capital.

10 Eira Paunu, *Torsten Thure Renvall: Elämä ja toiminta* (Helsinki: SKHS, 1952), 94–5; Eino Murtorinne, *Suomalainen teologia autonomian kautena, 1828–1918* (Helsinki: Gaudeamus, 1986), 135–8.

11 Kena, *Kirkon asema ja asenteiden muotoutuminen itsenäistyneessä Suomessa*, 341–5. Also see Ahonen, *Antisemitismi Suomen evankelis-luterilaisessa kirkossa*, 35–42; and Jorma Marjokorpi, "Kirkollisen lehdistön levikki itsenäisyyden alkuvuosikymmeninä," in *Kirkko suomalaisessa yhteiskunnassa 1900-luvulla*, eds. Markku Heikkilä and Eino Murtorinne (Helsinki: Kirjapaja, 1977), 187–9.

12 Santeri Jacobsson, *Taistelu ihmisoikeuksista: Yhteiskunnallis-historiallinen tutkimus Ruotsin ja Suomen juutalaiskysymyksen vaiheista* (Jyväskylä: Gummerus, 1951), 288–92; Torvinen, *Kadimah*, 70.

13 Jacobsson, *Taistelu ihmisoikeuksista*, 285–95, 320–1; Torvinen, *Kadimah*, 70–71.

14 Jacobsson, *Taistelu ihmisoikeuksista*, 111–12, 244–8; Torvinen, *Kadimah*, 59–60. In February 1888, sixteen families (sixty deportees) from Helsinki, and in August 1888, twelve families from Turku, thirty-four families from Vyborg (125 deportees), and nine other deportees.

15 Torvinen, *Kadimah*, 75–6, 88–9. Despite the unclear societal status of the Jews, the construction work of the Synagogue of Helsinki was completed in 1906 and the Synagogue of Turku in 1912.

16 Between 1918 and 1920, the Municipal Court of Helsinki gave 456 verdicts on crimes related to speculation. Eight of the convicted were Jews (1.8%); see National Archives of Finland (KA), Archives of the Justice Department of Commission of Trade and Industry (KTKOA), Bb:1.

17 "Juutalaiset lakia kiertämässä," *Työkansa*, 23 February 1920.

18 "Från allmänhäten," *Hufvudstadsbladet*, 22 February 1920; Ahonen, *Antisemitismi Suomen evankelis-luterilaisessa kirkossa*, 70–2; Paavo Haavikko, *Kansakunnan linja: Kommentteja erään tuntemattoman kansan tuntemattomaan historiaan 1904–1975* (Helsinki: Otava, 1977), 55–68; Kaija Junkkari, *Suomen juutalaiset uskonnollis-etnisenä vähemmistönä: tutkimus vuosilta 1918–1944* (MA thesis, University of Helsinki, 1973), 47–54; Torvinen, *Kadimah*, 104–6.

19 Pietilä's article was sent to the provincial newspapers by the Press Office of Central Association for Parish Work of the Church of Finland (SKSK). It was published at least in *Aamulehti*, the main newspaper of Tampere. See KA Archives of the Central Association for Parish Work of the Church of Finland (SKSKA), Hda:1; and "Juutalaiskysymys," *Aamulehti*, 9 September 1921.

20 "Kristillisyys ja liike-elämä."*Kotimaa*, 29 June 1920.

21 "Juutalaiskysymys," *Kotimaa*, 9 September 1921.

22 Albert S. Lindemann, *Esau's Tears: Modern Anti-Semitism and the Rise of the Jews* (Cambridge: Cambridge University Press 1997), 81–2.

23 "Juutalaiskysymys," *Kotimaa*, 9 September 1921.

24 Ulrich Herbeck, "National Antisemitism in Russia during the 'Years of Crisis,' 1914–1922," *Studies in Ethnicity and Nationalism* 3 (2007): 177–79; Sam Johnson, "Russia and the Origins of Twentieth-Century Antisemitism," *History Compass* 1 (2003): 2; Lindemann, *Esau's Tears*, 396–7, 424. The allegation of Jewish overrepresentation in the Bolshevik movement was not entirely unfounded, as many of Bolshevik leaders had a Jewish background. However, the argument is problematic, in that the key Jewish Bolshevik leaders were completely alienated from Judaism. Moreover, many politically active Jews chose to join the Jewish Labor Bund instead.

25 Ahonen, *Antisemitismi Suomen evankelis-luterilaisessa kirkossa*, 63–70, 97–8;

Andre Gerritz, *The Myth of Jewish Communism: A Historical Interpretation* (New York: Peter Lang, 2009), 9–10; Hannu Soikkanen, *Sosialismin tulo Suomeen: Ensimmäisen yksikamarisen eduskunnan vaaleihin asti* (Helsinki: WSOY, 1961), 28–33. Hungarians and Finns are the two most numerous Finno-Ugric peoples, and many churchmen had personal relations with their Hungarian "brothers."

26 Ahonen, *Antisemitismi Suomen evankelis-luterilaisessa kirkossa*, 101–2. Despite the fact that Lenin's closest "Jewish" ancestor was his mother's grandfather, a Christian convert who was adamant about not passing his Jewish heritage to his children, Lenin was often considered a Jew.

27 "Miksi on juutalaislähetystyö nykyaikana erikoisen tärkeä?," *Kotimaa*, 17 June 1919. See also Ahonen, *Antisemitismi Suomen evankelis-luterilaisessa kirkossa*, 87–96, 101.

28 Ahonen, *Antisemitismi Suomen evankelis-luterilaisessa kirkossa*, 99–110. The conservative *Herättäjä* did not make a connection between Bolshevism and the Jews in the early 1920s, as the paper focused on religious subjects.

29 Ahonen, *Antisemitismi Suomen evankelis-luterilaisessa kirkossa*, 110.

30 Malin wrote the book under the pseudonym "Kansalainen" (citizen).

31 Artur Malin Kansalainen, *Mitä on Bolshevismi?* (Helsinki: Kirkollis-kansallinen valistustoimisto, 1919), 14–15. See also Ahonen, *Antisemitismi Suomen evankelis-luterilaisessa kirkossa*, 111–14.

32 It is not clear whether Pärnänen adopted his antisemitic views during the last few years before his flight in 1921 or whether he had a strong anti-Jewish mindset even before the Revolution.

33 Ahonen, *Antisemitismi Suomen evankelis-luterilaisessa kirkossa*, 115.

34 Eevertti Pärnänen, *Bolshevikit: Suomalaisen silminnäkijän havaintoja* (Porvoo: WSOY, 1922), 98–9.

35 Pärnänen, *Bolshevikit*, 93–9.

36 Already in the same year, an eyewitness testimony was published in which Jews were accused of causing the famine in Russia. According to the book, the Jews intended to kill the people by starvation to make room for a Jewish state. Such accusations went too far and were not accepted without criticism in Finland's ecclesiastical press. Ahonen, *Antisemitismi Suomen evankelis-luterilaisessa kirkossa*, 123–4.

37 KA Archives of Suomen suojelusliitto (SSL), Kansio 11, Suomen suojelusliiton kiertokirje N:o 73; Ahonen, *Antisemitismi Suomen evankelis-luterilaisessa*

kirkossa, 120–1; Kari Immonen, *Ryssästä saa puhua: Neuvostoliitto suomalaisessa julkisuudessa ja kirjat julkisuuden muotona 1918–1939* (Helsinki: Otava 1987), 383–4.

38 Ahonen, *Antisemitismi Suomen evankelis-luterilaisessa kirkossa*, 149–50, 159–61, 184–6.

39 Ibid., 148–9.

40 Otto von Kursell and Dietrich Eckart, *Totengräber Russlands* (Munich: Deutscher Volksverlag Dr Ernst Boepple, 1921), 2. This booklet consists of thirty-two caricatures by von Kursell, with mockery verses written by Eckart and a three-page essay with the title "Der Jüdische Bolschevismus" (Jewish Bolshevism) by Alfred Rosenberg.

41 Johan Wilhelm Wartiainen, *Juutalaisten maailmanhistoriallinen merkitys: entisaikaan Jumalan kansana ja nykyään saatanan joukkona* (WSOY: Porvoo, 1922), 5–6.

42 Ibid., 6–12.

43 Ibid., 13–14.

44 Ibid., 15–25.

45 George Brandes (1842–1927) was a Danish critic, whose modern and liberal views were considered a threat among the Scandinavian clergy, especially in the last decades of the nineteenth century. Brandes was born into a Jewish family, and though he did not identify himself as a Jew, Finnish churchmen regarded him as the embodiment of the radical liberalism and negative rationalism they believed the Jews represented. Ahonen, *Antisemitismi Suomen evankelis-luterilaisessa kirkossa*, 150–1.

46 Wartiainen, *Juutalaisten maailmanhistoriallinen merkitys*, 26.

47 KA Archives of WSOY (WSOY), Kirjailijakirjeenvaihto, Wartiainen to WSOY, 22 May 1922; Ahonen, *Antisemitismi Suomen evankelis-luterilaisessa kirkossa*, 152–3.

48 "Juutalaiskysymys," *Kotimaa*, 3 October 1922.

49 Wartiainen, *Juutalaisten maailmanhistoriallinen merkitys*, 28.

50 Ahonen, *Antisemitismi Suomen evankelis-luterilaisessa kirkossa*, 161–2.

51 Later, Kaila was the bishop of Vyborg (1925–35) and then the archbishop of Finland (1935–44).

52 KA Diaries and Notebooks, 1905–1944 (EK1), 29 March 1918.

53 KA EK1, 9 April 1920."

54 Turku University Library (TYK), Archives of Erkki Kaila Kirjeet, Letters

(EK), 1.3, Yksityiskirjeet, 2 September 1932. The book sold more than 2,000
copies, which was a decent number in Finland in the 1920s. Also see
Ahonen, *Antisemitismi Suomen evankelis-luterilaisessa kirkossa*, 184–6.

55　Erkki Kaila, *Aikojen murroksessa: Ajatuksia Euroopan kohtalosta* (Helsinki:
Otava, 1921), 45–9, 58–60.

56　Ibid., 57–8.

57　Ibid., 46–7, 59–61.

58　Ibid., 61–2.

59　Ibid., 67–77.

60　Ibid., 75. Otto Dickel led several fascist organizations that were rivals of the
NSDAP. The best-known was *Deutsche Werk-Gemeinschaft*. In the summer
of 1921, Dickel negotiated with NSDAP founder Anton Drexler for a merger
of the *Werk-Gemeinschaft* with the NSDAP – unsuccessfully, as it turned out.
On this point, see Thomas D. Grant, *Stormtroopers and Crisis in the Nazi
Movement: Activism, Ideology, and Dissolution* (New York: Routledge, 2004),
32–3.

61　Ahonen, *Antisemitismi Suomen evankelis-luterilaisessa kirkossa*, 187–202.

62　Ibid., 327–9.

63　Until the 1970s, convocations were held in every diocese of the Church of
Finland every five years. In addition to the congregational issues, the meetings prepared for the General Synod held the following year. On this point,
see Esko Häkli, *Pappeinkokouskirjallisuuden luettelo 1807–1957* (Helsinki:
Helsingin yliopiston kirjasto, 1962), 7–8.

64　For example, the 1922 reports focused on Jews four times. The bishop of
Porvoo, Jaakko Gummerus, used only one sentence to refer to the Judeo-
Bolshevik reign in Hungary. Jaakko Gummerus, *Yleiskatsaus tärkeimpiin
ilmiöihin kirkon ja teologian alalla 1917–1922* (Porvoo: Porvoon hiippakunta,
1922), 36.

65　Gustaf Johansson, *Merkillisimmät ilmiöt kristillisen kirkon ja jumaluusopin
alalla viimeisen pappeinkokouksen jälkeen* (Turku: Turun arkkihiippakunta,
1922), 58.

66　Ahonen, *Antisemitismi Suomen evankelis-luterilaisessa kirkossa*, 140–2. Jews
were not the only party interested in world domination. Johansson also
implied the same about the pope and the Catholic Church.

67　Ahonen, *Antisemitismi Suomen evankelis-luterilaisessa kirkossa*, 140–2. Archbishop Johansson did not specify the role Jews had played in the First

World War; however, he referred to it as "bad" in his next review in 1927. Gustaf Johansson, *Merkillisimpiä ilmiöitä kristillisen kirkon ja jumaluusopin alalla*, 11.

68 Johansson, *Merkillisimmät ilmiöt kristillisen kirkon ja jumaluusopin alalla*, 58–9. Johansson regarded Zionists as an unrighteous people because the movement aimed at practising nationalism regardless of religion. He did not claim that only the Jews aimed at world domination. He compared the Jewish plans to the similar aspirations of the Catholic Church and the pope, both overshadowed by the twisted relationship vis-à-vis the true faith.

69 Kalevi Toiviainen, *Muurinvartija: O.I. Colliander Kuopion ja Savonlinnan hiippakuntien piispana 1897–1924* (Helsinki: SKHS 2005), 270–1.

70 O.I. Colliander, *Nykyinen murrosaika: Pyhän Raamatun ilmoittaman Jumalanvaltakunnan historian valossa* (Savonlinna: O.I Colliander, 1922), 76–80.

71 Colliander, *Nykyinen murrosaika*, 80.

72 Toiviainen, *Muurinvartija*, 47–8.

73 Ibid., 270–1.

74 J.R. Koskimies, *Kertomus Kuopion hiippakunnan tilanteesta vv. 1917–1922: ynnä piirteitä kristillisen kirkon ja jumaluusopin alalta* (Oulu: Kuopion hiippakunta, 1922), 51.

75 Ahonen, *Antisemitismi Suomen evankelis-luterilaisessa kirkossa*, 325–9. Even though many Finnish priests considered Jews a race, the concept of "race" remained vague. None of the churchmen underscored any interracial hierarchy, and Jews were not considered or written about as a lower race. Presumably, "race" as a concept was understood as similar to "nation" or "nationality."

76 Hannu Mustakallio, "Oulun hiippakunnan johto ja oikeistoradikalismi 1929–1939 J. R. Koskimies, J.A. Mannermaa ja Elias Simojoki," in *Suomen kirkkohistoriallisen seuran vuosikirja 1999–2001*, ed. Hannu Mustakallio (SKHS: Helsinki, 2002), 252.

77 A short educational video on the history of antisemitism, part of the permanent exhibit of the United States Holocaust Memorial Museum in Washington, DC, features Martin Luther prominently.

78 For a comprehensive examination of this question with evidence from Luther's writings for the exegetical roots of antisemitism, see Brooks Schramm and Kirsi Stjerna, *Martin Luther, the Bible, and the Jewish People* (Minneapolis: Fortress Press, 2012). Luther did not express racially driven

or oriented arguments against Jews, but his fundamental and consistent argument throughout his career was that the Jewish religion as such was dead and that the Christian reading of the Scriptures was superior to that of the rabbis. Near the end of his life, he argued vehemently for the expulsion of all Jews and the extinguishing of their religion.

79 In predominantly Lutheran Finland, Martin Luther's views are part of the landscape. While the evidence so far points to minimal engagement with Luther's explicitly anti-Jewish writings, there were notable exceptions, such as the 1939 Finnish translation of one of Martin Luther's most vitriolic anti-Jewish texts, "On Jews and Their Lies" (1543). While the text was apparently rejected by most Lutherans, it gained an audience beyond the Lutheran clergy, in radical right-wing circles. See Martin Luther, *Juutalaisista ja heidän valheistaan*, preface by Toivo Tuomas Savolainen (Helsinki: Varsara, 1939) [Translation of the preface from Finnish to English by Kirsi Stjerna, June 2017, available at United States Holocaust Memorial Museum Archives, Washington, DC]. On the rejection of this work, see Paavo Ahonen, "Juutalaisvastaisuus Kotimaa- ja Herättäjä -lehdissä 1930–1939" (MA thesis, University of Helsinki 2008), 86–8; and Ahonen, *Antisemitismi Suomen evankelis-luterilaisessa kirkossa*, 306–8.

8

"The Converts Were Just Delighted": Dynamics of Religious Conversion as a Tool of Genocide in the Independent State of Croatia

Danijel Matijević

Ivan Zubić was born in 1909 in Đurđevac, northern Croatia. He became a Franciscan friar, taking the name Silvestar, in 1925, and was ordained a priest in 1933. In 1934, he was assigned to teach at Virovtica High School, as a catechist in the Catholic faith.[1] In 1936, he was transferred to Vukovar High School.[2] In December 1938, for unknown reasons, state officials dismissed him from his teaching position.[3] In 1939, he was appointed to teach catechism at Slavonski Brod High School.[4] In 1940, he returned to Vukovar and assumed residency at the Franciscan friary there.[5] At some point, before the Ustaša movement was installed in power in April 1941, Zubić became active in Vukovar's underground Ustaša cell, promoting the movement among the city's youth.[6] High school students Antun Gölis, Tomislav Stanišić, and Vladimir Radauš, for example, became involved with the Ustaša movement before the war.[7] As the Ustaša reign began, Zubić officially resumed his teaching at Vukovar High School.[8]

Father Zubić's story serves as a leitmotif of the dynamics of religious conversion and violent population engineering in the Independent State of Croatia, drawn from local research. As we explore fascist Croatia's campaign

of forced religious conversion and the way it fit into a larger project of ethnonational consolidation, Father Zubić's path through the upheavals of his
time will serve as a poignant example of how the Catholic Church involved
itself in genocide. His story also draws attention to the essential role that
local actors played in campaigns of mass violence.

In April 1941, the German army invaded the interwar Kingdom of
Yugoslavia; shortly afterward, in consort with Fascist Italy, the Germans established the Independent State of Croatia (Nezavisna Država Hrvatska, or
NDH). This was a Greater Croatia, encompassing most of today's Croatia,
Bosnia and Herzegovina, and parts of northern Serbia. The NDH's estimated population was 6,285,000; the three largest groups were Croats
(3,300,000, or 53 per cent, virtually all Catholic), followed by Serbs (1,925,000,
or 31 per cent, nearly all Eastern Orthodox), and Bosnian Muslims (700,000,
or 11 per cent).[9] To head the new country, the Germans installed the fascist
Ustaša movement.

Croats numbered only slightly more than half of the NDH population,
which made population policy essential for an insurgent, newly empowered
fascist movement like the Ustaša. Bosnian Muslims were immediately
"nationalized" as Croats. Serbs, seen as tentacles of Serbia's interwar imperialism, were to be either removed or assimilated. Other groups were of
lesser concern; the ethnic Germans were seen as allies, the Jews as an easy
and lucrative target, and Czechs, Slovaks, and Slovenians as no threat.[10] The
"Serbian question" thus became the main focus of the regime's population
engineering efforts.

Even as some of its dignitaries expressed serious concerns about certain
state policies, the Catholic Church in Croatia remained a loyal supporter of
the Ustaša regime until the end of the war. The Church's support extended
into the postwar period as well; hundreds of Ustaša perpetrators escaped
capture by the Allies with the assistance of the Croatian subcommittee of
the Vatican Relief Commission.[11] During the war, the most damning form
of collaboration undertaken by the Catholic Church in Croatia was its participation in the campaign of forced religious conversion that the Ustaša
regime unleashed on NDH's Serbian population. This campaign was part of
a homegrown, Ustaša-designed genocide against the Serbs, which also included forced deportations, mass executions, and concentration, labor, and

death camps.[12] Focusing mainly on events in and around the town of Vukovar between 1941 and 1945, this chapter argues that the Catholic Church in
Croatia served as an obedient tool in the hands of a regime bent on trans-
forming the NDH from a diverse society into a virtually monoethnic state
by any means necessary. Facing grave *realpolitik* concerns in a highly turbu-
lent time, with a large number of virulently nationalist clerics in its ranks,
and opting to pursue a cooperative course in its relations with the Ustaša
movement, the Catholic Church in Croatia became a crucial accomplice in
a genocidal campaign that violated both canon law and Christian morality.
The Ustaša regime, for its part, placed less importance on the converts' religious conversion than on their consequent *ethnonational* transformation.
Indeed, the Serbs were subjected to a "double conversion" – *religious* conversion from Serbian Orthodoxy to Catholicism (or, later, to "Croatian" Orthodoxy), and a *legal*, state-decreed conversion from Serbian to Croatian
ethnonationality. Contrary to the high hopes the Church had in 1941, the Ustaša regime was less interested in reinforcing Catholicism than in its primary
aim, Croatia's ethnonational consolidation. By tracing the power dynamics
between the Catholic Church and the Ustaša regime, this chapter examines
how religion, political ideology, and mass violence intertwined in the NDH.

I

After Nazi Germany crushed the Kingdom of Yugoslavia in April 1941, there
were many reasons for the Catholic Church in Croatia to greet with con-
tentment the founding of the NDH. Headquartered in Zagreb, now the capital of a country with a Catholic majority and Catholic leaders, the Catholic
Church in Croatia would be the most influential religious institution in the
NDH, with more political influence and social authority than any other
non-government entity. Moreover, the Ustaša was a socially and politically
conservative movement, viewed as having "resurrected" an independent
Croatian state and won freedom from Serbia, which dominated the interwar
Kingdom of Yugoslavia. In addition, the regime was fiercely anti-communist
and, unlike the dominant strain of fascism – German National Socialism –
professed devout Catholicism, according the Church a prominent place in
the Ustaša-envisioned Croatian national project.

During the interwar period, the Church had been dissatisfied with its position, as well as that of the Croatian people within the Kingdom of Yugoslavia. Many Croats portrayed the kingdom as their prison and saw themselves as having been forced into an unholy and unwanted union with the imperialistic and backward Serbian nation. In addition to this, Serbs represented the westernmost outpost of Eastern Orthodox Christianity in Europe, whereas Croat nationalists saw their nation as the Antemurale Christianitatis – Bulwark of Christendom – that had defended "the Roman Catholic faith and Western Civilization" not only against the Ottoman conquest but also against Eastern Orthodox heresy.[13] Croatia thus went from being the cradle of Yugoslavism in the seventeenth century to its staunchest enemy by 1941. With the founding of the Kingdom of Serbs, Croats, and Slovenes in 1918 (renamed the Kingdom of Yugoslavia in 1929), Serbia became the centre of Yugoslavism. In the interwar period, Serb nationalists used that ideology to strengthen Serbia's hegemony within the new state.[14] Unsurprisingly, Croatia's Catholic elites viewed foreign domination by an Orthodox nation as a threat. Especially for clerics, the borderland created by the 1054 Great Schism between Catholicism and Orthodoxy, in terms of both people and territory, remained as contested in the interwar period as it had been in the eleventh century. Croat nationalists, therefore, viewed interwar Yugoslavism as synonymous with both Greater Serbianism and the looming onslaught of the heretical Eastern rite.[15]

Against Greater Serbianism stood Greater Croatianism, the most notorious bone of contention between the two expansionist national projects being the arrogation of Bosnia-Herzegovina. The Catholic Church in Croatia was staunchly nationalist, often espousing Greater Croatianism. The Zagreb Archbishopric's *Katolički list* (Catholic paper), for example, regularly referred to Bosnia-Herzegovina as a historically Croat territory and to the Slavic Muslim population there as "Muslim Croats," juxtaposing them with "Catholic Croats."[16] Nationalist Serbs, of course, claimed the same Muslim population for the Serbian nation.

The Catholic Church in Croatia saw another fault in the Kingdom of Yugoslavia: its liberal socio-economic system, which had been modelled on that of the progressive Western democracies. One article in *Katolički list*, referring to "modern culture," said that the "source of that evil lies in the pagan humanism of the fifteenth and the sixteenth centuries, which led humans away from the Christian domain into the domain of materialism."[17] In another article, a two-part travelogue titled "Along the Adriatic Coast," the Catholic priest Father Franjo Pipini commented negatively about the impact of the Eastern Orthodox minority along the Croatian coast, implying that Croats in both the Yugoslav and Italian sectors of the Adriatic were living under unjust foreign domination. He then identified more general, systemic problems with the contemporary social contract. Observing material progress – asphalt roads, cars, buses – and the diversity of foreigners summering on the Adriatic, he noticed most prominently the "half-naked" women, "everywhere ... in the streets, beaches, bars, and steamboats." Pipini invoked Bishop Josip Srebreni and his fight against "nudity," and told an anecdote in which "foreign women seductively came before his eminence Srebreni , and when he protested, they dared insult him too." He proceeded to complain about the demographic decline of Croats in the area – "the white plague" – blaming it all on lack of faith, a consequence of "all kinds of ideas" sown among the people. As examples of this modern decay, he listed "village women wearing modern dresses, hair cut short, on Sundays dancing the modern dances ... and every young man must have his own bicycle even if the last cow is gone from the stable." Pipini also reported popular complaints about the "gentry," who could "afford everything" while the majority lived in misery. He lamented that money was plentiful yet unavailable, "frozen."[18]

Pipini saw communist radicalism as perhaps even more dangerous. He told of a man who returned to the coast from Slavonia and who "every day teaches Marx's theory" and "after a few years poisoned the entire male youth and repelled it from the church." For Pipini , the transnational discourse around class and world revolution stood in stark contrast to the supranational, conservative traditions of the Catholic religion. As he noted further on, the men mentioned above who complained about the wealthy gentry felt that "all gentry should be eradicated" if a political upheaval were to occur.[19] Figures like Pipini viewed the Church as a binding regulatory force for Croatian society. They thus fought back against ideologies that sought to incite social change, especially communism, which they feared would smite the Church together with the gentry.

Indeed, the popularity of communism was rising both globally and locally. The Catholic Church, including its Croatian branch, followed with anxiety the Soviet measures against the Orthodox Church and other religions. For example, a news item in *Katolički list* titled "Soviet Russia: The Number of Catholic Clerics" reported that 137 Catholic priests remained in Soviet Russia, 135 of whom were in "dungeons or concentration camps."[20] Communism had spread to Yugoslavia as well. It had been made illegal in 1920, but that measure only increased its mystery, as it was difficult to gauge its actual strength in local society.

In the years leading up to the Second World War, *Katolički list* also regularly printed enthusiastic reports about the victories of Francisco Franco in Spain, laced with outrage at the alleged crimes of the Spanish "reds." One news article described the agonies of specific priests in dramatic detail, including a new method of torture that the "reds" had allegedly invented: "The victims [were] rolled into hay soaked in gasoline and then burned ... as a torch."[21] In another article, *Katolički list* published a telegram that Pope Pius XII had sent to "General Franco," expressing support for "His Excellency" the *caudillo* and "praying to God for [his] new successes."[22]

Fascist anti-communism appealed to the Church. At the same time, however, the Catholic Church in Croatia followed with apprehension the developments in Italy and Germany. In a series of articles with titles such as "Italy: Fascist Press Continues with Slanderous Attacks against Italian Clergy,"[23] "Germany: Imprisonments of Catholic Priests,"[24] and "Germany: Propaganda for Dropping Out of Church,"[25] *Katolički list* expressed serious alarm about the Italian Fascist and especially the German National Socialist attitude toward the Catholic Church.

In this context, going the way of either Nazi Germany or the Soviet Union was undesirable in the eyes of the Church, as was the preservation of decadent liberal democracy, especially in union with hegemonic, Orthodox Serbia. Therefore, an independent Greater Croatia, led by a fascist regime that was nationalist, socially and morally conservative, anti-communist, and devoutly Catholic must have appeared like a fairly good score in the political crapshoot of those unpredictable times.

II

On the eve of the Second World War, Father Silvestar Zubić was already involved in the Ustaša movement. He participated in the Ustaša takeover of Vukovar during the first days of the German attack on Yugoslavia, as did a number of

Figure 8.1 Father Silvestar Zubić with his class. Zubić served as eighth-grade headroom teacher during the school year 1943–44. Sitting next to Zubić is Josip Meštrović, Vukovar High School principal during the NDH.

his students, including Antun Gölis and most likely Tomislav Stanišić and Vladimir Radauš as well.[26] *Between 1941 and 1944, Zubić served the regime as Adjutant for Civil Affairs at the Ustaša headquarters in Vukovar.*[27] *In postwar testimony, lawyer Josip Herčik listed Zubić among "the main Ustaša authorities in Vukovar."*[28] *He regularly participated at Ustaša Youth meetings at the high school, where he delivered speeches against communism and in support of fascism and the Ustaša movement. He taught his students in a similar manner. After his most ardent Ustaša students such as Stanišić and Radauš graduated and joined an elite army unit called "Poglavnik's Bodyguard," the Ustaša spirit in the high school waned, at which time Zubić organized student spies to clamp down on anti-Ustaša activity among students and teachers.*[29] *His efforts led to the expulsion of three female students from the high school for criticizing the Ustaša movement and failing to use the Ustaša salute.*[30]

The Catholic Church in Croatia was a crucial partner of the Ustaša movement during the establishment of its regime in April 1941. The Church's support for the Ustaša came rather naturally. The movement was aligned with the Church's main interests – or fears – and it was popular among the clergy. The Catholic clergy in Croatia was an elite borne of "the Croatian people" –

the dominant group of Slavic speakers in the region, hitherto marked most prominently by its Catholicism, as opposed to Eastern Orthodoxy or Islam. During the Croatian nation-building process in the nineteenth and twentieth centuries, the Catholic clergy had a capillary presence in what would evolve into the national Croatian society. In this predominantly rural society, the Church was one of the key carriers of Croatian nationalism from literate elites to the rural masses.

In the interwar period, the Ustaša movement won favour with many Croat nationalists, including Zubić, because of its opposition to union with Serbia. The movement's popularity grew steadily in the 1930s as the interwar state struggled economically and became riven with internal divisions. It made loud splashes in the country and internationally with strikes against the state such as the short-lived 1932 Velebit uprising in western Croatia and the 1934 assassination of the Serb king, Alexander I "the Unifier," in Marseille, France. Illegal Ustaša cells littered Croat-populated lands, assisted by Church-affiliated organizations such as the "Great Brotherhood and Sisterhood of the Crusaders."[31] By 1941, many dozens, probably hundreds, of clerics had become involved in the Ustaša movement, assisting it in a multitude of ways, from organizing cells and mobilizing new members to distributing illegal pamphlets and acting as couriers between the exiled Ustaša leaders in Italy and the organization in Yugoslavia.

As one of many documented examples, Father Pipini , mentioned earlier as the author of the *Katolički list* article "Along the Adriatic Coast," was a member of the Ustaša cell in his parish in Slavonska Požega, attending meetings and, later, organizing the disarming of the Yugoslav army during the German attack in April 1941.[32]

Thus, on the eve of the German attack, the Ustaša movement had a well-organized core constituency[33] – while far from enjoying support of the majority of the Croat population, it was radicalized, extremely passionate about its goals, and eager to act against the perceived doom of the Croatian nation. Within this core constituency, Ustaša clerics formed a significant factor in practical, mobilizational, and political terms when the German attack finally came. First, they lent the Ustaša movement their skills and education in organizational terms, by assisting the takeover of local political authority and the disarming of retreating Yugoslav units. Second, as a result of their grassroots and public involvement in the Ustaša takeover, the many clerics who participated in the establishment of Ustaša authority were able to inspire locals to join the cause themselves, thus boosting Ustaša mobilization. But the Ustaša clerics' most significant contribution to the Ustaša takeover of Croatian society had to do with the *legitimacy* they provided to the nascent regime in the eyes of the undecided Croat majority. The presence of ordained Catholic clerics in local Ustaša units and the NDH administration was a powerful asset for the movement that had just stepped into the daylight and was in the process of taking political control over a Catholic society. Indeed, Catholic priests and friars conveyed an image of trust, community, as well as Croat particularity and unity within the larger body of the "Whatcha-macallit" linguistic space.[34]

The Church leadership greeted the founding of the NDH with enthusiasm. On 14 April, the head of the Catholic Church in Croatia, archbishop of Zagreb Alojzije Stepinac, made an official visit to General Slavko Kvaternik, who had declared the state's founding four days earlier. The archbishop "expressed his congratulations for the restoration of state independence."[35] On 16 April, Stepinac had an official audience with "Poglavnik" Ante Pavelić.[36] *Katolički list*, in its issue of 21 April, reported that event on its front page in an editorial titled "The Independent State of Croatia." The week of the founding of the NDH was also the first week of the Easter season, and 1941 was the 1,300th anniversary of the Croats' conversion to Christianity. The omens seemed promising. The editorial noted pointedly that the Croatian troops had rebelled "on Easter Thursday," that the "Poglavnik" had arrived "on Easter," and that the new government had taken an oath of service to "almighty God," "the Croatian people," "the NDH," and "Ustaša principles." "A Croatian state is, therefore, a fact," the editorial continued, "an ideal that our ancestors carried in their souls for centuries. It has been realized by the Almighty Providence in the year of a great national jubilee. The Catholic Church ... follows with happiness these days of the rise of the Croatian people and the restoration of its independent state."[37] As one historian put it, Croats "considered the new Croatian government, dominated by Ustaše, as being eminently theirs. All previous governments had been foreign and oppressive, and now for the first time, the Croats had come into power."[38]

As the Ustaša began implementing its policy of violence against Serbs and Jews, the Church acted cautiously. Its social influence was significant, but it had no decision-making authority, and in the context of the troubles the

Catholic Church was facing in Nazi Germany, it surely wanted to avoid losing favour with the regime. As we will see, under Stepinac's leadership the Church seems to have taken an official stance of measured criticism and avoidance of direct conflict with the regime, but never to the point of withdrawing its support, for the NDH was now an independent Croatian state, and other political alternatives seemed much worse.

On 23 April 1941, Stepinac wrote to Andrija Artuković, the NDH's interior minister, to advocate for baptized Jews to be exempted from the recently decreed racial laws. On 14 May, days after the Ustaša massacre of 388 Serbs in the village of Prekopa,[39] Stepinac wrote to Pavelić demanding "all measures to be taken that not another Serb is killed, if he has not committed any proven acts that deserve a death sentence."[40] On 22 May, he again wrote to Artuković to protest passionately against the new measure forcing Jews to wear the Star of David.[41] However, Stepinac's Archbishopric's media mouthpiece, *Katolički list*, continued publishing anti-Serbian and antisemitic comments and texts. One article compared the struggle of "anti-communists" against "communists" during the Second World War to the struggle of Christ and his followers against the Jews "2000 years ago" and, in no uncertain terms, "reminded" readers that it was the Jews that killed Christ. "'We want his death no matter what,'" the author wrote, putting words into ancient Jews' mouths, "'even though he is innocent ... And we are conscious ... that the revenge for the crime will be enormous. So be it. If the punishment is so big that we, who ask for his blood, cannot bear it, let it fall on our children too ... His blood be on us and on our children.' (Matthew 27:23–5)."[42]

Notwithstanding the racial laws, the multiplying massacres, and Stepinac's private protests, the Church's official attitude toward the Ustaša movement remained unchanged. *Katolički list*'s editorial of 3 June 1941, whose authors were apparently still drunk on the gift of political independence and an apparently God-fearing, Catholic leadership, stated that the relationship between the regime and the Church would be "a relationship of complementarity, where the clergy lays and builds the foundations of an orderly and faithful family life." The same editorial praised the regime's conservative stance on public morality, relieved, for example, that "foreign ideologies will be removed without sentimentality" from Croatian theatres. The editorial then ran its fingers deeper into the dirt, dabbling in hidden motives and conspiracies: "Secret forces of powerful freemasonry, assisted profusely by fiercely anti-Catholic currents in the Eastern Orthodox hierarchy, could not stand the free development of the Catholic Church ... Although it would be logical to expect that opposite currents, such as freemasonry and fierce Orthodoxy, cannot come together ... freemasonry, especially Serbian, saw [in Orthodoxy] a natural ally against the Catholic Church." Running its fingers still deeper, the editorial applauded the regime's decree simplifying religious conversions,[43] so that "in a short time, those painful losses that the Catholic Church suffered in former Yugoslavia are corrected, when all those sons, and even more daughters, left their ancestors' faith for marriage. These are now returning to the Church's lap."[44]

On 26 October 1941, Stepinac delivered a public sermon in which, among other things, he spoke against actions based on hatred, calling instead for "love for a human no matter what his name is." "It is distressing," he declared, "that even those who boast their Catholicism, even those in a spiritual profession, become victims of passionate hate and forget the law that is the most beautiful characteristic of Christianity, the law of love."[45] It was a suggestive sermon, but still mild, delivered in general terms, referring to trends of the "last few decades" and naming no culprits.

As the war progressed, Stepinac issued increasingly strident protests against the excesses of the regime and its German overlord.[46] But his objections, public or private, passionate or mild, could not defeat the facts on the ground. Scores of his clergy eagerly involved themselves in the Ustaša "revolution" as members of the movement, local administrators, and even members of the armed forces, as well as outside supporters ready to offer a helping hand.[47] Across the NDH, the unimpeded mass involvement of the Catholic clergy with the Ustaša movement carried far more weight than Stepinac's protests to the Ustaša bigwigs. Stepinac and the Church authorities never directly encouraged the clergy to join the Ustaša, but neither did they ever make a serious effort to discourage them. Instead, the foundations Stepinac set for his clergy's engagement with the new state in April 1941, calling on them to "guard and advance" the NDH,[48] remained in place. Without concrete action that would have curbed the grassroots support the regime received from Catholic clergy across the NDH, Stepinac's protests remained mainly symbolic.

As a consequence of the grassroots support the regime enjoyed among clerics across the NDH, a number of individuals took pro-Ustaša initiatives

in their local communities, confronting the Church with a reality that made
any policy of curbing that trend even harder to contemplate. In the Vukovar
district, for example, besides Father Zubić, several Ustaša clerics were active
in the Ustaša movement: Pavle Gvozdanović, pastor of the Catholic parish
in the village of Kukujevci, was appointed head Ustaša officer in the village
of Berkasovo;[49] Vilko Anderlić, pastor of the parish in the village of Sotin,
became editor-in-chief of the sole newspaper in Vukovar, written in a fierce
Ustaša tone; and the list continues.[50] In Vukovar, Father Dionizije Andrašec,
the Guardian (religious superior) of the Franciscan friary, never joined the
movement itself, but was a frequent participant in Ustaša events. He performed mass conversion services in the Vukovar district, pressing local Serbs
to convert to Catholicism even when they had other options.[51] For example,
on 8 March 1942, he presided over the conversion ceremony of 250 Serbian
families in the village of Bršadin, assisted by Zubić.[52]

The Ustaša regime began its reign of terror against Serbs and Jews in the
first weeks of its government. On 17 April, the new regime issued the *Decree
for the Defence of the People and the State*.[53] The law was loosely worded, allowing for arrests based on "anti-Croatian" activity, but without naming
specific crimes. Between April and July 1941, thousands of Serbs and Jews
were arrested across the NDH, and hundreds killed. In Vukovar, just days
after the Ustaša took power, prominent Serbs and Jews were ordered to report to the police on a daily basis.[54] Mistreatment was commonplace; for
example, one of Father Zubić's high school students mentioned earlier,
Tomislav Stanišić, beat up a Jewish woman.[55] On 10 May 1941, around twenty
Serbs and Jews were arrested, beaten, and taken to nearby Vinkovci,[56] where
101 people were arrested the same day and taken to Zagreb.[57] The arrestees
from Vukovar were dispatched to the Danica concentration camp, except
for three men who were released; the men taken to Danica never returned.[58]

In this context, requests for conversion from Orthodoxy and Judaism to
Catholicism saw a sharp spike. On 19 August 1941, the inhabitants of the village of Rujnice in central NDH, where a number of Ustaša massacres of Serbs
had already been committed, sent a request for conversion to Catholicism
directly to Pavelić, asking "Poglavnik to protect us and spare our lives and
the lives of our children … swearing that in every way we will act as real,
honest, and sincere Croats."[59]

As we have seen, the legal foundations for mass conversion were already in place by May 1941. *Katolički list* first mentioned religious conversions on 15 May, explaining the rules of admittance to Catholicism, since "recently, in certain parishes, many people have asked about 'crossing' into Catholic Church."[60]

The months between April and September 1941 saw not only a rise in conversion requests but also the crushing of the Serbian Orthodox Church in the NDH as well as regime-organized mass deportations of Serbs from the NDH to Serbia. In June, all Orthodox schools and community organizations were ordered closed, the name "Serbian Orthodox faith" was banned and replaced with "Greek-Eastern faith," and Serbs in NDH cities were ordered to wear a blue armband with the letter "P" for "Pravoslavac" (Orthodox).[61] At the same time, tens of thousands of Serbs were being deported to Serbia.[62] Between June and August, *all* Serbian Orthodox priests in the NDH, except those who had been killed or who had fled on their own accord, were interned to await deportation to Serbia.[63] These deportations furthered the goal of decapitating the Serbian community, removing elements seen as unyieldingly Serbian from the NDH, and creating conditions conducive to mass conversion. The Catholic Church, in Croatia or Rome, issued no comment.[64]

The Catholic leadership in Croatia was undoubtedly aware of the mass arrests and deportations of Serbs. In May 1941, the Bishopric of Đakovo, which included Vukovar, printed a handbill titled "Friendly Advice" that targeted the bishopric's Orthodox population and explicitly told potential converts, "as Catholics, you will be able to stay in your homes,"[65] implying that they would not be imprisoned or deported to Serbia. On 8 August 1941, Archbishop Stepinac wrote to the Education Ministry asking for additional funding for Catholic seminaries. Referring to the Banja Luka bishopric, Stepinac wrote that it "cannot send only 2–3 boys to the seminary ... when the number of Catholics in the Bishopric increased fourfold, it is very insufficient."[66] Stepinac knew that such a sharp increase in conversions was certainly not normal, and hardly voluntary or legitimate in terms of canon law; as he stated in his postwar trial, "these were not conversions, but comedies for which the Church cannot bear responsibility ... I know very well that had I not approved and made possible conversions on the repeated insistence of the converts themselves, I would be accused today of not having had the heart and not wanting to save the Serbs from being massacred."[67] Educating additional priests, however, amounted to planning for a future in which the converts would remain Catholic and, as we will see, were no longer Serbs.

III

Father Silvestar Zubić helped organize the Ustaša regime's campaign to forcibly convert Orthodox Serbs to Catholicism. He summoned Serbian students to meetings devised to convince them to convert.[68] *Budimir Mirković, one of Zubić's students, who had been converted to Catholicism, remembers Zubić punishing the converted students for errors in reciting Catholic prayers by beating their hands with a stick: "When he [got] mad, he would raise his habit and on one side he had a stick [hanging from his belt] and on the other side a pistol. But he had to lift the cloth higher up for [the pistol] to be visible; he wanted to scare the students."*[69]

As the Church established the framework for forced conversions, its leaders negotiated with the regime over specific policies. But, as we will see, the state retained firm control over the campaign. On 14 July 1941, the NDH Ministry of Justice and Religious Worship issued a memorandum instructing local bishoprics not to allow conversions to Catholicism for "Orthodox priests, teachers, also intelligentsia in general, and finally the rich merchants, shopkeepers, and rich peasants."[70] Furthermore, crucial to the approval of each individual conversion request was a "rectitude confirmation" – that is, a background check – which could only be conducted by the local Ustaša authorities.[71] The state was making it clear that *it* would decide who was allowed to convert. Moreover, the state did not hesitate to persecute the clerics who opposed it. For example, on 22 August, a state court sentenced canon lawyer Dr Pavle Lončar to death – later remitted to twenty years in prison – "for insulting the state leader and for anti-state and anti-Ustaša propaganda."[72]

The Ustaša regime also prepared the ground for the Serbs' conversion. The agency in charge of the campaign was the Faith Department of the State Directorship for Renewal.[73] The Faith Department sent "missionaries" to municipalities across the NDH to prepare "Greek-Easterners" for conversion. For example, on 22 October 1941, it sent two "missionaries" to the Crkveni Bok municipality, a priest and a schoolteacher, instructing the local Ustaša authorities to pay their honorariums and to transform the Orthodox church building into a Catholic one.[74]

On 17 November 1941, the leadership of the Catholic Church in Croatia made its most vigorous attempt to reclaim some authority over conversions to Catholicism. The most relevant "resolutions" it issued stated that only the Church was authorized "by divine right and canonical decrees" to issue directives regarding conversion and that "missionaries" could be appointed only by Church authorities, not by "municipal bureaucrats, Ustaša functionaries, or the Faith Department." The document also referred to a missive from the Vatican, sent by Cardinal Eugène Tisserant, Secretary for the Congregation of the Oriental Churches. The Cardinal wrote that "the disunited/ outcasts" should be allowed to convert to the Catholic Eastern rite if they had belonged to it before but abandoned Catholicism "under threat and pressure from the Orthodox." By communicating these instructions to other Croatian bishops, Tisserant said, Stepinac will have made "a precious contribution for the proper development of Catholicism, where so much hope exists for converting the 'disunited.'"[75] Tisserant's words revealed the interest-driven attitude of the Vatican, which corresponded to the cooperative relationship that the Church in Croatia pursued with the Ustaša regime.[76]

The Church's "resolutions" were careful not to spark a conflict with the regime. The latter part of the document explained carefully that no blame was being cast on Pavelić or state policy.[77] Indeed, on 3 December 1941, Archbishop Stepinac wrote to Rome to report that "the best prospects appear to exist" for the conversion of the Orthodox.[78] It seems that the regime wanted to preserve its friendly relations with the Church, for it apparently approved one of the resolution's requests. On 14 February 1942, it was the Đakovo Bishopric, rather than the Faith Department, that appointed as "missionaries" Vukovar Franciscans Stjepan Rade and Pavao Dodić to provide religious instruction for local converts and transform Orthodox churches into Catholic ones.[79] Of course, the change in authority for appointing "missionaries" made little difference to the people being forced to convert.

Despite such compromises, the conversion campaign remained under firm Ustaša control. "Rectitude confirmations" were still a requirement, so the state still had the final say on each conversion. In addition, on 2 November 1941, the government had instructed local municipalities that their Serb employees must submit proof of conversion to Catholicism in order to keep their jobs.[80]

And on 30 December 1941, Serb retirees were ordered to provide proof of conversion to Catholicism to continue receiving retirement payments.[81]

IV

Father Silvestar Zubić was involved in "missionary" activity among the Serbian inhabitants of villages around Vukovar. To help with this work, Vice-Governor Luka Aždajić lent Zubić a car.[82] Zubić's high school church choir performed at a number of mass conversion ceremonies.[83] On at least one occasion, Zubić assisted the priest performing the mass baptism.[84] In late 1941, Vukovar's municipal authorities organized three public gatherings for the city's Serbs at the Orthodox church. Zubić presided over these gatherings. An unknown priest assisted him and delivered speeches contending that Catholicism and Orthodoxy were essentially the same faith, that conversion was also in line with the desires of the government, and that "this was not a forcible conversion, yet adding that whoever does not convert ... can count with worst consequences and that the Catholic Church would not be able to protect and guard them against regime persecution."[85]

As noted earlier, the Church issued strict instructions for the clergy involved in the conversion campaign.[86] However, much looser standards were applied on the ground. Without a doubt, the most egregious breaches of Church instructions and canon law involved forcing the Orthodox to convert by issuing threats and performing conversion ceremonies en masse.

Father Pipinić, mentioned several times before in this chapter, was active in the Ustaša conversion campaign, engaging in both threats and mass conversion ceremonies. Witnesses from the village of Crkveni Vrhovci remember his visit in late 1941, when he told them, "the law says you have to convert because, if not, you will be taken into camps." In January 1942, Pipinić converted around 150 Crkveni Vrhovci inhabitants in a mass ceremony.

As a rule, however, open threats were issued mainly by local Ustaša authorities. In the village of Bobota, for example, the head of the Vukovar district, Vladimir Šipuš, told the family members of thirty-two people taken to Jasenovac concentration camp that their relatives would be released if the entire village converted to Catholicism; if they did not, another fifty villagers would be arrested. Serbs from Bobota stopped inquiring about their family members when "we learned through secret channels that our children have been killed."[87]

Archbishop Stepinac's directives tacitly approved fear-motivated conversions. His circular of 2 March 1942 stated that converts must have "pure intent, without dishonorable motivations, with belief in the truthfulness of Catholicism. That must be the first and main motivation for conversion. Should the convert have other, secondary motivations, they should not hinder the conversion unless they are sinful."[88] Considering his statements in the paragraphs above, it is likely that Stepinac here counted on hitting two birds with one stone: if these conversions stuck, the Church would have won a major victory in its centuries-old struggle with "eastern heresy"; if they did not, conversions would have saved innocent lives.

In tandem with fear-induced conversion requests came the mass ceremonies. As one example among many in Vukovar area, on 25 March, catechist David Pohl conducted the mass conversion of more than 165 Serbs in the town of Ilok; priest Valentin Mekovec gave "a beautiful sermon to the converts … placing on their hearts love toward the Church and the homeland where they are located;" "all converts," *Hrvatski Borac* reported, were "just delighted" on their way home.[89] As for Serbs who remained in Vukovar and did not convert, their situation was clear:

ANNOUNCEMENT

All male Greek-easterners [Eastern Orthodox] born between 1887 and 1918, who have not converted to Roman Catholic faith, are called to report for registration to the military department of this Authority, before noon on business days.

This order also concerns those who are not indigenous in Vukovar, as well as those who are foreign citizens. Whoever does not respond to this call will be severely punished and taken to a concentration camp.

City Council
in Vukovar, March 27, 1942
City Mayor: **Türk**[90]

V

Father Silvestar Zubić remained committed to his Ustaša ideals throughout the
war. He investigated and denounced the high school students whom he suspected
of collaborating with the resistance.[91] *In 1943, communist resistance fighters*
caught Zubić in a village near Vukovar. They questioned him, then carved a
five-pointed star, the size of a hand, on his chest, and released him. Budimir
Mirković, a fifth grader at the time, remembers Zubić showing the star-shaped
wound to his class.[92] *In 1944, members of two Orthodox families, Likić and*
Lončarić, were discovered brutally slain in their households. It was rumoured
around Vukovar that Zubić was linked to the murders. However, Zubić's name
was never mentioned at the sham trial the Ustaša authorities organized to pacify
the citizenry shocked by such senseless violence on their doorstep.[93] *For the oc-*
casion of the third anniversary of the NDH, *the state awarded Zubić a medal,*
the "Order of Merit of 2nd Degree."[94]

Underlying the forced conversion campaign was a widely publicized claim
that "the great majority of Serbs" were, in fact, Croats-of-old who had become Orthodox (and thus Serbian) as a result of the evil schemes of the
Serbian Orthodox Church and Greater Serbian machinations; the Ustaša
conversion campaign was, therefore, merely the Orthodox returning to
"the faith of their fathers."[95] The regime presented this theory as having been
legitimized by the Vatican, given that its academic foundation was a doctoral dissertation defended by a Croatian cleric, Krunoslav Draganović, at
the Pontifical Institute in Rome in 1937.[96] In its diplomatic contacts with the
NDH, the Vatican indeed appeared to have approved the Ustaša thesis and
the campaign to reclaim the "strayed" Orthodox for the Catholic Church.[97]
In support of this theory, the Saint Jerome Society in Zagreb, a Catholic
group, published a pamphlet titled "Return to the Fathers' Faith," in which
it stated that "unreasonable people wanted to impose the shameful and hu-
miliating name 'Serb' on Croats of Greek-Eastern faith ... Hence, no Croat,
of any faith, will be called by that name."[98] For the Ustaša regime, therefore,
the crucial element of the campaign of forced conversion was not the Serbs'
religious identity but rather their *ethnonational* one. Several facts make this
clear: regime instructions regarding the converts' ethnicity, the range of religions available to the persecuted population, and the creation of the Croatian Orthodox Church.

On 13 January 1942, Pavelić's office sent a memo to the Ministry of Internal Affairs specifying that "Serb converts to Catholicism are considered Croats, hence are to be written in as Croats. Notify regional offices."[99] This directive indicates that Serbs were, in fact, being subjected to a "double conversion" – *religious* conversion from Serbian Orthodoxy to Catholicism (or, as we will see, to "Croatian" Orthodoxy) as well as a *legal*, state-decreed conversion from Serbian to Croatian *ethnicity*.

Identical rules applied to Serb converts to Islam. On 10 February 1942, the Ministry of Internal Affairs sent a follow-up memo to lower levels of the administration: "Our memo of January 20, 1942 … naturally applies to Greek-Easterners/Serbs who convert to the Muslim religion, hence are also … to be logged as Croats."[100] Indeed, "Greek-Easterners/Serbs" were permitted to convert to Islam, to Evangelicalism, or even, after the intervention of the Catholic Church, to Greek Catholicism.[101] Even if the Ustaša movement preferred that they convert to Catholicism, absorbing Croatia's Serbs into the body of the Croatian nation was more important than bringing them under the wing of the Catholic Church. Clearly, the regime was engaging in proper fascist population engineering rather than any kind of misguided religiosity.

So it is not surprising that, after the above-mentioned mass conversion ceremony performed by Pipini on 150 Serbs from Crkveni Vrhovci, Ustaša captain Petranović gave a speech to the converts, who until just hours before had trembled before Ustaša units, calling on them to *join* those very Ustaša units; these people were now considered Croats.[102]

In the Ustaša population engineering imagination, Serbs appear to have represented an abstract, malleable concept: they could be killed, deported, or converted to Catholicism and recast as Croats. By contrast, Jews and Roma remained a fixed, inescapable "category" in the eye of the regime. Regarding the Jews, it first appeared that racial definitions might be bendable, since the NDH authorities allowed them to convert to Catholicism; the converts hoped their baptism would allow them to evade persecution and deportation.[103] But these were empty hopes for Jews. Vukovar attorney Dr Daniel Klein and his wife Leona Lili were baptized as Catholics on 8 April 1942;[104] their daughter Elizabeta had been baptized earlier, on 12 December 1941.[105] All three were eventually murdered in the Jasenovac death camp.[106] All the Jews of Vukovar, baptized or not, suffered a similar fate, except for a handful of survivors.[107] As the regime's 30 July 1941 instructions on conversion specified, the Jews' conversion meant nothing, because in their case, the racial laws took precedence.[108] While the murder of the NDH's Jews was clearly an Ustaša policy, it seems that many in the Church agreed in principle that anti-Jewish measures should be taken.[109]

The policy against Roma was more chaotic. The regime's blanket approach was annihilation, but Roma were of less concern to the Ustaša. They were seen as a nuisance – as beggars, thieves, hustlers, prostitutes – and as a threat to the purity of Croatian "blood," as well as an obstacle to the Ustaša's vision of public order and morality.[110] Unlike Jews and Serbs, however, they were not seen as an imminent threat to the Ustaša national project.[111] In the Vukovar area, the "cleansing" of Roma began in the spring of 1942. Nikola Dimitrijević was one of 860 Roma from the village of Novi Jankovci, all of whom were arrested on 15 August 1942 and taken to Jasenovac. The first day at the camp, Dimitrijević's mother, wife, and two children were killed before his eyes; within fifteen days, 845 Roma from Novi Jankovci were dead.[112]

The Ustaša genocide against the Jews and Roma, who numbered only in the tens of thousands, was logistically incomparable to the genocide against the Serbs, whose population approached 2 million. The anti-Serbian policy necessitated a flexible, contingent approach. By early 1942, it was clear that the campaign of conversion to Catholicism was not yielding the hoped-for results. One Ustaša source, allegedly relying on the words of Archbishop Stepinac, estimated that 100,000 Orthodox had been converted by early 1942[113] – perhaps some thousands more when those who converted to Islam or Protestantism are added, but still far less than the "one million" that the Faith Department had expected.[114] The Serbs had not been convinced by the "faith of their fathers" theory, they resisted conversion even in the face of force,[115] and the flames of rebellion against the NDH – generated primarily by the genocidal campaign against the Serbs that included these very conversions – were already problematic by early 1942. On 3 April 1942, therefore, the regime unveiled its final large-scale attempt to "convert" the NDH's Serbs into Croats: the founding of the Croatian Orthodox Church (Hrvatska pravoslavna crkva, or HPC).[116] The HPC represented a desperate attempt by a zealously fascist but also weak and incompetent regime to solve the "Serbian question" once and for all by rubber-stamping all Serbs into Croats with the stroke of a pen.

Indeed, when the HPC was declared one of the NDH's "approved" religions in April 1942, "Serbs" and "Greek-Easterners" disappeared as an official population category; they had become Orthodox Croats or, more commonly, "the Orthodox." Bosnian Muslims had been counted as Croats from the start, so converting Serbs into either Catholics or the "Croatian Orthodox" turned the NDH into a picture-perfect monoethnic state, with "Croats" forming roughly 94 per cent of its population.[117]

To illustrate, on 27 August 1942, when Vukovar High School student Maksim Stanišić and two of his schoolmates filed registration forms for the coming school year, they entered "Serb" as their ethnicity; two days later, the principal called them into his office, where he told them that Serbian ethnicity did not exist and instructed them to correct their entries by writing "Croat," which they did. The next day, the three students were summoned to the local Ustaša headquarters, where they were beaten, as well as threatened with revolvers and a "space at Dudik," the nearby Ustaša mass shooting site.[118]

Even so, forced conversions to Catholicism continued. The Ustaša movement drew its strength mainly from Catholic Croats, and this was reflected on the ground. For instance, Muslim members of the movement complained that their Catholic counterparts were forcing Serbs to convert specifically to Catholicism and harassing those who opted for Islam.[119] It appears that after the HPC was created, the regime left significant freedom for local activists to continue with Catholic proselytization. As Pavelić announced the establishment of the HPC, the previously mentioned head of Vukovar's Franciscan friary, Guardian Dionizije Andrašec, told a delegation of local Serbs that he had gone to Zagreb to inquire on this matter. There, he reported, the relevant minister had told him personally that Pavelić's statement was for "foreign affairs and diplomatic representatives, to show that there is no violence with conversions," but that it "has no bearing on the conversion campaign itself." Andrašec advised the men not to withdraw from conversion since their lives and property would "again be in great insecurity." The men took his advice and converted.[120] Note that Andrašec justified his continued proselytization by referring to state authorities rather than official Church policy or canon law. It appears that the activist clergy continued the forced conversion campaign according to Ustaša guidelines, which was thus mainly a continuation of existing arrangements.[121]

Unsurprisingly, the HPC received a cold welcome from the Catholic Church.[122] Croats had become a people of three faiths, with Catholicism as undoubtedly the most important faith in practice, but not in theory. Had it continued to rule beyond 1945, it is impossible to say whether the Ustaša regime, in cooperation with loyal clerics, would have pursued conversion to Catholicism until the HPC ceased to exist. Most "former" Serbs, however, did remain "Orthodox Croats" until the end of the war. In the short term, even if preferring Catholicism, the Ustaša nation-building policy was essentially *ethnonational* rather than religious.

Regardless of the Church's support and level of involvement, the Ustaša ethnonational consolidation project was doomed to failure. Ustaša mass violence against the Serbs generated armed resistance, which led to repression, which generated further resistance, and this vicious cycle could not be stopped by ethno-religious machinations. Most Serbs had no illusions about the kind of state the NDH was, and eventually, neither did most Croats, Bosnian Muslims, and others. The NDH had joined in the Nazi genocide against the Jews and the Roma, it had launched its own genocide against the Serbs, and it was unable to reign in the chaos of internal warfare that, at one time or another, ravaged almost the entire country. The regime, then, was turning its citizens into enemies, and as doubts took hold about the Ustaša national project, Serbs remained the main target of desperate Ustaša attempts to quash resistance to its rule. The regime continued treating them as second-class citizens regardless of their membership in the Catholic Church or the HPC, effectively defeating the entire point of the conversions.

In the Vukovar area, for example, the hostages the NDH and German forces took from the local population in response to partisan attacks, and those among them who were later shot in retribution, were almost all newly minted Catholics or "Orthodox Croats," or Jews.[123] In 1943, those Serbs from Crkveni Vrhovci whom Father Pipinić had converted into Croats the year before were taken to concentration camps, and their village was razed. No voice was raised to protect them, neither by Pipinić nor the Church.[124]

CONCLUSION

After the collapse of the NDH, Father Zubić went into hiding until his arrest in 1950. The communist authorities of the re-established Yugoslavia sentenced him to twenty years' imprisonment with hard labour. In 1951, the head office of the Franciscan order in Zagreb filed a demand for the release of Zubić and several other Franciscans, but Zubić remained in prison. However, the communist authorities later reduced his sentence, first to fifteen years and then to ten. In 1958, after positive testimonials from the administration of Stara Gradiška prison, Zubić was freed and the remainder of his sentence was remitted. Zubić continued serving the Catholic Church in various towns as a catechist, parish priest, and librarian. He died in 1970.[125] His former high school student Vladimir Radauš disappeared during the final days of the Second World War.[126] Radauš's former classmate Antun Gölis disappeared after being arrested by the communist authorities in May 1945.[127] Former student Tomislav Stanišić fled to Argentina in 1948, returning to Croatia in 1996.[128]

For the Ustaša regime, the forced conversion campaign, like the genocide against the Serbs in general, was essentially an ethnonational project. Serbs who before April 1941 had lived alongside Croats were primarily "undesirables" in the eye of the Ustaša regime and were turned into "Greek-Easterners," "Croats-of-old," "new Catholics," "new Muslims," or "Orthodox Croats" only as a tool of genocide. To achieve ethnonational uniformity for the NDH, the Ustaša regime subjected the Serbs to a process of "double conversion," first religious and then legal; the latter – creating Croats – was the regime's ultimate aim. It thus turned out that Ustaša fascism was more similar to the German and Italian variants than the Catholic Church might have hoped – the nation ranked above all else, including the Church.

Many Catholic clerics took part in the Ustaša movement before and during the Second World War. Like Father Zubić, they had chosen to serve the aims of the Ustaša movement, often in contradiction to the fundamental principles of Christianity. Still, many Ustaša clerics probably did not seek genocide. Moreover, the participation of Catholic clerics in the Ustaša movement is perhaps less shocking than one would expect. Belief that they have in their grasp the absolute truth and a duty to save one's group, or all humanity, from a looming precipice is a trait that most Christian denominations, indeed most organized religions, share with totalitarian ideologies. We would do well to remember that at this time in history, Catholics sincerely believed that conversion to Catholicism would save a person's soul for eternity. But we would also do well to remember that genocides are rarely if ever the result of a long-standing evil plan. On the contrary, genocides tend to arise from a process of gradually radicalizing "solutions" for a perceived population problem on the ground, usually in pursuit of a future utopian society, a new Eden, always imagined in terms of unity, happiness, and abundance – all of these aims imagined as eventually *total*.

It is important to understand the perceived threats and serious dilemmas that the Catholic Church in Croatia faced in these tumultuous years; from the perspective of the time, both domestic and international, the Church's fears appeared indeed to have a basis in reality. Having carefully considered its options, the Church prioritized the Croatian state- and nation-building projects and the Catholic anti-Schismatic drive over the questionable nature of the Ustaša movement, which had begun exhibiting its tyrannical nature in the very first months after its rise to power. Still, in Ustaša Croatia, the Catholic Church was not involved in state affairs to the extent that the label "clero-fascist," which has been used to describe the NDH, would suggest. The Church left space for its clerics to be active in the Ustaša movement, and, as a rule, it followed regime directives, but it was not directly involved in Ustaša decisions. Nonetheless, the Church ended up cutting a multitude of moral, ethical, and canonical corners in pursuit of its perceived interests during this era, ultimately becoming an intermittently willing but always obedient accomplice in Ustaša campaigns of forced assimilation and, by extension, genocide.

NOTES

1 Miroslav Akmadža and Slađana Josipović Batorek, *Stradanja svećenika Đakovačke i Srijemske biskupije 1944.–1960.* (Slavonski Brod: Hrvatski institut za povijest, 2012), 373.

2 *Report for School Year 1936–7* (Vukovar: Državna realna gimnazija u Vukovaru, 1937), 4.

3 *Report for School Year 1938–9* (Vukovar: Državna realna gimnazija u Vukovaru, 1939), 3.

4 Akmadža and Batorek, *Stradanja svećenika Đakovačke*, 373.

5 Mirko Kovačić, *U potrazi za istinom: Martirij Hrvata u Vukovaru 1941–1945* (Vukovar: Matica hrvatska, 2004), 354.

6 Testimony of Poljac Miroslav, Archive of Yugoslavia (hereafter SR-AJ), 110, 677–293/4; and testimony of Herčik Josip, SR-AJ 110, 677–94.

7 Testimony of Reisendorf Stjepan Junior "Ceca," SR-AJ 110, 677–98; testimony of Poljac Miroslav, SR-AJ 110, 677–293/4, and Stanišić Maksim, SR-AJ 110, 677–142. Witness Stjepan "Ceca" Reisendorf became active in the Ustaša

movement in fall of 1941.

8 *Report for School Years 1941–42, 1942–43, and 1943–44* (Vukovar: Državna realna gimnazija u Vukovaru, 1944), 16. See also testimony of Stanišić Maksim, SR-AJ 110, 677–142.

9 Based on a 1941 German Foreign Ministry estimate, cited in Fikreta Butić-Jelić, *Ustaša i NDH* (Zagreb: SN Liber/Školska knjiga, 1977), 106. There were also around 150,000 Germans (2 per cent), 65,000 Czechs and Slovaks (1 per cent), 40,000 Jews (0.6 per cent), and 30,000 Slovenians (0.5 per cent). The German estimate was probably slightly higher than the actual numbers.

10 Over 80 per cent of Jews in the NDH perished under the murderous policy of the Ustaša regime, which eagerly embraced the Nazi "solution to the Jewish question."

11 Gerald Steinacher, *Nazis on the Run: How Hitler's Henchmen Fled Justice* (New York: Oxford University Press, 2011), 129–30. As Steinacher notes, "the Croatian subcommittee of the PCA [Vatican relief commission] was particularly active in issuing denazification certificates and falsified passports" (114). See also Steinacher, 101–58, for more information on the Vatican ratlines, including the Croatian network.

12 On the Ustaša genocide against the Serbs, see Paul Mojzes, *Balkan Genocides: Holocaust and Ethnic Cleansing in the Twentieth Century* (Lanham: Rowman & Littlefield, 2011), 52–64. See also, Butić-Jelić, *Ustaše i NDH*, 162–77.

13 "Celebration of the 1300th Anniversary of the Baptism of Croats in Ilok," *Srijemski Hrvat* 2, no. 5 (27 January 1940), 2.

14 See Christian Axboe Nielsen, *Making Yugoslavs: Identity in King Aleksandar's Yugoslavia* (Toronto: University of Toronto Press, 2014), Part I.

15 For a history of Yugoslavism, see John R. Lampe, *Yugoslavia as History: Twice There Was a Country* (Cambridge: Cambridge University Press, 2000), Chapters 1–3.

16 "Numerical Development of Croats over Nine Decades," *Katolički list* 90, no. 9 (2 March 1939), 115. Translation mine. For issues of space, this chapter will draw mainly from articles from *Katolički list*, Croatia's leading contemporary Catholic publication.

17 "Christian Elements in Culture," *Katolički list* 90, no. 14 (6 April 1939), 175.

18 Franjo Pipinić, "Along the Adriatic Coast," *Katolički list* 90, no. 34 (24 August 1939), 415–17; Pipinić, "Along the Adriatic Coast (End)," *Katolički list* 90, no. 35 (31 August 1939), 429–31.

19 Pipinić, "Along the Adriatic Coast," *Katolički list* 90, no. 34; Pipinić, "Along the Adriatic Coast (End)," *Katolički list* 90, no. 35.

20 "Soviet Russia: Number of Catholic clerics," *Katolički list* 90, no. 8 (23 February 1939), 103.

21 "Spain: Bestial Rampage of the Reds," *Katolički list* 90, no. 18 (4 May 1939), 231.

22 "Spain: Telegram from Pius XII to General Franco," *Katolički list* 90, no. 11 (16 March 1939), 143.

23 "Italy: Fascist Press Continues with Slanderous Attacks against Italian Clergy," *Katolički list* 90, no. 3 (19 January 1939), 34.

24 "Germany: Imprisonments of Catholic Priests," *Katolički list* 90, no. 3 (19 January 1939), 35.

25 "Germany: Propaganda for Dropping Out of Church," *Katolički list* 90, no. 11 (16 March 1939), 142.

26 Testimony of Reisendorf Stjepan Senior, SR-AJ 110, 677–98.

27 Miroslav Akmadža, *Katolička crkva u Hrvatskoj i komunistički režim, 1945.–1966.* (Rijeka: Otokar Keršovani, 2004), 351.

28 Testimony of Herčik Josip, SR-AJ 110, 677–94.

29 Testimony of Poljac Miroslav, SR-AJ 110, 677–293/4; and testimony of Reisendorf Stjepan Junior "Ceca," SR-AJ 110, 681–30. "Poglavnik's Body-guard Unit" (Poglavnikov tjelesni sdrug, or PTS) was an independent army unit within the armed forced of the NDH. Membership in the PTS was considered a great honour. Witness Stjepan "Ceca" Reisendorf joined the PTS himself after graduation from Vukovar High School.

30 Testimony of Stanišić Maksim, SR-AJ 110, 677–142. "Za dom spremni!" ("For home, ready!") was the Ustaša equivalent of the Nazi "Sieg heil!"

31 See Joža Horvat and Zdenko Štambuk, *Dokumenti o protunarodnom radu i zločinima jednog dijela katoličkog klera* (Zagreb: Zaklada August Cesarec, 2008), 292–303. Silvester Zubić led the Crusaders' chapter in Vukovar High School (testimony of Reisendorf Stjepan Junior "Ceca," SR-AJ 110, 681–30).

32 For Pipinić's activities during the war, see Horvat and Štambuk, *Dokumenti*, 18.

33 The concept of "core constituency" was developed by sociologist Michael Mann in his book *Dark Side of Democracy: Explaining Ethnic Cleansing* (Cambridge: Cambridge University Press, 2012).

34 "Whatchamacallit" is the provisional name I adopted for the former "Serbo-Croatian" language, today recognized by four distinct names stem-

ming from the linguistic politics of the four successor states of former Yugoslavia (Croatia, Serbia, Bosnia-Herzegovina, and Montenegro). The provisional name avoids the politicization involved in calling the language by any of the four variants or, should one decide to list them all, the order in which they are listed. In addition, the provisional name serves to point out a fascinating political and sociolinguistic phenomenon and carries with it a well-earned dose of ridicule.

35 "Visit of His Eminence Archbishop to General Kvaternik," *Katolički list* 92, no. 16 (21 April 1941), 195.

36 "His Eminence Mr. Archbishop in Audience with the Poglavnik of the State of Croatia," *Katolički list* 92, no. 16 (21 April 1941), 195. "Poglavnik" is an Ustaša equivalent of "Duce," "Führer," or "Caudillo."

37 "Independent State of Croatia," *Katolički list* 92, no. 16 (21 April 1941), 185–7.

38 Jure Krišto, "The Catholic Church in Croatia and Bosnia–Herzegovina in the Face of Totalitarian Ideologies and Regimes," in *Religion under Siege I: The Roman Catholic Church in Occupied Europe (1939–1950)*, eds. Lieve Gevers and Jan Bank (Leuven: Peeters, 2007), 59. While Krišto's framing of the historical narrative, as well as his conclusions and analyses, are in places highly problematic, entering the territory of historical revisionism, his work is a good source for facts on the perspectives, political engagement, and suffering of the Church, its clergy, and Catholic organizations in Croatia during this era.

39 See Branko Vujasinović, Čedomir Višnjić, and Đuro Roksandić, *Glina 13. maja 1941: u povodu 70. godišnjice ustaškog zločina* (Zagreb: SKD Prosvjeta, 2011).

40 Vinko Nikolić, ed., *Stepinac mu je ime: zbornik uspomena, svjedočanstava i dokumenata*, vol. 1 (Zagreb: Kršćanska sadašnjost, 1991), 316.

41 Krišto, "The Catholic Church," 64.

42 "History Repeats," *Katolički list* 92, no. 44 (6 November 1941), 519–20.

43 The *Decree on Conversion from One Faith to Another* of 3 May 1941.

44 "Labor on Inner Renewal," *Katolički list* 62, nos. 21–2 (3 June 1941), 245. In another article, *Katolički list* says that Jews "founded" the "anti-Christian" Freemasons and were its "most active members." On this point, see "History Repeats (End)," *Katolički list* 92, no. 46 (27 November 1941), 552.

45 "Jesus, King of Hearts, Have Mercy on Us," *Katolički list* 92:, no. 3 (30 October 1941), 502.

46 See Jozo Tomasevich, *War and Revolution in Yugoslavia, 1941–1945: Occupation*

and Collaboration (Stanford: Stanford University Press, 2001), 556–8. Tomasevich writes that Stepinac may have remained primarily neutral also for
humanitarian reasons, afraid of being unable "to continue supporting and
protecting about 7,000 orphaned, mostly Orthodox children."

47 For examples of activist clerics across the NDH, see Horvat i Štambuk,
Dokumenti, 181–90. In *War and Revolution*, 555, Tomasevich states: "A considerable number of Catholic priests and a large number of well-known
Catholic intellectuals openly sided with the regime and assumed responsible positions in it … On June 2, 1945 … Abbott Marcone, papal legate in
Zagreb [said] that the Catholic Church in Croatia tended to identify itself
too closely with the Ustaša movement during the war."

48 "Circular to the Honorable Clergy of the Zagreb Archbishopric," *Katolički
list* 92, no. 17 (29 April 1941), 197.

49 Testimony of Daražac Ivan, SR-AJ 110, 677–42; testimony of Đorđević Lazar,
SR-AJ 110, 677–63/64.

50 See *Hrvatski Borac*, in circulation between December 1941 and June 1942.

51 As we will see, Andrašec pushed Serbs to convert to Catholicism even after
the Ustaša regime created the Croatian Orthodox Church. See testimony
of Pojić Savo, SR-AJ 110, 677–298.

52 "Conversion of Greek-Easterners to the Faith of Their Fathers in Bršadin,"
Hrvatski Borac 2, no. 12 (20 March 1942), 3.

53 "Zakonska odredba za obranu naroda i države," *Hrvatski narod* 65 (18 April
1941), 2.

54 Testimony of Herčik Josip, SR-AJ 110, 677–94.

55 Testimony of Poljac Miroslav, SR-AJ 110, 677–293/4.

56 Testimony of Herčik Josip, SR-AJ 110, 677–94.

57 Filip Škiljan, *Organizirana prisilna iseljavanja Srba iz NDH* (Zagreb: SNV,
2014), 79.

58 Testimony of Herčik Josip, SR-AJ 110, 677–94.

59 "Village Rujnice Asks for Conversion to Catholicism" (3033-B-1941), Croatian State Archives (hereafter HR-HDA), NDH Ministry of Justice and Religious Worship (herafter, MPB NDH) – Religious Worship ("Bogoštovlje")
section, kut. 11/218.

60 "Circular," *Katolički list* 92, no. 19 (15 May 1941), 221.

61 Viktor Novak, *Magnum Crimen: pola vijeka klerikalizma u Hrvatskoj*
(Zagreb, 1948), 603.

62 See Škiljan, *Organizirana*, 109–34.

63 Škiljan, *Organizirana*, 161–4. Škiljan calculated that 354 Orthodox priests were deported, not counting their families. Estimates on the number of killed range between 370 and 515. See also Tomasevich, *War and Revolution*, 570.

64 Tomasevich, *War and Revolution*, 555.

65 "Friendly Advice," SR-AJ 110, 677–295.

66 Document 309-B-1941, HR-HDA MPB NDH – Religious Worship section, kut. 4/218.

67 As quoted in Tomasevich, *War and Revolution*, 578.

68 Testimony of Stanišić Maksim, SR-AJ 110, 677–142.

69 Budimir Mirković, interview by author (Vukovar, 5 July 2019), Centre for Oral History and Digital Storytelling Archive (COHDS), Concordia University, 2020–04.

70 HR-HDA MPB NDH memo 42.678-B-1941 (14 July 1941), SR-AJ 110, 677–317. Serbian elites were as a rule slated for physical removal, by deportation or imprisonment, the latter likely to result in death. As with the Jews and Orthodox priests, the option of conversion was not open to them; they were ostensibly seen as manageable in relation to their numbers, as well as unfit for "Croatization."

71 "Circular," *Katolički list* 92, no. 31 (8 August 1941), 367.

72 "Judgment against canon scholar Dr Pavle Lončar," *Katolički list* 92, no. 34 (28 August 1941), 403.

73 Vladimir Dedijer, *Vatikan i Jasenovac: Dokumenti* (Belgrade: IRO Rad, 1987), 454, 456.

74 Horvat and Štambuk, *Dokumenti*, 109.

75 "Resolutions" (235/41), SR-AJ 110, 677–292.

76 For more on the role the Vatican played in the way the Catholic Church in Croatia manoeuvred the dilemmas of the era, see Michael Phayer, *The Catholic Church and the Holocaust, 1930–1965* (Bloomington: Indiana University Press, 2000), 31–40, 83–6.

77 "Resolutions" (235/41), SR-AJ 110, 677–292.

78 Tomasevich, *War and Revolution*, 539.

79 Bishopric of Đakovo memo 848/42-a (14 February 1942), SR-AJ 110, 677–314.

80 MPB NDH memo 83490-41, SR-AJ 110, 677–305; testimony of Türk Dragutin, SR-AJ 110, 677–297.

81 Testimony of Bošnjaković Jelka, SR-AJ 110, 677–309; testimony of Mrkšić Katica, SR-AJ 110, 677–311.

82 Akmadža, *Katolička crkva*, 351.

83 Testimony of Poljac Miroslav, SR-AJ 110, 677–293/4.

84 "Conversion of Greek-Easterners to the Faith of their Fathers in Bršadin," *Hrvatski Borac* 2, no. 12 (20 March 1942), 3.

85 Testimony of Pojić Savo, SR-AJ 110, 677–298; testimony of Novaković Stevan, SR-AJ 110, 677–308.

86 "Zagreb Archbishop on Admittance to the Catholic Church," *Hrvatski Borac* 2, no. 11 (13 March 1942), 1; "Circular: Instruction of Converts," *Katolički list* 93, no. 14 (2 April 1942), 164.

87 Testimony of Janković Nikola, Vukajlović Mladen, Jovičić Blagoje, Jelić Savo, and Mitrović Damjan, SR-AJ 110, 677–40. Akin to Auschwitz, Jasenovac was a camp complex, serving as labour, concentration, and death camp.

88 "Circular of March 2, 1942," cited in Novak, *Magnum Crimen*, 699.

89 "Conversion of Greek-easterners in Ilok," *Hrvatski Borac* 2, no. 15 (10 April 1942), 3.

90 "Announcement," *Hrvatski Borac* 2, no. 14 (3 April 1942), 4.

91 Akmadža, *Katolička crkva*, 351.

92 Interview with Budimir Mirković, COHDS, 2020–04.

93 Testimony of Herčik Josip, SR-AJ 110, 681–7.

94 Dedijer, *Vatikan*, 179.

95 Jere Jareb, "A Word on Conversions," *Ustaša* 18 (30 November 1941), 3.

96 Tomasevich, *War and Revolution*, 390–1, 539. See also Krunoslav Draganović, *Massenubertritte von Katholiken zur 'Orthodoxie' im kroatischen Sprachgebiet zur Zeit der Turkenherrschaft* (Rome: Pontifical Institute, 1937). Conversion from Catholicism to Orthodoxy in the region during Ottoman rule is based in historical fact, but to a far lesser extent than the Ustaša propaganda claimed. After the war, Draganović served as chairman of the Croatian subcommittee of the Vatican Relief Commission and became the main operative of the Vatican ratlines for former Ustaša officers. On this point, see Steinacher, *Nazis on the Run*, 114–15, 128–39.

97 Dedijer, *Vatikan*, 464–5.

98 "Return to the Fathers' Faith," cited in Novak, *Magnum Crimen*, 692n209.

99 Head Secretariat of the Presidency Memorandum of 13 January 1942 (818-XI-2-1942), SR-AJ-110, 677–25.

100 Ministry of Internal Affairs Memorandum of 19 February 1942 (830 I.A.1942.), SR-AJ-110, 677–24.

101 NDH Ministry of Internal Affairs Circular 3049-B-1941, HR-HDA MPB NDH, kut. 11/218.

102 Horvat i Štambuk, *Dokumenti*, 66.

103 See Ivo Goldstein and Slavko Goldstein, *The Holocaust in Croatia* (Pittsburgh: University of Pittsburgh Press, 2016), 405–16.

104 Lidija Barišić-Bogišić, "Tri biografije – tri popisa – isti ishod. Vukovarsko međuraće kroz tri židovske biografije," RADOVI – *Zavod za hrvatsku povijest* 43 (2011): 313–42, here 324.

105 Ibid., 323.

106 Ibid., 324–5.

107 The Jewish community of Vukovar archive lists twenty-three survivors of the Holocaust, Croatian State Archive in Vukovar (DAVU), Jewish Community of Vukovar Collection – "Survivors" section.

108 Circular 2636-B-1941, HR-HDA MPB NDH, kut. 10/218.

109 For example, see "History Repeats," *Katolički list* 92, no. 44 (6 November 1941), 519–20. For a prewar example, see "Catholics and Jews," *Katolički List* 90, no. 20 (18 May 1939), 249, a virulently antisemitic article published two years before the Ustaša movement came to power.

110 See Tomasevich, *War and Revolution*, 608–610. Tomasevich puts NDH's Roma population at around 25,000 in April 1941. Tomasevich writes: "The fact that the 1948 census counted only 847 [Roma] in the Socialist Republics of Croatia and Bosnia and Herzegovina would indicate that the Ustashas succeeded in destroying most of the [Roma] in their state."

111 "Gypsy Women and Begging in Villages," *Hrvatski Borac* 2, no. 13 (27 March 1942), 3.

112 Testimony of Dimitrijević Nikola, SR-AJ 110, 681–41.

113 Reports from Nikola Rušinović, NDH representative in the Vatican, as quoted in Dedijer, *Vatikan*, 464.

114 Horvat i Štambuk, *Dokumenti*, 117.

115 For example, between November 1941 and April 1942, Ustaša functionaries had to come to the village of Novi Jankovci at least four times, accompanied by armed units, until they finally succeeded in coercing the Serbian residents to "sign up" for conversion. A Catholic priest, Dr Marko Baličević, once came alone for the same purpose, "but he didn't threaten anyone."

Testimony of Vunduk Marko, Mitrović Živko, and Teofilović Stevan, SR-AJ
110, 677-143/144.

116 "Decree on the Establishment of the Autocephalous Croatian Orthodox
Church," *Hrvatski narod* 394 (3 April 1942).

117 Approximate calculation based on the population estimate listed in Jelić-
Bultić, *Ustaše i. NDH*, 106. The remaining 6 per cent were Germans, Czechs,
Slovaks, Slovenes, and a plummeting number of Jews. As we have seen,
another group whose numbers plummeted were the Roma.

It should here be noted that the Ustaša policy regarding the HPC was
updated at the meeting of top NDH officials on 2 July 1942. The memo
containing the conclusions of the meeting stated that the HPC was not the
successor of the Serbian Orthodox Church, that the Orthodox population
could not be forced to join the HPC, and that those who decided not to join
but "are fulfilling their citizens' duties must be treated as equal with other
citizens." These conclusions were in essence of declaratory nature, since
"Serbs" remained officially absent from the NDH population categories and
the Serbian Orthodox Church remained banned, keeping "the Orthodox"
who did not explicitly join the HPC in an ethno-religious twilight zone
where they appeared to have neither a Church nor an ethnicity. Still, after
creating the HPC, the regime routinely counted "the Orthodox" as Croats,
regardless of whether they had explicitly joined the HPC and thus officially
underwent the consequent ethnonational conversion. See Nikica Barić, "Relations Between the Chetniks and the Authorities of the Independent State
of Croatia, 1942–1945," in *Serbia and the Serbs in World War Two*, ed. Sabrina
P. Ramet and Ola Listhaug (London: Palgrave Macmillan, 2011), 181, 191.

118 Testimony of Stanišić Maksim, SR-AJ 110, 677–142.

119 Tomasevich, *War and Revolution*, 504–6, 543.

120 Testimony of Pojić Savo, SR-AJ 110, 677–298. It should be noted that Andrašec's successor, Guardian Kulundžić, adopted a different attitude and
"in 1943 or 1944" joined several notables from Vukovar in a deputation to
Governor Jakob Elicker to "ask for arrests of Serbs to end." On this point,
see testimony of Žitvaj Eugen, SR-AJ 110, 681–18.

121 In his report to the pope of 18 May 1943, Archbishop Stepinac estimated
around 240,000 conversions up to that time, a large increase from the
100,000 estimated in early 1942. Much of this increase surely occurred after

the proclamation of the HPC. On this point, see Tomasevich, *War and Revolution*, 578.

122 Only two terse mentions of the HPC were published in *Katolički list* in all of 1942, announcing its creation ("Formation of the Croatian Orthodox Church," *Katolički list* 93, no. 15 [9 April 1942], 178) and its constitution ("Constitution of the Croatian Orthodox Church," *Katolički list* 93, no. 24 [11 June 1942], 286).

123 Dušan Lazic-Gojko and Brana Majski, *Dudik* (Vukovar: Odbor memorijalnog parka Dudik, 1977), 59, 124, 154, 176. Jews were another target favoured for retributive executions until summer 1942, when the last Jews in the Vukovar area were taken to the camps. Before that time, "units" of arrested Jews were also used for digging execution pits, moving and stacking corpses, and covering them with quicklime, a highly caustic material that speeds up decomposition.

124 Horvat i Štambuk, *Dokumenti*, 66.

125 Akmadža and Batorek, *Stradanja*, 373–4.

126 Kovačić, *U potrazi za istinom*, 183.

127 Ibid., 199.

128 Ibid., 278.

PART THREE

Critiquing Ethnonationalism
and Antisemitism

9

Learning as a Space of Protection: The Hochschule für die Wissenschaft des Judentums in Nazi Berlin

Sara Han

On 7 November 1819, seven young Jewish intellectuals met in Berlin to explore the possibilities of taking action against the antisemitic Hep-Hep riots that had erupted in the summer and autumn of 1819.[1] They consequently founded the Berlin Verein für Cultur und Wissenschaft der Juden (1819–24; Association for Jewish Culture and Science, or Culturverein), which eventually encompassed scientific, pedagogical, and synagogal activities besides urgent political ones.[2] Using methods of source-critical research and modern scholarship to systematically explore Judentum in its entirety was the major concern of founders Leopold Zunz (1794–1886), Isaak Levin Auerbach (1791–1853), Eduard Gans (1797–1839), Isaak Markus Jost (1793–1860), Joel Abraham List (1780–1848), Moses Moser (1797–1838), and Josef Hilmar (1767–1828); who were later joined by Immanuel Wohlwill (born: Wolf, 1799–1847), Abraham Geiger (1819–1874), Zacharias Frankel (1801–1875), Moritz Steinschneider (1816–1907), and Heinrich Graetz (1817–1891).[3] These scholars strove to articulate the lasting significance of Judaism in the modern age so as to advance the social standing of Jews and establish Judaism as a subject of historical investigation.[4]

After a brief discussion of the founding of the Wissenschaft des Judentums in the nineteenth century, this chapter examines the question of continuity and discontinuity for the Hochschule für die Wissenschaft des
Judentums and considers how, during the persecution of the Jews in Nazi
Berlin, the learning and teaching within its walls provided a spiritual shelter
for Jews.[5] As Jews experienced increased persecution in their daily lives, the
Hochschule became a space of protection. In the face of the German state's
antisemitic legislation, it offered the only opportunity for professors and
students in the fields of history and religion to continue their scholarly endeavours in Berlin. For many students, the Hochschule became a part of
their survival story.

I

In 1818, Leopold Zunz published "Etwas über die rabbinische Litteratur"
(Something about Rabbinical Literature), which later became the blueprint
for the Wissenschaft des Judentums.[6] In that work, he abandoned the nor-
mative content of rabbinic literature and sought to define "a concept of Ju-
daism that includes all, or most, aspects of human thought."[7] In 1822,
Immanuel Wohlwill followed Zunz's groundbreaking work with an essay,
"Über den Begriff einer Wissenschaft des Judenthums" (Concerning the
Concept of a Study of Judaism),[8] published in the first edition of the
Zeitschrift für die Wissenschaft des Judenthums,[9] in which he asserted that the
Wissenschaft des Judentums must consider "the word Judenthum in its most
comprehensive meaning."[10]

Wohlwill argued that to explore and portray the religion of the Jews in
its entirety, scholars needed to organically integrate Judentum into the fields
of Jewish history, philosophy, language, and literature. He added that the
Hebrew Scriptures required a source-critical examination. Wohlwill defined
the Culturverein's ideals in his 1822 essay, and a few years later (1845),[11] Zunz
formulated a critical method in the context of the Wissenschaft des Judentums. Zunz's formulation affected Wissenschaft both internally by
challenging traditional learning methods in Rabbinic Judaism and externally by critiquing the predominant "Christian-theological vision," which
encouraged only a Christological reading of the Hebrew Bible.[12] Zunz critiqued both Jewish and Christian approaches to Judentum in the hope of

shifting the discourse away from a limited religious sphere of interpretation, which he considered a counter-response to Christian theology, and more toward Wissenschaft.

As heirs of the Haskala, the Jewish Enlightenment, younger Jewish scholars interpreted rabbinical literature as one part of a comprehensive body of Jewish literature. Through source-critical research, Zunz intended to protect rabbinic literature from "disappearance and oblivion."[13] At the same time, he wanted to prevent Judaism from being reduced to a religion, so he formulated an appeal in his 1845 essay, "Zur Geschichte und Litteratur" (On History and Literature), in which he wrote that "our *Wissenschaft*, therefore, needs first to emancipate itself from the theologians."[14] As Wohwill also stressed, one should not view Judentum in a "limited sense in which it means only the religion of the Jews."[15]

For Zunz, Judentum needed to be recognized as an integral part of European culture and literature. He advocated that scholars use modern scientific methods to reveal how Judaism was intertwined with European culture. He also believed that such a study would expose centuries-old anti-Jewish prejudices. In "Etwas über die rabbinische Litteratur" and "Zur Geschichte und Literattur," Zunz investigated the works of Christian Hebraists, who examined Jewish source materials from the perspective of theological anti-Judaism. Christian scholars tended strongly to employ Jewish sources mainly to illustrate the fulfillment of Christian expectations in the New Testament and to accentuate what they saw as a wide chasm between Christian belief and a Jewish "hardness of heart." Zunz argued that these representations had nourished laws against the Jews and led to "hatred and contempt."[16] Only when scholars recognized Jewish literature – especially post-biblical literature – as an equal part of philosophy and poetry would equality for the Jews develop. For Zunz, equality for Jews would come about only when both Jews and Christians recognized the Wissenschaft des Judentums.

Zunz exposed a superiority complex inherent in Christian anti-Judaism, which understood Judaism as an inferior and outdated precursor to Christianity. In this way he revealed its rhetoric of contempt, which characterized Jews as "the Other." By applying the methods of scientific inquiry to emphasize that the Jews were an integral part of European culture and literature, Zunz exposed theological anti-Judaism, which had excluded Jewish literature since the patristic period. Note that the reappraisal of this "teaching of contempt" within Christian theology began only after the Holocaust.[17]

Zunz's ideas were confronted with criticisms from Jews themselves. Orthodox leaders such as Samson Raphael Hirsch feared that such Wissenschaft might lead to a break with Jewish law and undermine the written and oral Torah. Other leaders argued that such scientific methods were elitist and threatened to replace religious Judaism.[18] Hirsch affirmed German culture and literature but emphatically rejected any application of historical criticism to the Torah and the Talmud.

Zacharias Frankel was open to a source-critical analysis of the Mishna but contended that the borders of the scientific method must stop at the Pentateuch, which must remain untouchable – talmudically speaking, *the fence around the Torah* must be maintained. Abraham Geiger, by contrast, was willing to apply the methods of source-critical investigation to the entire body of Jewish literature, the Torah and the Talmud, to promote the adaptability of Judaism.[19] Geiger also believed that Wissenschaft needed to include an examination of the writings of the New Testament, since these contained historical insights about the first-century Jewish world. In 1938, Rabbi Leo Baeck (1873–1956) published "Das Evangelium als Urkunde der jüdischen Glaubensgeschichte" (The Gospel as a Document of the History of the Jewish Faith), in which he analyzed different "layers" in the Christian Gospel and "excavated" them to return to the Jewish core, what he called the "old Gospel." Baeck placed it within the Pharisaic tradition and classified it "as a testimony of the Jewish faith." As Susannah Heschel has written about Abraham Geiger, "the more Jewish Jesus could be shown to have been, the more Christians would respect Judaism – or so many of the German Jews hoped. ... For [the Christians], the more Jewish Jesus was shown to be, the less original and unique he was. Geiger's writings were nothing less than an assault based on Christianity."[20] The establishment of such Wissenschaft inherently contained the possibility of challenging Christian self-assurance in its demarcation from Judaism by entering into a historical-critical examination of Jesus and the New Testament. As Heschel concluded, it was "an intellectual revolution against Europe and its conception of the role of Judaism within Western civilization."[21]

Frankel and Geiger characterized Jewish theology as a form of religious study and thus defined it as an integral part of the Wissenschaft des Judentums. This alignment of Wissenschaft brought about a new Jewish educational elite who wanted to measure successful emancipation in terms of the recognition of the Wissenschaft des Judentums within the German university system. Despite differing scholarly emphases, they premised their common concern on "the bond of scientific method"[22] to promote Jewish self-discovery and emancipation "through the medium of academic scholarship."[23]

On 25 July 1848, Zunz called for the creation of an academic chair for the "History and Literature of Jews from the Period of the Last Two Thousand Years" at the University of Berlin to prevent Judaism being treated as an inferior research subject. The approval committee's rejection of his application reflected a refusal by the Christian dominated academic world to support and strengthen the Wissenschaft des Judentums.[24] German universities continued to refuse the calls of Jewish scholars for equal treatment of the Wissenschaft des Judentums.

II

The Wissenschaft des Judentums remained excluded from academia. Some of its supporters turned to rabbinical seminars as places to implement this new conception of learning. Leopold Zunz and Moritz Steinschneider rejected such an approach, fearing it might result in the construction of a "new ghetto of Jewish scholarship."[25] Many Jewish scholars tried to free themselves from the boundaries of such an academic ghettoization by establishing a Wissenschaft des Judentums and gaining a place in university circles; non-Jewish academics continually blocked such efforts. Zunz succinctly described the situation: "The ghetto has been torn asunder, but the banishment has not yet been revoked."[26]

Disagreements among members, financial debts, and low membership caused the Culturverein to dissolve after five years. Nevertheless, the ideas of its founders remained, and they led to the founding of the Hochschule für die Wissenschaft des Judentums on 5 May 1872; that body initially became associated with the Jewish Theological Seminary in Breslau (Jüdisch-Theologisches Seminar Fraenckel'sche Stiftung, 1854–1938) and the Orthodox Rabbinical Seminary in Berlin (1873–1938).[27] The founding of independent institutions for the Wissenschaft des Judentums demonstrated both the reality of scholarly and institutional discrimination for German-Christian academia and the institutionalization of the Wissenschaft des Judentums and its historical-critical methods.[28]

As the Hochschule stood in the tradition of the Culturverein and its bond to Wissenschaft, the founders declared the independence of the Hochschule from any Jewish congregational or governing authority. Neither religious confession nor gender would prevent scholars and students from teaching, researching, and studying at the Hochschule. Both male and female faculty and students associated with or enrolled in other institutions would be allowed to participate. The only requirement for students was proof of university enrolment. The Hochschule was not associated with any particular Jewish denomination but rather was grounded in its commitment to Wissenschaft. The Hochschule's faculty had to present professional qualifications and proof of scientific competence. To ensure a broad spectrum of approaches, the professors would represent "different Jewish religious currents."[29] In 1922, on the occasion of the Hochschule's fiftieth anniversary, Ismar Elbogen (1874–1943), professor of history and biblical exegesis and a prominent faculty member, recalled that the faculty's intention was not to create artificial uniformity but to "showcase individuality in complete freedom."[30]

The Hoschschule's focus was solely on free and critical scholarship. It based its recruitment of teachers and the admission of students on the principles of science, diversity, and independence. Studying at both a university and the Hochschule, where education was not limited to rabbinical studies, offered an interdisciplinary approach to the transfer of knowledge. It also led to the recognition of the Wissenschaft des Judentums within the traditional academic disciplines, as Zunz had demanded, albeit in reverse, in that this integration came not from German universities but from Hochschule regulations. The appreciation of modern historical criticism combined with the popularization of Jewish knowledge and the principles of independence and diversity fostered a unique climate within the Hochschule at the end of the nineteenth century.[31]

In 1907, an increase in members and donations made it possible to move the Hochschule to Artilleriestrasse,[32] closer to the University of Berlin. With this move, the visibility and popularity of the Wissenschaft des Judentums, especially among scholars, in the metropolis of Berlin, continued to grow.

For example, Hugo Gressmann (1877–1927), a Protestant and a professor of the Old Testament at the University of Berlin, invited his Jewish colleagues to a lecture series in the winter term of 1925–26. In his introductory address, Gressmann described this lecture series as an expression of the "recognition of Jewish scholarship."[33] However, this remained an isolated case in the official interactions between the Hochschule and the faculty of the University of Berlin. Official parity for the Wissenschaft des Judentums with the traditional academic disciplines was still missing.

III

Mere weeks after Hitler's ascendancy to the chancellorship, a German student movement began its campaign of terror. Founded in 1926, the National Socialist German Student Union had a profound impact on university students; eventually, in 1931, it took over an umbrella organization of the German Students Union (Dachverband der deutschen Studentenschaften). They mobilized against so-called "anti-regime" professors and endeavoured to advance the nazification of German universities.[34] While most professors initially rejected the "introduction of party politics" in university affairs, by the summer semester of 1933, 20 per cent of the faculty had joined the NSDAP.[35]

In April 1933, the Law for the Restoration of the Professional Civil Service was passed, and by December 1935, around 250 scientists in Berlin and 800 scientists throughout Germany, all of whom were Jews, had lost their jobs. The Central Office for Jewish Economic Aid set up a department and was able to raise funds to support these newly unemployed university teachers.[36] The department set out to support financially those who had not emigrated for various reasons and to integrate them into Jewish (adult) education.

On 25 April 1933, the German government, under a largely National Socialist administration, expelled Jewish students from academia by passing the decree Against the Overcrowding of German Schools and Universities. After 23 April 1938 the government allowed matriculation only for those with an "Aryan Certificate."[37] For Jewish students of the Hochschule, obligatory enrolment at a German university was no longer possible, and therefore the compulsory dual study was no longer feasible. The German state had designed its antisemitic regulations to end education for German Jews.[38]

In response to these discriminatory measures, the Reichsvertretung der deutschen Juden (Reich Representation of German Jews) founded a Task Force for General Scientific Lectures, which oversaw a "reorganization" of the Hochschule.[39] In his depiction of the Hochschule, Richard Fuchs (1886–1970) described this process: "The idea was to broaden the activities of the Hochschule by teaching there, in addition to the traditional subjects, non-Judaistic matters of various kinds to transform the Hochschule gradually and in a non-obtrusive manner into a Jewish university."[40] Members of the working group included Arthur Lilienthal (1899–1942), a lawyer and since 1934 secretary-general of the Reichsvertretung, and Otto Toeplitz (1881–1940), a well-known mathematician. Toeplitz organized emigration for Jewish students out of Nazi Germany and then immigrated to Jerusalem in 1939, where he worked as an adviser to the rector of the Hebrew University in Jerusalem. They were joined by the philosopher and cultural Zionist Martin Buber (1878–1965) and the historian Ernst Kantorowicz (1895–1963), who represented the Center for Jewish Adult Education and contributed indispensable insights into this process of "reorganization." Ernst Simon (1899–1988), a student of the Freie Jüdische Lehrhaus (Free House of Jewish Studies) and later Buber's assistant at the centre, immigrated to Palestine in 1928, then returned to Germany for one year in 1934 at the request of Buber and Leo Baeck to work in Jewish adult education at the centre.[41] Simon later described their work as "construction amid doom."[42] By 1936, all Jewish professors had lost their professorships at German universities, and this provided the task force with a pool of scholars from which to draw lecturers to teach non-Judaic subjects; in this way, some were able to resume their activities as university instructors. The task force was interested mainly in younger scientists and was "determined to find the best among them."[43] It emphasized a particular approach to Judaism: instructors should be able to teach a general student population and also reveal new possibilities of connection between Jewish and non-Judaic fields of research in their teaching and research.

After more than a year, the Hochschule found itself on the radar of the Berlin Gestapo, which made an official inquiry into its purpose. Richard Fuchs recommended answering "that its object was the training of rabbis and teachers of the Jewish religion."[44] In the broadest sense, this statement was consistent with the work of the Hochschule faculty. In a way, they were

following the founders of the Wissenschaft des Judentums and their aspiration to explore the "entirety" of Judentum through the discipline of the
Wissenschaft des Judentums.

As the reorganization did not align with Nazi interests, the Hochschule
disguised its courses under traditional subjects, such as history and philosophy.[45] By the summer semester of 1936, philosophy was being taught by
Arnold Metzger, Hans Friedländer, and Fritz Kaufmann, history by Eugen
Täubler (Antiquity), Hans Liebesschütz (Middle Ages), and Arnold Berney
(Modern), and Islamic Studies by Moses Goldmann. The following winter
semester, sociology was included in the curriculum, taught by Franz Oppenheimer, Paul Eppstein, and Friedrich Caro. Ernst Grumach taught classical philology and literature, and Franz Rosenthal, the Semitic languages.[46]

Due to its unavoidable change in profile, the Hochschule enjoyed its
largest number of students and teachers during the first six years of Nazi
rule. In 1936, the number of teachers increased to fifteen; by 1938, it had risen
to twenty-two. After this point, emigrations, arrests, detentions, and deportations caused these numbers to decrease.[47] Still, the Hochschule offered the
only opportunity for disenfranchised German Jews to study in Berlin after
their exclusion from German universities, an action that had robbed Jewish
youth of their educational opportunities and futures.

The transformation of the Hochschule was a form of resistance and an
attempt to create a semblance of normal life by offering young students a
place where they could briefly settle down and pursue their studies. A lasting
educational ideal from a time that no longer existed externally marked this
process of transformation. In his report on the Hochschule, Herbert A.
Strauss (1918–2005), one of the last students at the Hochschule and, since
1971, professor of history at the City College of New York and first head of
the Center for Research on Antisemitism in Berlin, wrote that the curriculum and examination regulations "remained completely traditional" until
the closure of the Hochschule.[48]

For some Jewish high school graduates who did not plan on emigrating
or who were not involved in Zionist youth associations with an educational
focus on agricultural and craft trades, the Hochschule was all that remained
of university study after 1938. The Jewish Youth Federations worked out an
agreement with the university to provide matriculation certificates for students without university entrance qualifications so that they could acquire

Figure 9.1 Students on the steps of the Lehranstalt für die Wissenschaft des Judentums (1935).

Jewish knowledge and language skills for emigration during their undergraduate studies.[49]

Jewish schools and rabbinical seminars were among the great achievements of Jewish organizations that, unfortunately, the Nazis largely closed after the 1938 November pogrom. The Gestapo forced the Jewish Theological Seminary in Breslau and the Orthodox Rabbinical Seminary in Berlin to close in November 1938; however, the faculty of the Hochschule für die Wissenschaft des Judentums was able to resume teaching a few weeks after the pogrom. Why the Nazi government allowed the Hochschule to stay open is not entirely clear. Its connection to the Reichsvereinigung possibly offered it protection. It appears that the Gestapo also believed it was only a theological seminary. Either way, it belongs to what Herbert A. Strauss concluded was part of the state's "eerie politics of false normality."[50]

The continued existence of the Hochschule reflects Marion Kaplan's thesis about the "tension between the normal and abnormal" in the everyday lives of Jews in Nazi Germany. Kaplan described the various ways in which Jewish women structured their family's daily life in an attempt to maintain "abnormal normality." But she makes clear that "daily life came to a standstill on November 9, 1938" (Reichskristallnacht). Before the November 1938 pogrom, the self-structured daily life of the mothers "gave some false hope and allowed ... the dangerous assumption of some normalcy amid the hostility of Nazi Germany."[51] After the pogrom, the resumption of teaching at the Hochschule might have also produced false hope and dangerous assumptions. Because the Hochschule was heavily impacted by the despotic Nazi legislation as well as by the whims of the Gestapo, the false normality fostered a tactical pretence of normality among the perpetrators.

I V

Ernst Ludwig Ehrlich (1921–2007) began his studies at the Hochschule in 1940. He belonged to the generation of Jewish high school graduates in Berlin for whom this space offered the only opportunity for academic training. At that time, the Hochschule had eleven to thirteen students enrolled full-time. Only three of the final students of Hochschule besides Ehrlich survived the Shoah. Herbert A. Strauss fled to Switzerland with Ehrlich in 1943.[52] Wolfgang Hamburger (1919–2012) hid in Berlin until the war ended and, in 1947, immigrated to Cincinnati, where he graduated from Hebrew Union College in 1957. Hamburger spent the rest of his life in the United States, where he served several Jewish Reform Congregations. In 1941, Nathan Peter Levinson (1921–2016), fled with his family to the United States and enrolled as a student at Hebrew Union College. In 1950, he returned to Germany as a rabbi and helped rebuild Jewish communities there.[53]

In a history of the Hochschule, Marianne Awerbuch described studying there during the Nazi era as a "survival strategy."[54] However, it would be too one-sided to describe the enrolment of students merely from a perspective of hopelessness or survival. Despite the dire circumstances, many students looked toward a more positive future. For example, Ernst Ludwig Ehrlich on his high school graduation certificate stated that he planned to become a theologian.[55] Most children of acculturated families had no religious ties; thus Ehrlich was exceptional, given the liberal environment of his "German-Jewish parental home." This had fundamental implications for his future studies.[56]

In 1940, Ehrlich attended Leo Baeck's lectures on Midrash and homiletics. Three years later, on 27 January 1943, Baeck was deported to Theresienstadt. After that ghetto's liberation, he immigrated to London, where he became the most prominent Jewish voice after 1945.[57] Eugen Täubler taught history until 1941, when with his wife, the historian Selma Stern (1890–1981), he immigrated to the United States, where he joined the faculty of Hebrew Union College in Cincinnati.[58] Rabbi Leopold Lucas (1872–1943) succeeded Täubler in Berlin. On 17 December 1942, Lucas and his wife were deported to Theresienstadt, where he died on 13 September 1943; his wife Dorothea Lucas was murdered in Auschwitz on 12 Oktober 1944.[59] Rabbi Heinrich Mikhael Gescheit (1887–1945), a Talmudic scholar, was deported to the Buchenwald concentration camp and presumably was murdered there. Manfred Gross (1918–1943), a biblical scholar, was deported and murdered in Auschwitz in March 1943.[60] On 12 March 1943, Rabbi Julius Lewkowitz (1876–1943), an instructor in the philosophy of religion, was also deported to Auschwitz, with his wife Selma Lewkowitz, and murdered there.[61] Ernst Grumach (1902–1967), a lecturer in philosophy and the Greek language, survived the Holocaust because of his "non-privileged mixed marriage," according to the Nazi racist categories.[62] After the closure of the Hochschule, he was used for forced labour, assigned to the central library of the Reich Security Main Office (Reichsicherhauptamt or RSHA) to catalogue stolen Jewish books. The stage actor and director Otto Bernstein (1887–1943), lecturer in theatre and oration, was deported with his wife Jenny Schaffer (1888–1943) and murdered in Auschwitz on 26 February 1943.[63] Fritz Wisten, director of the Jewish Cultural Association in Berlin and instructor of elocution, survived the Holocaust.[64] On 7 September 1945, he staged Gotthold Ephraim Lessing's "Nathan the Wise" as the first postwar performance at the Deutsches Theater Berlin.[65]

After the successful emigration of Ismar Elbogen, Leo Baeck became the representative figure of the Hochschule during the last two years of its existence. Together with the teachers still living in Berlin, he endeavoured to provide the students with "a full program of studies."[66] In addition to the enrolled students, the university offered a threefold number of auditing students an "everyday" space away from persecution. The growing number of attendees proved to historian Marianne Awerbuch that the university offered "an emotional shelter from the ever-increasing difficulties of daily life."[67]

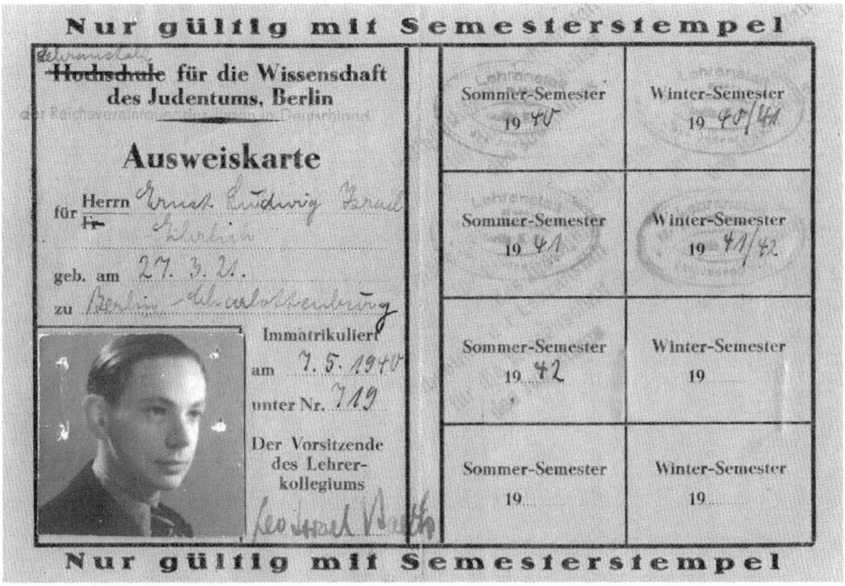
Nur gültig mit Semesterstempel

~~Hochschule~~ für die Wissenschaft des Judentums, Berlin

Ausweiskarte

für Herrn Ernst Ludwig Israel Ehrlich

geb. am 27. 3. 21.

zu Berlin-Charlottenburg

Immatrikuliert am 7. 5. 1940 unter Nr. 719

Der Vorsitzende des Lehrerkollegiums

Sommer-Semester 19 40	Winter-Semester 19 40/41
Sommer-Semester 19 41	Winter-Semester 19 41/42
Sommer-Semester 19 42	Winter-Semester 19
Sommer-Semester 19	Winter-Semester 19

Nur gültig mit Semesterstempel

Figure 9.2 Ernst Ludwig Ehrlich, student ID of the Hochschule.

The memory of Peter Nathan Levinson, who impressively described the asynchronism experienced by him and his fellow students, reinforces this interpretation. While their dire situation deprived them of academic opportunities, they were able to participate in a learning space at the Hochschule inhabited by the great intellectuals among German Jews. Long after the Holocaust, Levison gave a striking testimony in his obiturary for his teacher Leopold Lucas:

> Jews were no longer allowed to visit theaters, cinemas, cafés, and, of course, universities. The synagogues had been destroyed in November 1938. Thus, the *Lehranstalt* remained almost the only place where Jews could engage in spiritual activity … In fact, this *Hochschule* was an island within a surging sea. Outside was the violence, the horror, the intimidation, the disenfranchisement. Inside the walls and the *Hoch schule*, one experienced the feeling of being in another world, the spiritual world, which cannot be defeated.[68]

Likewise, Herbert A. Strauss, referring to the task force, described this spiritual world of protection as a "university in inner exile," a paradox he did not deny within the framework of historical reflection after the Holocaust.[69]

In 1937, Fritz Bamberger expressed the difficulty of being a Jewish teacher in Nazi Germany: "Assimilated Jewish children objected to learning a new curriculum that emphasized Hebrew and Jewishness, feeling that it branded them as Jews against their will."[70] Ehrlich later described this time as one thrown back on "being Jewish."[71] Placed alongside each other, these statements suggest a dichotomy of alienation among acculturated Jewish children, youths, and students in Nazi Germany. Antisemitic policies had completely excluded them from the existing social and cultural structures, but at the same time they were introduced to a deep Jewish religiosity and culture unknown to many of them. In Germany, especially in Berlin, many Jewish families had deliberately distanced themselves from any form of Jewish religiosity as they acculturated themselves. At the same time, academic study and learning at the Hochschule counterbalanced the fear and insecurity triggered by every new Gestapo degree. Wolfgang Hamburger's memories about the lecture themes and atmosphere hint at this dichotomy between community and insecurity. He described how Leo Baeck could evoke an understanding of democracy that spanned from biblical times to the modern era. Such lectures enabled Hamburger to "forg[e]t for an hour that he was living in the realm of a lawless and brutal dictatorship."[72] Amid the destruction, professors and students continued to teach and study at the Hochschule. During their classes and discussions, the faculty and students did not talk about the threats "outside," instead following Baeck's dictum "by concentrating on their work, on 'the task of the day.'"[73]

By contrast, Ernst Ludwig Ehrlich recalled that he and his fellow students heard from an employee of the Hochschule that "there were camps in Poland with huge 'basins' filled with gas instead of water."[74] Inevitably, study at the Hochschule did not shield students from hearing about the persecution and murder of Jews. Still, when discussing ancient or medieval primary sources, professors would make only indirect comparisons to their own experience of disenfranchisement. As the question of "how to get out of Germany as soon as possible" became more urgent,[75] some faculty and students came to view the intensive study at the Hochschule as "inner freedom amid external bondage."[76]

Alongside the Hochschule courses, a preaching ministry continued to function at the remaining synagogues in Berlin; it also began "at homes for the elderly."[77] By September 1941, the Gestapo was enforcing ordinances that completely abolished the Jews' freedom of movement[78] and prohibited Jews who were wearing the yellow star from using public transportation.[79] Such "everyday" places of learning and refuge were thereby lost. In the presence of National Socialist leadership and persecution of Jews, these spaces had regularly felt, in retrospect, as "uncanny" and "unreal."[80] On 19 February 1941, Leo Baeck expressed a similar motif in a letter to his colleague, Ismar Elbogen, who was already, fortunately, living in Cincinnati: "The diligence of our students is admirable; one must occasionally slow them down."[81] Until the university's forced closure on 19 June 1942, the faculty of the Hochschule used all the resources at their disposal to maintain and promote the pursuit of unimpeded research within the Wissenschaft des Judentums. As Ehrlich wrote to Rudolf Schottlaender (1900–1988) after the war, "It may be of interest to you that immediately after 1933 a wealth of professors and lecturers from the universities came to the *Lehranstalt* ... So, for a relatively short time, the school became a Jewish substitute university."[82]

V

From the founding of the Culturverein to the institutionalization of the historical-critical projects of the Wissenschaft des Judentums and until the forced closure of the Hochschule in 1942, the Wissenschaft des Judentums had been shaped and transformed in various ways. Its critical scholarly approach to transferring knowledge, which prioritized reflection on Judentum, remained constant. Judaism no longer was an object but rather a subject of reflection and study.

The Hochschule was ultimately able to create a zone of protection for its numerous students, auditors, and professors, and eventually it became a place of asynchronism. This asynchronism is apparent in Ehrlich's observation that as students at the Hochschule, they not only were educated in the Wissenschaft des Judentums but also were taught by a rabbi about Christianity, Jesus, and Paul, an "eerie thought when one realizes when this took place."[83]

During this time of hardship, the Mittelstelle für jüdische Erwachsenenbildung (Central Office for Jewish Adult Education), a bureau founded in

1934 by Martin Buber and led beginning in 1937 by Abraham Joshua Heschel, sought to link together various Jewish learning institutions. Its focus was on Jewish adult education, and it was characterized by the Lehrhaus method of "new learning." The office's influential work in mobilizing Jewish teachers and working with the faculty of the Hochschule was perhaps a significant reason why the number of guest students increased so greatly. Wolfgang Hamburger supported this interpretation when he wrote:

> They belonged to all age groups and came from every walk of life. A rabbi emeritus sat next to a widow, a former lawyer shared his Bible with a former merchant, while a dismissed civil servant, after the lecture, discussed a point of interest with a former bank official and a physician. This participation of men and women in the academic work of the *Lehranstalt* had a very wholesome influence on the enrolled students.[84]

Though the curriculum and examinations remained traditional, the learning community "from every walk of life" created a unique educational environment for the younger students who attended the Hochschule during its final years.[85]

In Judaism, dialogue between teacher and student is one of the essential forms of learning; it constitutes a teaching situation of flat hierarchies that establishes a community, which focuses on the point of interest, that is, the discourse. The atmosphere of refuge created at the Hochschule flowed from the Jewish tradition, which had prevailed over many centuries, given the mutual learning approach and the teacher–pupil relationship. In the Talmudic writings of *Makkot 10a*, it is written: "Much Torah have I studied from my teachers, and I have learned more from my colleagues than from them, and I have learned more from my students than from all of them."

And the *Pirkei Avot* compilation begins with the maxim and tradition of passing on knowledge: "Moses received Torah at Sinai and transmitted it to Joshua, Joshua to the elders, and the elders to the prophets, and the prophets to the Men of the Great Assembly. They said three things: Be patient with justice, raise many disciples, and make a fence around the Torah." The tradition of the chain of teachers and calls to establish a discipleship protect what has been handed down, namely the Torah, which reveals the reciprocity of knowledge acquisition, learning, the transfer of knowledge, and teaching.

Figure 9.3 Ismar Elbogen with students, Lehranstalt für die Wissenschaft des Judentums (1938).

This understanding of learning and teaching as a maxim and as one that does not end with the teacher because it has a circular dynamic – from teacher to student and back – had already been written in the Jewish sources of the Talmud. Teachers at the Hochschule were able to draw on this understanding of learning during a time of disenfranchisement and persecution. Jewish knowledge, thinking, tradition, and culture need not be taught solely from the "pulpit"; they can also be imparted through "sitting in the presence of scholars" (Pirkei Avot 2.7).

In a time of disenfranchisement, repression, and persecution within a predominately German-Christian environment, this learning motif became an *asynchronistic* reinforcement and protection mechanism. As Wolfgang Hamburger recalled, this atmosphere had a "wholesome influence" on the students and auditors at the Hochschule. After the Hochschule was closed in 1942, those individuals who remained in Berlin were now as unprotected as any other Jew in Nazi Germany and were forced into labour or exile.[86] The shelter the Hochschule tried to maintain during the war years had been lost.

For the lecturers, the enrolled students, and the auditors, the Wissenschaft des Judentums provided a place where they could "recover" from the daily harassment of the Nazis, a space of protection borne out of "learning." The memories of the last students and employees of the Hochschule confirm that this form of Jewish existence was strengthened between 1938 and 1942. Ehrlich remembered that, with the phrase "the task of the day," Leo Baeck embodied the instruction and learning spaces at the Hochschule and thus created an "admirable calm."[87] Nevertheless, even for Ehrlich, who remembered his teacher Leo Baeck with immense gratitude, a question remained: How much did his teacher know about the cruel and murderous reality at the concentration camps? Even if the dictum "the task of the day" had a calming effect, Ehrlich framed it this way: "Considering the rapidly deteriorating situation, this pastoral behavior may have been healing at the moment, but could not have a lasting effect."[88] Baeck's role as "a teacher and helper,"[89] however, bore more weight in the memories of his students. Richard Fuchs captured them by describing the atmosphere in which he lived and studied: "From the desolate misery of their daily life with its deprivations and the ever-growing danger to their liberty and existence, they found in this place a refuge and encouragement by devoting themselves to study and learning."[90]

The Hochschule became a space of protection, just as studying served as a "survival strategy," a foundation from which to build after the destruction years of the Holocaust. As Wolfgang Hamburger wrote, "Indeed, it was saved not only for the few who still hoped to leave it with a rabbinical diploma, but also for those who, by law, had lost their right to engage in their various occupations, and who found at the Lehranstalt an island where they could give their shattered existence a new meaning."[91] The combination of "rabbinical diploma" with the phrase "hoped to leave with" affords space to the pre-existing potential of a possible future. For the last students of the Hochschule, the "rabbinical diploma" was linked to the history of the Hochschule during Nazi Germany and, therefore, inevitably, with their personal history of violent persecution and exclusion. Yet it also remained a part of their survival story and their memory of this protective space. The motivation to obtain an academic certificate has an innate quality that points to a possible future and that can be evoked by learning – as the Hochschul-student Wolfgang Hamburger pictured it, "with the ever-growing forebodings of terrible things to come, all academic studies became ever more activities for their own sake, learning for the sake of heart and mind amid a hurricane which otherwise made purposeless what until then had purpose and meaning."[92]

Though they were "learning for the sake of heart," students still had traditional exams to take, including an opportunity to take a preliminary rabbinical examination. A passing certificate on this exam was one of the few things Ehrlich took in his briefcase with him when he fled to Switzerland in March 1943. Though taking only one briefcase was part of his escape plan to reach the Swiss border unrecognized, his Hochschule certificate and student ID became "things of exile."[93] These objects revealed one aspect of what Hans Sahl called "the generation of 'no more' and 'not yet.'"[94] The Hochschule's "rabbinical diploma" will always be a witness to the theft of education perpetrated by the Nazis. For Ernst Ludwig Ehrlich, this same certificate played an essential role after his successful escape to Switzerland, in that it made it possible for him to resume his studies at the University of Basel.

After the destruction of the European Jews, the gap between the intellectual concerns of the Wissenschaft des Judentums and the Holocaust remains.[95] Learning protected the students and lecturers at the Hochschule for a time and created a space of asynchronism for its members, but it certainly could not shelter them from the murderous machinations of the Nazis. Only through early emigration or a late escape from Nazi Germany could Jews protect their lives.

Nathan Peter Levinson recalled the time shortly before his emigration:

In 1940, when I started studying at the rabbinical seminary, I truly didn't want to emigrate. I was nineteen years old, and even though all the horror was going on around us, we at the seminary were on a kind of island ... I went to Baeck and asked him, "Should I really go? The nightmare has to end soon." And Baeck said very seriously, "You have to get out of here."[96]

The Culturverein's pursuit of social and scientific equality remained audible as a *basso continuo* and persisted in methodical variations until the end of Nazi rule, but was "not discovered in Germany until the phenomenon of

German Jewry no longer existed."[97] The asynchronism at the Hochschule in
Berlin between 1933 and 1942 shaped the memories of those who survived,
and the methods of Wissenschaft des Judentums continued to influence
their activities in academia and the development of Jewish communities in
South America, England, North America, and, after 1945, Germany. By 1938,
an existential bond had developed between professors and students at the
Hochschule. At the time, this relationship was unusual for a German university setting, and for "some this created an intensively experienced educational landscape and friendship that survived disaster."[98]

NOTES

1 See Jacob Katz, *Die Hep-Hep-Verfolgungen des Jahres 1819* (Berlin: Metropol,
   1994); Eleonore Sterling, "Anti-Jewish Riots in Germany in 1819: A Displacement of Protest," in *Historica Judaica* 12, no. 2 (1950): 105–42; and Manfred
   Gailus, "Anti-Jewish Emotion and Violence in the 1848 Crisis of German
   Society," in *Exclusionary Violence: Antisemitic Riots in Modern German History*, eds. Werner Bergmann, Christian Hoffmann, and Helmut W. Smith
   (Ann Arbor: University of Michigan Press, 2002), 43–65.
2 See Alfred Abraham Greenbaum, "The Verein für Cultur und Wissenschaft
   der Juden in Jewish Historiography: An Analysis and Some Observations,"
   in *Texts and Responses: Studies Presented to Nahum N. Glatzer on the Occasion of His Seventieth Birthday by His Students*, eds. Michael A. Fishbane and
   Paul R. Flohr (Leiden: Brill, 1975), 173–85; Michael Graetz, "Renaissance des
   Judentums im 19. Jahrhundert. 'Der Verein für Cultur und Wissenschaft der
   Juden' 1819 bis 1824," in *Bild und Selbstbild der Juden Berlins zwischen Aufklärung und Romantik*, eds. Marianne Awerbuch and Stefi Jersch-Wenzel (Berlin: Colloquium, 1992), 211–27; Ismar Schorsch, "Breakthrough into the Past:
   The Verein für Cultur und Wissenschaft der Juden," *Leo Baeck Institute Yearbook* 33 (1988): 3–28; Kerstin von Krone, "Verein für Cultur und Wissenschaft der Juden," in *Enzyklopädie jüdischer Geschichte und Kultur* (EJGK),
   vol. 6 (Stuttgart: J.B. Metzler, 2015), 256–9; Ricardo Haase, "Suche nach
   dem Judentum: zur Geschichte des 'Vereins für Cultur und Wissenschaft
   der Juden,'" *Tribüne* 174 (2005): 126–34; Rachel Livneh-Freudenthal, "From
   'a Nation Dwelling Alone' to 'a Nation Among the Nations' or, 'The Return
   to History' – between Universalism and Nationalism," in *Streams into the*

Sea: Studies in Jewish Culture and Its Context, Dedicated to Felix Posen, eds. Rachel Livneh-Freudenthal and Elchanan Reiner (Tel Aviv: Alma College, 2001), 153–77; Michael A. Meyer, *Von Moses Mendelssohn zu Leopold Zunz. Jüdische Identität in Deutschland 1749–1824* (Munich: C.H. Beck, 1994); Michael A. Meyer, *Judaism within Modernity: Essays on Jewish History and Religion* (Detroit: Wayne State University Press, 2001), 21–63; Max Wiener, "The Ideology of the Founders of Jewish Scientific Research," *YIVO Annual for Jewish Social Sciences* 5 (1950): 184–96; Nahum N. Glatzer, "The Beginnings of Modern Jewish Studies," in *Studies in Nineteenth-Century Jewish Intellectual History*, ed. Alexander Altmann (Cambridge, MA: Harvard University Press, 1964), 27–45; Rachel Heuberger, *Aron Freimann und die Wissenschaft des Judentums, Conditio Judaica* (Berlin: De Gruyter, 2004); Christian Wiese, "Hochschule für die Wissenschaft des Judentums," in *EJGK*, vol. 3 (Stuttgart: J.B. Metzler, 2012), 75–81; Christian Wiese, *Challenging Colonial Discourse: Jewish Studies and Protestant Theology in Wilhelmine Germany* (Leiden: Brill, 2005); Christian Wiese, Walter Homolka, and Thomas Brechenmacher, eds., *Jüdische Existenz in der Moderne. Abraham Geiger und die Wissenschaft des Judentums* (Berlin: De Gruyter, 2013); Yosef Hayim Yerushalmi, *Zakhor: Jewish History and Jewish Memory* (Seattle: University of Washington Press, 1982), 77–103; and Christina von Braun, ed., *Was war deutsches Judentum? 1870–1933* (Berlin: Brill, 2015). On the situation of the Jews at German universities, see Monika Richarz, *Der Eintritt der Juden in die akademischen Berufe. Jüdische Studenten und Akademiker in Deutschland 1678–1848* (Tübingen: Mohr, 1974).

3 For a list of the founders, see Gründungsurkunde, Leopold Zunz Archive, Sig. ARC 4 792/B1-2, http://www.jewish-archives.org/content/titleinfo/2742.

4 For example, see Jonathan Frankel and Steven J. Zipperstein, eds., *Assimilation and Community: The Jews in Nineteenth-Century Europe* (Cambridge: Cambridge University Press, 1992); Pierre Birnbaum and Ira Katznelson, eds., *Paths of Emancipation: Jews, States, and Citizenship* (Princeton: Princeton University Press, 1995); Walter Homolka, *Jewish Jesus Research and Its Challenge to Christology Today* (Leiden: Brill, 2016), 42–9; Stefi Jersch-Wenzel, "Minderheiten in der burgerlichen Gesellschaft. Juden in Amsterdam, Frankfurt und Posen," in *Burgertum im 19. Jahrhundert*, vol. 2, ed. Jürgen Kocka (Göttingen: Vandenhoeck & Ruprecht 1995), 392–420; George L. Mosse, *German Jews beyond Judaism* (Cincinnati: Hebrew Union College

Press, 1985); Reinhard Rurup, "The Tortuous and Thorny Path to Legal Equality," *Leo Baeck Institute Yearbook* 31 (1986): 3–33; Reinhard Rurup, *Emanzipation und Antisemitismus. Studien zur Judenfrage der bürgerlichen Gesellschaft* (Göttingen: Vandenhoeck & Ruprecht, 1975); David Sorkin, *The Transformation of German Jewry, 1780–1840* (New York: Oxford Unversity Press, 1987), 113–23; and Shulamit Volkov, "Die Verburgerlichung der Juden in Deutschland als Paradigma," in *Judisches Leben und Antisemitismus im 19. und 20. Jahrhundert. Zehn Essays,* ed. Shulamit Vokov (Munich: C.H. Beck, 1990), 111–30.

5 In 1883, after passing the state examination for the equivalent to a university institution, the Hochschule was renamed a "teaching institution" (Lehranstalt) until 1922. From 1933 to 1942, the Nazis renamed the Hochschule a second time to Lehranstalt für die Wissenschaft des Judentums. See the handwritten deletion of "Hochschule" and the handwritten heading of "Lehranstalt" on the student card of Ernst Ludwig Ehrlich. This paper uses the honorific title *Hochschule*. In addition, the term *Judentum* is also not translated, since debates about the meaning of this term within the Wissenschaft des Judentums had a utility different from concept of culture to a concept of religion.

6 Leopold Zunz, "Etwas über die rabbinische Litteratur" (Berlin, 1818), in *Gesammelte Schriften von Dr. Leopold Zunz. Herausgegeben vom Curatorium der Zunzstiftung,* vol. 1 (Berlin: Louis Gerschel, 1875), 1–31.

7 Glatzer, *The Beginnings of Modern Jewish Studies,* 36.

8 Immanuel Wolf, "Über den Begriff einer Wissenschaft des Judenthums," *Zeitschrift für die Wissenschaft des Judenthums* 1 (1822): 1–24.

9 See Kerstin von Krone, *Wissenschaft in Öffentlichkeit. Die Wissenschaft des Judentums und ihre Zeitschriften* (Berlin: De Gruyter, 2012).

10 Wolf, "Über den Begriff," 1.

11 Leopold Zunz, *Zur Geschichte und Literatur* (Berlin: Veit, 1845), 41–59; see also Guiseppe Veltri, "A Jewish Luther? The Academic Dreams of Leopold Zunz," *Jewish Studies Quarterly* 7 (2000): 1–8; Gianfranco Miletto, "Leopold Zunz and the Hebraisten," *European Association of Jewish Studies* 15 (2004): 50–60.

12 Peter Schäfer, "Judaistik – judische Wissenschaft in Deutschland heute. Historische Identität und Nationalität," in *Saeculum Jahrbuch fur Universalgeschichte* 42, no. 2 (1991): 199–216, here 203.

13 Christoph Schulte, *Die jüdische Aufklärung: Philosophie, Religion, Geschichte* (Munich: C.H. Beck, 2002), 116.

14 Michael A. Meyer, "Jewish Religious Reform and Science of Judaism: The Positions of Zunz, Geiger, and Franke," *Leo Baeck Institute Year Book* 16 (1971): 19–41, here 26.

15 Wolf, "Über den Begriff," 1.

16 Zunz, "Zur Geschichte und Literatur," 21.

17 Jules Isaac, *The Teaching of Contempt: Christian Roots of Anti-Semitism* (New York: Holt, Rinehart and Winston, 1964).

18 See Michael A. Meyer, *Response to Modernity: A History of the Reform Movement in Judaism* (New York: Oxford University Press, 1988), 77–84.

19 Michael A. Meyer, "Jüdische Wissenschaft und jüdische Identität," in *Wissenschaft des Judentums. Anfänge der Judaistik in Europa*, ed. Julius Carlebach (Darmstadt: Wissenschaftliche Buchgesellschaft, 1992), 3–20, here 10.

20 Susannah Heschel, "Revolt of the Colonized: Abraham Geiger's Wissenschaft des Judentums as a Challenge to Christian Hegemony in the Academy," *New German Critique* 77 (1999): 61–85, here 74.

21 Heschel, "Revolt of the Colonized," 69.

22 Wolf, "Über den Begriff," 24.

23 Schäfer, "Judaistik - Jüdische Wissenschaft in Deutschland heute," 204.

24 See Ludwig Geiger, "Zunz im Verkehr mit Behörden und Hochgestellten," *Monatsschrift für Geschichte und Wissenschaft des Judentums* 60 (1916): 245–62, 321–47; Wiese, *Hochschule für die Wissenschaft des Judentums*, 432.

25 See Michael Brenner, "Jüdische Geschichte an deutschen Universitäten - Bilanz und Perspektive," *Historische Zeitschrift* 266 (1998): 1–21, here 3.

26 Geiger, "Zunz im Vekehr mit Behörden und Hochgestellten," 335.

27 Wiese, *Hochschule für die Wissenschaft des Judentums*, 428.

28 See, for example, Wiese, *Challenging Colonial Discourse*, 78–85; and Mirjam Thulin, *Kaufmanns Nachrichtendienst. Ein jüdisches Gelehrtennetzwerk im 19. Jahrhundert* (Göttingen: Vandenhoeck & Ruprecht, 2012).

29 Irene Kaufmann, *Die Hochschule für die Wissenschaft des Judentums (1872–1942)* (Berlin: Hentrich & Hentrich, 2006), 9. Abraham Geiger taught Oriental studies, Jewish philosophy, history, and rabbinical Bible exegesis; David Cassel (1818–1893) took over Bible exegesis, Jewish history, and literature; Heimann Steinthal (1823–1899) taught philosophy of religion; and Israel Lewy (1841–1917) taught Talmud and rabbinical literature. The board

of trustees of the university was represented by Moritz Lazarus, Albert
Mosse (1846–1925), Oscar Wassermann (1889–1934), Martin Philippson
(1846–1916), Heinrich Stahl (1868–1942), Gotthold Weil (1882–1960), and
Bernhard Weiß (1880–1951).

30 Ismar Elbogen, *Ein Jahrhundert Wissenschaft des Judentums* (Berlin: Philo,
    1922), 8.

31 On the "popularization" of the *Wissenschaft des Judentums*, see Chapter 4,
    "The Science of Judaism and Its Popularization," in Michael Brenner, *Jüdis-che Kultur in der Weimarer Republik*, 2nd ed. (Munich: C.H. Beck, 2016),
    114–41.

32 Today, Tucholskystraße 9 in Berlin Mitte is called Leo-Baeck-Haus and is
    the seat of the Central Council of Jews in Germany.

33 See Meyer, *Jüdische Wissenschaft und jüdische Identität*, 16.

34 See Werner Treß, *Wider den undeutschen Geist. Bücherverbrennung 1933*
    (Berlin: Vorwarts, 2003).

35 Michael Grüttner, "Nationalsozialistische Wissenschaftler: ein Kollektivpor-trät," in *Gebrochene Wissenschaftskulturen. Universität und Politik im 20.
    Jahrhundert*, eds. Michael Grüttner, Rüdiger Hachtmann, Konrad H.
    Jarausch, Jürgen John, and Matthias Middell (Göttingen: Vandenhoeck
    & Ruprecht, 2010), 149–65, here 150.

36 See Chaim Weizmann, *Trial and Error: The Autobiography of Chaim
    Weizmann* (London: Hamish Hamilton, 1950).

37 Gesetz gegen die Überfüllung deutscher Schulen und Hochschulen vom 25.
    April 1933, in *Reichsgesetzblatt* (RGB1) I 1933, 225; 1. Verordnung zur Durch-führung des Gesetzes gegen die Überfüllung deutscher Schulen und
    Hochschulen vom 25. April 1933, in RGB1. I 1933, 226; Albrecht Götz von
    Olenhusen, "Die 'nichtarischen' Studenten an den deutschen Hochschulen.
    Zur nationalsozialistischen Rassenpolitik 1933–1945," *Vierteljahrshefte für
    Zeitgeschichte*, 14 (1966): 175–206.

38 On the discrimination and exclusion of Jewish students, professors, and
    researchers at German universities after 1933, see Michael Günter, "Wissen-schaftspolitik im Nationalsozialismus," in *Geschichte der Kaiser-Wilhelm-Gesellschaft im Nationalsozialismus. Bestandsaufnahme und Perspektiven
    der Forschung*, ed. Doris Kaufmann (Göttingen: Wallstein, 2000), 557–85;
    Michael Günter, "Die deutschen Universitäten unter dem Hakenkreuz," in
    Zwischen Autonomie und Anpassung in den Diktaturen des 20. Jahrhunderts,

eds. John Connelly and Michael Grüttner (Paderborn: Ferdinand Schoningh, 2003), 67–100; Michael Grüttner and Sven Kinas, "Die Vertreibung von Wissenschaftlern aus den deutschen Universitäten 1933," *Vierteljahrshefte für Zeitgeschichte* 55 (2007): 123–86; Christoph Jahr, "Die nationalsozialistische Machtübernahme und ihre Folgen," in *Die Berliner Universität zwischen den Weltkriegen 1918–1945*, ed. Michael Grüttner (Berlin: Akademie, 2012), 295–324; Ursula Ferdinand, "Vertreibung im Umgestaltungsprozess der Medizinischen Fakultäten an deutschen Universitäten im 'Dritten Reich,'" in *Jüdische Ärztinnen und Ärzte im Nationalsozialismus. Entrechtung, Vertreibung, Ermordung*, eds. Thomas Beddies, Susanne Doetz, and Christoph Kopke (Berlin: De Gruyter, 2014), 117–48; Reinhard Rürup and Michael Schüring, *Schicksale und Karriere. Gedenkbuch für die von den Nationalsozialisten aus der Kaiser-Wilhelm-Gesellschaft vertriebenen Forscherinnen und Forscher* (Göttingen: Wallstein, 2008); and Sabine Schleiermacher and Udo Schagen, eds., *Wissenschaft und Politik. Hochschule in den politischen Systembrüchen 1933 und 1945* (Stuttgart: Franz Steiner, 2009).

39　See Richard Fuchs, "The 'Hochschule für die Wissenschaft des Judentums' in the Period of Nazi Rule: Personal Recollections," *Leo Baeck Institute Year Book* 12 (1967): 3–31; and Marianne Awerbuch, "Die Hochschule für die Wissenschaft des Judentums," in *Geschichtswissenschaft in Berlin im 19. und 20. Jahrhundert. Persönlichkeiten und Institutionen*, eds. Reimer Hansen and Wolfgang Ribbe (Berlin: De Gruyter, 1992), 517–52.

40　Fuchs, "The 'Hochschule für die Wissenschaft des Judentums,'" 10.

41　See Ernst Simon, "Pädagogik in Selbstdarstellung," in *Pädagogik in Selbstdarstellungen*, vol. 1, ed. Ludwig J. Pongratz (Hamburg: Felix Meiner, 1975), 272–333; and Michael Bühler, *Erziehung zur Tradition – Erziehung zum Widerstand. Ernst Simon und die jüdische Erwachsenenbildung in Deutschland* (Berlin: Selbstverlag Institut Kirche und Judentum, 1986).

42　Ernst Simon, *Aufbau im Untergang. Jüdische Erwachsenenbildung im nationalsozialistischen Deutschland als geistiger Widerstand* (Tübingen: C.B. Mohr, 1959).

43　Fuchs, "The 'Hochschule für die Wissenschaft des Judentums,'" 15.

44　Ibid., 14.

45　Awerbuch, "Die Hochschule für die Wissenschaft des Judentums," 548.

46　See Fuchs, "The 'Hochschule für die Wissenschaft des Judentums,'" 16.

47　Richard Fuchs called it a "voluntary transformation" to have the teacher and *Arbeitskreis* perspective in mind. But for this chapter, in which the historical matrix of the Nazi era is in mind, one must identify it as an inevitable transformation.

48 Herbert A. Strauss, "Die letzten Jahre der Hochschule (*Lehranstalt*) für die *Wissenschaft des Judentums*, Berlin: 1936–1942," in *Wissenschaft des Judentums. Anfänge der Judaistik in Europa*, ed. Julius Carlebach (Darmstadt: Wissenschaftliche Buchgesellschaf, 1992), 36–52, here 47. See also Herbert A. Strauss, *Über dem Abgrund. Eine jüdische Jugend in Deutschland 1918–1943* (Frankfurt: Campus, 1997).

49 See Awerbuch, "Die Hochschule für die Wissenschaft des Judentums," 548; Herbert A. Strauss, "Jewish Emigration from Germany: Nazi Policies and Jewish Responses: Part I," *Leo Baeck Institute Year Book* 25 (1980): 313–61; and Herbert A. Strauss, "Jewish Emigration from Germany: Nazi Policies and Jewish Responses: Part II," *Leo Baeck Institute Year Book* 26 (1981): 343–409.

50 Strauss, "Die letzten Jahre der Hochschule," 40.

51 Marion A. Kaplan, *Between Dignity and Despair: Jewish Life in Nazi Germany* (New York: Oxford University Press, 1998), 10, 94–118.

52 See Hartmut Bomhoff, *Ernst Ludwig Ehrlich – prägende Jahre. Eine Biographie* (Berlin: De Gruyter, 2015); Herbert A. Strauss, *Über dem Abgrund. Eine jüdische Jugend in Deutschland 1918–1943* (Frankfurt: Campus, 1997); Lotte Strauss, *Uber den grunen Hugel. Erinnerungen an Deutschland* (Berlin: Metropol, 1997); and interview with Ernst Ludwig Ehrlich, in *"Wo es hell ist, dort ist die Schweiz." Flüchtlinge und Fluchthilfe an der Schaffhauser Grenze zur Zeit des Nationalsozialismus*, ed. Franco Battel (Zurich: Chronos, 2001), 334–8.

53 Nathan Peter Levinson (born Lewsinki, 1921–2016) was able to leave Nazi Germany in 1941 and emigrate to the United States. At Hebrew Union College in Cincinnati, he resumed his rabbinate studies, and in 1948, after his ordination, he took up his first rabbinical post in Selma, Alabama. Between 1950 and 1953 he held the position of State Rabbi of Berlin. See Levinson, *Ein Ort ist, mit wem Du bist. Lebensstationen eines Rabbiners* (Berlin: Schriften der Stiftung Neue Synagoge Berlin, Centrum Judaicum, 1996); and Michael Brenner, *After the Holocaust: Rebuilding Jewish Lives in Postwar Germany* (Princeton: Princeton University Press, 1999), 107–11.

54　Awerbuch, "Die Hochschule für die Wissenschaft des Judentums," 549.

55　Zeugnis der Reife. Private höhere Schule der Jüdischen Gemeinde Berlin, Ernst Ludwig Ehrlich, 06.03.1940, Archiv für Zeitgeschichte ETH Zürich: NL Ernst Ludwig Ehrlich/25.

56　Ibid.

57　See Leonard Baker, *Days of Sorrow and Pain: Leo Baeck and the Berlin Jews* (New York: Oxford University Press, 1980).

58　Irene Aue-Ben-David, *Deutsch-jüdische Geschichtsschreibung im 20. Jahrhundert. Zu Werk und Rezeption von Selma Stern* (Göttingen: Vandenhoeck & Ruprecht, 2017).

59　Julius Carlebach and Michael Brocke, eds., *Die Rabbiner im Deutschen Reich 1871–1945* (Munich: K.G. Saur, 2009), 415–16.

60　Andrea Löw, *Deutsches Reich und Protektorat September 1939–September 1941*, (Berlin: De Gruyter, 2012), Document 37, n. 21, 142.

61　Joseph Walk, ed., *Kurzbiographien zur Geschichte der Juden 1918–1945* (Berlin: De Gruyter 1988), 232.

62　Anna Holzer-Kawaiko, "Jewish Intellectuals between Robbery and Restitution: Ernst Grumach in Berlin, 1941–1946," *Leo Baeck Institute Year Book* 63 (2018): 273–95.

63　Kay Weniger, *Zwischen Bühne und Baracke. Lexikon der verfolgten Theater-, Film- und Musikkünstler 1933–1945* (Berlin: Metropol, 2008), 63–4.

64　Stephan Dörschel, *Fritz Wisten. Bis zum letzten Augenblick – ein jüdisches Theaterleben* (Berlin: Hentrich & Hentrich, 2009).

65　List of teachers in Ernst Ludwig Ehrlich, "Report on His Illegal Life by One of the Three Surviving Graduates of the Last Course of the 'Lehranstalt für die Wissenschaft des Judentums' in Berlin," Wiener Library London, P.III.d. (Berlin) No. 1141, 1959.

66　Prof. Dr Dr. H.C. Ernst Ludwig Ehrlich, *Verfolgung und Aufbruch - Jüdisches Leben nach dem Holocaust. Mein Engagement für den christlich – jüdischen Dialog (Erinnerungen 1940–1996)*; Archiv für Zeitgeschichte ETH Zürich: TA Kolloquien FFAfZ/140, Kolloquien "Zeugen der Zeit" (2005).

67　Awerbuch, "Die Hochschule für die Wissenschaft des Judentums," 549.

68　Nathan P. Levinson, "In memoriam Dr. Leopold Lucas," in *Ein Rabbiner in Deutschland. Aufzeichnungen zu Religion und Politik*, ed. Nathan P. Levinson (Gerlingen: Bleicher, 1987), 56.

69 Strauss, "Die letzten Jahre der Hochschule," 48.

70 Michael A. Meyer, "Scholarship and Worldliness: The Life and Work of Fritz Bamberger," *Leo Baeck Institute Year Book* 58 (2013): 143–58, here 150.

71 Rolf Vogel and Ernst Ludwig Ehrlich, "Ein Gespräch mit Ernst Ludwig Ehrlich," in *Ernst Ludwig Ehrlich und der christlich-jüdische Dialog*, ed. Rolf Vogel (Frankfurt am Main: Knecht, 1984), 13–69, here 44.

72 Wolfgang Hamburger, "Teacher in Berlin and Cincinnati," *Leo Baeck Institute Yearbook* 2 (1957): 27–34, here 31.

73 Fuchs, "The Hochschule für die Wissenschaft des Judentums," 30.

74 Ernst Ludwig Ehrlich, "Leo Baeck - Rabbiner in schwerster Zeit," in *Ernst Ludwig Ehrlich. Von Hiob zu Horkheimer. Gesammelte Schriften zum Judentum und seiner Umwelt*, eds. Walter Homolka and Tobias Barniske (Berlin: De Gruyter, 2009), 295–300, here 297.

75 Meyer, *Scholarship and Worldliness*, 151.

76 Strauss, "Die letzten Jahre der Hochschule," 48.

77 Ehrlich, Report (P.III.d. No. 1141/1959).

78 See Diemut Majer, "Rassistisches Recht in NS-Deutschland: From the Legislation to the Police Regime 1941–1944," in *Gesetzliches Unrecht. Rassistisches Recht im 20. Jahrhundert, Jahrbuch zur Geschichte und Wirkung des Holocaust*, eds. Micha Brumlik, Susanne Meinl, and Werner Renz (Frankfurt am Main: Campus, 2005), 95–110, here 97–9.

79 Ehrlich, Report (P.III.d. No. 1141/1959).

80 Fuchs, "The Hochschule für die Wissenschaft des Judentums," 30.

81 Leo Baeck to Ismar Elbogen, 19 February 1941, in "Letters From War-Time Berlin," *Leo Baeck Institute Year Book* 5 (1960): 351–8, here 354.

82 Ehrlich to Schottländer, 4 November 1965, in Nachlass 359 Rudolf Schottländer Mappe 658 Ehrlich, Ernst Ludwig; Staatsbibliothek zu Berlin – Preußischer Kulturbesitz.

83 Ernst Ludwig Ehrlich, "Begegnungen - Menschen auf meinem Weg des christlich-jüdischen Gesprächs, First Publication: Speech on the occasion of the awarding of the Buber Rosenzweig Medal at the opening of the *Woche der Brüderlichkeit* in Düsseldorf on March 7, 1976," in *Ernst Ludwig Ehrlich und der christlich-jüdische Dialog*, ed. Rolf Vogel (Frankfurt am Main: Knecht, 1984), 171–90, here 180.

84 Hamburger, "Teacher in Berlin and Cincinnati," 31.

85 See Strauss, "Die letzten Jahre der Hochschule," 44.

86 Fuchs, "The 'Hochschule für die Wissenschaft des Judentums,'" 31.

87 Ehrlich, "Leo Baeck – Rabbiner in schwerster Zeit," 296.

88 Ibid.

89 Hamburger, "Teacher in Berlin and Cincinnati," 34.

90 Fuchs, "The 'Hochschule für die Wissenschaft des Judentums,'" 31.

91 Hamburger, "Teacher in Berlin and Cincinnati," 30.

92 Ibid., 31.

93 See Doerte Bischoff and Joachim Schlör, eds., *Dinge des Exils, Exilforschung 31. Jahrbuch der Gesellschaft für Exilforschung* (Munich: edition text + kritik, 2013); Johannes F. Evelein, "Erste Dinge - Reisegepack im Exil. Eine phanomenologische Lekture," *Exilforschung* 31 (2013): 23–34; and Joachim Schlor, "Dinge der Emigration. Eine Projektskizze," *Exilforschung* 23 (2005), 222–38.

94 Hans Sahl, *Memoiren eines Moralisten. Das Exil im Exil* (Munich: Luchterhand, 2008), 225.

95 See Strauss, "Die letzten Jahre der Hochschule," 58.

96 Brenner, *After the Holocaust*, 107.

97 Ernst Ludwig Ehrlich, "Rezension of Hans J. Bach, 'The German Jew.' A Synthesis of Judaism and Western Civilization 1730-1930," *Freiburger Rundbrief*, 37–38 (1985–86): 109.

98 Strauss, "Die letzten Jahre der Hochschule," 50.

10

Ethnonationalism as a Theological Crisis: Metropolitan Andrey Sheptytsky and the Greek Catholic Church in Western Ukraine, 1923–1944

Kateryna Budz and Andrew Kloes

For more than four decades, from 1901 to 1944, Andrey Sheptytsky led the Greek Catholic Church in western Ukraine as he exercised the ecclesiastical offices of metropolitan of Halych, archbishop of Lviv, and bishop of Kamianets-Podilskyi.[1] During the interwar period, Greek Catholicism was the religious identity of most of the 5.8 million inhabitants of Galicia, where there were an estimated 3.6 million lay members of the Church.[2] Providing pastoral care and local religious leadership to the Greek Catholic faithful were around 2,350 parish clergy and 140 monastic priests (*hieromonks*).[3] In recent years, the life and work of Metropolitan Sheptytsky has received renewed interest and recognition from various community organizations, religious leaders, and scholars, both in Ukraine and around the world.[4]

On 31 October 2013, the national director of the American Anti-Defamation League, Abraham Foxman, posthumously awarded Metropolitan Sheptytsky his organization's highest honour, the Jan Karski Courage to Care Award. In conferring this award, Foxman cited how Sheptytsky had taken "great risk upon himself, upon the priests and nuns in his charge, and upon his entire Church to save Jewish men, women and children ... The courage of his clandestine acts was matched by the bravery of his public statements."[5] The Yale University historian Timothy Snyder delivered a similar assessment of Sheptytsky in his remarks at the 14 November 2014 presentation of the eponymous Sheptytsky Award, which is bestowed jointly by the Ukrainian Jewish Encounter organization and the Jewish Confederation of Ukraine. Snyder observed that in writing to Adolf Hitler, Heinrich Himmler, and Pope Pius XII to protest the German atrocities against Jews in Ukraine, the metropolitan was unique among his contemporary European church leaders. According to Snyder, Sheptytsky carried out, "probably, the most consistent opposition to the Holocaust undertaken by a public figure during the Second World War."[6]

Citing Sheptytsky's pioneering ecumenical overtures to bridge differences that Greek Catholics had with Roman Catholics and with the Orthodox, his pastoral work in Ukraine under periods of communist and Nazi occupation, and his efforts on behalf of Jews during the Nazi occupation, Pope Francis signed a decree on 16 July 2015 that recognized Sheptytsky as "venerable." This declaration, the first step toward canonization in the Catholic Church, identified Sheptytsky as having lived a life that heroically exemplified the theological virtues of faith, hope, and love and the cardinal virtues of prudence, justice, fortitude, and temperance.[7] Lastly, at an event in Kyiv on 1 November 2015, which commemorated the 150th anniversary of Sheptytsky's birth, the chief rabbi of Ukraine, Yaakov Dov Bleich, remarked: "Metropolitan Sheptytsky is an example of love for his people, an example of the desire for the unity of all the Churches, religions, and nations and a model of conduct for modern citizens, especially young people. During the Second World War, Metropolitan Andrey not only saved hundreds of Jewish families through his own efforts from looming death, but united believers and clergy to help Jews."[8] As the previous statements indicate, Sheptytsky was a historically exceptional figure on the interwar and Holocaust-era religious landscape. In various ways, he worked to promote peace and understanding between the different religious and ethnic groups in Galicia.

When Sheptytsky joined the monastic Order of Saint Basil the Great on 29 May 1888, at age twenty-three, he had an unusual background for a Greek Catholic monk, in that he had already earned a law doctorate from the University of Kraków and had learned to read, write, and speak Hebrew.[9] Fifteen years later, in 1903, the leaders of one Jewish community wrote to the young

Metropolitan to ask for financial assistance on behalf of an older man who had fallen suddenly into dire need. Besides sending a monetary gift, Sheptytsky enclosed a letter written in Hebrew that "displays an astonishing familiarity with Jewish texts such as the Talmud and the Siddur and a deep sensitivity for Jewish customs and religious conventions. The letter is replete with allusions to classic Jewish works, and the calligraphy is exemplary."[10] The warm relations that the archbishop of Lviv later had with the Jewish religious community are further conveyed by the birthday wishes he received from the chief rabbi of Lviv, Ezekiel Lewin, on the occasion of his seventieth birthday, in 1935. Writing in *Chwila*, the Polish-language newspaper that primarily served Lviv's Jewish community, Lewin praised Sheptytsky as a "real representative of culture and of the highest ethical values, who had always assumed an attitude of understanding and justice toward Israel."[11] One of the children whom Sheptytsky helped hide during the Holocaust related in video testimony he gave to the United States Holocaust Memorial Museum in 1995: "Sheptytsky had proven himself, over a number of years that he had been Archbishop of that area, as a friend of the Jews," and "on Passover, he used to send potatoes for poor Jews so they would have something to eat."[12]

Sheptytsky was also an early advocate for the Christian ecumenical movement in Eastern Europe. As the founder of the ecclesiastical Congress of Velehrad, which met seven times between 1907 and 1936, symbolically in the town where the ninth-century Byzantine missionaries Cyril and Methodius, the "Apostles to the Slavs," had resided, Sheptytsky pursued the interrelated goals of reconciliation between the various Catholic and Orthodox churches of Eastern Europe and peaceful relations between the different national groups that composed their membership.[13]

Despite the failure of Sheptytsky's diplomatic missions to the victors in the First World War regarding independence for the West Ukrainian People's Republic (Zakhidnoukrayins'ka Narodna Respublika), the Metropolitan consistently condemned the use of violence by Ukrainian nationalist groups in their pursuit of political independence in the years between March 1923 and his death in November 1944.[14] Indeed, Sheptytsky reminded the members of his church that, based on several texts from the New Testament, they had an obligation to God to obey the Polish government, up to the point that their obedience to state authorities would require them to disobey God. Sheptytsky later reiterated this spiritual counsel to Ukrainian Greek

Catholics after the Soviets occupied Lviv in late September 1939, and again after the Germans entered the city in late June 1941.[15]

The rest of this chapter examines how Sheptytsky drew upon the theological resources of his Greek Catholic tradition to formulate alternatives to ethnonationalism and antisemitism and how he worked, with limited success, to promote adherence to them among the ordained and lay members of his church. Between 1923 and 1944, he published hundreds of pastoral letters, which priests read out on Sundays to those assembled for worship in the churches under his pastoral oversight.[16] These documents, along with other writings and public statements by him, provide a rich source base for examining Sheptytsky's responses to the social and economic problems that church leaders across Europe grappled with during the years after the First World War. This chapter also examines the episode in Shepytysky's life for which he is today, arguably, best-known outside his church context – his organization of efforts to save the lives of at least 150 Jews, mostly children, during the Holocaust.[17] New information on this topic is drawn from sworn affidavits from one Greek Catholic rescuer who worked for Sheptytsky and from ten Jews whom Sheptytsky and other Greek Catholics rescued, which have been deposited in the archives of the United States Holocaust Memorial Museum.

THE RISE OF UKRAINIAN RADICAL NATIONALISM IN INTERWAR GALICIA

After its proclamation by Ukrainian troops in Lviv on 1 November 1918, a short-lived West Ukrainian People's Republic existed until July 1919, when its soldiers were defeated and its territory occupied by Polish forces.[18] During the conflict, Poles and Ukrainians committed atrocities against each other, which included the killing of prisoners of war and the detention of civilians in internment camps.[19] After their victory, Polish authorities placed 100,000 Ukrainians who had been living in East Galicia in camps and prisons, where around 20,000 died from infectious diseases.[20]

After the independence proclamation in November 1918, Metropolitan Sheptytsky had supported political independence for his national community of West Ukraine, as did other leaders of ethnic, linguistic, and religious communities in Europe, whose people had formerly had a subordinate status within Austria-Hungary and the German, and Russian empires.[21] As John-Paul Himka has observed, during the second half of the nineteenth century, "Greek Catholic clergy created a Ukrainian intelligentsia" in the historic region of Galicia, and in the absence of an independent Ukrainian state, the Greek Catholic Church functioned as a symbol of Ukrainian nationhood.[22] After the military defeat in the summer of 1919, between 1920 and 1923, Sheptytsky travelled widely throughout Europe, North America, and South America as an apostolic delegate, an official representative of the Vatican.[23] His fluency in French, German, Polish, and Ukrainian and additional language skills in English, Hebrew, and Russian enabled him to converse with many different kinds of people during his time overseas.[24] While abroad, Sheptytsky endeavoured to raise funds from the Ukrainian diaspora and Catholic churches in the United States for the relief of those in Galicia whom the war had impoverished and to build international diplomatic support for the West Ukrainian independence movement.[25]

Shortly after arriving in New York City, Metropolitan Sheptytsky sent a letter dated 23 November 1921 to the U.S. secretary of state, Charles Evans Hughes, in which he sharply criticized the Allies' decision to permit the Polish army to occupy East Galicia.[26] The Metropolitan wrote: "This unusual condition is gravely unjust to the population of the country, of which 72 percent is Ukrainian and 12.5 percent Jewish, because the Polish authorities are using their power, not for the benefit of the people, but adversely to their interests, by colonizing and Polonizing the country, thus artificially changing its ethnographic character."[27] He also maintained that sectarian religious aims were animating Polish policy: "the Polish authorities, in their efforts to denationalize the Ukrainian population, who are Greek Catholics, forcibly compel them to accept the Latin rite [Roman Catholicism], and thus a kind of religious persecution has been carried on during this military occupation, in which hundreds of Ukrainian Greek Catholic churches have been desecrated and ruined and hundreds of Greek Catholic priests imprisoned and maltreated by the soldiers."[28]

Nearly a year later, on 10 November 1922, Metropolitan Sheptytsky secured a meeting in Washington, DC, with Hughes at which he presented him with a memorandum that outlined the historical and international legal

Figure 10.1 Archbishop Andrey Sheptytsky
in Philadelphia in October 1910.

arguments for "the organization of East Galicia and Northern Bukovina into a separate state, the West Ukrainian Republic."[29] In this document, he reiterated and intensified the charges he had made in his letter of the previous year: "The Polish regime in this unfortunate land is characterized by barbarous atrocities and national and religious persecution practiced upon the Ukrainian and Jewish populations of this country."[30] Sheptytsyky's calls for Hughes to intervene on behalf of a West Ukrainian People's Republic were of no avail. His audiences on this matter with the US president Warren Harding, French prime minister Aristide Briand, French president Raymond Poincaré, and British prime minister David Lloyd George were equally fruitless.[31] On 15 March 1923, the Conference of Ambassadors of the Principal Allied and Associated Powers recognized Polish sovereignty over the lands for whose independence Sheptytsky had been lobbying.[32] Upon his return home, the Polish government briefly detained the metropolitan, releasing him from custody only after he swore an oath of allegiance to the Polish state.[33]

After the Allies decided in 1923 against supporting the independence of West Ukraine, in favour of the Second Polish Republic's claims to the territory, militant nationalism grew into a potent political force in Ukrainian society. Most Ukrainians in East Galicia had boycotted the 1922 Polish parliamentary elections, and as a result, they had little representation in the Sejm (the Polish parliament).[34] In addition to their primary grievance regarding the failure of international diplomacy to bring about their self-determination, which was amplified by the Polish parliament's decision to officially rename "Galicia" as "Eastern Little Poland" ("Małopolska Wschodnia"), Ukrainian nationalists attracted a popular following through their opposition to several new domestic policies emanating from Warsaw.[35]

In 1918, under the Austro-Hungarian authorities, there had been around 3,000 primary schools in Galicia that taught in Ukrainian; by 1935, there were only 450. The others had introduced bilingual education, with primacy given to the Polish language.[36] A 1925 land reform law exacerbated ethnic tensions when it redistributed around 2 million acres of farmland to 200,000 former Polish soldiers, who subsequently settled in Eastern Galicia and Volhynia.[37] That same year, on 10 February 1925, Poland and the Vatican signed a concordat that, while it officially acknowledged the rights of the Greek Catholic

Church in Galicia, prohibited that church from ministering in Volhynia and the Chełm region.[38]

The discriminatory policies the Polish government had enacted against Ukrainians contributed to the radicalization of the Ukrainian nationalist movement and a broadening of its appeal.[39] As Sheptytsky himself observed: "Unfortunately, even the most serious people and those who keep farthest away from politics are often pushed out of their stance perhaps for no reason other than that they are Ukrainians. Those kinds of instances create a feeling of hopelessness and facilitate the work of emotional, senseless, and irrational elements that, in normal circumstances, would play a markedly lesser role."[40] By then, Ukrainian nationalists had launched a terrorist campaign targeting Polish officials, led by the Ukrainian Military Organization (Ukrainska Viiskova Orhanizatsia, UVO), founded in 1920. The following year, the UVO attempted to assassinate the leader of the new Polish state, Marshall Józef Piłsudski.[41] Led by Yevhen Konovalets, a former Ukrainian officer in the Austro-Hungarian army, the UVO was comprised mainly of other Ukrainian military veterans. By 1924, they had made another unsuccessful assassination attempt, this time on the Polish president, Stanisław Wojciechowski, and had committed thousands of other politically motivated acts of violence against people and property. These targeted both Poles and those Ukrainians whom they regarded as collaborators with the Polish authorities.[42]

Prominent among the nationalist ideologues then fomenting discontent in postwar Ukraine was Dmytro Dontsov, a journalist who edited a literary review financed by Konovalets.[43] Dontsov translated portions of Adolf Hitler's *Mein Kampf* into Ukrainian and published them in 1926, the same year that he published his own programmatic text, *Natsionalizm* (Nationalism).[44] In the latter, Dontsov set forth his vision of a "nationalism of action" and urged Ukrainians to discard the moral constraints that, he argued, had so far impeded its realization. As Grzegorz Rossoliński-Liebe has noted, Dontsov regarded the attainment of independent nationhood as the *summum bonum* for Ukrainians, the pursuit of which superseded all other ethical considerations:

A very fundamental concept of Dontsov's works was "amorality" … This concept reversed the "common" and "universal" system of values and morality. It justified all kinds of crimes and violence as long as they were conducted for the good of the nation, or in order to obtain a state. He argued that only fanaticism and amoral fighting could change history and the unfavorable status quo of not having a state.[45]

While he never joined the Organization of Ukrainian Nationalists (Orhanizatsia Ukrainskykh Natsionalistiv, oun), Dontsov's writings were the inspiration for many of the young men who gathered in Vienna in January 1929 to found the oun.[46] During that congress, the Group of Ukrainian National Youth (Hrupa ukrainskoi natsionalnoi molodi, hunm), the League of Ukrainian Nationalists (Legiia ukrainskykh natsionalistiv, lun), and the Union of Ukrainian Nationalist Youth (Soiuz ukrainskoi natsionalistychnoi molodi, sunm) amalgamated with the uvo.[47] The uvo's leader, Yevhen Konovalets, became the leader of the oun.[48] The new organization was composed largely of young men who had entered adulthood after the First World War. A number of its prominent younger members, including Stepan Bandera, were either the sons of Greek Catholic priests or the products of a Greek Catholic parochial education.[49]

At its founding congress, the oun passed a series of resolutions that outlined its political philosophy, political program, and domestic policy. It envisioned a "national dictatorship" that would eventually reorganize the Ukrainian economy, government, and society on behalf of the "liberation struggle."[50] For example:

General Outline, Resolution 1: Ukrainian nationalism is a spiritual and political movement arising from the inner nature of the Ukrainian Nation in the period of its fierce struggle for the foundations and goals of creative existence.

General Outline, Resolution 2: The Ukrainian Nation is the basis for every activity and the aim of every aspiration of Ukrainian nationalism.

General Outline, Resolution 13: In view of its state of political captivity, the chief aim of the Ukrainian Nation is the creation of a political-legal organization, to be called the Ukrainian Independent United State.

General Outline, Resolution 15: Ukrainian nationalism derives practical tasks for itself from the foremost principles of state organization. These tasks are to prepare for the realization of the national idea through the united efforts of Ukrainians committed to the ideas of a nation-state organized on the principles of active idealism, moral self-discipline, and individual initiative.

Its revolutionary nationalist resolutions made for a rather dense text. However, the OUN also issued a much more straightforward "Ten Commandments," which every member of the group was expected to memorize. This new decalogue rhetorically presented the Ukrainian nationalist cause as a religious one, but not one that was related to any of the churches in Ukraine. Instead, the OUN rhetorically styled Ukrainian nationalism itself as a god to be worshipped. In a deliberately provocative contrast to the biblical Ten Commandments, whose preamble runs, "I am the Lord your God, who brought you out of the land of Egypt, out of the house of slavery" (Exodus 20:2), the OUN's Ten Commandments began, "I am the spirit of the eternal natural force which protected you from the Tartar hordes and placed you on the frontier of two worlds to create a new life."[51] The spirit of Ukrainian nationalism gave the following commandments to OUN members:

1   You will attain a Ukrainian State, or die in battle for it.
2   You will not permit anyone to defame the glory or the honor of Your Nation.
3   Remember the Great Days of our struggles.
4   Be proud of the fact that You are the inheritor of the struggle for the glory of Volodymyr's Trident.
5   Avenge the deaths of the Great Knights.
6   Do not speak about matters with whom you can, but only with whom you must.
7   Do not hesitate to commit the greatest crime, if the good of the Cause demands it.
8   Regard the enemies of Your Nation with hate and perfidy.
9   Neither pleading, nor threats, nor death shall compel You to betray a secret.

10   Aspire to expand the strength, riches, and size of the
      Ukrainian State even by means of enslaving foreigners.

To be sure, the OUN's influence over Galicia's Ukrainians between 1929 and the Soviet occupation in 1939 should not be overstated. Its unofficial press organ, *Ukrainskyi Holos* (Ukrainian Voice), had a circulation of only 4,000. By contrast, newspapers published by the politically moderate Ukrainian National Democratic Alliance (UNDO), the largest Ukrainian party in the Second Polish Republic, reached more than 40,000 subscribers, and the various papers published by the Greek Catholic Church reached more than 50,000.[52] Nevertheless, through its terrorist campaigns, the OUN exercised an outsized influence on Galician Ukrainians.

In response to the OUN's acts of sabotage throughout the summer and fall of 1930 (e.g., burning crops and warehouses, damaging telephone and railway infrastructure, destroying bridges), Polish police and soldiers conducted a "pacification campaign" between 16 September and 30 October 1930 against 450 villages inhabited mainly by Ukrainians. This campaign was premised on their collective responsibility for the OUN's actions.[53] The OUN responded with more violence, and on 15 June 1934, it succeeded in assassinating the Polish government official who had led the pacification operations, the interior minister, Bronisław Pieracki.[54] The OUN's inflammatory expressions of nationalism, made in the service of political terrorism to a population disappointed by the international community and with its own attempts to achieve self-determination through diplomacy, constituted the historical context in which Sheptytsky issued his public statements regarding nationalism and political violence.

METROPOLITAN SHEPTYTSKY'S THEOLOGICAL CRITIQUE OF ETHNONATIONALISM AND POLITICAL VIOLENCE

Sheptytsky interpreted nationalism as a disordered love of country that led people into sin. As Stanisław Stępień has observed, Sheptytsky's views were echoed by the Catholic press in western Ukraine.[55] Thus, nationalism was a sin against God when the nation became an idol in a person's life that supplanted the love that was rightly due to God alone. Nationalism also led people into sin against their fellow men and women when it incited enmity in a person's heart and moved them to carry out malicious actions against those who were different. Against an exclusive kind of ethnonationalism, Sheptytsky encouraged the members of his church to adopt an inclusive kind of patriotism, whose scope extended to everyone living in the country, regardless of their religious or ethnic identity. He preached that such patriotism was a Christian virtue, one that he derived from Jesus's commandment to love one's neighbour.[56]

Sheptytsky's writings on this subject remained consistent over the nearly fifty years that he served in senior leadership positions in the Greek Catholic Church. The following examples of his criticisms of Ukrainian nationalism and his condemnation of political violence are drawn from his earlier years of episcopal ministry in the Austro-Hungarian Empire, the period following the formation of the OUN in 1929, and the five years of the Second World War, during which western Ukraine was incorporated first into the Soviet Union and then into the General Government of German-occupied Poland (1939 to 1944).

In 1897, when he was an abbot, Sheptytsky had founded *The Missionary*, a religious periodical pitched to a popular audience. It would continue to be published intermittently until 1944.[57] The purpose of this publication, according to John-Paul Himka, was to present to a lay audience "a Christian alternative to the radical periodicals in the countryside" and to combat "the increasingly irreligious character of the Ukrainian national movement."[58] In his first pastoral letter, which he issued shortly after becoming the bishop of Stanyslaviv in 1899, Sheptytsky adjured the members of his diocese:

A Christian can and should be a patriot. But his patriotism must not be hatred! And it must not impose duties that contradict the faith. That which would seem to be patriotism, but in fact be hatred or opposition to the faith, is not true patriotism.[59]

Likewise, in a 1904 pastoral letter addressed to Polish members of the Greek Catholic Church, Sheptytsky warned them against having the type of national pride that separated them from other church members from different national backgrounds:

I can only support you in your patriotic beliefs if this patriotism expresses a Christian love for the Motherland and comes from the love of God and neighbor. The Christian is obliged to love his Motherland and to care for the good of his people. The only thing he is not allowed to do, and has no right to do, even under the guise of patriotism, is to hate, and even more, he is not allowed to harm others.[60]

Domestic political violence in western Ukraine forced Sheptytsky to return to these themes in 1908 after Myroslav Sichynsky, a Ukrainian student, assassinated Andrzej Potocki, a Polish aristocrat, who was then serving as a senior Austro-Hungarian government official in Galicia. Sichynsky had murdered Potocki in retaliation for the killing of several Ukrainian peasant activists by the police.[61] Sheptytsky condemned Sichynsky's political murder in a Good Friday sermon on 24 April 1908:

A public crime must be publicly condemned. It must provoke a strong, vigorous protest among Christians, a protest of outrage and disgust at the disregard shown for the light of God's law ... Crime does not serve the people: a crime committed in the name of patriotism is a crime not only before God, but against one's own community, it is a crime against the Motherland.[62]

The UVO and then the OUN carried out acts of terrorism against people and property in Poland throughout the 1920s and 1930s. In response, Sheptytsky challenged the central premise of their political violence – that such actions would help Ukrainians attain a better future. In a pastoral letter he issued on 13 October 1930 in response to the Polish government's pacification campaign, Sheptytsky urged young Ukrainians to become "ant-like." That is, he encouraged them to commit themselves to the long-term work of building up ecclesiastical, economic, and educational organizations to improve the collective prospects of all Ukrainians.

You are young and hot-tempered. You have a strong sense of love for your native land, which demands action and which calls you to action. Persevere in that service and spare no sacrifice, but the sacrifices that the national cause requires at the present moment and which are those that are in accordance with the teaching of Christ and the good of the people ... We are weakened to an extreme degree; in order to be revived and to recover our health and energies, our people need daily, silent, ant-like constructive and productive work in all areas of life; they need agricultural and scientific work; they need Catholic organizations ... Do not allow anyone among you to be led into work for the underground. Whoever leads you away from positive work and inclines you toward conspiracy commits a crime against you and against our native land. Work openly for our people and subordinate that work always to the divine law.[63]

To provide structure and leadership in the pursuit of such social goals, in January 1931, Sheptytsky helped found two new organizations: the Catholic Union, and a Ukrainian chapter of Catholic Action.[64] The former was not a political party but rather a political pressure group created to influence all political parties to adopt policy positions that comported with Catholic social ethics.[65] The latter was meant to offer lay Christians an ecclesiastical alternative for channelling their nationalist sentiments in constructive ways.[66] As the first edition of its newspaper announced: "The task of Catholic Action is to prepare, create and gather Catholic associations for the aims of the lay apostolate, that is, for the intensification and extension, realization and defense of Catholic principles in the life of the individual, the family, and society, according to the teaching of the Catholic Church and the directives of the Apostolic See."[67] Ivan Buchko, who assisted Sheptytsky as an auxiliary bishop in Lviv, described the aim of Catholic Action as the cultivation of a "Christian nationalism" distinct from "heretical nationalism":[68] "Christian nationalism does not place the national idea above all else, but subordinates it to God's laws, to the eternal laws of the Catholic Church, which alone shows us the true way to truth, love, goodness, and beauty."[69]

Among those who worked for Catholic Action was Ivan Babii, a Ukrainian who directed the oldest academic secondary school in Lviv. Sheptytsky appointed him to lead the Archepiscopal Institute of Catholic Action and organize youth activities in the city. On 24 July 1934, a high school student belonging to the OUN murdered Babii, after which he turned his gun on himself and committed suicide.[70] The student committed the murder because Babii had made speeches that denounced nationalist organizations and discouraged young people from joining them. Babii had also, allegedly, cooperated with the Polish police.[71] The deaths of Babii and the student were a tremendous shock for Sheptytsky. In a pastoral letter concerning these events, he condemned the nationalists for "leading our youth astray and into the dead-end of crime." He wrote that if they wanted to murder people like Ivan Babii, who were opposed to their "criminal and stupid work," they would have to murder all of the mothers, fathers, teachers, politicians, priests, and bishops of Ukraine.[72]

The statements Sheptytsky issued concerning nationalism and political violence during earlier periods of his public ministry contextualize the remarks he made in the final years of his life, when the Soviets and the Germans occupied western Ukraine. His pastoral writings during the war years reflected the ethical and theological motifs found throughout his larger corpus as they addressed these new political developments.

The Soviet occupation touched Sheptytsky personally. In addition to placing restrictions on the churches under his care, in the autumn of 1939 the Soviet authorities confiscated his family's estate in Prylbychi, thirty miles west of Lviv. After first making them dig their own graves, the Soviets executed the Metropolitan's younger brother, Count Leon Sheptytsky, along with his wife.[73] Notwithstanding these events, in December 1939, Sheptytsky issued a pastoral letter in which he advised the members of the Greek Catholic Church to obey the new Soviet authorities: "This then is to be our programme. We shall obey the government and observe its laws in so far as they are not contrary to the law of God. We shall keep out of politics and purely secular activities, but we shall not cease to work zealously for the cause of Christ and our people."[74]

The following year, in 1940, Sheptytsky led the other senior bishops of the Greek Catholic Church in issuing a statement titled "The Profession of the Universal Faith," which reiterated his past opposition to nationalism and political violence:

Obedient to Christ's command, we love all nations of the world with neighborly love. We consider hatred to any nation, social stratum, or group as opposed to God's law and thus as harmful for our current and eternal good. Our Christian patriotism is only in that we love our people, the Ukrainian people, with a Christian love that is stronger than that which we have for other peoples, and we are ready to give for them the work of our entire life, and even life itself.[75]

When the German army entered Lviv twenty-two months after the Soviets, in late June 1941, Sheptytsky announced in another pastoral letter:

We welcome the victorious German Army as a liberator from the enemy. We give the appropriate obedience to the established authorities. We recognize Mr. Yaroslav Stets'ko as the head of the regional administration of the western provinces of Ukraine. We expect from the government that he has called to life, wise and just leadership and policies that will consider the needs and welfare of all the citizens who reside in our region regardless of the faith, nationality, or social class to which they belong. May God bless all your labours, Ukrainian People, and may he give all our leaders holy wisdom from heaven.[76]

The 28 March 1942 letter that Sheptytsky wrote, in French, to Pope Pius XII conveyed the Metropolitan's assessment of how the new authorities had governed during the preceding nine months.[77] Johannes Peters, a German who had become a priest in a Catholic monastic order in Ukraine, personally delivered Sheptytsky's letter to the Apostolic Nuncio in Berlin, Archbishop Cesare Orsenigo, who forwarded it to the Vatican.[78] Sheptytsky wrote this letter one day after issuing instructions to local clergy and parish members to place any church member who had committed murder under church discipline. Sheptytsky instructed the Greek Catholic faithful:

[By] repetitive admonitions, by avoiding association with them, by decisive avoidance of family ties with them, let them give murderers to understand that they consider them as a disease and danger for the village. If no one in the village greets a murderer, no one allows him to enter their home, no one speaks to him, no family agrees to become related with him, if even in church Christians will be on guard not to stand near him, if while walking people will avoid meeting with him, if no one sells him anything and no one buys anything from him, then perhaps he will be converted and will begin a life of repentance and work for improving.[79]

In his March 1942 letter to the pope, Sheptytsky informed Pius XII: "As they progress further eastwards, the Germans are becoming more and more willful, without having any regard as to how they are acting out an entirely unrestrained national egoism." The metropolitan contrasted the favourable treatment of the Germans toward his church, in lifting the restrictions on Catholic religious life that the Soviets had implemented, with how they treated Jewish communities in Ukraine. He wrote, "They regard all Jews as enemies of war and organize massacres in which thousands of Jewish men perish along with their wives and children. For example, in all of the large cities of Ukraine, they have exterminated all of the Jews who did not flee from their army, almost 130,000 in Kyiv according to seemingly accurate reports, and similar numbers in other cities."[80] Citing statistics that he had received from members of the Jewish community in Lviv, Sheptytsky reported to Pius XII that 15,000 Jews had been murdered in his own city.

Sheptytsky emphasized to the pope that he was especially concerned that Ukrainians had participated in the mass killings of Jews:

[The Germans] often ordered the local militia to execute hundreds of these condemned Jews without trial and photographed these executions ... From the outbreak of the war, crowds of young people joined local militias [Ukrainians], and it seems inevitable that they were used for such executioner services ... I published, in the only way possible at the time, a pastoral letter on the crime of homicide, and I tried, through the clergy, to warn the youth not to join militias or organizations, where their souls might be exposed to danger.[81]

In a second letter to the pope, dated 29–31 August 1942, Sheptytsky reiterated that "for at least a year, there has not been a day that [the German occupation forces] have not committed the most horrible crimes: murders, theft and robbery, confiscation and extortion. The Jews are the primary victims. The number of Jews killed in our small country has certainly exceeded 200,000."[82]

Two months later, on 21 November 1942, Sheptytsky issued what is, arguably, his best-known pastoral letter, "Thou shalt not kill." Having directed other senior Greek Catholic Church leaders in Ukraine to begin a series of pastoral letters on each of the Ten Commandments in 1941, Sheptytsky himself exposited the fifth commandment. In this letter, which was read out to those in attendance at Greek Catholic worship services, he did not specifically mention either the German occupiers or the Jewish community of Ukraine but instead emphasized to his church's members their universal obligation to love their neighbours: "True love embraces all one's neighbors ... The one who renounces this holy all-embracing Christian love of neighbor, for the sake of God, the worst, and destroys it within himself, is he, who permits the terrible, loathsome evil against the very commandment of God: do not kill!" In sections of the letter dedicated to the topics of "political murder" and "the murder of one's own countrymen," he upbraided the dullness of so many Ukrainians' consciences that they had either sanctioned or remained indifferent to the number of killings going on around them.

METROPOLITAN SHEPTYTSKY'S ASSISTANCE TO JEWS DURING THE HOLOCAUST

Across the five decades that he served as a bishop and metropolitan, Sheptytsky repeatedly reminded those Greek Catholics under his spiritual care that God had commanded them to obey those who governed them, whether that was the Austro-Hungarian Empire, the Second Polish Republic, the Soviet Union, or Nazi Germany. However, he emphasized that they were to obey only to the point at which the state would cause them to disobey God. Sheptytsky consistently condemned revolutionary nationalist violence committed in the cause of Ukrainian political independence as untenable from a Christian perspective. However, during the Holocaust, he encouraged the clergy under his supervision to engage in non-violent disobedience toward the German authorities in the General Government by helping Jews go into hiding.

Among those to whom Sheptytsky provided such help was Kurt Lewin, the son of the chief rabbi of Lviv, Ezekiel Lewin, who was murdered during the pogrom that occurred following the withdrawal of the Soviets and the arrival of the German army in Lviv in late June 1941.[83] In his memoir, Kurt Lewin described his relationship with Sheptytsky and how he was able to survive through the assistance he received from the Metropolitan and the members of several Greek Catholic monastic communities.[84] In the 1990s, Lewin also gathered sworn affidavits from other Jewish men and women, whom

Sheptytsky and other Greek Catholics had assisted, and deposited this collection in the archives of the United States Holocaust Memorial Museum.[85]

In his notarized affidavit of 8 August 1994, Kurt Lewin wrote how before the war, he had known Sheptytsky as a friend of his father and approached him in August 1942 to ask for assistance for him and his younger brother, Nathan Lewin. Sheptytsky introduced Kurt Lewin to his brother Clement Sheptytsky, who was the Superior General of the Studite Fathers, an order of Greek Catholic monks. Together with Marko Stek, a religious superior in the Studite Fathers, Fr Clement coordinated the placement of Jews in several monasteries and convents, issuing them with false identity documents. Specifically, Kurt Lewin moved through the St John the Baptist Monastery in Lychakiv, the Holy Dormition Lavra (a type of monastery) in Univ, the St Andrew's Skete (another type of monastery) in Luzhky, and the St Josaphat Monastery in Lviv. He recalled receiving help from many monks who knew that he was Jewish.

According to Lewin, the monks continued to assist Jewish children after the Germans retreated until they could be placed with suitable Jewish families, as identified by David Kahane, who, in late 1944, was the chief rabbi of the Polish People's Army.[86] According to an affidavit submitted by Kahane's daughter, Ruth Kahana-Geyer, Sheptytsky had arranged for her and her parents' safety in a convent. Likewise, Nathan Lewin reported that after he met Sheptytsky in his official residence, the Metropolitan Palace, opposite St George's Cathedral in Lviv, a monk took him to a convent that belonged to the Basilian Order of nuns in the village of Pidmykhailivtsi. From there, he moved to the home of a parish priest in Bachiv, an estate belonging to Sheptytsky in Yur, and finally to an orphanage in Lviv, where he remained hidden until the Soviets arrived.

Other survivors emphasized how Sheptytsky had similarly intervened on their behalf. For example, Zwi Barnea (formerly known as Herbert Chameides) wrote in his affidavit that his father, Rabbi Kalman Chameides, the former rabbi of Katowice, brought him to the Metropolitan Palace in September 1942, as Sheptytsky had made arrangements for him to go into hiding:

At a time when to help a Jew was to risk death, Archbishop Sheptytsky made the extraordinarily courageous decision to save the lives of a number of Jewish children and adults. In doing so, he exposed himself, his Church, and his religious and lay assistants to mortal danger. Their task, made excruciatingly difficult by the ubiquitous antisemitism of the populace, required considerable intelligence and organizational resources and raised painful moral dilemmas.

Barnea's brother, Leon Chameides, likewise survived the Holocaust, hidden first in a Greek Catholic orphanage and then in a monastery. In the video testimony he gave to the United States Holocaust Memorial Museum in 1995, Leon Chameides added that the Jewish community in Lviv had approached Sheptytsky about hiding 1,000 Torah scrolls. According to Chameides, Sheptytsky had agreed to do so, but the community was ultimately unable to think of a way to bring the scrolls to the monastery.[87]

Oded Amarant (born in August 1935) stated in his affidavit that his uncle found a way to take him out of the ghetto in Lviv and bring him to the Metropolitan Palace, where he met Sheptytsky. From there, monks hid Amarant in monasteries in Lviv and Univ, until the country was liberated and Rabbi Kahane helped him reach his parents in Palestine. He testified that "being Jewish, there is no doubt that I owe my life to the courage and goodwill of Metropolitan Sheptytsky, who instructed his priests to save Jewish lives, endangering themselves and the existence of the Greek Catholic religious order and its institutions." Edward Harvitt echoed Amarant's remarks: "If it were not for Metropolitan Andrej Sheptytsky, Mr Zurakowski, and Mrs Slavka Barycka, my mother and I most probably would not have survived the Holocaust." In his affidavit, Harvitt recounted how after the murder of his father in Stanisławów (Stanislaviv, present-day Ivano-Frankivsk), his mother fled with him to Lviv, where they met a Ukrainian man, Zurakowski, who sheltered them. In turn, he suggested that they visit Sheptytsky, who issued them with false identity papers. They survived the war staying with Barycka, the daughter of the Ukrainian man who had first helped them. After meeting Sheptytsky in his residence during the winter of 1943, Lilit Pohlmann credited Helena Witter (Olena Viter), the abbess of the convent in Ubocz (Uboch), with saving her life, her mother's life, and the lives of several other Jewish children.

One of the people whom Sheptytsky relied upon in his efforts to shelter Jews during the Holocaust was Ivan Hirnyj, who worked for the office of the

Metropolitan as a car and truck driver.[88] Through the work of Johannes Peters, a German who had become a priest in the Studite Fathers' monastic order, the metropolitan's office received permission from officials of the General Government to operate these two vehicles for official church business, which the German occupational authorities also supplied with gasoline. While the stated purpose of these vehicles was to transport communion wine and supplies for the church's printing office, as well as for Sheptytsky's personal travel (by 1941 he was unable to walk), Sheptytsky directed Hirnyj to use the vehicles to transport Jewish men, women, and children to orphanages, convents, monasteries, and other locations in Galicia.

CONCLUSIONS

Metropolitan Andrey Sheptytsky is celebrated by many today for his conceptualization of ethnonationalism as a theological crisis, in which the members of his church were tempted to disobey the divine command to love one's neighbour as oneself, and for the leadership role that he exercised in the rescue of around 150 Jewish men, women, and children during the Holocaust. A certain sense of tragedy hangs over the life of Sheptytsky. Despite all the decades during which he exhorted the members of his church not to engage in ethnic hatred and political violence, genocide on a staggering scale transpired in the lands over which he had so long served as a bishop. According to Alexander Kruglov, the four Soviet *oblasts* of Drohobych, Lviv, Stanyslaviv, and Ternopil, whose geographic areas primarily overlapped with the boundaries of Galicia, had had a Jewish population of 656,000 in 1939. Of these Jewish men, women, and children, the Germans, with the assistance of local Ukrainians and others, murdered approximately 566,000 (86 per cent) between 1941 and 1944; the remaining 90,000 survived in hiding or by fleeing eastward to Soviet territory.[89] The aforementioned civil rights activists, Catholic and Jewish religious community leaders, and scholars who call for Sheptytsky's remembrance today do so to draw attention to his opposition to ethnic hatreds and to remind contemporary audiences that such violence is not inevitable.

NOTES

The views expressed here are those of the authors and do not represent those of the United States Holocaust Memorial Museum.

1 Like the Roman Catholic Church, the Greek Catholic Church follows the spiritual leadership of the pope, the bishop of Rome, with whom it is in full communion. However, dating back several centuries to the decision of several Ukrainian Orthodox bishops to accept papal authority at the ecclesiastical Union of Brest in 1596, the Greek Catholic Church (or Uniate Church) remains distinct among Catholic churches, in that it retains the Byzantine liturgical tradition in its worship. After the First Partition of the Polish–Lithuanian Commonwealth in 1772, Galicia became a part of the Austrian Habsburg monarchy, whose rulers favoured the Uniate Church as a counterbalance to the Roman Catholic Church in the region. In 1774, by a special decree, the empress Maria Theresa replaced the term "Uniate," which already had a pejorative connotation, with the title "Greek Catholic." The introduction of this new term implied an equal status between the Byzantine-rite Greek Catholic Church and the Latin-rite Roman Catholic Church. In 1808, the Greek Catholic Church in Austrian Galicia regained the Galician Metropolitanate, whose seat was in Lviv. The organizational support the Habsburgs extended to the Greek Catholic Church, particularly in supporting education for future priests, resulted in the formation of the Ukrainian clerical elite. These church leaders played a dominant role in Ukrainian nation-building in the mid-nineteenth century. As John-Paul Himka has observed, the Ukrainian national identity in Austrian Galicia was forged predominantly by two institutions, the Habsburg dynasty and the Greek Catholic Church. On this point, see John-Paul Himka, *Religion and Nationality in Western Ukraine: The Greek Catholic Church and the Ruthenian National Movement in Galicia, 1867–1900* (Montreal and Kingston: McGill-Queen's University Press, 1999); John-Paul Himka. "The Greek Catholic Church and Nation-Building in Galicia, 1772–1918," *Harvard Ukrainian Studies* 8 (1984): 426–52; and Oleh Turij, "Hreko-Katolytska Tserkva ta ukrainska natsionalna identychnist v Halychyni," *Kovcheh. Naukovyj zbirnyk iz tserkovnoi istorii* 4 (2003): 67–85.

2 Bohdan Botsiurkiv, *Ukrainska Hreko-Katolytska Tserkva i Radianska derzhava (1939–1950)* (Lviv: Vydavnytstvo UKU, 2005), 25; Volodymyr Kubijovyč, "Galicia," in *Encyclopedia of Ukraine*, vol. 2, ed. Volodymyr Kubijovyč (Toronto: University of Toronto Press, 1988), 11–12.

3 Botsiurkiv, *Ukrainska Hreko-Katolytska Tserkva*, 24.
4 In July 2017, the Metropolitan Andrey Sheptytsky Institute of Eastern Christian Studies became affiliated with the University of Toronto, and in September 2017 the Metropolitan Andrey Sheptytsky Center opened at the Ukrainian Catholic University in Lviv.
5 "Speeches at ADL's recognition of Metropolitan Andrey Sheptytsky," *The Ukrainian Weekly*, 10 November 2013, 16.
6 "U.S. scholar Timothy Snyder at the Metropolitan Andrey Sheptytsky Award Ceremony," video of Timothy Snyder's remarks at the Sheptytsky Award ceremony, https://www.youtube.com/watch?v=8dT6_ydloY4.
7 "Decretum super virtutibus S.D. Andreae Szeptyckyj," *Acta Apostolicae Sedis* 109 (2017): 941–3.
8 "Ukraine Chief Rabbi named two things one needs to learn from Andrey Sheptytsky," Religious Information Service of Ukraine, Ukrainian Catholic University, https://risu.org.ua/en/index/all_news/confessional/religious_relations/61573.
9 Shimon Redlich, "Sheptyts'kyi and the Jews," in *Morality and Reality: The Life and Times of Andrei Sheptyts'kyi*, ed. Paul Robert Magocsi (Edmonton: University of Alberta Press, 1989), 145–64, here 149; Shimon Redlich, "Metropolitan Andrei Sheptyts'kyi, Ukrainians and Jews during and after the Holocaust," *Holocaust and Genocide Studies* 5, no. 1 (1990): 39–51, here 40. In his *Holocaust and Genocide Studies* article, Redlich mentions that Sheptytsky strongly denounced the Galician Socialist Soviet Republic, which existed for a few months in the summer of 1920, and characterized one of its leaders as a "Jew-dictator." This statement is cited in several subsequent English-language studies of Sheptytsky. Redlich's source for this statement was Edward Prus, *Władyka świętojurski. Rzecz o arcybiskupie Andrzeju Szeptyckim (1865–1944)* (Warszawa: Instytut wydawniczy zwiazkow zawodowych, 1985), 71. In an article that appeared in 2004 in the online journal of the East Central European Center of Columbia University, Rafał Wnuk, a scholar affiliated with the Institute of National Remembrance in Warsaw and the Polish Academy of Sciences and currently a professor at the Catholic University of Lublin, wrote that Edward Prus was unreliable as a professional historian. According to Wnuk, Prus badly distorted historical sources and had a strong bias against Ukrainians. See Rafał Wnuk, "Recent Polish Historiography on Polish-Ukrainian Relations during World War II

and Its Aftermath," *Intermarium* 7, no. 1 (2004), https://ece.columbia.edu/intermarium/intermarium-volume-7. Without access to the source that Prus cited in his book on Sheptytsky, it is not possible to ascertain whether Sheptytsky made the antisemitic remark that Prus attributed to him.

10 Henry Abramson, "Metropolitan Sheptyts'kyi's Hebrew Correspondence, 1903," *Harvard Ukrainian Studies* 15 (1991): 172–6, here 172.

11 Bohdan Budurowycz, "The Greek Catholic Church in Galicia, 1914–1944," *Harvard Ukrainian Studies* 26 (2002–3): 291–375, here 348; Redlich, "Metropolitan Andrei Sheptyts'kyi, Ukrainians and Jews during and after the Holocaust," 40.

12 Oral history interview with Leon Chameides, tape 3, United States Holocaust Memorial Museum Archives (USHMMA) RG-50.030.0350.

13 Augustyn Babiak, "Udział i rola Cerkwi greckokatolickiej w kongreseach welehradzkich (1907–1936)," *Studia Teologiczno-Historyczne Śląska Opolskiego* 34 (2014): 1537–77; Andrzej A. Zięba, "André Szeptyckyj: Actualité et mystère d'un grand prélat ukrainien," *Istina* 51 (2006): 153–6; Antoine Lambrecht, "Orthodoxes et Grecs-catholiques en Pologne: *La defense des biens de l'Église orthodoxe par le métropolite André Šeptyc'kyi*," *Irénikon* 64 (1991): 49–56.

14 John-Paul Himka, "Christianity and Radical Nationalism: Metropolitan Andrei Sheptytsky and the Bandera Movement," in *State Secularism and Lived Religion in Soviet Russia and Ukraine*, ed. Catherine Wanner (New York: Oxford University Press, 2012), 93–116. On the difficult conditions that Ukrainians sometimes faced in Poland, see Stefan Dyroff, "Minority Rights and Humanitarianism: The International Campaign for the Ukrainians in Poland, 1930–1931," *Journal of Modern European History* 12 (2014): 216–30.

15 Andrey Sheptytsky, "Pastoral letter on 1 July 1941," Marco Carynnyk, trans., European Holocaust Research Infrastructure Online Course in Holocaust Studies, https://training.ehri-project.eu/d01-pastoral-letter-1-july-1941. A copy of the original Ukrainian text of the 1 July 1941 pastoral letter is also held in USHMMA, Metropolitan Andrew Graf Szeptycki collection, Accession number 2004.609, folder 1. See also Denis Dirscherl, "The Soviet Destruction of the Greek Catholic Church," *Journal of Church and State* 12 (1970): 421–39, here 425; and Andrii Krawchuk, *Christian Social Ethics in Ukraine* (Toronto: Canadian Institute of Ukrainian Studies Press, 1997), 120–4, 131.

16 Sheptytsky's complete bibliography may be found in Krawchuk, *Christian Social Ethics in Ukraine*, 278-363.

17 Frank Golczewski, "Shades of Gray: Reflections on Jewish–Ukrainian and German–Ukrainian Relations in Galicia," in *The Shoah in Ukraine: History, Testimony, Memorialization*, eds. Ray Brandon and Wendy Lower (Bloomington: Indiana University Press in association with the United States Holocaust Memorial Museum, 2008), 114–55, here 144–6.

18 Paul Robert Magocsi, *A History of Ukraine* (Toronto: University of Toronto Press, 1996), 512–22. During the First World War, Galicia was temporarily occupied by the Russian Empire. With the collapse of Austria-Hungary in 1918, Ukrainians formed a Western Ukrainian People's Republic (Zakhidnoukrayins'ka Narodna Respublika), which existed from 1918 to 1919. After 1919, Eastern Galicia *de facto* belonged to the Second Polish Republic.

19 Jochen Böhler, *Civil War in Central Europe, 1918–1921. The Reconstruction of Poland* (New York: Oxford University Press, 2018), 76–82.

20 Piotr Wróbel, "The Seeds of Violence: The Brutalization of an East European Region, 1917–1921," *Journal of Modern European History* 1 (2003): 125–49, here 138.

21 Regarding the distinctive history and culture of this region, its so-called "Western-Ukrainianness," see John-Paul Himka, "Western Ukraine between the Wars," *Canadian Slavonic Papers / Revue Canadienne des Slavistes* 34 (1992): 391–412.

22 Himka, "Western Ukraine between the Wars," 395.

23 Budurowycz, "The Greek Catholic Church in Galicia, 1914–1944," 303–4.

24 Ann Slusarczuk Sirka, "Sheptyts'kyi in Education and Philanthropy," in *Morality and Reality: The Life and Times of Andrei Sheptyts'kyi*, ed. Paul Robert Magocsi (Edmonton: University of Alberta Press, 1989), 269–88, here 271.

25 Bohdan P. Procko, "Sheptyts'kyi and Ukrainians in the United States," in *Morality and Reality: The Life and Times of Andrei Sheptyts'kyi*, ed. Paul Robert Magocsi (Edmonton: University of Alberta Press, 1989), 349–62, here 355–7.

26 On Sheptytsky's visit to Canada and the United States, see Procko, "Sheptyts'kyi and Ukrainians in the United States," 354–8.

27 Sheptytsky to Hughes, 23 November 1921, Records relating to Jews in Ukraine during World War II, USHMMA, Accession number: 1995.A.0223.

28 Sheptytsky to Hughes, 23 November 23, 1921, Records relating to Jews in Ukraine. Similar accusations were published by officials from the government of West Ukraine, including the deportation of thousands of Ukrainians to internment camps in Poland. On this point, see Vladimir Temnitsky and Joseph Burachinsky, *Polish Atrocities in Ukrainian Galicia, a Telegraphic Note to M. Georges Clemenceau, President of the Paris Peace Conference* (New York: Ukrainian National Committee of the United States, 1919).

29 Records relating to Jews in Ukraine during World War II, Memorandum on the case of East Galicia, USHMMA, number: 1995.A.0223. See also Procko, "Sheptyts'kyi and Ukrainians in the United States," 356.

30 Records relating to Jews in Ukraine during World War II [...] USHMMA, number: 1995.A.0223.

31 Augustyn Babiak, "André Szeptyckj, Métropolite Ukrainien (1900–1944)," *Istina* 51 (2006): 125–45, here 131.

32 Andrii Krawchuk, *Christian Social Ethics in Ukraine* (Toronto: Canadian Institute of Ukrainian Studies Press, 1997), 91–2.

33 Bohdan Budurowycz, "Sheptyts'kyi and the Ukrainian National Movement after 1914," in *Morality and Reality: The Life and Times of Andrei Sheptyts'kyi*, ed. Paul Robert Magocsi (Edmonton: University of Alberta Press, 1989), 47–74, here 53; Athanasius D. McVay, "A Prisoner for His People's Faith: Metropolitan Andrei Sheptytsky's Detentions under Russia and Poland," *LOGOS: A Journal of Eastern Christian Studies* 50 (2009): 13–54.

34 Bohdan B. Budurowycz, "Poland and the Ukrainian Problem, 1921–1939," *Canadian Slavonic Papers / Revue Canadienne des Slavistes* 25 (1983): 473–500, here 480.

35 Stephen Rapawy, *The Culmination of Conflict: The Ukrainian–Polish Civil War and the Expulsion of Ukrainians after the Second World War* (New York: Columbia University Press, 2016), 82–5.

36 Hans-Jürgen Bömelburg, "Die polnisch-ukrainischen Beziehungen 1922–1939: Ein Literatur- und Forschungsbericht," *Jahrbücher für Geschichte Osteuropas* 39 (1991): 81–102, here 91. On the Ukrainians' loss of rights related to schools, see also Himka, "Western Ukraine between the Wars," 395–7.

37 Budurowycz, "Poland and the Ukrainian Problem, 1921–1939," 480.

38 Budorowycz, "The Greek Catholic Church in Galicia, 1914–1944," 307–8.

39 Alexander J. Motyl, *The Turn to the Right: The Ideological Origins and Devel-*

opment of Ukrainian Nationalism, 1919–1929 (New York: Columbia University Press, 1980).

40 Cited in Krawchuk, *Christian Social Ethics in Ukraine*, 134–5. See also "Rozmowa z J. E. Metropolit Szeptyckim," *Zeszyty Historyczne* 71 (1985): 119–21, here 120.

41 Gábor Lagzi, "The Ukrainian Radical National Movement in Inter-War Poland: The Case of the Organization of Ukrainian Nationalists (OUN)," *Regio-Minorities, Politics, Society* 7 (2004): 194–206, here 197.

42 Alexander J. Motyl, "Ukrainian Nationalist Political Violence in Inter-War Poland, 1921–1939," *East European Quarterly* 19 (1985): 45–55, here 48–50.

43 Mykhailo Sosnovs'kyi, *Dmytro Dontsov: politichnyi portret* (Toronto: Trident International, 1974), 170–82; Budurowycz, "Poland and the Ukrainian Problem, 1921–1939," 482–4. For a recent assessment of Dontsov, see Trevor Erlacher, "The Furies of Nationalism: Dmytro Dontsov, the Ukrainian Idea, and Europe's Twentieth Century" (PhD diss., University of North Carolina at Chapel Hill, 2017).

44 Grzegorz Rossoliński-Liebe, *The Fascist Kernel of Ukrainian Genocidal Nationalism*, Carl Beck Papers in Russian and East European Studies, no. 2402 (Pittsburgh: University of Pittsburgh Press, 2015), 11; Oleksandr Zaitsev, "Natsionalism iak relihiia: pryklad Dmytra Dontsova ta OUN (1920–1930-ti roky)," *Naukovi zapysky Ukrains'koho katolyts'koho universytetu* 1 (2010): 163–89.

45 Rossoliński-Liebe, *The Fascist Kernel of Ukrainian Genocidal Nationalism*, 11.

46 Renata Caruso, "Dmytro Dontsov's Ideology of Integral Nationalism in Post-Soviet Ukraine," in *Ukraine Twenty Years after Independence: Assessments, Perspectives, Challenges*, eds. Giovanna Brogi, Marta Dyczok, Oxana Pachlovska, and Giovanna Siedina (Rome: Aracne Editrice, 2015), 249–58; Myroslav Shkandrij, *Ukrainian Nationalism: Politics, Ideology, and Literature, 1929–1956* (New Haven: Yale University Press, 2015), 101–34.

47 Myroslav Yurkevich, "Organization of Ukrainian Nationalists," in *Encyclopedia of Ukraine*, vol. 3, ed. Danylo Husar Struk (Toronto: University of Toronto Press, 1993), 708.

48 "Yevhen Konovalets," *Biographical Dictionary of Central and Eastern Europe in the Twentieth Century*, eds. Wojciech Roszkowski and Jan Kofman (New York: Routledge, 2008), 485–6.

49 Oksana Volynets, "Metropolian Andrey Sheptycky on Communism, Fascism, and Extreme Nationalism Ideologies," *Humanitarian Vision* 1 (2015): 7–11.

50 "Resolutions of the First Congress of the Organization of Ukrainian Nationalists," trans. Taras F. Pidzamecky, Roman Waschuk, and Andriy Wynnyckyj, in *Ukraine during World War II: History and Its Aftermath*, ed. Yury Boshyk (Edmonton: Canadian Institute of Ukrainian Studies, University of Alberta, 1986), 165–72. Ukrainian original: OUN *v svitli postanov Velykykh zboriv, konferentsii ta inshykh dokumentia z borotby 1929-1955 r.* (n.p. 1955), 3–16.

51 "The Ten Commandments of the Ukrainian Nationalist," trans. Taras F. Pidzamecky, Roman Waschuk, and Andriy Wynnyckyj, in *Ukraine during World War II: History and Its Aftermath*, ed. Yury Boshyk (Edmonton: Canadian Institute of Ukrainian Studies, University of Alberta, 1986), 173–4. Ukrainian original: Petro Mirchuk, *Narys istorii Orhanizatsii ukrainskyh natsionalistiv 1920–1939* (Kyiv: Ukraïns ka vydavnycha spilka, 2007), 126–7. Note: in subsequent versions of their Ten Commandments, the OUN slightly altered the wording of some of the commandments.

52 Oleksandr Zaitsev, Oleh Behen, and Vasyl Stefaniv, *Natsionalism i relihiia: Hreko-Katolytska Tserkva ta ukrainskyi natsionalistychnyi rukh u Halychyni (1920–1930-ti roky)* (Lviv: Vydavnytstvo UKU, 2005), 109–10.

53 Lagzi, "The Ukrainian Radical National Movement," 201.

54 George Liber, *Total Wars and the Making of Modern Ukraine, 1914–1954* (Toronto: University of Toronto Press, 2016), 94.

55 Stanisław Stępień, "Krytyka teroru iak metodu vyrishennia natsionalnykh i politychnykh konfliktiv u pastyrskii nautsi mytropolyta Andreia Sheptytskoho," *Naukovi zapysky Ukrains'koho katolyts'koho universytetu* 1 (2010): 191–208, here 192.

56 Michał Wawrzonek, "Andrey Sheptytsky's 'Christian Patriotism' in Light of Ukrainian Nationalism," in *Beyond Imagined Uniqueness: Nationalisms in Contemporary Perspectives*, eds. Joan Burbick and William Glass (Newcastle: Cambridge Scholars, 2010), 191–206.

57 "Misionar," in *Encyclopedia of Ukraine*, vol. 3, ed. Danylo Husar Struk (Toronto: University of Toronto Press, 1993), 426–7.

58 John-Paul Himka, "Sheptyts'kyi and the Ukrainian National Movement before 1914," in *Morality and Reality: The Life and Times of Andrei Sheptyts'kyi*, ed. Paul Robert Magocsi (Edmonton: University of Alberta Press, 1989), 29–46, here 36.

59 A. Bazylevych, ed. *Tvory Sluhy Bozhoho Mytropolyta Andreia Sheptyts'koho: Pastyrs'ki lysty* (Toronto: Ukrainian Theological Society, 1965), 17.

60 Andrey Sheptytsky, "Pastyrske poslannia Mytropolyta Andreia 'Do poliakiv
    hreko-katolytskoho obriadu,'" in *Pastyrski poslannia 1899–1914*, eds. Oksana
    Haiova and Roman Terekhovskyi, vol. 1 of *Mytropolyt Andrei Sheptytskyi.
    Dokumenty i materialy. 1899–1944* (Lviv: ARTOS 2007), 482. See also Michał
    Wawrzonek, "Andrey Sheptytsky's 'Christian Patriotism' in Light of
    Ukrainian Nationalism," in *Beyond Imagined Uniqueness: Nationalisms in
    Contemporary Perspectives*, eds. Joan Burbick and William Glass (Newcastle:
    Cambridge Scholars, 2010), 199–203.
61 Himka, "Sheptyts'kyi and the Ukrainian National Movement before 1914,"
    36.
62 Cited in Stępień, "Krytyka teroru," 194.
63 Cited in Krawchuk, *Christian Social Ethics in Ukraine*, 95–9.
64 Andrew Sorokowski, "The Lay and Clerical Intelligentsia in Greek Catholic
    Galicia, 1900–1939: Competition, Conflict, Cooperation," *Harvard
    Ukrainian Studies* 26 (2002–3): 261–90, here 273–4.
65 Krawchuk, *Christian Social Ethics in Ukraine*, 129–130; Budurowycz, "The
    Greek Catholic Church in Galicia," 314.
66 Budurowycz, "The Greek Catholic Church in Galicia, 314–15.
67 Cited in Sorokowski, "The Lay and Clerical Intelligentsia in Greek Catholic
    Galicia," 276.
68 Ibid.
69 Cited in ibid.
70 Shkandrij, *Ukrainian Nationalism*, 30.
71 Krawchuk, *Christian Social Ethics in Ukraine*, 143; Zaitsev, "Natsionalism iak
    relihiia," 279.
72 Andrey Sheptytsky, "Pastyrske poslannia Mytropolyta Andreia do virnykh
    iz pryvodu vbyvstva dyrektora himnazii Ivana Babia ta z zasudzhenniam
    aktiv teroryzmu," in *Pastyrski poslannia 1918–1939*, eds. Oksana Haiova and
    Roman Terekhovskyi, vol. 2 of *Mytropolyt Andrei Sheptytskyi. Dokumenty
    i materialy. 1899–1944* (Lviv: ARTOS 2009), 177.
73 Cyril Korolevsky, *Metropolite Andre Szeptyckyj, 1865–1944* (Rome: Esse-
    Gi-Esse, 1964), 355.
74 Cited in Denis Dirscherl, "The Soviet Destruction of the Greek Catholic
    Church," 425.
75 Andrey Sheptytsky, "Dekret Arkhyparkhialnoho Soboru *Vyznannia Vselen-
    skoi Viry* ta pravyla do dekretu," in *Pastyrski poslannia 1939–1944*, eds. Ok-

sana Haiova and Roman Terekhovskyi, vol. 3 of *Mytropolyt Andrei Shepty-tskyi. Dokumenty i materialy. 1899–1944* (Lviv: ARTOS 2010), 369.

76 Andrey Sheptytsky, "Pastoral letter on 1 July 1941."

77 Report of Szeptycki to Pius XII, 28 March 1942, USHMMA, Metropolitan Andrew Graf Szeptycki collection, Accession number 2004.609, folder 1.

78 Johannes Peters was able to deliver a second letter from Sheptytsky, dated 31 August 1942, before he was arrested by the Gestapo in October 1942. See the statement made by Holocaust survivor Kurt I. Lewin, whom Sheptytsky helped hide in a monastery. See Reports of Szeptycki to Pius XII, 1942, USHMM, Metropolitan Andrew Graf Szeptycki collection, Accession number 2004.609, folder 1.

79 Pastoral Letter: "Thou Shall Not Kill," USHMM, Metropolitan Andrew Graf Szeptycki collection, Accession number 2004.609, folder 1. See also John-Paul Himka, "Metropolitan Andrey Sheptytsky and the Holocaust," *Polin* 26 (2013): 337–59, here 348.

80 Report of Szeptycki to Pius XII, 28 March 1942, USHMM [...] folder 1.

81 Ibid. This file contains two transcribed versions of Sheptytsky's originally handwritten letter, which differ in a significant way. The first transcription reads: "J'ai comme de raison protesté dans une letter écrite à Himler [*sic*] sans obtenir paraît-il aucun succès." The second transcription reads: "J'ai comme de raison protesté dans une letter écrite à Hitler sans obtenir paraît-il aucun succès." Without access to the original handwritten version, it cannot be determined whether Sheptytsky was referring to a letter that he sent to either Heinrich Himmler or to Adolf Hitler. Sheptytsky sent two other communications to Hitler of which scholars are aware: a 22 July 1941 telegram (also sent to Himmler and German foreign minister Joachim Ribbentrop), in which Sheptytsky argued against the annexation of Galicia into the Generalgouvernement, and a February 1942 protest letter to Hitler that was signed by all the members of the Ukrainian National Council. On this point, see Krawchuk, *Christian Social Ethics in Ukraine*, 211; Iaroslav Nahurs'kyi, "Die Tragödie der ukrainisch-katholischen Kirche," *Ukraine in Vergangenheit und Gegenwart* 1 (1952): 9–10; and Hansjakob Stehle, "Sheptyts'kyi and the German Regime," in *Morality and Reality: The Life and Times of Andrei Sheptyts'kyi*, ed. Paul Robert Magocsi (Edmonton: University of Alberta Press, 1989), 125–41, here 132. In his August 1942 letter to Pope Pius XII, Sheptytsky mentioned that he had previously written a letter of

protest to Himmler. Kurt Lewin, the son of the chief rabbi of Lviv, Ezekiel Lewin, claimed that during the winter of 1943–44 he had seen a copy of a letter that Sheptytsky had sent to Himmler and Himmler's dismissive response to it. Kurt I. Lewin, "Andreas Count Sheptytsky, Archbishop of Lviv, Metropolitan of Halych, and the Jewish Community in Galicia during the Second World War," *Annals of the Ukrainian Academy of Arts and Sciences in the United States* 7 (1959): 1656–67, here 1661.

82 "Le métropolite de Léopol des Ruthènes Szeptyckyj au pape Pie XII," in *Le Saint Siège et la Situation Religieuse en Pologne et dans les Pays Baltes, Deuxième Partie 1942–1945*, vol. 3 of *Actes et Documents, du Saint Siège Relatifs à la Seconde Guerre Mondiale*, eds. Pierre Blet, Robert A. Graham, Angelo Martini, and Burkhart Schneider (Vatican City: Libreria Editrice Vaticana, 1967), 625.

83 John-Paul Himka, "The Lviv Pogrom of 1941: The Germans, Ukrainian Nationalists, and the Carnival Crowd," *Canadian Slavonic Papers* 53 (2011): 209–43.

84 Kurt I. Lewin, "Andreas Count Sheptytsky, Archbishop of Lviv, Metropolitan of Halych, and the Jewish Community in Galicia during the Second World War," *Annals of the Ukrainian Academy of Arts and Sciences in the United States* 7 (1959): 1656–67; and Kurt I. Lewin, *A Journey through Illusions* (Santa Barbara: Fithian Press, 1993).

85 Sworn statements regarding the Metropolitan's rescue work, USHMM, Metropolitan Andrew Graf Szeptycki collection, Accession number 2004.609, folder 2.

86 On Kahane, see Arieh J. Kochavi, *Post-Holocaust Politics: Britain, the United States, and Jewish Refugees, 1945–1948* (Chapel Hill: University of North Carolina Press, 2001), 170; and David Kahane, *Lvov Ghetto Diary*, trans. Jerzy Michalowicz (Amherst: University of Massachusetts Press, 1990).

87 Oral history interview with Leon Chameides, tape 3, USHMM, RG-50.030.0350.

88 See Iwan Hirnyji's affidavit in USHMMA, number: 1995.A.0223, Records relating to Jews in Ukraine during World War II, Memorandum on the case of East Galicia.

89 Alexander Kruglov, "Jewish Losses in Ukraine, 1941–1944," in *The Shoah in Ukraine*, eds. Ray Brandon and Wendy Lower, 272–90, here 284.

11

To Murder or Save Thy Neighbour? Romanian Orthodox Clergymen and Jews during the Holocaust (1941–1945)

Ionuț Biliuță

In its support of the persecution and deportation of Romanian Jews, the Romanian Orthodox Church generally stands apart from other churches in the region.[1] By far the majority of the Church's hierarchy and clergy, led by the patriarch, Miron Cristea, supported the antisemitic measures of the National Christian Party government (28 December 1937–10 February 1938), including the revocation of citizenship for Jews and the exclusion of Jews from the civil service and public office.[2] After the collapse of the Royal Dictatorship (10 February 1938–6 September 1940), the Orthodox Church failed again to condemn the pogroms orchestrated by the Legionaries during the short-lived National Legionary State (September 1940–February 1941).[3] Moreover, some clergymen participated in the abuse and murder of Jews and the looting of Jewish property during the Holocaust.[4]

While scholars have convincingly portrayed Romanian Orthodox clergymen as Holocaust perpetrators,[5] they have made little effort to examine the efforts of ordinary clergy in the rescue of Jews.[6] The reasons for this are varied.[7] Most significant is the lack of access to Romanian Orthodox Church

archives coupled with the church's refusal to face responsibility for its nefarious actions against Jews, especially those committed in Transnistria. To
reconstruct this history, I have used personal interviews and state archives
to uncover cases of Orthodox clergymen in Bessarabia and Transnistria
who, between 1941 and 1944, spoke out against the persecution of Jews or
intervened directly to rescue them. Rather than establishing a typology of
the Orthodox rescuer, this chapter discusses what motives drove Orthodox
priests, in direct contradiction to the state's official antisemitism, to stand
up for Jews in numerous ways – for example, by preaching positively about
Jews, providing baptism certificates, supplying Jews with necessities, or
serving as couriers. It also addresses the post-1945 fate of these Orthodox
clergymen and how they were able – or not – to survive the violent purges
unleashed by the Communist regime.[8] Their prior fascist activism and
anti-communist views rendered these clergymen vulnerable to the Securitate, the communist secret police, who was eager to purge Romanian society of such individuals or exploit them as informants.[9] Historians and
popular opinion have readily demonized these clergymen as communist
informants rather than acknowledging their efforts to save Romanian Jews
during the Holocaust.

The Orthodox clergy who resisted the state's antisemitic policies were a
minority among the priests in the Romanian Orthodox Church. Given that
some prominent representatives of the hierarchy were complicit in the
persecution of Jews, these clergymen acted alone and not as part of a plan
sanctioned by church superiors. Their moral choices and actions during
the Holocaust reveal that resistance was possible. They opted to engage in
resistance, yet most of them harboured radical ethnonationalist views and
supported the antisemitic Iron Guard and the extremist National Christian
Party. In them, ethnonationalism and antisemitism coexisted with the
Christian command to love neighbour.

This chapter has three parts. The first discusses why some clergymen,
such as Father Gala Galaction (1879–1961), a professor at Bucharest University and the Chișinău Department of Orthodox Theology, resisted the state's
antisemitic policies and inspired future Orthodox clergymen to behave
humanely toward Jews. Father Galaction's influence on his students enabled
them to view Jews in a more positive light, one different from the dominant
antisemitic and ultranationalist narrative of the traditional theological mi-

lieu. The second offers several case studies of priests and monks who defended Jews during the Holocaust. The third discusses the lives and the professional trajectories of these resistant clergymen in the postwar era and how their imprisonment or recruitment as informers by the communist government discredited them so that they could not easily participate in any discussion of Romania's complicity in the Holocaust.

I

The rescue of Jews in Romania during the Holocaust must be approached on a case-by-case basis and analyzed with caution, given the limited sources.[10] In 28 December 1937 the Romanian government introduced antisemitic legislation that infringed upon Jews' civil rights, confiscated Jewish property, and prohibited Jews from working as civil servants, including as doctors and lawyers (whose salaries were state-paid). On 12 January 1938, the state rounded out its antisemitic laws by stripping Romanian Jews of their citizenship.[11] Most of the Orthodox clergy greeted these measures with either satisfaction or indifference.[12] Nevertheless, the legislation did trouble a small group of clergymen, who individually sympathized with Jews and who spoke out publicly in a positive way about them or assisted them directly. One must ask: how did such sympathies arise? And did the clergy act on their sympathies because of the Christian teaching of universal love or some other theological principle? Or were there other cultural or contextual factors at play?

Historians have written much about Christians' motives for saving Jews during the Holocaust.[13] In the case of Romanian Orthodox Christianity, many factors contributed to a clergyman's decision to help or rescue Jews during the Holocaust, including their proximity to Jews in Bessarabia, Bucharest, and northern Moldavia and their mutual economic and cultural interests.[14] Indeed, various overlapping factors were at work, and some of their reasons were far from altruistic. To complicate matters further, some clergymen, such as Fathers Theodor Petcu and Gheorghe Petre-Orleşti, had fascist pasts and openly sympathized with various ultranationalist movements that outwardly professed antisemitism.[15] Likewise, many of these same Orthodox clergymen placed equal value on ethnonationalism and anti-communism, even while also saving Jews from the murderous hands of the Romanian government. Those clergymen with no declared political affiliation remained indifferent to antisemitism even when state policies toward Jews escalated from persecution to murder.[16]

The clergymen who spoke in favour of or rescued Jews relied on their ability to deliberately manipulate the military prefects, mayors, and officers in the Romanian police and field gendarmerie to protect themselves and save Jews.[17] Such acrobatics involved deceiving both their ecclesiastical superiors and state officials. The clergymen benefited from the administrative inconsistencies of the government, which was unable to keep up with the paper trails while it attempted to establish a functional bureaucratic apparatus in the newly conquered territories on both banks of the Dniester.[18] The establishment of the Romanian Orthodox Mission in Tiraspol on 15 August 1941 – and, soon after, in Odessa – for re-Christianization of the Slavs across the Dniester provided Orthodox clergymen with the necessary means and the legal framework to pursue missionary activity among the Slavs and the Jews.[19]

One of the most undervalued factors in the case of the Orthodox clergymen was the theological education the clergy had received during the interwar period.[20] While most of the faculty held deeply entrenched antisemitic and ultranationalist sympathies, in the interwar years there were some clergymen who rejected such views. Several prominent theologians and professors publicly voiced their concerns about the increased spread of antisemitism in universities and in Romanian society more generally.[21]

Father Gala Galaction, the pen name of Grigore Pișculescu, was a biblical scholar who taught his students to uphold the values of love of neighbour and who criticized antisemitism as a modern heresy.[22] Galaction, professor of New Testament in the Theology Faculty at Chișinău and, beginning in 1941, professor of Old Testament at the University of Bucharest, authored numerous bestselling novels and short stories that earned him many national accolades and prizes.[23] Popular among his students due to his progressive views, he also publicly supported the Jewish community, speaking against the rise of antisemitism and violent ultranationalism in his articles and scholarly publications.[24] His statements and writings highlighted the antisemitism of Romanian fascists, and this drew the attention of the Legionaries, who considered him one of their greatest enemies and labelled him a tool of international "Jewish Freemasonry."[25] Throughout his life, Galaction remained patriotic while also expressing sympathy for Romanian Jews in cultural periodicals, such as *Adam*.[26] At the same time, in his sermons, he professed moderate ethnonationalist views consistent with the prevailing nationalist position of the Orthodox clergy during the interwar years.[27]

On several occasions, Galaction joined Jews in their efforts to unmask the danger of antisemitism in Romanian society. He publicly repudiated the *Protocols of the Elders of Zion*, one of the primary inspirations for the members of both the Iron Guard and the National Christian Defence League.[28] Likewise, in his 1923 book *Sionismul la prieteni* (Zionism among Friends), he wrote positively about Zionism and the idea of a Jewish state, arguing that a true Christian must support the idea of Israel as an indepedent nation and sympathize with the Zionist struggle.[29] With the advent of modernization and the cultural avant-garde, he reminded his readers that Orthodox Christians were unaware of the importance of Christianity for Romanian culture and neglected to acknowledge the common heritage their faith shared with Judaism.[30] For those who professed antisemitism, Galaction had much stronger words:

In the street, in the square, in public meetings, the usual antisemite is the common man. Who knows if he even graduated high school! Who knows if, during his university years, he read anything except newspapers and textbooks to prepare for exams! Today, he is a householder; he has political views and party allegiances, and an important job … When does he have the time and the disposition to alter his antisemitic feelings? He is Christian (because he is baptized) and goes to Church on Easter and Christmas, and maybe when he becomes a godfather … Aside from such events, his Christianity is a hollow void, plagued and filled with rationalist trash. He never read the Bible! Never held a Bible containing both the Old and New Testament! This type of Christian is representative of Christianity in Old Romania![31]

Galaction went even further in his judgment against Romanian antisemites who declared themselves to be good Christians yet professed hatred toward their Jewish neighbours. He condemned their antisemitism and propagation of radical ethnonationalism and declared their Christian faith to be "dead."[32] According to Galaction, no Christian, regardless of denomination, could pretend to be a true follower of Jesus Christ if he or she professed antisemitic views.

On 10 February 1938, after the Iron Guard made substantial electoral gains in the 1937 elections (16.4 percent of the vote), King Carol II appointed a new government led by Patriarch Miron Cristea (1868–1939) as prime minister and Bishop Nicolae Colan (1893–1967) as minister of public education.[33] Galaction reprimanded these leading representatives of the Orthodox Church in the government for maintaining the Goga government's antisemitic legislation and for their silence on the unfortunate state of the Jewish minority.[34] He then criticized the entire hierarchy of the Romanian Orthodox Church for their support of the government's antisemitic legislation, their silence when confronted with antisemitic violence, and their promotion of fascist political parties such as the Front of National Regeneration (December 1938), later renamed the Party of the Nation (21 June 1940), and the underground Iron Guard.[35] At the same time, Galaction made it clear that he stood firmly on the side of the persecuted Jews:

> Today's trials should be welcomed with joy. If malice, prejudice, and disillusionment are powerful elements, goodness, clarity, and true justice can never be disarmed. Good times will come! Our love and wisdom cannot disappear! The plight of the Jewish people is a question both for individuals and for the consciousness of nations. Let us fight forever to solve this question. History proves that both individually and collectively goodwill shown toward Israel is not wrong but right. Let us fight onward, without rest, until we are victorious![36]

In his diary, he also decried the interwar violence against Jews as well as Jewish suffering during the Holocaust.[37] After the Second World War, Wilhelm Filderman (1882–1963), the chairman of the Federation of the Jewish Communities in Romania, praised Gala Galaction as one of the Gentiles who had helped the Jews during the Shoah.[38] In 1947, the Romanian Academy elected him a member for his literary achievements, including a new translation of the Bible, and for his adamant support of the Jews before and during the Shoah.[39]

Although Romanian fascists, including many clergymen, despised him, Galaction did have supporters among his students and fellow priests. For example, Father Theodor Petcu (1897–1957), a priest from Bessarabia, Father Athanase Negoiță (1903–1994), an Old Testament scholar and Galaction's friend, and Hieromonk Paul Paulin Lecca (1914–1996), a young theology student from Chișinău, embraced Galaction's stance on Jews.[40] In his postwar recollections, Lecca claimed that he had refused to participate in the abuse of Jewish women and to force their husbands to build churches or monasteries while serving as a monastic novice and Russian translator with the Romanian Orthodox Exarchate in Transnistria during the Second World War because of the discussions he had with "Moșul," the nickname of Gala Galaction among his students.[41] Archival documents, including his Securitate personal file and postwar survivors' testimonies, support Lecca's claims.[42] For other clergymen, such as Bishop Antim Nica (1908–1994) and Father David Portase-Prut, the Securitate files meticulously documented their crimes committed against Jews and the local population in Transnistria.[43]

Following the abdication of King Carol II (5–6 September 1940), General Ion Antonescu (1882–1946), took over as prime minister. Horia Sima (1906–1993), the leader of the resurrected Iron Guard, supported Antonescu. The antisemitic legislation passed by the governments of Goga-Cuza and King Carol II paved the way for the brief but murderous National Legionary State (14 September 1940–23 January 1941), which resulted in the increased persecution of Jews and the confiscation of Jewish property.[44] In January 1941, this antisemitism culminated in a pogrom, during which 125 Jews were murdered in Bucharest alone.[45] Simultaneously, the Legionaries rebelled against their ally, General Antonescu, in an attempt to overthrow the government and secure a Legionary government.[46] Antonescu responded by implementing measures to prevent further antisemitic violence by the Iron Guard.[47] Some Iron Guard clergymen, such as Father Constantin Palaghiță and Father Spiridon Cândea, played substantial roles in the crimes committed against Jews during the rebellion; yet the violence led some priests who had initially supported the Legionaries to reconsider their antisemitic stance.[48] While they did not wholly reject antisemitism, they began to soften their stance toward Jews.

Following the legionaires' rebellion, the bellicose public discourse of some clergymen, such as Patriarch Nicodim Munteanu (1864–1948) and Metropolitans Nicolae Bălan (1882–1955), Irineu Mihălcescu (1874–1948), and Nifon Criveanu (1890-1970), began to backfire.[49] Many clergymen moved to the newly acquired territories in the East (Bessarabia, Northern Bukovina, Southwestern Ukraine) as missionaries, where they soon became disenchanted with the hateful rhetoric unleashed by the church's hierarchy in Bucharest, who attacked Jews as the source of all evil, as being in league with the devil, and as Christianity's greatest enemy.[50] By contrast, the priests found Jews to be in dire poverty, defenceless, and deprived of all property; they were victims, not opponents, of Christianity. Following the advance of the Romanian army across the Dniester and the Tighina Conference (18 August 1941, where the Romanian governors of northern Bukovina, Bessarabia, and Transnistria discussed the Romanization of these territories), Antonescu displaced large numbers of Jews, accusing them of being "Bolshevik agents," "agitators," and "enemies of the Romanian nation." The displacement of Jews from Moldavia, northern Bukovina, and Bessarabia to Transnistria wrought havoc on local commerce, school systems, and the economy. The ensuing difficulties led to dissatisfaction and tensions among the Christian inhabitants.[51]

II

In the summer of 1941, the first few cases of Orthodox priests assisting Jews occurred in Bessarabia following the Romanian armed forces' repossession of that region. In Bessarabia, relations between Jews and Gentiles had always proved challenging, with outbursts of antisemitic violence taking place both before and after the First World War.[52] Despite this hostile climate, a few Orthodox clergymen had defended Jewish rights and shielded Jews from discrimination. This pattern continued after the Romanian government established the Chișinău ghetto on 25 July 1941, along with other ghettos across Bessarabia.[53] By autumn 1941, the ghettos had become the focal point for deportations of Jews from Romania, northern Bukovina, and Bessarabia.[54] Father Vasile Gumă (1865–1954), a retired priest from Chișinău, opposed these developments by appealing to General Constantin Voiculescu (1890–1955) to exempt Moise Preigher, a merchant, and Avram Nemirovschi/Nimirovschi, a goldsmith, from ghettoization.[55] Before the war, Gumă had intervened with Romanian authorities on behalf of his Jewish neighbours. In 1941, his appeal fell on deaf ears. Preigher and Nemirovschi had to remain behind the barbed wire of the Chişinău ghetto.[56] Nemirovschi eventually perished in the Holocaust.[57]

Although Orthodox priests might not have succeeded in their efforts to intercede for Jews to keep them out of ghettos, some priests did succeed in assisting Jews by issuing them baptism certificates.[58] This practice was a sensitive issue in the Orthodox Church. Many priests saw it as a part of their broader effort to convert people to the Orthodox faith in territories where atheist Bolshevism had supposedly uprooted Christianity.[59] Yet priests initially were uncertain whether their church and the government would permit them to baptize former communists and Jews in the newly claimed territories, so they approached the Romanian Ministry of Religious Denominations and the Patriarchy of the Orthodox Church seeking clarification.[60] While Orthodox clergy took this step, other religious groups such as Baptists and Seventh-day Adventists provided Jews with baptismal certificates that attested to their reception of the sacrament before the Second World War began.[61]

In March 1941, the Romanian government issued Decree no. 711/4 declaring invalid all baptism certificates issued after 21 March 1941. Despite this decree, Orthodox clergy continued to baptize individuals and to issue baptism certificates, while other priests refused to baptize and issue baptismal certificates for Jews. In October 1941, Father Iordăchescu, initially a parish priest at St Mary Church (Craiova) and then at Miron Cristea Church (Bucharest), provided a baptism certificate to Rahil Froim Haim Golfberg, a seamstress by trade. It appears this action saved Golfberg from imprisonment and deportation by the local military authorities.[62]

In Transnistria, priests followed similar patterns when baptizing or encountering Orthodox Christians of Jewish heritage. For example, Father Ioan Sârbu, a missionary priest in Golta, baptized a Jewish woman and administered first communion to her, contrary to the state's regulations, in an attempt to save her life.[63] Despite being rebuffed by the authorities and his ecclesiastical superiors, Sârbu continued to minister as a priest in Transnistria.[64] One factor that likely spared him further persecution was his close prior relationship with Colonel Modest Isopescu (1895–1948), the prefect of Golta county, near the Bug River.[65] The existing documents do not provide any additional information on the fate of the woman Sârbu baptized.

Like Sârbu, Father Theodor Petcu helped Jews during the Holocaust.[66] Although suspected by the Romanian authorities before the war of Legionary sympathies, in the interwar years he was recognized as a priest engaged in charity work among the poor in his parish at Stahnaia village in Bessarabia.[67] After Romanian forces reoccupied Bessarabia, he volunteered for missionary service, becoming a parish priest in the Orthodox churches in Țăreni and Rezeni.[68] According to the testimonies of Jewish survivors, from July to September 1941, Petcu began providing the Jews in the Râbnița ghetto and those deported from Bessarabia and crossing the Dniester into Transnistria with food and medicine paid for from his personal income.[69]

Another relevant case is that of the Metropolitan of Bukovina, Tit Simedrea (1886–1971), and Gheorghe Russu (1880–1977), a theologian and icon painter, hired as a counsellor to the Metropolitan See of Bukovina.[70] In the first days of October 1941, the Romanian military authorities in Czernowitz/ Cernăuți confined the Jewish population in a ghetto in preparation for their deportation to Transnistria.[71] On 10 October, the mayor of Czernowitz, Traian Popovici (1892–1946), a lawyer and the son of an Orthodox priest, protested without success to General Corneliu Calotescu (1889–1970), the governor of Bukovina, against the arbitrary decision. Two days later, Popovici appealed directly to General Antonescu. As a result, Antonescu exempted 20,000 Jews and their family members from the lists of deportees. He considered these Jews to be indispensable economic experts, working in sectors that were important for the Romanian military, such as heavy industry, railways, telephony, and textiles.[72] Because the military authorities considered artists and liberal professions unnecessary for the war effort, David Slacman, a printer, escaped from the ghetto and asked his friend, Russu, to intercede with Metropolitan Simedrea to obtain a pass for him and his family so that they could avoid deportation. Metropolitan Simedrea approached Governor Calotescu for a pass but was refused. Then Metropolitan Simedrea suggested to Russu that he ask Mayor Popovici to issue the pass.[73] Within a few days, Russu had obtained the pass from Popovici.[74]

In June 1942, the state began investigating the activities of Mayor Popovici that ultimately led to his removal from office. After that, the Romanian authorities resumed deporting Jews in Transnistria.[75] David Slacman now appealed again to his friend Russu to hide Slacman, his wife, Ida, and their two children, Meir and Beatrice.[76] In turn, Russu sought help from Metropolitan Simedrea, who agreed to hide the Slacman family in his residence. Simedrea was taking a serious risk, for he knew that hiding Jews was punishable by death.[77] The Orthodox prelate threatened the Ukrainian policeman guarding his residence with excommunication should he denounce the presence of the Slacman family on the metropolitan premises to the Romanian authorities.[78]

Father Gheorghe Petre-Orleşti, who between 1937 and 1939 had served as the local president of the Govora branch of the antisemitic and ethnonationalist National Christian Party, became a courier for the Jews in the Transnistrian ghettos.[79] Assigned on 1 December 1942 as a missionary priest in Sîrova, Transnistria, Petre-Orleşti incessantly preached against communism and local religious splinter groups, such as Inochentists, the Evangelicals, and the Old Calendarists. During his tenure in Sîrova, he built a new church and cultural houses for the Romanian and Russian populations. He also baptized 124 children, witnessed the sacrament of marriage for 37 couples, and taught religious classes in local schools.[80] In May 1943, en route to his church after visiting family, he delivered a letter to a Jewish woman in Bucharest from her husband, who was in the Crivoi Ozero ghetto in Transnistria. In turn, he received a package from her containing three pairs of winter socks, a flannel shirt, a pair of boots, and a kilogram of candy to deliver to the woman's husband.[81] While returning to his parish in Transnistria, he encountered Captain Giurescu Gheorghe, an officer in the Romanian Army serving as the "Crimea" train's military commander, who asked Petre-Orleşti to smuggle money, letters, and photos belonging to Jews from Iaşi to their relatives in the Crivoi Ozero and Trei Dube ghettos.[82] Three days after he arrived in Sîrova, a lieutenant from the Golta gendarmerie warned Petre-Orleşti that local authorities were going to search his house and that he should discard any incriminating items.[83] Petre-Orleşti burned the letters and the photos but managed to deliver the package and the money.[84] The following day, confronted by the police searching his house, he acknowledged that he helped Jews. State authorities charged him with conspiracy for delivering prohibited goods.[85] On 16 February 1944 the Tiraspol Military Court acquitted him of all charges.[86]

These cases show clergymen directly assisting Jews. While their motivations are not always entirely clear, their actions reveal that they were willing to run afoul of state authorities to do so. Sometimes they agreed to assist

Jews they knew personally. Other times, the clergymen appear to have been motivated by the possibility of converting Jews to the Orthodox faith, even though, in doing so, they risked persecution by the state. In their minds, they were offering Jews salvation through the sacrament of baptism, while also indirectly providing them with a means to avoid persecution, deportation, or death at the hands of the state. The following accounts of efforts by Orthodox clergymen to assist Jews are more dubious.

Some clergymen exploited Jewish labour during the Holocaust, but in doing so, provided them with better chances for survival. For example, in 1942, Hieromonk Varlaam Chiriţă (1909–1989) used Jewish prisoners to erect monasteries and churches in Transnistria.[87] In doing so, Chiriţă was acting on the encouragement he had received from the leaders of the Orthodox Mission in Transnistria, namely, from Archimandrite Antim Nica (1909–1993), the administrative vicar of the mission.[88] Others, like Hieromonk Antim Tabacu, the abbot of St Anthony Monastery in Dubăsari (Transnistria), gave free rein for violence to be used against forced labourers, Jewish or otherwise, without incentives from the central administration of the Romanian Orthodox Mission in Transnistria.[89] Forcing Jews to perform hard labour is condemnable, especially since the work was often dangerous and cost many Jewish lives. Nevertheless, the opportunity enabled some individuals to survive and avoid deportation across the Dnieper into the hands of the Germans.[90]

A former survivor from the Djurin ghetto in Transnistria recalled that to procure food for themselves and their families, even children and adolescent teens had to work on the local farms, some owned or managed by Romanian priests.[91] While hunger, disease, and torture affected anyone confined in ghettos and concentration camps, in some cases the Jews who toiled as slaves on the estates belonging to the Transnistrian Exarchate and its clergymen enjoyed limited freedoms and access to essential commodities.[92] Despite such factors, the clergy's motives remain unclear. The priests might have provided the Jews under their charge with food and reprieve from the concentration and death camps, but they were still exploiting them as slaves to profit the church and thereby acted as perpetrators.

III

After the collapse of the Eastern Front and reoccupation of Eastern Ukraine by the Soviet Red Army in the early months of 1944, the missionaries and local clergymen from Bessarabia and Transnistria were repatriated.[93] Like most of those in Romania who perpetrated the Holocaust and profited by stealing from deported Jews, the clergymen who persecuted Jews were not held accountable. With the support of the communist secret police, who recruiteded them as informants or undercover agents, these priests easily integrated themselves into new parishes while also climbing the ladder of promotion in the Orthodox Church. In doing so, they also received the protection of their church.[94] To further remove doubts about the church's actions during the Second World War, the central administration of the Orthodox Church began to assist Jews who had returned to Romania as part of an unsuccessful effort to mend its relationship with the Jewish community and to counter any allegations that it had participated in the Holocaust.[95] During the early communist years, the rescuers' participation in missionary undertakings in Bessarabia and Transnistria and their efforts to save Jews could prove detrimental to their survival.[96] At the same time, those whose stories became known to the state or continued their anti-communist activism experienced persecution and imprisonment.

After returning to Romania, Father Theodor Petcu resumed his activities as a priest in the village of Murgași in southern Romania.[97] In 1949, the Securitate detained him and transferred him to Chișinău, then in the Soviet Union. In a sham trial, a Soviet court condemned him for "espionage in favour of a foreign power, an enemy of the USSR," and sentenced him to nine years' hard labour.[98] After the trial, the Soviet authorities deported Petcu to the Gulag, where he remained until June 1956, when he was transferred to Gherla prison in Romania to complete the rest of his sentence.[99] Although Petcu's family tried to arrange for some of the Jews Petcu assisted to give testimony, the court rejected their request on the basis that Petcu had committed treason against the Soviet Union and Romania. The court did not consider him a war criminal.[100] Nor would the court admit any mention of his efforts to help Jews while a missionary in Râbnița.[101] On 12 March 1957 Petcu died in a Romanian prison, ending any possibility for him to redeem his name or tell his story outside his family circle.[102]

Unlike Petcu, Father Ioan Sârbu survived the postwar years generally unnoticed. One cannot say the same of Hieromonk Paulin Lecca, a reputed translator of Russian literature and theology, who published a memoir that described both his personal experiences and those of other priests deployed to Transnistria.[103] Fashioning an exemplary autobiography for himself, in his postwar recollections he neglected to recall the harsh treatment and sexual abuses inflicted on Jews by the Orthodox clergy in missionary territory. He focused instead on his role in the re-evangelization of Transnistria.[104]

Father Gheorghe Petre-Orleşti took a different path than Sârbu or Lecca. In 1970, the Securitate recruited him as an informant with the code name "Pintilie Dorel."[105] Over several years, he delivered reports on the activities of the Govora Jehovah's Witnesses and the political and social views of his fellow clergymen.[106] Petre-Orleşti also shared relevant information about any Jews he encountered with the Securitate, especially those returning from Israel to visit family and friends. For example, he reported about Carol Bercovici, a Jew he had earlier saved from arrest and deportation during the Antonescu era for illegal delivery of radios.[107] In 1979, while visiting Govora with a friend, Bercovici visited Petre-Orleşti. Afterwards, the priest informed the Securitate about the visit. The Securitate used this information later to persecute Bercovici's friend, who had accompanied Bercovici without permission from the authorities.[108] In July 1984, he reported on his conversation with a Jewish family visiting Romania, whom he had met while travelling by train from Bucharest to Govora. Their conversation touched upon Israeli politics and the country's nuclear capability.[109]

CONCLUSION

The rescue of Jews reveals the complexity of the choices made by Romanian Orthodox clergy during the Holocaust. Defying a myopic narrative describing the clergy as either perpetrators or bystanders, the examples of individual clergymen assisting Jews gives new meaning to the contemporary understanding of the Romanian Holocaust. Still, the actions of these individual clergymen failed to change the dominant antisemitic views of Romanian Orthodox clergy and laity.

Whether for charity or personal profit, the efforts of some priests to assist Jews during the Holocaust subverted, at least in minor ways, the state's persecution of Jews in Transnistria. After the war and the communist takeover, both the perpetrators and the rescuers became targets for the Securitate and were subject to arrest and imprisonment, or forced to become informants. As the archives and the testimonies of the survivors reveal, the story of those Orthodox clergymen who assisted Jews ended tragically. With the onset of the communist regime and its terror against fascist clergymen, war criminals, and state employees deployed in the former territories of the Soviet Union, the wave of discretionary violence also affected those priests who had attempted to assist Jews. Their stories remain unknown today, for church leaders still refuse to recognize both their clergymen's acts of violence against Jews and these men's efforts to assist Jews during the Holocaust. The silence from the Holy Synod of the Romanian Orthodox Church and the ambiguity of the archival sources in revealing the contribution of Orthodox clergymen remains one of the main shortcomings of Holocaust research in contemporary Romania.

NOTES

1 Michael Bar-Zohar, *Beyond Hitler's Grasp: The Heroic Rescue of Bulgarian Jews*, 3rd ed. (New York: Adams Media, 1998), ch. 13; Panteleymon Anastasakis, *The Church of Greece under Axis Occupation* (New York: Fordham University Press, 2015); Ion Popa, *The Romanian Orthodox Church and the Holocaust* (Bloomington: Indiana University Press, 2017), 59–62.

2 Henry Eaton, *The Origins and Onset of the Romanian Holocaust* (Detroit: Wayne State University Press, 2013), 43–55; Paul A. Shapiro, "Prelude to Dictatorship in Romania: The National Christian Party in Power, December 1937–February 1938," *Canadian–American Slavic Studies* 8, no. 1 (1974): 45–88; Dov B. Lungu, "The French and British Attitudes towards the Goga-Cuza Government in Romania, December 1937–February 1938," *Canadian Slavonic Papers / Revue Canadienne des Slavistes* 30, no. 3 (1988): 323–41; Ion Mezarescu, *Partidul Național Creștin 1935–1938* (Bucharest: Paideea, 2018), 250–4.

3 For the Legionary pogroms, see Matatias Carp, *Cartea neagră. Fapte și documente. Suferințele evreilor din România (1940–1944)*, vol. 1: *Legionarii și rebeliunea* (Bucharest: Socec, 1946), 242–5; *Comisia internațională pentru Studierea Holocaustului în România, Raport Final*, eds. Tuvia Friling, Radu

Ioanid, and Mihai E. Ionescu (Iași: Polirom, 2004), 10; Gerhard Köpernik, *Faschisten im KZ: Rumäniens Eiserne Garde und das Dritte Reich* (Berlin: Frank & Timme, 2014), 84; and Roland Clark, *Holy Legionary Youth: Fascist Activism in Interwar Romania* (Ithaca: Cornell University Press, 2015), 229–32.

4 Ahiva Consiliului Național pentru Studierea Arhivelor Securității [ACNSAS], Informativ, file 264668, vol. 1, 14; ACNSAS, Penal, file 010618, vol. 1, 172; *Pe marginea prăpastiei, 21–23 Ianuarie 1941*, vol. 2, 2nd ed. (Bucharest: Scripta, 1992), 56–8, 76.

5 For a definition of the Holocaust perpetrator, see Gunther Lewy, *Perpetrators: The World of the Holocaust Killers* (Oxford: Oxford University Press, 2017), 45–60. For the European churches and their participation in the Holocaust, see Michael Phayer, *The Catholic Church and the Holocaust, 1930–1965* (Bloomington: Indiana University Press, 2000), 41–67; Robert P. Ericksen, *Complicity in the Holocaust: Churches and Universities in Nazi Germany* (Cambridge: Cambridge University Press, 2012), 94–139; and Dagmar Pöpping, *Kriegspfarrer an der Ostfront: Evangelische und katholische Wehrmachtseelsorge im Vernichtungskrieg, 1941–1945* (Göttingen: Vandenhoeck & Ruprecht, 2017), 140–73. For the Romanian Orthodox Church's participation in the Holocaust, see Veaceslav Ciorbă, *Biserica Ortodoxă în Basarabia și Transnistria (1940–2010)* (Chișinău: Pontos, 2011), 107–23; Jean Ancel, *The History of the Holocaust in Romania*, trans. Yaffah Murciano (Lincoln: University of Nebraska Press, 2017), 430–6; Diana Dumitru, *The State, Antisemitism, and Collaboration in the Holocaust: The Borderlands of Romania and the Soviet Union* (Cambridge: Cambridge University Press, in association with the United States Holocaust Memorial Museum, 2016); and Popa, *The Romanian Orthodox Church and the Holocaust*, 41–72.

6 Evgeny Finkel, *Ordinary Jews: Choice and Survival during the Holocaust* (Princeton: Princeton University Press, 2019); Stefan Kühl, *Ordinary Organizations: Why Normal Men Carried Out the Holocaust* (London: Wiley, 2016); Pearl M. Oliner, *Saving the Forsaken: Religious Culture and the Rescue of Jews in Nazi Europe* (New Haven: Yale University Press, 2008); Diana Dumitru and Carter Johnson, "Constructing Interethnic Conflict and Cooperation: Why Some People Harmed Jews and Others Helped Them during the Holocaust in Romania," *World Politics* 63, no. 1 (2011): 1–42. For the help that Christian denominations offered to the Jews during the Holocaust, see

Kevin P. Spicer, *Resisting the Third Reich: The Catholic Clergy in Hitler's Berlin* (DeKalb: Northern Illinois University Press, 2004), 120–39; Suzanne Vromen, *Hidden Children of the Holocaust: Belgian Nuns and Their Daring Rescue of Young Jews from the Nazis* (Oxford: Oxford University Press, 2008); Susan Zuccotti, *Père Marie-Benoît and Jewish Rescue: How a French Priest together with Jewish Friends Saved Thousands during the Holocaust* (Bloomington: Indiana University Press, 2013); and Jan Bank with Lieve Gevers, *Churches and Religion in the Second World War* (London: Bloomsbury, 2016), 419–69. For the Romanian case, see Radu Ioanid, *The Holocaust in Romania: The Destruction of Jews and Gypsies under the Antonescu Regime, 1940–1944* (Chicago: Ivan Dee, 2000), 238–59.

7   For the rescue of the Jews during the Holocaust, see Roy G. Koepp, "Holocaust Rescuers in Academic and Historical Scholarship," in *Unlikely Heroes: The Place of the Holocaust Rescuers in Research and Teaching*, eds. Ari Kohen and Gerald J. Steinacher (Lincoln: University of Nebraska Press, 2019), 15–30.

8   Vladimir Tismăneanu, *Stalinism for All Seasons: A Political History of Romanian Communism* (Berkeley: University of California Press, 2003), 107–36; Dennis Deletant, *Romania under Communism: Paradox and Degeneration* (Abington: Routledge, 2019), 89–114.

9   Lucian Leustean, *Orthodoxy and the Cold War: Religion and Political Power in Romania, 1947–1965* (Basingstoke: Palgrave, 2009), 76–120; Anca Maria Şincan, "Of Middlemen and Intermediaries: Negotiating the State Church Relationship in Communist Romania: The Formative Years" (PhD diss., Central European University, 2011), 91–6.

10 Popa, *The Romanian Orthodox Church*, 50–3; Ionuţ Biliuţă, "The Making of 'Christian' Transnistria: Fascist Orthodox Priests as Perpetrators, Bystanders, and Beneficiaries during the Holocaust," *Holocaust and Genocide Studies* 34, no. 1 (Spring 2020): 18–44.

11 For an account of the antisemitic measures, see Lya Benjamin, ed., *Legislaţia antievreiască din România 1938–1944: Documente* (Bucharest: Hasefer, 2008).

12 Vladimir Solonari, *Purifying the Nation: Population Exchange and Ethnic Cleansing in Nazi-Allied Romania* (Baltimore: Johns Hopkins University Press, 2009); Ancel, *The History of the Holocaust in Romania*, 430–6.

13 Bob Moore, *Victims and Survivors: The Nazi Persecution of the Jews in the Netherlands, 1940–1945* (London: Arnold, 1997); Bob Moore, *Survivors: Jewish Self-Help and Rescue in Nazi-Occupied Western Europe* (Oxford: Oxford

University Press, 2010); Marianné Ruel Robins, "A Grey Site of Memory: Le-Chambon-sur-Lignon and Protestant Exceptionalism on the Plateau Vivarais-Lignon," *Church History* 82, no. 3 (2013): 317–52. For Eastern Europe, see Nechama Tec, *Resistance: Jews and Christians Who Defied the Nazi Terror* (Oxford: Oxford University Press, 2013), 16–47.

14 Direcția Muncipiului București a Arhivelor Naționale, Sfântul Sinod, file 1/1919, 5; Direcția Județeană a Arhivelor Naționale Suceava, Mitropolia Bucovinei, Diverse, file 2124/1851–1938, 32v.

15 ACNSAS, Penal, file 011520, 11. See Mihai I. Poliec, *The Holocaust in the Romanian Borderlands: The Arc of Civilian Complicity* (Abingdon: Routledge, 2019), 84–114; Roland Clark, "Fascists and Soldiers: Ambivalent Loyalties and Genocidal Violence in Wartime Romania," *Holocaust and Genocide Studies* 33, no. 1 (2019): 408–32.

16 Dennis Deletant, "Transnistria and the Romanian Solution to the 'Jewish Problem,'" in *The Shoah in Ukraine: History, Testimony, Memorialization*, eds. Ray Brandon and Wendy Lower (Bloomington: Indiana University Press, in association with the United States Holocaust Memorial Museum, 2018), 156–90.

17 ACNSAS, Informativ, file 233982, vol. 1, 2. ACNSAS, Informativ, file 233982, vol. 2, 87.

18 "Archimandrite Scriban to the Department of the Religious Denominations," ANR, MCA, file 106/1942, 243; Svetlana Suveică, "The Local Administration in Transnistria and the Holocaust: Two Case Studies," *Holocaust: Studii și cercetări* 7, no. 8 (2015): 97–111.

19 Jean Ancel, *Transnistria*, vol. 3, trans. Doina Uricariu (Bucharest: Atlas, 1998), 183–8, 208–12; Alexander Dallin, *Odessa, 1941–1944: A Case Study of Soviet Territory under Foreign Rule*, (Iași: Center for Romanian Studies, 1998), 163. On the Orthodox missionarism in Russia under Nazi patronage in August 1941 manifested in the German-controlled territories in the Baltic states and Western Russia, see Johannes Due Enstad, "Prayers and Patriotism in Nazi Occupied Russia: The Pskov Orthodox Mission and Religious Survival, 1941–1944," *Slavonic and East European Review* 94, no. 3 (July 2016): 468–96.

20 For the impact of theological education, fascism, and the antisemitism of Orthodox theologians, see Ionuț Florin Biliuță, "Sowing the Seeds of Hate: The Antisemitism of the Romanian Orthodox Church in the Interwar

Period," *S.I.M.O.N. – Shoah: Intervention, Methods, Documentation* 3, no. 1 (2016): 20–34; and Ionuț Biliuță, "The Fascist Newsroom: Orthodox 'Ecumenism' in the Interwar Transylvanian Press," *Review of Ecumenical Studies* 10, no. 1 (2018): 46–88.

21 Mardarie Popinciuc, *Pentru Sfânta Cruce, Pentru Țară* (Freiburg: Coresi, 1985), 55–75; Clark, *Holy Legionary Youth*, 58.

22 See Mircea Păcurariu, *Dicționarul Teologilor Români* (Bucharest: Enciclopedic , 2002), 363–6.

23 Gheorghe Perian, *Despre Gala Galaction* (Cluj-Napoca: Limes, 2005), 35; Sabin Preda, "Preotul Profesor Grigore Pișculescu-Gala Galaction (1871–1969)," in *Profesorii noștri, învățătorii noștri*, vol. 1, ed. Ioan Moldoveanu (Bucharest: Basilica, 2020), 435–51. For the theological milieu of Galaction in interwar Romania, see Vasile Mihoc, "Dezvoltarea studiilor biblice," in *Teologia ortodoxă în secolul al XX-lea și începutul secolului al XXI-lea*, ed. Viorel Ioniță (Bucharest: Basilica, 2011), 175–87.

24 Gala Galaction, *Piatra din capul unghiului: Scrisori teologice* (Bucharest: Tipografiile Române Unite, 1926); Gala Galaction, *Scrisori către Simforoza. În pământul făgăduinței* (Bucharest: Cugetarea, 1927), 10–11. See also Gala Galaction, *Jurnal*, vol. 1 (Bucharest: Albatros, 1996), 52–3.

25 Arhivele Naționale ale României [ANR], Ministerul de Interne, Diverse, file 5/1931, 34.

26 Gala Galaction, "De pe treptele palatelor irodiane," *Adam* 1, no. 1 (15 April 1929): 5; Gala Galaction, "Sinagoga de lângă Tibru," *Adam* 3, no. 43 (1 November 1931): 1–2; Gala Galaction, "La moartea lui Adolf Ștern," *Adam* 3, no. 44 (1 December 1931); Gala Galaction, "Duhul poeziei lui A. Tomi," *Adam* 3, no. 47 (15 March 1932): 6–7; Gala Galaction, "Cuvântul cel etern și neisprăvit," *Adam* (10 July 1932): 7–8.

27 Ion C. Butnaru, *The Silent Holocaust: Romania and Its Jews* (New York: Greenwood Press, 1992), 54; Lucian Leuștean, "'For the Glory of Romanians': Orthodoxy and Nationalism in Greater Romania, 1918–1945," *Nationalities Papers* 35, no. 4 (2007): 717–42.

28 Gala Galaction, "Introduction," in *Impotriva urei. Numerus clausus, antisemitismul, Protocoalele Înțelepților Sionului* (Bucharest: Editura ziarului "Cuvântul nostru," 1938), 4–7. For the *Protocols of the Elders of Zion*'s impact on Romanian fascism and theological antisemitism, see Paul A. Shapiro, "Faith, Murder, Resurrection: The Iron Guard and the Romanian Orthodox

Church," in *Antisemitism, Christian Ambivalence, and the Holocaust*, ed.
Kevin P. Spicer (Bloomington: Indiana University Press, in association with
the United States Holocaust Memorial Museum, 2017), 136–73; and Ionuț
Biliuță, "The 'Jewish Problem' in the Light of the Scriptures: Orthodox Biblical Studies and Antisemitism in Interwar Transylvania," in *Modern Anti-
semitisms in the Peripheries: Europe and Its Colonies, 1880–1945*, eds. Raul
Cârstocea and Éva Kovács (Vienna: New Academic Press, 2019), 161–79.

29 His anti-fascist and anti-xenophobic ideas were similar to those coming
from the Jewish intellectual milieu. See Isac Ludo, *În jurul unei obsesii. Pre-
cizările unui evreu pentru românii de bună credință* (Bucharest: Adam,
1936), 394–412; and Avram Leib Zissu, *Logos, Israel, Biserica. Viciile organice
ale Bisericii și criza omenirii creștine* (Bucharest: n.p., 1937), 384–401.

30 Gala Galaction, *Sionismul la prieteni* (Bucharest: Mântuirea, 1919), 51.

31 Ibid., 58.

32 Ibid., 62.

33 Maria Bucur, "Carol II of Romania," in *Balkan Strongmen: Dictators and Authoritarian Rulers of Southeast Europe*, ed. Bernd J. Fischer (West Lafayette:
Purdue University Press, 2007), 87–118; Constantin Iordachi, "A Continuum
of Dictatorships: Hybrid Totalitarian Experiments in Romania, 1937–1944,"
in *Rethinking Fascism and Dictatorship in Europe*, eds. António Costa Pinto
and Aristotle Kallis (Houndmills: Palgrave, 2014) 246–53; Cristian Vasile
Petcu, *Guvernarea Miron Cristea* (Bucharest: Enciclopedic , 2009), 235–6.

34 For the 1938 antisemitic turn of the Romanian government, see Rebecca
Ann Haynes, *Romanian Policy towards Germany, 1936–1940* (Basingstoke:
Palgrave, 2000), 43–66; Solonari, *Purifying the Nation*, 48–51; Ancel, *History
of the Holocaust in Romania*, 25–39; Rebecca Haynes, "Reluctant Allies? Iuliu
Maniu and Corneliu Zelea Codreanu against King Carol II of Romania,"
Slavonic and East European Review 85, no. 1 (2007): 121; and Eaton, *The
Origins and the Onset of the Romanian Holocaust*, 43–55.

35 Gala Galaction, *Jurnal*, vol. 2 (Bucharest: Minerva, 1977), 184.

36 Gala Galaction, "Introduction," in *Împotriva urei*, 7. He even went so far as
to claim that the calamitous earthquake on 10 November 1940 was a divine
punishment for the sufferings of the Jews inflicted by the fascist regime.
See Gala Galaction, *Jurnal*, vol. 4 (Bucharest: Albatros, 2000), 62.

37 Gala Galaction, *Jurnal*, vol. 3 (Bucharest: Albatros, 1999), 209; Gala Galaction, *Jurnal*, vol. 4, 142–3, 172–3, 192.

38 Wilhelm Filderman, *Memorii & Junale*, vol. 2: 1940–1952 (Bucharest: Hasefer / Editura Institutului pentru Studierea Holocaustului din România "Elie Wiesel," 2017), 620.

39 Gala Galaction, "Epistola lui Aristeia. Discurs de recepție la Academia Română," *Biserica Ortodoxă Română* 64: 5–8 (1948): 272–83.

40 At the behest of Gala Galaction, during the Second World War, Father Athanase Negoiță, one of his closest students, went incognito to bring food to various Jewish families in Bucharest. On this point, see Alexandru Mihăilă, "Părintele Athanase Negoiță (1903–1994). Preocupări biblice și orientalistice," in *Profesorii noștri, învățătorii noștri*, 398.

41 Paulin Lecca, *De la moarte la viață* (Bucharest: Paideea, 1999), 19–21.

42 ACNSAS, Informativ, file 005220, vol. 1, 42. For another secondary source that considers Archimandrite Paulin Lecca as authentic, see Vladimir Solonari, *A Satellite Empire: Romanian Rule in Southwestern Ukraine, 1941–1944* (Ithaca: Cornell University Press, 2019), 135.

43 ACNSAS, Informativ, file 000701, vol. 1, 33; ACNSAS, Informativ, file 233982, vol. 1, 2.

44 ANR, Centrala Evreilor, file 3/1940, 3; *Raport Final*, 108–9.

45 Iancu Guttman, *Slove de martiri... Publicate de părintele lor Rabin H. Guttman* (Bucharest: Institutul de Arte Grafice "Cartea de Aur," 1945), 290–1.

46 Matatias Carp, *Cartea neagră. Fapte și documente. Suferințele evreilor din România (1940–1944)*, vol. 1: *Legionarii și rebeliunea* (Bucharest: Socec, 1946), 242–5, 247–88; F. Brunea-Fox, *Orașul măcelului. Jurnalul rebeliunii și crimelor legionare*, 2nd ed. (Bucharest: Hasefer, 2004), 31–3; Emil Dorian, *Jurnal din vremuri de prigoană, 1937–1944* (Bucharest: Hasefer, 1996), 146–7; *Raport Final*, 125.

47 Dumitru Lungu, *Luptă și temnițe* (Bucharest: Ramida, 1996), 74; Ana Maria Marin, *Prin poarta cea strâmtă*, 2nd ed. (Bucharest: Evdokimos, 2018), 67; Dumitru Banea, *Acuzat, martor și apărător în procesul vieții mele* (Sibiu: Puncte Cardinale, 1994), 89.

48 ACNSAS, MFI (Sibiu), 12197, vol. 1, reel 146, 2, 26; ACNSAS, informativ, file 264668, 43; Ancel, *The History of the Holocaust*, 157; Florin C. Stan, *Situația evreilor din România între anii 1940–1944* (Cluj-Napoca: Argonaut, 2012), 341.

49 Metropolitan Irineu Mihălcescu, *Preoțimea și războiul sfânt: Contra hidrei bolșevice* (Iași: Tipografia Alexandru Țerek, 1941), 7; Metropolitan Nicolae

Bălan, "Înoirea forțelor morale ale națiunii," *Revista Teologică* 31, nos. 9–10 (1941): 397–9.

50 Gheorghe Secaș, *Pentru sufletul Basarabiei: Ierarhii și preoții din Ardeal în misiune la frații din Basarabia dezrobită* (Sibiu: Tipografia Arhidiecezană, 1944), 8, 16; Bishop Nicolae Popovici, "Misiunea Bisericii Ardelene în Basarabia și Transnistria," in Nicolae Popovici, *Lespezi de altar: În slujba Bisericii ișa Neamului la granița de vest a țării* (Beiuș: Tipografia Eparhială, 1942), 141–7.

51 "Informative Notification," ANR, MCA, file 102/1942, 6. See also "Report of the Golta Legion of Gendarmes, June 1943," 2178, Opis 1, Delo 57, 184, RG-31.008, Nikolaev Oblast Archives, United States Holocaust Memorial Museum Archives (USHMMA); Dennis Deletant, *Hitler's Forgotten Ally: Ion Antonescu and His Regime, Romania, 1940–1944*, (Basingstoke: Palgrave, 2007), 42; *Raportul Final*, 43.

52 Shlomo Lambroza, "The Pogroms of 1903–1906," in *Pogroms: Anti-Jewish Violence in Modern Russian History*, ed. John Dolye Klier and Shlomo Lambroza (Cambridge: Cambridge University Press, 2002), 195–248; Steven J. Zipperstein, *Pogrom: Kishinev and the Tilt of History* (New York: Liveright, 2018); Viorica Nicolenco, *Extrema dreaptă în Basarabia (1923–1940)* (Chișinău: Civitas, 1999), 12–43; Dumitru, *The State, Antisemitism*, 53–93.

53 For the Kishinev ghetto, see Paul A. Shapiro, *The Kishinev Ghetto, 1941–1942: A Documentary History of the Holocaust in Romania's Contested Borderlands* (Tuscaloosa: University of Alabama Press, in association with the United States Holocaust Memorial Museum, 2015), 14–27.

54 "Order no. 11 A from 18 September 1941, The Military Headquarters from Chișinău to the General Governor of Bessarabia," 706, Opis no. 1, Delo no. 22, 4, RG. 54.001M, reel 1, National Archives of Moldova, USHMMA. On deportations across the Dniester, see "Annex no. 4. The Organization of the Deportation of the Jews," 706, Opis no. 1, Delo no. 22, 44–5; 47–9; 53–60, RG. 54.001M, reel 1, National Archives of Moldova, USHMMA.

55 "Annex no. 2," 706, Opis no. 1, Delo no. 22, 35, RG. 54.001M, reel 1, National Archives of Moldova, USHMMA. On Gumă, see Ioan Lisnic, *Clerici ortodocși din Basarabia și Bucovina de Nord în închisorile comuniste* (Chișinău: Cuvântul ABC, 2018), 177–8.

56 Ibid.

57 Yad Vashem Archives, pages of Testimony Names Memorial Collection, 380705.

58 For the issue of baptizing Jews during the war by Orthodox clergymen, see Ancel, *Transnistria*, 182–9; and Popa, *The Romanian Orthodox Church*, 53–62.

59 Archimandrite Iuliu Scriban, Archimandrite Antim Nica, "Report about the Activity of the Romanian Orthodox Mission in Transnistria from 15 August 1941 until 31 December 1941," *Transnistria creştină* 1, no. 1 (1941): 25. See also ACNSAS, Informativ, file 000701, vol. 3, 25–8. For the situation of the Bessarabian Orthodox Church before the start of the war, see Sergiu C. Roşca, "Biserica basarabeană sub ocupaţie sovietică şi primele realizări ale nouei stăpîniri romîneşti în Basarabia," *Misionarul* 13, no. 1 (1942): 34–40.

60 "Report no. 197/1941, Judge of the Cabinet 4, Ilfov Tribunal to the Ministry of Justice," ANR, MCA, file 106/1942, 34.

61 "Informative Report," 666, Opis no. 2, Delo no. 165, 206, RG. 54.001M, reel 2, National Archives of Moldova, USHMMA. See also Ion Popa, "Sanctuary from the Holocaust? Roman-Catholic Conversions of Jews in Bucharest, Romania 1942," *Holocaust and Genocide Studies* 29, no. 1 (2015): 39–56.

62 "Informative Report," 706, Opis no. 1, Delo no. 22, 273, RG. 54.001M, reel 2, National Archives of Moldova, USHMMA.

63 "Note nr. 86, 12 September 1942, Colonel Modest Isopescu, Golta County Military Prefect, to Archimandrite Antim Nica," 2178, Opis 1, Delo 2, 178, RG-31.008, Nikolaev Oblast Archives Records, USHMMA; "Informative Report on Transnistria, July 1942," 2242, Opis no. 4C, Ed. Hr. no. 28/1942, 74, reel 1, RG-31.004M, Odessa Oblast Archives, USHMMA.

64 "Isopescu to Nica," 2178, Opis 1, Delo 2, 178, RG.31.008, Nikolaev Oblast Archives, USHMMA; "Order no. 2144, April 9, 1942, Golta Prefecture to Deanery Golta County," 2178, Opis 1, Delo 4, 331, RG.31.008, Nikolaev Oblast Archives, USHMMA. According to the documents remitted by the Orthodox Patriarchate to the government, thirty-three Jews were baptized in Bucharest alone after 4 March 1941. On this point, see "The Evidence of baptized Jews in the Parishes of the Metropolitan See of Ungro-Walachia," ANR, MCA, file 120/1943, 4–7.

65 Ancel, *Transnistria*, 234–5.

66 Toma Rădulescu, "Petcu, Theodor," in *Martiri pentru Hristos din România, în perioada comunistă*, ed. Mircea Păcurariu (Bucharest: EIMBOR, 2007),

545–8; Ana Maria Iancu, "File din suferinţa preoţilor basarabeni în secolul al XX-lea. Cazul părintelui Theodor Petcu," in *Pătimitori şi pătimire în închisorile comuniste*, ed. Florin Dobrei, (Deva/Alba Iulia: Editura Episcopiei Devei şi Hunedoarei/Reîntregirea, 2015), 307–28.

67 ACNSAS, Penal, file 011520, 13.

68 ACNSAS, Informativ, file 004847, vol. 2, 2–8; Rădulescu, "Petcu, Theodor," 546.

69 "Letter, January 2008, Drăgan-Petcu to Rădulescu," Toma Rădulescu Archive, Craiova in Iancu, "File din suferinţa preoţilor basarabeni," 310.

70 For Metropolitan Tit Simedrea, see Alexandru M. Ioniţă, *Tit Simedrea Mitropolitul: repere biografice* (Constanţa: Ex Ponto, 2002), 45–8; Popa, *The Romanian Orthodox Church*, 65–7. For the survivors' testimonies regarding the collaboration between Simedrea and Russu during the Holocaust in saving Jews, see Marius Mircu, *Ce s-a întâmplat cu evreii în şi din România*, vol. 3: *O altă faţă a prigoanei* (Bucharest: Glob, 1996), 95. For Russu's theological studies, see Yad Vashem Archives, M. 31, file 10818, 45.

71 Jean Ancel, "The Romanian Way of Solving the 'Jewish Problem' in Bessarabia and Bukovina, June–July 1941," *Yad Vashem Studies* 19 (1988): 127–232; Vladimir Solonari, "Patterns of Violence: The Local Population and the Mass Murder of the Jews in Bessarabia and Northern Bukovina, July–August 1941," *Kritika: Explorations in Russian and Eurasian History* 8, no. 4 (2007): 749–87. For the testimonies of the Jewish survivors, see Jewgenjia Finker and Markus Winkler, *Juden aus Czernowitz: Ghetto, Deportation, Vernichtung 1941–1944; Überlebende berichten* (Konstanz: Hartung-Gorre Verlag, 2004).

72 Yad Vashem Archives, M. 31, file 499, 1, 5; Traian Popovici, *Spovedania* (Bucharest: Editura Fundaţiei Dr Wilhelm Filderman, 2002), 28–9, 39.

73 Yad Vashem Archives, M. 31, file 10818, 18; Mircu, *Ce s-a întâmplat cu evreii în şi din România*, 96.

74 Yad Vashem Archives, M. 31.2, file 10818, 3; Mircu, *Ce s-a întâmplat cu evreii în şi din România*, 95.

75 Yad Vashem Archives, M. 31, file 499, 40.

76 Yad Vashem Archives, M. 31, file 10818, 12.

77 Mircu, *Ce s-a întâmplat cu evreii în şi din România*, 96–7.

78 Yad Vashem Archives, M. 31, file 10818, 19.

79 ACNSAS, Informativ, file 375002, vol. 1, 1. On the antisemitic views of the National Christian Party, see Cristian Sandache, *Doctrina national-creştină*

în România (Bucharest: Paideea, 1997), 36–47; and Mezarescu, *Partidul Naţional Creştin*, 119.

80 ACNSAS, Informativ, file 375002, vol. 1, 12, 36, 39.

81 Yad Vashem Archives, M. 31, file 10060, 1.

82 Ibid., 3; "Informative Note," ANR, Inspectoratul General al Jandarmeriei, file 29/1943, 112–13. Captain Giurescu was also arrested by the Golta Legion of Gendarmes following the arrest of Father Gheorghe-Orleşti.

83 Yad Vashem Archives, M. 31, file 10060, 3.

84 Ibid.

85 Ibid.

86 Ibid., 17; ACNSAS, Penal, file 061490, 12.

87 Matatias Carp, *Cartea neagră. Fapte şi documente. Suferinţele evreilor din România (1940–1944)*, vol. 3: *Transnistria* (Bucharest: Socec, 1948), 199–206.

88 ACNSAS, Informativ, file 000701, vol. 1, 33.

89 ACNSAS, Informativ, file 547926, vol. 1, 7.

90 Viorel Achim, *Munca forţată în Transnistria. "Organizarea muncii" evreilor şi romilor. Decembrie 1942–Martie 1944* (Târgovişte: Cetatea de Scaun, 2015); Alexandru Florian, "Munca obştească sau limbajul eufemistic al Holocaustului," in *Munca obligatorie a evreilor din România (1940–1944). Documente*, eds. Ana Bărbulescu, Alexandru Florian, Alexandru Climescu, and Laura Degeratu (Iaşi: Polirom, 2013), 13–31; Dallas Michelbacher, *Jewish Forced Labor in Romania, 1940–1944* (Bloomington: Indiana University Press, 2020).

91 Miriam Korber-Bercovici, *Jurnal de Ghetou* (Bucharest: Curtea Veche, 2017), 95.

92 Sarah Rosen, "The Djurin Ghetto in Transnistria through the Lens of Kunstadt's Diary," in *Romania and the Holocaust: Events–Contexts–Aftermath*, ed. Simon Geissbühler (Stuttgart: ibidem Verlag, 2016), 131–51.

93 Dennis Deletant, *Hitler's Forgotten Ally: Ion Antonescu and His Regime, Romania 1940–1944* (Basingstoke: Palgrave, 2006), 230–45. For the postwar position of the Orthodox Church regarding the coup and the Jews, see Bishop Antim Nica, "Pe urmele apostolatului românesc," *Biserica Ortodoxă Română* 11–12 (1945): 571–89; Teodor N. Manolache, "Din dragoste şi din simţul datoriei: Fapte puţin cunoscute din activitatea Î.P.S. Patriarh Nicodim în timpul războiului," *Biserica Ortodoxă Română* 11–12 (1945): 672.

94 ACNSAS, Informativ, file 261033, vol. 3, 10; ACNSAS, Informativ, file 233981,

vol. 1, 2. See Lavinia Stan and Lucian Turcescu, "Collaboration and Resistance: Some Definitional Difficulties," in *Justice, Memory and Redress in Romania: New Insights*, eds. Lavinia Stan and Lucian Turcescu (Newcastle: Cambridge Scholars, 2017), 24–45. ACNSAS, Fond Informativ, file 261884, 1.

95 D. Lungulescu, *Problema evreiască în lumina Revelației divine* (Craiova: Ramuri, 1944), 100–5; the German Church acted similarly. On this point, see John Pollard, *The Papacy in the Age of Totalitarianism, 1914–1958* (Oxford: Oxford University Press, 2014), 365–6; Mark Edward Ruff, *The Battle for the Catholic Past in Germany, 1945–1980* (Cambridge: Cambridge University Press, 2017), 15–16; and Giuliana Chamedes, *A Twentieth-Century Crusade: The Vatican's Battle to Remake Christian Europe* (Cambridge, MA: Harvard University Press, 2019), 235–41.

96 Popa, *The Romanian Orthodox Church*, 83–98.

97 Lisnic, *Clerici ortodocși*, 233.

98 ACNSAS, Penal, file 011522, 13.

99 Ibid.

100 Ibid., 14.

101 Ibid., 13.

102 Iancu, "File din suferința," 313.

103 Lecca, *De la moarte la viață*, 156.

104 Ibid., 173.

105 ACNSAS, Rețea, file 303520, vol. 1, 2. Father Paulin Lecca became an informant for the Securitate as well. See ACNSAS, Rețea, file 001456, 1-5; ACNSAS, Rețea, file 228170, 2.

106 ACNSAS, Rețea, file 303520, vol. 1, 56.

107 ACNSAS, Rețea, file 303520, vol. 2, 82.

108 ACNSAS, Rețea, file 303520, vol. 1, 47.

109 ACNSAS, Rețea, file 303520, vol. 2, 41.

12

Racist, Brutal, and Ethnotheist: A Conservative Christian View of Nazism in the Korntal Brethren

Samuel Koehne

In recent work, scholars have considered the question of how individual Christian communities, including those outside the main Protestant and Catholic churches, viewed the Nazi Party. This is based on a desire to examine the question of Nazism and religion "from below" – including at the congregational level – and forms part of a much larger historiographical trend toward understanding the full diversity of German Protestant responses to the rise of the Nazis.[1] There was "an immense profusion of opinions and voices" within German Protestantism such that "each individual, each theological trend, each church group, and even the *Landeskirchen* (state churches) had to seek their own guidelines, and make a decision" on Nazism.[2]

One continuing question about these decisions is: Why did Christians support the Nazis?[3] In 1933, Henry Leiper, an American who was heavily involved in the ecumenical movement, prepared a confidential report in which he identified this very problem: "The thing we cannot understand from the outside is why so many Christians acclaim Hitler as a prophet of the Lord and proceed not only to hand over their consciences to the State but to seek to justify it by rewriting Christian theology."[4] He detailed the situation in Germany as he understood it: there was an atmosphere of fear and censorship, and the Nazis had launched an "Anti-Jewish Crusade" that was "sickening and unforgettable" and a "head-on collision between two religions": Christianity and Nazism.[5] We historians also approach this topic "from the outside," which is why it is so important to turn to responses from *within* German Protestantism – some of which closely paralleled Leiper's observations.

In this chapter I am particularly interested in an important analysis of Nazism from 1930, in which the author asked: Why are Christians voting for the Nazis? This work came from within a theologically conservative Protestant group called the Korntal Brethren, whose faith might be considered fundamentalist.[6] It characterized Nazism as anti-Christian on the basis that it was violent, revolutionary, neo-pagan, and defined religion by race. These views were almost identical to the conclusions reached by members of the theologically liberal Temple-Society at around the same time: that Nazism was antisemitic, dictatorial, and an ersatz religion.[7] It confirms that Germans with very different theological views could readily grasp the Nazis' antisemitism and racial ideology and that Nazism might form a "political religion."[8] What is most valuable in such assessments is that they were *contemporary* and written by people who lived within the German Protestant traditions. Thus, they suggest why some Protestants were drawn to the Nazi Party.[9]

To understand the Korntal Brethren's response to Nazism, some context is necessary. Founded in 1819 under royal privilege as a kind of theocracy in Württemberg, the Brethren's foundational views were aligned with those of Württemberg Pietism. These included a strong millenialist focus and a belief that the will of God could be read in contemporary events. They believed that members should engage in a "lived" Christianity, and their village was developed as a political-religious community that sought to emulate the communality of the first Christians. They had a literal interpretation of the Bible, with a strong emphasis on the Old Testament and prophetic tradition. The Brethren served as a central "node" for both mission work and Pietist networks.[10]

The years after the First World War were quite difficult for the Brethren, particularly as their combined "political-religious" community was forced to divide in 1919. They also lost their royal privilege, as the monarchy had been abolished, and experienced an influx of "outsiders": non-Brethren who settled in Korntal.[11] Some of these "new" Korntalers later became leaders of the local chapter of the NSDAP when it was founded in July 1927.[12] Indeed, the first time that a Nazi Party event was held in Korntal (1924), the participants were described as rowdy outsiders who had mostly come from Stuttgart; they were criticized for causing a disturbance in the community. Despite the Beerhall Putsch in Munich in November 1923, the Nazi Party was still relatively unknown in Korntal, where it was consistently referred to as the "NSAPD" rather than the NSDAP, showing confusion even about the party's name.[13]

The Brethren attempted to maintain the original Christian "character" of Korntal as well as control over the village. From 1919 to 1933, at least nine of the twelve seats on the municipal council were held by members of the Brethren. From 1919 to 1935, Korntal's mayor was a member of the Brethren and sat on the Brethren Council.[14] Given this, it is unsurprising that the Korntal Council was similarly concerned about maintaining the village's religious character, as the "soil of a healthy and sensible Christian culture, that also permeates through public life."[15]

What makes the village of Korntal fascinating is that two of the inhabitants, Christian Mergenthaler and Wilhelm Simpfendörfer, both became state ministers of education – albeit with vastly different views on Christian faith. Mergenthaler, a fanatical National Socialist, was minister of education and premier of Württemberg from 1933–1945. Simpfendörfer, a member of the Brethren, was Baden-Württemberg minister of education in 1946–47 and again in 1953–58. He took part in the founding of the Christian Democratic Union (CDU) after the Second World War.

It is not surprising that Wilhelm Simpfendörfer and others were politically engaged. Those living in Korntal had consistently studied current events and politics through a religious lens. As a result, Korntal was also the birthplace of a Christian political party, the Christian Volk-Service (Christlicher Volksdienst, CVD) which became the Christian Social Volk-Service (Christlich-sozialer Volksdienst, CSVD). That party sought to advance the notion of a "lived" Christianity into the political sphere.[16]

The Brethren's faith remained solidly conservative and biblically grounded. They also felt that their faith was under siege. In part this was owing to a general decline in church life; the Brethren held that Germans had "sunk into the idolatry of mammonism and materialism."[17] Also, there was a clear sense in the community that neo-paganism was a rising force in German society. This reflected the fact that there were movements seeking to establish "new religions," including the neo-pagan "German Faith" movement – one of whose leaders, Jakob Wilhelm Hauer, came from Württemberg.[18] In 1930, Korntal was described as a place of "living Christianity" that would be significant "in the coming battles between Christianity and neo-paganism."[19] In the early 1930s, the Brethren became increasingly aware of the anti-Christian and anti-church ideas of such groups and were determined that neo-paganism not be spread in "sacred Korntal."[20] They viewed Nazis as advocates for neo-paganism, and the Nazis understood that this was the Brethren's perspective.

The history of the Korntal NSDAP was published in 1934 in a special edition newspaper, which ran a photograph of Korntal members as "old fighters." The group in that photo numbers twenty-six, barely an *Ortsgruppe* (local NSDAP group), but it is significant because it includes Christian Mergenthaler, who had settled in Korntal in 1926.[21] Interestingly, one article in this same publication described a time of "godlessness" in which "German piety" was failing. While this matched the Brethren's concerns, the Nazis' proposed solution was very different from theirs. The Nazi paper advocated a salvational nationalism: culture was to be purified in order to achieve a renewal of the "German soul." The "foundation" of this "German soul" was to be racial – "namely, the purity of the blood." Moreover, "sin against the blood" meant that "the German *Volk* in large measure had lost its soul."[22] The paper itself stated that the Nazi Party had been strongly opposed in Korntal, on the basis that it was connected to "neo-paganism."[23]

In this respect, the Brethren fitted into a much broader trend toward viewing the Nazis as neo-pagan. At the time, the question of how to respond to them was a major concern for "positive Christians." It should be noted that I am using "positive Christianity" according to its commonly understood meaning by the 1920s – as orthodox and doctrinal Christian faith, which Hartmut Lehmann described as "conservative, fundamentalist and nationalistic."[24] The Nazis in their party program stated that they stood for "positive Christianity," but this had no cohesive meaning in the NSDAP and was a political ploy.[25] The Brethren, by contrast, understood "positive Christianity" as fundamentalist Christian faith and as the opposite of liberal-rationalist theology.

One major point of concern for theologically conservative Christians was that the Nazis had arisen from the *völkisch* movement, and there were clear instances of neo-pagan groups in this German subculture, such as the Thule Society, the Order of Odin's Children, and the Germanic Order, all of which used the swastika and the expression "Sieg Heil" or "Heil und Sieg." Catholic authors like Erhard Schlund believed that the National Socialists were part and parcel of a "religious wave" that would draw people away from the churches and into "anti-Christian, neo-Germanic-*völkisch* straits."[26] As an anonymous critic put it when discussing the "Wodan-cult" or cult of Odin in Austria, "where one has rejected positive Christianity generally one ends up in the deepest swamp of superstition!"[27]

Alfons Steiger, who was heavily involved in the Catholic Centre Party, was a vocal critic of the Nazis as a "neo-pagan" group. He explained "positive Christianity" according to its generally accepted meaning at the time: "the faithful acceptance" of the "doctrines and moral precepts of the Christian religion, as they are laid down in Holy Scripture and dogma." He noted that the Nazis were certainly not "positive Christians," given that they even advocated measuring religion by the "moral feelings of the Germanic race."[28] It is clear that this kind of "ethnotheism" was the core focus in the official Nazi views on religion and that religious teachings were to be measured against a "racial yardstick."

"Ethnotheism," a common conceptual approach adopted by the Nazis, meant that they defined religion in terms of race and the spiritual or moral characteristics supposedly "inherent" in race.[29] This explains why diverse religious perspectives existed in the Nazi Party and why they often freely blended paganism with Christianity. Nazis also followed an ethnotheist approach to try to explain how Christianity, with its clear roots in Judaism, became the dominant religion in Germany. These explanations varied, from the view that Jesus was somehow "Aryan" to a kind of reverse logic that stated that the very success of Christianity meant it had to be "Nordic" because "[a] teaching that does not come from Nordic blood and which does not have a Nordic spirit, cannot spread among Nordic peoples."[30] The Nazi leadership was less concerned with types of religion (paganism, Christianity) than with ensuring that religious teachings aligned with a "racial soul."

At the time, this same point was identified and strongly attacked by Catholics like Erhard Schlund and Alfons Steiger, as well as by Protestants like Hermann Sasse and Richard Karwehl.[31] In the period when the Nazi

Party was making major political gains (1930–31), "the ideological foundations of the party" remained a key issue for Protestants, particularly its
"völkisch ideology."[32] The most detailed analyses of the Nazi Party that were
provided in Korntal came from the CSVD, which was seen as a "local" party
that embodied the values of the Korntal Brethren.[33]

The CSVD began its life as the Christian-Social Association (Christlich-
soziale Gesinnungsgemeinschaft, CSG), founded in Korntal on 7 April 1924.
Its manifesto outlined what it desired: "not the re-establishment of fallen
idols, the restoration of our nation's external greatness, but the restoration
of its [inner] health, its moral renewal." The group supported the Weimar
Republic through its participation in the democratic system and opposition
to the Nazis' revolutionary aims.[34] The main impetus for the Christian-Social Association was Pastor Samuel Jaeger's call (issued 13 March 1924) for
the formation of Christian groups to provide direction for Protestants in
contemporary politics.

The CSG anticipated that its members would be politically active, though
initially such involvement was meant to be limited to promoting Christianity
and examining policies in the light of faith. The CSG aimed to be a Christian
pressure group, one that would bring the Gospel into every aspect of public
life and work as witnesses to God within the German nation. These aspirations were summed up in their slogan, taken from the Lord's Prayer: "Your
Kingdom come, Your will be done also on earth."[35] Over and above the clear
connections to ideas within the Brethren, influence was exerted in Korntal
by the position of the CSG/CVD founders (Wilhelm Simpfendörfer and Paul
Bausch) in the community. Both men were locals and members of the
Brethren – unlike those who had founded the Korntal branch of the Nazi
Party.[36] Wilhelm Simpfendörfer was an influential figure, especially as a
Brethren member on the Korntal Council (1919–30). Both he and Bausch
were teachers.

The CSG did not set out to stand candidates for election, but this soon
changed. In 1925, the CSG became the Christian Volk-Service (CVD), a Christian political party. It formed a coalition with the "Stöcker" Christian Socialists on 28 December 1929, bringing the CSVD into existence.[37] Across
these distinct periods the group stood for the ideal of a Christian state, while
rejecting the idea of turning Christianity into policy. They hoped to apply
"Christian values" to political debate; where the Nazis saw race as the key to

community, this group wished to use "Christian love" to bridge the divide between parties and overcome "the god Mammon."[38]

When the CSVD was founded, Paul Bausch stated: "[It] has to be the state-political exponent of the people of God, those united faithful communities of Jesus Christ." The CSG's aims remained as guidelines for the CSVD – to bring the "strengths of the Gospel" into public life "in obedience to the will of God, in faith to Jesus Christ our Lord and in living connection to His community."[39] The group consistently stood for many of the same issues that were important to the Brethren. The CVD and CSVD supported Christian politics in a perceived anti-Christian time and viewed the period as one driven by rampant materialism.[40] Hence they focused on moral and ethical issues such as alcoholism and "shame and smut" in German cultural life – sometimes referred to as "cultural bolshevism."[41] They shared most of these ideas with the Nazis, though the Nazis viewed them all as "racial" issues.

Consciously formed within Pietism, the CVD found its supporters primarily among the "Free Churches" (*Freikirchen*) and saw God's will at work in the world, especially in Germany's postwar distress. The first issue of the CSG paper began: "The one true God stands against us," with the writer describing national and spiritual salvation as only possible through God's grace. Wilhelm Simpfendörfer assessed the year 1924 as a time when "God's hand lies heavy upon us."[42] In this regard, the CVD also aligned with the apocalyptic tradition of Württemberg Pietism, and a 1930 election poster depicted the grim reaper descending upon Germany, with the slogan "Shall it come to pass? Shall death and horror reign in Germany?"[43] Though it was later claimed that this poster predicted the impact of National Socialism, at the time it was far more indicative of a belief that without a return to God, Germany would descend into chaos.[44]

Their solution was "active" Christianity, an intersection of the temporal and spiritual based on an idea of Christians performing their duty as members of the state. This was summarized by a prominent member of the group, Hermann Kling: "The CSVD stands neither right nor left, nor in the middle, but will be a bridge. The enemy stands neither right nor left, but beneath, and help comes not from the swastika nor from the soviet-star, not from black-white-red nor black-red-gold, but from above."[45] Another article noted that "service, love, God" provided the answers to political problems, not counter-revolution, nationalism, or fascism.[46]

Many of the CSVD's policies also catered to popular nationalism. For example, it rejected the Treaty of Versailles and the "lie of war-guilt," and it sought to reclaim lost German territory.[47] The CVD and the later CSVD were relatively significant minor parties, and they managed to gain fourteen seats in the Reichstag in 1930 (the first time they ran in federal elections).[48] From its inception, the organization was associated with Korntal and the Brethren. This was because it had been founded there and also because of the support it gave to Christian politics.[49] Lehmann viewed the CVD's impact on Korntal as limited due to the Brethren's reticence regarding support for political parties, and because the CVD was only once allowed to advertise in the church newsletter. This alone might be seen as promoting a strong alignment of the Brethren with the group, given that no other party was allowed to advertise in this bulletin.[50] In addition, the CVD's newspaper served for a time as Korntal's official community gazette.[51]

The Nazis did not underestimate the CSVD, viewing it as their strongest opposition in Korntal. There were anti-Nazi articles throughout the group's newspapers (*Christlich-soziale Blätter*, CSB; *Christlicher Volksdienst*, CV) – some of them triggered by the NSDAP's strong opposition to religious political parties. Wilhelm Simpfendörfer stated openly at the time of the CSVD's founding that the greatest dangers to the German state were left-wing and right-wing radicalism. The party openly opposed the extremes of Bolshevism and fascism.[52] By its own formulation, it wished to be "just Christian." Yet the CSVD did see some "good" in the NSDAP and found points in common with its own political aims. Even in several of the strongest anti-Nazi articles, it was noted that the CSVD could agree with the Nazis on conservative and nationalist desires: the rejection of Germany's war guilt, "family values," and the purification of cultural and political life.[53]

While there was a perceived similarity of political goals, there was also differentiation as to the methods for achieving them. Bausch wrote of his belief that the CSVD, like the Nazi Party, had emerged from the experience of the war and was fighting for moral values and against "the politics of class and interests." But while the Nazis sought a "racial" community, the Christian party's vision was of a society under God, bound together by Christian faith.[54] What CSVD writers could not abide was the NSDAP's basis in hatred, its violence, and its anti-Christian attitude.

Simpfendörfer, in response to a Nazi attack on the csvd, counter-attacked the Nazis' claim to be supporting a "Christianity of deed." National Socialism cultivated hatred, and thus he called it a "blasphemy" for "hate-filled" Nazis to claim that they stood for Christianity, in light of Christ's commandment to love one's enemies. "Blasphemy" was an extremely powerful term to use when addressing conservative Christian readers, for it indicated that something was both obscene and fundamentally against God. The cv challenged the Nazi claim to "positive Christianity"; one contributor believed that its "practical meaning [was] cloaked in an openly intended mystical darkness." Such articles showed the group itself to be opponents of "hate-filled" Nazism. But the most influential publications in Korntal were the csvd pamphlets.[55]

They produced numerous pamphlets, but it is unclear how widely these were distributed in Korntal. However, we can confirm that there were two publications that were disseminated in Korntal, both of which attacked the Nazi Party. One was *The Swastika or Christ's Cross?* (1930), and the other was Paul Bausch's anti-Nazi pamphlet *What Is the Truth?* (1932). By Bausch's own account, this latter pamphlet was delivered "fresh from the printer" to every inhabitant of Korntal, including Christian Mergenthaler, an influential Nazi.[56] Though *The Swastika or Christ's Cross?* was published anonymously, it seems likely that Bausch wrote it, for he used sections of it in his 1932 publication *What Is the Truth?*

The Swastika or Christ's Cross? was produced around the time of the 1930 national elections (when the Nazis won 107 seats in the *Reichstag*). Bausch observed that "broad sections of the populace stare – as if hypnotised – at the banner of the swastika, hoping that it will bring salvation," and part of the pamphlet's purpose was political, aiming to win over Protestants from voting National Socialist.[57] However, it was also written out of a genuine concern that Nazism was fundamentally anti-Christian.[58] This was an attempt to understand and counter the reasons why Protestants were turning to Nazism. To that end, Bausch identified four major factors: a belief that the Nazis were "protectors" of Christianity, the political nature of Hitler (and people's capacity to see what they wished to), sheer faith in the Nazis' capacity to revive Germany, and an indifference to or even support for antisemitism, based on the widespread acceptance of a "Jewish question." He also believed that many people were turning to the Nazi Party out of despair, owing to Germany's political and economic situation.

Bausch began by noting that the Nazis were winning ever greater numbers of adherents, especially among Protestants, partly due to blind hope: "Yes, even faithful Christians ... see Adolf Hitler and his following as the saviours of Germany."[59] The problem that many Protestants agreed with right-wing groups had been acknowledged by 1925. At that time, Wilhelm Simpfendörfer cited Adam Röder, a Christian conservative, who wrote that "the politics of the current right-wingers are *not* oriented towards Christianity," and who saw such people as either materialistic or heading toward a "cleaned-up cult of Odin" and "flirting with a 'German god,' a 'German religion.'"[60]

Bausch recognized that Christians were asking: "But doesn't National Socialism profess a positive Christianity?" This was based on Point 24 of the Nazi Program, the second paragraph of which began "the Party as such stands for a positive Christianity."[61] Yet Nazis themselves placed greater emphasis on the first paragraph, which derived from the original *Grundsatz* (party platform) of the Nazi Party: "We demand freedom for all religious confessions in the state so long as they do not endanger its existence or offend the ethical and moral feelings of the Germanic race."[62] Bausch pointed out that nearly every German political party paid at least "lip service" to being Christian, and he compared the Nazi Party to Satan: "Satan is also 'religious.' He also appears in the raiment of an angel of light. By their fruits shall you know them! [Matthew 7:15–17]."

Bausch sought to examine the "fruits" of Nazism against "the word of God," arguing that "Christ is the Lord of Christians also in politics!" and that Christians remained bound to the gospel.[63] He attacked the idea that Nazis were "protectors of religion and Christianity," and already by 1930 he believed it was clear that the fruits of Nazism were brutality, hatred, and violence. His criticism was also based on what he saw to be the foundational ideas of Nazism, for which he relied on articles from the *Völkischer Beobachter* (*VB*), on statements by leading Nazis, and on writers whose works had influenced Nazi ideology: Paul de Lagarde, Houston Stewart Chamberlain, and Hans F.K. Günther.[64]

Based on such publications, he described National Socialism as a racial utopianism where people were categorized according to whether they belonged to a "superior" or "inferior" race. He also described the Nazi belief that superior races were perfect so long as they maintained a purity of blood. He quoted Hans Günther's view that "pure-blooded ancient Germans were fundamentally capable, fundamentally good, and not originally sinful"; from this, Günther argued that the Christian conception of original sin was only appropriate to a "morally dubious people like the Jews."[65] This formed part of a larger discussion of "Jewry," in which Günther argued that "original sin" could only arise from a race "that acknowledges it has questionable blood, that feels as a whole that in the blood-inheritance itself there is something terrible." Although Bausch did not cite this, Günther even argued that "alien Christian morality" had corrupted Germanic concepts.[66]

Bausch did quote a contemporary Nazi article stating that "the Teuton" was "a heroic example in every age" and possessed a "healthy world-view." The same article claimed that following "the collapse" in the First World War, "[a] miracle occurred: a kind God sent the *Volk* a saviour. Adolf Hitler rose up and created a new confession for the German *Volk* in National Socialism."[67] Bausch rejected these ideas outright, noting that "Christianity teaches otherwise" in the doctrine of original sin and that to take God's grace and salvation and attribute it to race was materialistic. He preferred to stand with Martin Luther, and quoted him: "I wish to be in a church … in which there are the weak and sick and those of little courage, who recognise their sin, sorrow and wretchedness."[68]

It was precisely the focus on race that Bausch believed was leading National Socialists into viewing "the fatherland" as a new god, so that the core of National Socialism was pagan: "religious glorification of the fatherland is completely of pagan origin." He cited another Nazi article that talked of the "German century" in which "the heroic body and spirit of a *Volk* will rise from the ruins of an ancient world, [and] will march across the Earth under the symbol of the victorious sun."[69] The Nazis' radicalism, aggressive militarism, and "pagan intoxication with a materialistic race-fanaticism" were contrasted to the CSVD's "old conservatism [built] upon the Christian responsibility for a *Volk* given by God." This rejection of racism in conjunction with a belief in God-created peoples can be traced back to the early days of the CSG, which rejected "all class- and race-hatred" while simultaneously holding that the German *Volk* was a "God-given, indispensable member in the ranks of the peoples … with its own German character, German homeland and independence." By contrast, the Nazis were preaching a determinist "gospel of race and power" in which spiritual matters became "a function of blood."[70]

The same point was made by leading Nazis like Hans Schemm, who became minister of culture after the "seizure of power" in 1933. While he opposed the notion of Nazism as "race materialism," Schemm believed in the "racial soul" and that "spiritual values" and the "form of soul" were intrinsically bound to and carried "with the blood." This was the same kind of ethnotheism expressed by other Nazis, and Schemm argued directly that "morality is obedience to the laws of blood."[71]

In opposing the Nazis' racial ideology, Bausch rejected their "excessive, un-Christian hatred of the Jews." The use of the term "excessive" indicated an acceptance of the idea that there was a "Jewish question" in Germany.[72] But here, too, we must recognize the complexity of what this meant. For leading Nazis, the "Jewish question" was fundamental to their worldview, and it consisted of a core paranoid belief that there was a racial struggle between "culture-creating Aryans" and "culture-destroying Jews" and an international "Jewish conspiracy" to dominate the world. Nazi leaders believed that this "battle" had been going on since ancient times, that it was being fought through "blood intermixture," and that it had led to the ruin of the supposedly "Aryan" civilizations of the ancient Greeks, Persians, and Romans. They also believed that Jews were using Freemasonry, Bolshevism, and Christianity as tools for their own ends. All of these ideas can be readily found in Hitler's writings and speeches.[73] He was remarkably consistent in arguing that "the Jew" had become the "greatest promoter" of Christianity in order to destroy the state, arguing this from 1920 through to 1941: "Christianity was the Proto-Bolshevism, the mobilisation of the enslaved masses by the Jews for the purpose of undermining the state."[74]

Bausch was a man of his time, and he grasped that many Germans – Christians among them – accepted the idea of a "Jewish question," a supposedly "excessive" Jewish influence in German public life, and that cosmopolitan or modernist views were having a negative impact on cultural life. On this level too, the Nazis were able to exploit assumptions and prejudices.[75] The belief that Jews in Germany wielded an "undue influence" was rife. They certainly played a role in the five "rationalizations" identified by Beck in considering why Protestant leaders made no open statement against Nazi antisemitic violence in 1933.[76] One prominent Protestant figure, Otto

Dibelius, defended the Nazi boycott of Jewish businesses (1 April 1933) partly out of a belief in the "extraordinary degree" of Jewish influence in law, politics, and the civil service.[77] *The Swastika or Christ's Cross?* argued that even if a person sought to defend his position by arguing "with complete correctness" that Jews exercised "an excessive, largely disastrous influence" in "contemporary public life, in trade, in industry … in public opinion, in theatre and art," the "hatred that is cultivated by National Socialism can never be approved of."[78]

These points may have links to the religious antisemitism of the Christian Socialists, whose founder Adolf Stöcker was later described as a Nazi precursor.[79] Indeed, Reinhard Mumm (leader of the Christian Socialists) stated that the CSVD's work was "the struggle against the Jewish-bolshevist destruction of all Christian cultural life." This was after the amalgamation of the Christian Socialists with the CVD and clearly represented one side's views.[80] Bausch claimed that the antisemitism "in which Stöcker had been in error" played no part in the CSVD, but it had played at least some role at its inception.[81]

The Christian Socialist pamphlet accepted the idea of excessive Jewish influence in Germany but did not accept the Nazis' "most bitter, venomous hatred" and persecution of "Jews as foreigners, as members of an inferior race," arguing that this was the opposite of Christian views and that Nazism "through its racial hatred places the Jews outside of any ethics."[82] A strong contrast was drawn between Christian teachings "that no person is irredeemable" and "National Socialist racial teaching" that Jews would never be able to redeem themselves, but would always be bound by "their Jewish blood." Hence, Nazism was rejected on the grounds of brotherly love: "Following Christian teachings all of humankind emanates from the creative desire of God; Christianity teaches the equality of all people. Hatred – in any form – against other people is to be rejected as un-Christian."[83]

Bausch rejected hatred itself as un-Christian and disparaged the Nazis for their "brutal violence." Violence, he believed, would also come to be used in enforcing ideas such as those of Wilhelm Frick, education minister in Thuringia, whom Bausch cited as wishing to remove anything relating to the Old Testament from schools.[84] Frick was the first Nazi to be made a minister, and he served as an interesting example of how the Nazis might operate in government, with his ideas about fighting "Negro" culture, destroying "degenerate" art, and maintaining racial purity.[85] Frick was viewed as a rather comical figure by *The Times*, which reported that he had issued a decree that "aims at 'de-jazzing' Thuringia and attempts to put into practice the peculiar political beliefs of his party ... that all ills come from Jews, Jesuits, Freemasons, foreigners, Socialist and Communists."[86]

The Times also reported that Frick had launched a motion to achieve the Nazis' racial goals, which "would imprison for 'racial treason those who injure or impede the natural fertility of the German race or who by interbreeding with members of the Jewish or coloured races contribute to the racial deterioration and disintegration of the German people.'" In addition, it was reported that "in Thuringia, if the National-Socialists have their way, religious instruction in the Old Testament is to be cut to a minimum because of its essentially Jewish character."[87]

Frick had become infamous for such statements, including five controversial prayers that he proposed for use in schools, three of which were later quoted by the Nazi leader Gottfried Feder.[88] These "German school prayers" were "recommended" in an official ministerial bulletin. Frick's introduction in the bulletin was clearly antisemitic: "For a long time, forces that are foreign to our nation and race have sought to destroy the spiritual-moral-religious foundations of our German thought and feeling, in order to uproot the German *Volk* and to make it much easier to rule."[89]

The "German school-prayers" were widely reviled as anti-Christian (including by the CSVD), partly because of their attacks on "Marxists and Jews."[90] The prayers also illustrated the complex relationship between Christians and Nazism, as the authors (though anonymous) apparently included "a Protestant Pastor," a "Protestant teacher," and "a Catholic teacher."[91] All of the prayers were nationalistic, and many writers pointed out that a major emphasis was hatred.[92] Indeed, some believed that the authors could only be "genuine National Socialists," that their prayers "slapped the spirit of Christianity in the face," and that "the National Socialists will never grasp, that their teaching of hatred and pride, that their pseudo-scientific Materialism has absolutely nothing to do with Christianity. When they say God, they blaspheme Him."[93]

Referring to the prayer controversy, Bausch concluded that Frick's ideas were so far removed from Christianity that all that was left was to get schoolchildren to pray to "the old Germanic god Wotan." He quoted Frick as stating that part of his task was "as far as possible to remove Old Testament materials from schools."[94] In stark contrast, Bausch argued that Christians saw "the revelation of God in the Old Testament." Rather than rejecting the Old Testament, Christians rejected "worship of one's 'ancestors,'" which Bausch believed was advocated in one of the "German" prayers: "I believe in the strength and honour of our ancestors."[95]

Because of these kinds of views and statements of faith, Bausch saw National Socialism as an ersatz religion. He believed that it was becoming a religion and that its ideology was creating the basis for a religion of "race." Reminding readers that "the First Commandment reads 'I am the Lord your God, you shall have no other gods before me,'" Bausch asked them to compare this to the "salvational doctrine of National Socialism," which claimed that "we SA-men live in the spirit of our Adolf Hitler. The sermons of our speakers fill the stores of our soul with strength."[96] For Bausch, taking the "fatherland as religion" meant raising "the state, nation, and race" to objects of worship, so that it became "paganism and idolatry." This is not to say that the CSVD rejected the importance of the state or the nation – rather, these were subordinate to Christian faith. It was on this basis that Bausch rejected Nazi revolutionary views: "Christianity is in any case *fundamentally anti-revolutionary*. Whoever is a Christian must reject any violent overthrow of legal order."[97] He made it very clear that the NSDAP was antisemitic and violent and that it sought to overthrow the state.

There was also a sense of futility in Bausch's pamphlet, for he stated (in some despair) that the belief in the rise of a "glorious Third Reich" appeared to have robbed many Protestants and pastors of their critical judgment. He readily identified that part of the problem was that Hitler was politically astute and willing to adapt himself and his policies to his audience. This has led some authors to describe Hitler as a "religious chameleon."[98] Bausch's larger point was that the uncertainty about what Hitler actually meant to do should cause Christians a great deal of concern, both because of the inherent dishonesty that this implied and because many of his statements and actions were un-Christian. Thus, Bausch asked who the "real" Hitler was: the man who swore "to uphold the Weimar Constitution, or the revolutionary?" Even more troubling, would Hitler prove to be a leader who confessed to "positive Christianity" or an opponent of Christian faith "who calls the Book of Books the Bible of Satan"?[99]

On this last point, Bausch appears to have confused Hitler with his mentor, Dietrich Eckart, who wrote in the *Völkischer Beobachter* in 1921: "To the Devil with the Jewish influence on our Christian tradition, so that – as Kant once said – we can finally have religion. Tear the evil Bible of Satan, the *Old Testament*, to shreds!"[100] Eckart was referring to Kant's views on Judaism in *Religion within the Limits of Reason Alone* (1793). There, Kant argued several points that later became common among antisemites in Germany, including the idea that "Judaism was really not a religion at all, but merely a political entity," that it was "not essentially religious," that it was limited to "external acts" and "limiting reward and punishment to this world."[101]

Similar ideas could be found in Eugen Dühring and his writings on "the Jewish question." As George Mosse noted, Dühring's consideration was "in terms of racial categories," which meant that he "condemned the Jew as a whole, not just some of his characteristics," and that he "linked depravity in culture, morals and manners to inherent racial traits possessed by all Jews."[102] Dühring argued that the "religious communities of the Jews" were "political formations" and that "the religion of the Jew is a racial religion, just as the morality of the Jew is a racial morality."[103] The idea that the Jews were fundamentally "materialists" and *incapable* of religion could be found in any number of *völkisch* and antisemitic texts, including *Mein Kampf* and Houston Stewart Chamberlain's highly influential *Foundations of the Nineteenth Century*. In Hitler's view, Jewish religious precepts had no moral or religious value whatsoever, as they were supposedly just the means by which to keep "the blood of Jewry pure."[104] By 1930, Bausch had concluded that there was an "irreconcilable opposition between Christianity and National Socialism." This later appeared prescient, given Martin Bormann's statement of 9 June 1941: "National Socialist and Christian concepts are irreconcilable."[105]

What this chapter has demonstrated is that groups with remarkably different theological bases could come to similar conclusions about the Nazi Party by 1933. In a manner comparable to that of the theologically liberal Temple-Society, Brethren members understood that the Nazi Party was revolutionary and antisemitic and that it might form a replacement faith or ersatz religion. This last point was in line with several other assessments at the time. Yet the Korntal Brethren, like others in Württemberg, were attracted to the "Protestant experience" of 1933 – the notion that Germany was experiencing both a national and church revival under the Nazis.[106] Members of the Brethren were certainly attracted to many of the perceived "benefits" of the Nazi state that had proved attractive to other Christians in Germany: a supposed return to morality, traditional family values, and law and order, as well as a regime that promised "to clear the streets of vice and corruption, prostitution, pornography, and homosexuality."[107]

Interestingly, there were also two strong ideological "constants" in Nazism that critics had identified in the 1930s: a diversity of forms of religious belief (including paganism), together with a commonly accepted notion that race was the sole "arbiter" or defining characteristic of *religiosity*. Critics viewed this ideological constant as the "glorification of race"; the Nazis repeatedly spoke of it in terms of the "racial soul." Such ethnotheism was clearly part of the Nazi program. This attempt to turn ethnonationalism into the font of religion was also a principally negative ethic in practice. It created new religions and religious positions by attacking anything deemed "Jewish," up to and including Christianity as a whole.

NOTES

1 Manfred Gailus, "Overwhelmed by Their Own Fascination with the 'Ideas of 1933': Berlin's Protestant Social Milieu in the Third Reich," *German History* 20, no. 4 (2002): 462–93; Manfred Gailus, *Kirchengemeinden im Nationalsozialismus: Sieben Beispiele aus Berlin* (Berlin: Hentrich, 1990); Kyle Jantzen, *Faith and Fatherland: Parish Politics in Hitler's Germany* (Minneapolis: Fortress Press, 2008).

2 Klaus Scholder, *The Churches and the Third Reich: Preliminary History and the Time of Illusions, 1918–1933*, vol. 1 (London: SCM Press, 1987), 135.

3 A work that consolidates much of the research is Robert P. Ericksen, *Complicity in the Holocaust: Churches and Universities in Nazi Germany* (New York: Cambridge University Press, 2012).

4 Henry Smith Leiper, *Personal View of the German Churches under the Revolution: A Confidential Report based on Intimate Personal Contact with the Leaders on both Sides of the Church and State Controversy in the Third Reich* (New York: American Section, Universal Christian Council for Life and Work, 1933). On such efforts to rewrite Christian theology, see Susannah Heschel, *The Aryan Jesus: Christian Theologians and the Bible in Nazi Germany* (Princeton: Princeton University Press, 2008); and Doris L. Bergen, *Twisted Cross: The German Christian Movement in the Third Reich* (Chapel Hill: University of North Carolina Press, 1996).

5 Leiper, *Personal View of the German Churches*, 12.

6 The best account of the Korntal Brethren in the Weimar era and Nazi period is Hartmut Lehmann, *Pietismus und weltliche Ordnung in Württemberg
   vom 17. bis zum 20. Jahrhundert*. (Stuttgart: W. Kohlhammer, 1969), 338–41. I
   use the term "fundamentalist" to indicate that the Brethren believed in a literal interpretation of the Bible, which included a strong belief in being able
   to interpret contemporary events through the Scriptures and to predict the
   return of Christ. They consistently opposed liberal theology or rationalist
   trends within the church.

7 Samuel Koehne, "Nazism, Political Religion, and 'Ordinary' Germans,"
   Agora 49, no. 3 (2014): 21–8.

8 Hans Maeir, *Totalitarismus und politische Religionen: Konzepte des Diktatur-
   vergleichs*, vol. 2 (Paderborn: Ferdinand Schöningh, 1996); Michael
   Burleigh, *Sacred Causes: The Clash of Religion and Politics, from the Great
   War to the War on Terror* (London: HarperCollins, 2007).

9 Interestingly, other small groups formed around a shared common "faith"
   could also form a node of resistance to Nazi ideas, See Mark Roseman's
   consideration of the leftist *Bund*, a "circle of vegetarian, teetolating utopi-
   ans," and their opposition to Nazi rule. Roseman, *Lives Reclaimed: A Story
   of Rescue and Resistance in Nazi Germany* (Oxford: Oxford University
   Press, 2019).

10 Protokolle, 5 March 1937 and 26 April 1937, Brüdergemeinderatsprotokoll
   (BRP).

11 *Wegweiser von Korntal* 6 (1930): 2; *Aus der Jugendzeit (AdJ)* JG-7 (1919): 4;
   Evangelisches Gemeindeblatt Korntal (EGK) (March 1919): 4.

12 *1. Kreiskongreß der* NSDAP, *Kreis Leonberg*, Special Edition, *Leonberger Tagblatt* (1934): 3. See File SAM101, Stadtarchiv Korntal-Münchingen (SAKM)
   (hereafter NSDAP-*Kreiskongreß*). Two leading figures were Wilhelm Hilden-
   brand (who arrived in Korntal in 1915) and Friedrich Kochendörfer (who
   arrived in 1922).

13 NSDAP-*Kreiskongreß*: 3; Protokolle, 22 July 1924, 19 May 1925, 5 June 1925, 30
   June 1925, Korntal Gemeinderatsprotokoll (KGRP). See also Letters, 26 June
   1925 and 8 July 1925, NSDAP to Korntal Council, file KB14, SAKM; file PL
   504/29, SAL.

14 *Wegweiser* Nr. 1 (1924): 3; "Rücktritt des Gemeindevorstehers Daur von
   Ortsvorsteher," 24 February 1922, file 12c, Korntal Brethren Archive (KBA);
   "Neuwahl eines Ortvorstehers Korntal," 27 June 1922, file E 180 II Bü 755, SAL.

15 The mayor spoke publicly of this as Korntal's character: *AdJ* JG-18, nos. 3–4 (1930): 39.

16 Günther Opitz, *Der Christlich-soziale Volksdienst: Versuch einer protestanti-schen Partei in der Weimarer Republik* (Düsseldorf: Droste Verlag, 1969); Heinz Sproll, "Katholische und evangelische Parteien in Württemberg seit dem 19. Jahrhundert," in *Die CDU in Baden-Württemberg und ihre Geschichte*, ed. Paul-Ludwig (Stuttgart: W. Kohlhammer, 1978), 71–80. The group changed from the *Christlich-soziale Gesinnungsgemeinschaft* (1924) to CVD (1925) to the CSVD (1929).

17 *AdJ* JG-10, nos. 1–2 (1922): 7; *Wegweiser* 4 (1927): 18–19.

18 Shaul Baumann, *Die Deutsche Glaubensbewegung und ihr Gründer Jakob Wilhelm Hauer*, trans. Alma Lessing (Marburg: Diagonal, 2005); Irving Hexham and Karla Poewe, "Jakob Wilhelm Hauer's New Religion and National Socialism," *Journal of Contemporary Religion* 20, no. 2 (2005): 195–215; Karla O. Poewe, *New Religions and the Nazis* (New York: Routledge, 2006).

19 EGK (August 1930): 4. See also EGK (November 1931): 3; EGK (August 1932): 1–2; *AdJ* JG-19 (1931): 41.

20 EGK (November 1931): 3; (August 1932): 1–2; Protokolle, 25 November 1931; 30 December 1931; 15 January 1932; 18 March 1932; 30 March 1932; 7 April 1932; and 13 May 1932, BRP.

21 NSDAP-*Kreiskongreß*, 7; Michael Stolle, "Der schwäbische Schulmeister: Christian Mergenthaler, Württembergischer Ministerpräsident Justiz- und Kultminister," 452. *Alte Kämpfer* joined the NSDAP before 1933, and an *Ortsgruppe* required twenty-five members.

22 NSDAP-*Kreiskongreß*, 6.

23 Ibid., 9.

24 Hartmut Lehmann, "The Germans as a Chosen People: Old Testament Themes in German Nationalism," *German Studies Review* 14, no. 2 (1991): 261–73, here 269.

25 On "positive Christianity" and the extraordinary confusion that has arisen from Richard Steigmann-Gall's characterization of "positive Christianity," see Samuel Koehne, "Nazism and Religion: The Problem of "Positive Christianity,'" *Australian Journal of Politics and History* 60, no. 1 (2014): 28–42.

26 *Allgemeine Rundschau* (1923), folder 1466 *Hauptarchiv der* NSDAP, Hoover Institution on War, Revolution, and Peace (hereafter HA-folder#).

27 See the 1923 article "Wodankultus," *Bayerischer Kurier*, HA-1466.

28 Alfons Steiger, *Der neudeutsche Heide im Kampf gegen Christen und Juden*, 2nd ed. (Berlin: Germania, 1924), 185–8.

29 Samuel Koehne, "The Racial Yardstick: 'Ethnotheism' and Official Nazi Views on Religion," *German Studies Review* 37, no. 3 (2014): 575–96.

30 *Der Stürmer* 15 (April 1938). See also Heschel, *The Aryan Jesus*.

31 Othmar Plöckinger, *Geschichte eines Buches: Adolf Hitlers "Mein Kampf"* *1922–1945* (Munich: R. Oldenbourg, 2006), 272; *Kirchliches Jahrbuch 1932*, 65–6; Richard Karwehl, "Politisches Messiastum: Zur Auseinandersetzung zwischen Kirche und Nationalsozialismus," in *Zwischen den Zeiten: Eine Zweimonatsschrift*, ed. Georg Merz (Munich: Christian Kaiser, 1931), 526.

32 Scholder, *The Churches and the Third Reich*, vol. 1. 135.

33 The initial newspaper for the CSG was the *Christlich-soziale Blätter* (CSB, 1924–26), then came the paper of the CVD and CSVD: *Christlicher Volksdienst* (CV, 1927–33). Wilhelm Simpfendörfer was editor from 1925, the previous editor being Arthur Staege. The CSB yearbooks ran from August to August. I have used the original numbering.

34 CSB 1 (1924): 3. See also David Diephouse, *Pastors and Pluralism in Württemberg, 1918–1933* (Princeton: Princeton University Press, 1987), 286.

35 CSB JG-1 (1924): 1–3; it was also the CVD's slogan: *Was will der Christliche Volksdienst?*, 4.

36 *NSDAP-Kreiskongreß*, 2–3; file PL 501 I Bü 11, SAL.

37 Paul Bausch, *Lebenserinnerungen und Erkenntnisse eines schwäbischen Abgeordneten* (Korntal: P. Bausch, 1969): 75. There was opposition to the CVD by some of the CSG's founding members (including Georg Michaelis and Samuel Jaeger), who rejected the idea of a Christian party (72, 78–9). On the amalgamation with the Christian Socialists, see CV JG-6, no. 1 (1930): 1–3; *Um die neue Front*. For their goals, see *Was will der Christliche Volksdienst?*, 1–4.

38 CSB JG-1 (1924): 5, 21; CV JG-4, no. 3 (1928): 1; CV JG-6, no. 1 (1930): 3–4; (1930): 3.

39 CV JG-6:1 (1930): 1, 3; *Um die neue Front*, 11.

40 On spiritual–moral crisis, see CV JG-6, no. 3 (1930): 3; JG-6, no. 4 (1930): 3; JG-6, no. 12 (1930): 1. On materialism and mammonism, see CSB JG-1 (1924): 21; JG-1 (1925): 27–8; CV JG-6, no. 3 (1930): 1; JG-6, no. 30 (1930): 2.

41 CSB JG-1 (1924): 5–6; CSB JG-1 (1925): 27; CV JG-6, no. 11 (1930): 1. On "cultural bolshevism," see CV JG-6, no. 1 (1930): 1; JG-6, no. 21 (1930): 3; JG-6, no. 30 (1930): 2.

42 CSB JG-1 (1924): 1; CSB JG-1 (1925): 24. On support for the party, see CV JG-6, no. 16 (1930): 3; JG-6, no. 10 (1930) (2nd ed.): 1. For "free church" support, see Karl Zehrer, *Evangelische Freikirchen und das "Dritte Reich"* (Göttingen: Vandenhoeck & Ruprecht, 1986), 15, 110, 135.

43 File 29e, KBA, CV JG-6, no. 35 (1930): 4.

44 *Was will der Christliche Volksdienst?*(Korntal: Reichsgeschäftsstelle des Christlichen Volksdienstes, 1927), 3.

45 CV JG-6, no. 4 (1930): 3. On temporal-spiritual duty, see CV JG-6, no. 2 (1930): 3.

46 CV JG-4, no. 4 (1928): 2. See also CV JG-6, no. 30 (1930): 2. On participation in the Republic and opposition to revolution, see CV JG-4, no. 17 (1928): 1; JG-6, no. 1 (1930): 2; CV JG-6, no. 3 (1930): 3.

47 CV JG-4, no. 5 (1928): 1; JG-4, no. 17 (1928): 1; JG-6, no. 3 (1930): 1. CSB JG-1 (1925): 39.

48 The NSDAP had been a minor party in the parliament. It won 14 seats in the Reichstag in 1924 and 12 seats in 1928. In 1930, during economic crisis, it won 107 seats.

49 The CV and most pamphlets were published in Korntal. After the 1929 coalition with the Christian Socialists, Paul Bausch proudly declared the CVD's connection to Korntal and the Brethren; see CV JG-6, no. 2 (1930): 3. In Korntal, support was expressed for those considered "Christian politicians": EGK (February 1920): 4; *AdJ* JG-12 (1924): 38–9.

50 *Für alle Korntaler* JG-2, no. 1 (1927); Lehmann, *Pietismus in Württemberg*, 306, 313, 319.

51 Protokolle, 23 December 1926, 15 March 1927, and 5 April 1927, KGRP.

52 CV JG-6, no. 3 (1930): 3; JG-6, no. 10 (1930): 3. Other right-wing groups were also attacked, such as *Stahlhelm* and the DNVP: CV JG-4, no. 10 (1928): 1–2; JG-4, no. 15 (1928): 1–2; JG-4, no. 40 (1928): 1; JG-4, no. 43 (1928): 1. On their "anti-Marxist" attitude, see CV JG-6, no. 7 (1930): 1; JG-6, no. 9 (1930): 1; Gustav Hülser, *Der Christlich-soziale Volksdienst und die Parteien* (Berlin: Reichsgeschäftstelle des Christlich-Sozialen Volksdienstes, 1931), 7–8. The Catholic Centre Party was a Nazi target, as was the CSVD. On this point, see Alfred Rosenberg, *Blut und Ehre: Ein Kampf für deutsche Wiedergeburt; Reden und Aufsätze von 1919–1933*, ed. Thilo von Trotha, 7th ed. (Munich: Zentralverlag der NSDAP, 1935), 61–4.

53 CV JG-6, no. 21 (1930), (2nd ed.): 1. See also CV JG-6, no. 50 (1930): 1.

54 Bausch, *Lebenserinnerungen und Erkenntnisse eines schwäbischen Abgeordneten*, 315.

55 CV JG-6, no. 21 (1930) (2nd ed.): 1; Hülser, *Der Christlich-soziale Volksdienst und die Parteien*, 12. See also CV JG-6, no. 50 (1930): 1; JG-6, no. 52 (1930): 3.

56 *Hakenkreuz oder Christuskreuz?*, file 29c, KBA; Bausch, *Lebenserinnerungen und Erkenntnisse eines schwäbischen Abgeordneten*, 104, 315–16 (*Was ist Wahrheit?*).

57 *Hakenkreuz oder Christuskreuz? Eine ernste Frage an die evangelische Christenheit* (Korntal: Christlicher Volksdienst Verlag, 1930), 1.

58 Bausch, *Lebenserinnerungen und Erkenntnisse eines schwäbischen Abgeordneten*, 93, 101.

59 *Hakenkreuz oder Christuskreuz?*, 1. It is well-established that a greater proportion of Protestants voted for the Nazis than Catholics. On this point, see Manfred Gailus, "1933 als protestantisches Erlebnis: Emphatische Selbsttransformation und Spaltung," *Geschichte und Gesellschaft* 29, no. 4 (2003): 481–511. Wolfram Pyta, *Dorfgemeinschaft und Parteipolitik 1918–1933: Die Verschränkung von Milieu und Parteien in den protestantischen Landgebieten Deutschlands in der Weimarer Republik* (Düsseldorf: Droste, 1996), 324–432; and Thomas Childers, *The Nazi Voter: The Social Foundations of Fascism in Germany, 1919–1923* (Chapel Hill: University of North Carolina Press, 1983), 188–91.

60 CSB JG-1 (1925): 27–8. Also see CV JG-6, no. 1 (1930): 3. Röder pointed out it was extraordinarily superficial for Nazis to identify Jews with capital finance: CV JG-6, no. 15 (1930) (2nd ed.): 1. See Adam Röder, *Reaktion und Antisemitismus, zugleich ein Mahnwort an die akademische Jugend*, 2nd ed. (Berlin: C.A. Schwetschke & Sohn, 1921).

61 *Hakenkreuz oder Christuskreuz?*, 1.

62 Koehne, "The Racial Yardstick," 576, 580–2.

63 *Hakenkreuz oder Christuskreuz?*, 1.

64 All of these were major influences on Nazi ideology; see Geoffrey G. Field, *Evangelist of Race: The Germanic Vision of Houston Stewart Chamberlain* (New York: Columbia University Press, 1981); and Elvira Weisenburger, "Der 'Rassepapst': Hans Friedrich Karl Günther, Professor für Rassenkunde," in *Die Führer der Provinz: NS-Biographien aus Baden und Württemberg*, eds. Michael Kißener and Joachim Scholtyseck (Konstanz: Universitätsverlag Konstanz, 1997), 161–99. On Lagarde, see Fritz Stern, *The Politics of Cultural Despair: A Study in the Rise of the Germanic Ideology* (Berkeley: University

of California Press, 1974), 35–94; and Uwe Puschner, Walter Schmitz, and Justus H. Ulbricht, eds, *Handbuch zur "Völkischen Bewegung," 1871–1918* (Munich: K.G. Saur, 1996), 45–93.

65 *Hakenkreuz oder Christuskreuz?*, 1; quoting Günther. This section can be found in Hans F.K. Günther, *Rassenkunde des deutschen Volkes* (Munich: J.F. Lehmann, 1922), 398–9.

66 Günther, *Rassenkunde des deutschen Volkes*, 398–9.

67 *Hakenkreuz oder Christuskreuz?*, 1–2, citing *Völkischer Beobachter* (VB) (15 February 1930).

68 *Hakenkreuz oder Christuskreuz?*, 1–2. By contrast, other Protestants used Luther's statements against Jews and linked these to racial antisemitism. On this point, see Christopher J. Probst, *Demonizing the Jews: Luther and the Protestant Church in Nazi Germany* (Bloomington: Indiana University Press, in association with the United States Holocaust Memorial Museum, 2012).

69 *Hakenkreuz oder Christuskreuz?*, 2. citing VB (10 May 1930). This referred to the swastika; the raising of the swastika flag for the Munich Putsch had also been described as the "victory of the sun." VB (9 November 1923).

70 *Hakenkreuz oder Christuskreuz?*, 2. He argued the "insanity" of the desire for "German world-domination in the advent of the Third Reich," VB (3 May 1930).

71 Hans Schemm, *Hans Schemm spricht: Seine Reden und sein Werk*, ed. G. Kahl-Furthmann (Bayreuth: Gauverlag Bayerische Ostmark, 1935), 49–50.

72 One work published in the First World War considered the "Jewish Question" as a European phenomenon and argued that there had been "manifold expressions of antisemitism in public life" before the war. See Max Simon, *Der Weltkrieg und die Judenfrage* (Leipzig: B.G. Teubner, 1916), 7–8. The same book argued that the defeat of Germany "would in no way mean the destruction of German antisemitism," but the contrary (79).

73 For example, see Hitler's chapter on "Volk and Race" in *Mein Kampf* (Munich: Franz Eher/Zentralverlag der NSDAP, 1936), 311–62.

74 See Hitler's speeches of 13 August 1920 in Adolf Hitler, *Sämtliche Aufzeichnungen: 1905–1924*, eds. Eberhard Jäckel and Axel Kuhn (Stuttgart: Deutsche Verlags-Anstalt, 1980), 191–2; and Richard C. Carrier, "Hitler's Table Talk: Troubling Finds," *German Studies Review* 26, no. 3 (2003): 561–76, here 571–2. Carrier queried this 1941 statement, but it is entirely in line with Hitler's early views.

75 Shulamit Volkov, "Antisemitism as a Cultural Code: Reflections on the History and Historiography of Antisemitism in Imperial Germany," *Leo Baeck Institute Yearbook* 23, no. 1 (1978): 25–46.

76 Hermann Beck, "Anti-Semitic Violence 'from Below': Attacks and Protestant Church Responses in Germany in 1933," *Politics, Religion, and Ideology* 14, no. 3 (2013): 395–411. Another powerful aspect was "outright fear of incurring Nazi wrath" (408), which was presumably only heightened by acts of violence.

77 Wolfgang Gerlach, *And the Witnesses Were Silent: The Confessing Church and the Persecution of the Jews*, trans. Victoria Barnett (Lincoln: University of Nebraska Press, 2000), 13–16. Dibelius was General Superintendent in Berlin.

78 *Hakenkreuz oder Christuskreuz?*, 2.

79 EGK (December 1935): 1–3; he was called a "Christian National Socialist" (1). Also see CV JG-4:, no. 3 (1928): 1; Günther Brakelmann, Martin Günther, Martin Greschat, and Werner Jochmann, eds. *Protestantismus und Politik: Werk und Wirkung Adolf Stoeckers* (Hamburg: Christians, 1982).

80 CV JG-6, no. 3 (1930): 2; CV JG-6, no. 12 (1930): 3.

81 Bausch, *Lebenserinnerungen und Erkenntnisse eines schwäbischen Abgeordneten*, 88.

82 *Hakenkreuz oder Christuskreuz?*, 2.

83 Ibid.

84 Ibid., 3. The Old Testament was defended in an article about neo-paganism: CV JG-6, no. ,21 (1930): 1.

85 Donald Tracey, "The Development of the National Socialist Party in Thuringia, 1924–30," *Central European History* 8, no. 1 (1975): 23–50, here 43 and 45. There was a "struggle with the University of Jena" over appointing Hans F.K. Günther to a position there. See *The Times*, 10 June 1930.

86 "De-Jazzing Thuringia," *The Times*, 10 April 1930, quoting Frick.

87 Ibid.

88 "Deutsches Schulgebet," *Amtsblatt des Thüringischen Ministeriums für Volksbildung"* 9, no. 6 (22 April 1930): 39–40; Gottfried Feder, *Hitler's Official Programme and Its Fundamental Ideas* (New York: H. Fertig, 1934), 122.

89 "Deutsches Schulgebet," 39–40.

90 Tracey, "The Development of the National Socialist Party in Thuringia," 23, 45. See reports on this issue in *The Times*, "Prayers and Politics in Thuringia," 25 April 1930; *Jenaer Volksblatt* 41 (25 April 1930).

91 "Deutsches Schulgebet," 40.

92 CV JG-6, no. 23 (1930), 2.

93 "Thüringische Streiflichter," *Jenaer Volksblatt* 41 (25 April 1930).

94 *Hakenkreuz oder Christuskreuz?*, 4; These ideas had already been part of antisemitic notions in the *Völkischer Beobachter:* Samuel Koehne, "Were the National Socialists a Völkisch Party? Paganism, Christianity and the Nazi Christmas," *Central European History* 47, no. 4 (2014): 760–90, here 773.

95 *Hakenkreuz oder Christuskreuz?*, 4.

96 Ibid.; citing VB, 18 February 1930.

97 *Hakenkreuz oder Christuskreuz?*, 2–3; relying on Romans 13.

98 Richard Weimkart emphasized the political aspect of Hitler's statements on religion in *Hitler's Religion: The Twisted Beliefs That Drove the Third Reich* (Washington, DC: Regnery History, 2016).

99 Bausch, *Lebenserinnerungen und Erkenntnisse eines schwäbischen Abgeordneten*, 315.

100 VB, 11 August 1921.

101 Translation in Sidney Axinn, "Kant on Judaism," *Jewish Quarterly Review* 59, no. 1 (1968): 9–23, here 9–10.

102 George L. Mosse, *The Crisis of German Ideology: Intellectual Origins of the Third Reich* (New York: Schocken Books, 1981), 131.

103 In Theoor Fritsch, *Antisemiten-Katechismus: Eine Zusammenstellung des wichstigsten Materials zum Verstaendniß der Judenfrage*, 25th ed. (Leipzig: Hermann Beyer, 1893), 94–5.

104 Adolf Hitler, *Mein Kampf*, trans. Ralph Manheim (London: Pimlico, 2004).

105 *Hakenkreuz oder Christuskreuz?*, 4; compare to Bormann in *Kirchliches Jahrbuch 1933–1944*, 450.

106 Manfred Gailus, "1933 als protestantisches Erlebnis: Emphatische Selbst-transformation und Spaltung," *Geschichte und Gesellschaft* 29, no., 4 (2003): 481–511.

107 Robert P. Ericksen, "Emerging from the Legacy? Protestant Churches and the 'Shoah,'" *Kirchliche Zeitgeschichte / Contemporary Church History* 17, no. 2 (2004): 360–1.

13

Ecumenical Protestant Responses to the Rise of Nazism, Fascism, and Antisemitism during the 1920s and 1930s

Victoria J. Barnett

The responses of the international Protestant ecumenical movement[1] to the rise of fascism and ethnonationalism after the First World War are relatively underexplored in the historiography of interwar Europe. Yet the ecumenical movement played a significant role during the Nazi era, and its interwar activities are essential for understanding its motives and strategies after 1933. With few exceptions, the criticisms of Nazi anti-Jewish policies that came from international Christian circles were from mainline Protestant church leaders and ecumenists.[2] The ecumenical world became particularly focused on the divisions within the German Protestant churches under Nazism. Throughout the 1930s, ecumenical representatives made frequent visits to Nazi Germany, and there were significant partnerships between ecumenists and Jewish organizations.[3]

Ecumenical engagement with events in Nazi Germany in the 1930s grew out of initiatives that had begun during the 1920s when ecumenical officials became involved in transnational efforts to address refugee issues and the strengthening of postwar peace. These activities led to ecumenical relationships across Europe with the different churches as well as with international Jewish and refugee organizations. Particularly after 1939, these connections made ecumenical offices important points of contact for the International Committee of the Red Cross, the Jewish Joint Distribution Committee, and the United States War Refugee Board.[4]

In many respects, the Protestant ecumenical movement between 1918 and 1945 offered a rare example of solidarity with the Jews of Europe; however, the record is complex. Ecumenical officials clearly opposed the various forms of nationalism and fascism that were taking root in the interwar period, and many of them became outspoken about the Nazis' anti-Jewish policies and involved themselves in refugee efforts. But their responses to events in Nazi Germany during the 1930s were complicated by competing agendas. First and foremost was their desire to prevent another European war, which, after some clear condemnations of Nazi policies in early 1933, led over time to greater caution and ambiguity in ecumenical statements. There was also much debate, particularly among German ecumenical officers in Switzerland, about how to assess and respond to the situation in Germany, as well as disagreement about whether and how to maintain ties to the opposing factions in the German Protestant church struggle. After 1939 the balancing act became even more delicate because of ecumenical connections to different resistance groups throughout Europe.[5]

Finally, although there were some notable ecumenical ties to Jewish organizations and their staffs, including the American Jewish Joint Distribution Committee and the World Jewish Congress,[6] Jews felt an immediate sense of urgency and vulnerability in 1933 that was not shared and often not understood by non-Jews. Particularly in the early period of National Socialism, Protestant ecumenists focused on what they saw as a twofold threat: (1) the threat to political civil liberties in the countries affected, and (2) the broader threat to European peace. Nor were ecumenists immune to the deeply rooted antisemitism that pervaded Christian theology and Western culture. Although several ecumenical statements before 1945 referenced the long Christian history of anti-Jewish teaching, only after 1945 was there a more widespread acknowledgment by Christian churches of the obvious link between that legacy and the openly Christian antisemitism of interwar ethnonationalist movements, notably the Deutsche Christen (German Christians) in Germany.

Ecumenists also tended to view discrimination against the Jews in the context of the broader persecution of religious minorities that occurred in some regions after the First World War. Even those who were outspoken about the persecution of German Jews sometimes showed a striking lack of sensitivity toward their Jewish colleagues and partners between 1933 and 1945. Indeed, all too often, Christian leaders, including ecumenical leaders, interpreted the threats to the Jewish community as one component of a broader threat to religion in general and Christianity in particular. As Uriel Tal noted in his introduction to *The Grey Book*, an early collection of ecumenical and church protests against Nazi anti-Jewish measures:

> The well-attested facts presented to us in this volume are a clear confirmation of the Church's repudiation of Nazi doctrines, not only when these doctrines were directed against the Jews but, first and foremost, when they threatened the very existence of the Church itself, both as a system of theological doctrines and beliefs and as an historical institution. The Church regards freedom, freedom of man as well as its own, as an inalienable right rooted in the nature of man as a rational being created in God's image. Hence, when the Church was deprived of the right of self-determination, it felt its very existence endangered, and it was then that it recognized the full symbolic import of the persecution of the Jews ... It is obvious that the Church was provoked to raise its voice in protest chiefly because the Nazis appropriated the messianic structure of religion which they exploited to their own ideological and political ends.[7]

It was only in the aftermath of the Holocaust that international church bodies and their leaders acknowledged the historical failures of Christian churches during the Nazi era as well as the deeper theological and historical roots of antisemitism.

This chapter examines these dynamics, focusing on how several issues that became central during the interwar period influenced subsequent ecumenical responses to National Socialism and the persecution and genocide of European Jews. This analysis begins with a brief overview of the ecumenical movement in the early twentieth century.

THE EARLY ECUMENICAL MOVEMENT

The ecumenical movement emerged as an interdenominational and international movement of Protestant churches, comprised primarily of representatives from the mainline Protestant churches in North America and the state Protestant churches in Europe. The birth of ecumenism coincided with the rise of the Social Gospel movement in the United States (which placed a theological emphasis on Christian social and political involvement as a public expression of faith) and the international pacifist movement, which in the wake of the First World War consisted of both religious and non-religious organizations. Many of the early ecumenists came from the international missionary movement. They were characterized by a strong internationalist consciousness, a commitment to building Christian unity among the world's various Christian communities, and an idealistic sense of mission that encompassed liberal democracy as well as "Christian universalism."[8]

The birth of the ecumenical movement coincided with the founding of several similar international organizations. Many early ecumenists had ties to international Christian bodies such as the YMCA/YWCA (founded in the mid-nineteenth century), the Student Christian Movement (1919), the World Student Christian Federation (1895), the World Alliance for International Friendship through the Churches (1914), and the World Missionary Conference (1910). Before and immediately after the First World War, a number of non-religious international organizations with similar orientations were founded as well, including the pacifist International Fellowship of Reconciliation (1914) and the League of Nations (1920), whose first high commissioner for refugees, Fridtjof Nansen, was named in 1920.

The European ecumenical movement was comprised of two organizations established during the 1920s. In 1925, the Universal Christian Council on Life and Work (which addressed social and political issues) was founded in Stockholm; two years later, the Council on Faith and Order (which focused on theological and ecclesial issues) was founded in Lausanne. By the early 1930s, these two organizations constituted the ecumenical offices in Geneva (the so-called World Council of Churches in Process of Formation, hereafter WCCipof), which became the World Council of Churches in 1948. There were parallel developments in the United States, where the ecumenical Protestant Federal Council of Churches (FCC) was founded in 1908. The FCC was supported by mainline Protestant denominations (by 1933, there were thirty-three member churches in the FCC).

The FCC and WCCIPOC were not representative bodies of the different member churches; that is, neither organization could claim to speak or act on behalf of individual member churches, and the leadership of individual member churches was not always formally involved. This allowed ecumenical bodies a certain freedom, since they could work with different church officials and staffs on social and political issues without having to reach theological consensus on doctrine or gain official denominational approval. During the interwar years, this enabled European ecumenists to work with leaders of some of the Eastern European Orthodox churches (despite doctrinal differences that remain unresolved to this day). Precisely because of such doctrinal limitations, there was no formal relationship between the Protestant ecumenical organizations and the Roman Catholic Church, although there was non-official communication between individuals in both bodies.

The WCCIPOF and the FCC focused primarily on various social and political concerns. During the 1920s, for example, FCC officials worked with organizations such as the National Association for the Advancement of Colored People (NAACP, founded in 1909) and the American Civil Liberties Union (1920). They also became engaged in interfaith issues, and the National Conference of Christians and Jews was founded in 1928 as an office within the FCC, becoming an independent organization in 1932.[9] Throughout the 1920s, staff involved in these different organizations worked together to address the challenges of the interwar period.[10]

It was not coincidental that many of these groups emerged immediately after the First World War. Particularly in Europe, the years after 1918 were marked by a sober political mood, social and cultural upheaval, and urgent humanitarian needs. In the United States, church leaders were confronted by a mix of "post-war disillusionment, of resurgent denominationalism in religion, and normalcy in politics and business, of heresy trials and ethical culture societies."[11] On both continents, social, political, and religious divisions intensified.

Nonetheless, ecumenists were filled with idealism, optimism, and the conviction that they had an important role to play in addressing these challenges. The young Dutch theologian and ecumenist Willem Visser 't Hooft, who arrived in Geneva in 1924 to begin his career, later recalled that "there was a deep conviction that the world had made a new start."[12] The US ecumenist Samuel Cavert – who led the FCC from 1921 to 1950 – held a similar perspective and a strong sense of international mission. An army chaplain in the First World War, Cavert became a pacifist after the war and joined the Fellowship of Reconciliation. He also became an outspoken critic of US isolationism and viewed it as the direct counterpart of the rising nationalism in Europe. In 1923, he wrote: "The question for America is whether we will re-enforce these forward-looking groups in the European countries or whether, by remaining coldly aloof, we let the forces of the older order prevail."[13]

These developments marked the creation of an internationally minded network of mainline Protestants.[14] The first half of the twentieth century was the heyday of liberal Protestantism. Western culture was predominantly Christian and largely Protestant. In the United States, Protestant church leaders enjoyed a privileged and prominent place in society from which they could address the social, cultural, and political issues of the day. In 1900, the US Protestant magazine *The Christian Oracle* was renamed *The Christian Century* (it was published by the Disciples of Christ, becoming nondenominational in 1908). Its managing editor, C.A. Young, explained the change by writing optimistically: "May not the coming century be known as the Christian century?" That goal was based upon "the God-fearing, liberty-loving brotherhood that pleads for the unity of God's children."[15]

In the wake of the First World War, Protestant ecumenists, international church leaders, and theologians believed that they could be instrumental in building the foundation for European peace. From their perspective, Christian leadership was essential for this and Christian teachings were fully consistent with liberal political aims. In Europe, one British layman described the League of Nations as "a Christian community the members of which solve their conflicts by friendly methods," and a French ecumenist described the same body as "a milestone on the road to the Kingdom of God."[16] In the United States, "having dreamed for the past generation of a new world order of mutually cooperating states, the social gospelers wanted to use their country's enhanced standing to promote the League of Nations, world democracy, and an international pact to 'outlaw' war."[17]

THE CHALLENGES OF THE INTERWAR PERIOD

Despite this optimism and the conflation of Christian mission and universalism with a liberal and internationalist political agenda, some ecumenists maintained a more cautionary vision, one that acknowledged the significance of other religions and the need for a different approach in addressing the challenges of the post-1918 world. Visser 't Hooft later recalled hearing J.H. Oldham, the British secretary of the International Missionary Council, warn at a 1929 meeting against "illusions" about the role the church should or could play in the modern world and advocate "a searchingly critical discussion with ourselves, with Christianity as it is."[18]

These ecumenical developments coincided with the beginnings of interfaith and ecumenical Jewish–Christian engagement. Although an international inter-religious movement already existed by the turn of the century (the first World Parliament of Religions convened in Chicago in 1893 and was attended by 5,000 international delegates), it was during the interwar years that two primary areas of interaction between ecumenical Protestants and Jews emerged. These would play an important role in shaping ecumenical responses to the rise of ethnonationalism and fascism as well as subsequent responses to the persecution of Jews and the refugee crisis under Nazism.

The first area of interaction was the development of parallel and, in a few cases, cooperative Jewish and Christian engagement around socio-political and international issues, particularly the humanitarian and refugee problems that followed the First World War. The American Jewish Joint Distribution Committee (hereafter the Joint) was founded in 1914 to assist Jews living in Palestine but soon began to hire staff in Europe to help Russian Jews. An early staff member was a Swedish-born Jewish physician, Bernhard Kahn, who had immigrated to Germany at the turn of the century and founded the Aid Association of German Jews (Hilfsverein der deutschen Juden) to assist Eastern European Jews who were fleeing pogroms. By the end of the First World War, Kahn was known for his work in Poland, Russia, and France, and in 1920, the Joint asked him to work on its behalf among European Jewish refugees.[19]

Throughout the 1920s, Kahn's activities internationally and in Germany brought him into contact with progressive German circles, European ecumenists, and, eventually, the US interfaith movement. A notable contact whose work began to intersect with these circles as well was a Swiss Protestant pastor, Adolf Keller. An early ecumenical activist, Keller in 1919 became the Swiss churches' liaison with the FCC.[20] Keller saw the need for an international organization that would help European Protestants, particularly Protestant minority populations in Eastern Europe. He worked not only on humanitarian issues but also on providing assistance to minority churches that were coming under state pressure or were struggling due to newly established borders and growing ethnic divisions. With financial support from the FCC in New York (which paid his salary) as well as European church organizations, in 1922 Keller founded the European Central Bureau for Relief (later called the Office for Inter-Church Aid). He travelled throughout Europe to assess the conditions in the different Protestant communities and began to raise funds internationally, thus developing ties in the United States that would become even more important for ecumenical work after 1933.[21] By 1923–24, he was able to distribute 1.7 million Swiss francs among Protestant communities in sixteen countries, including Poland, Romania, Russia, Lithuania, Latvia, Czechoslovakia, Estonia, and Yugoslavia.[22] Keller also developed close ties to Orthodox church leaders throughout the region.

Keller's first-hand experiences in Eastern Europe, as well as his relationships with Orthodox leaders, gave him considerable influence over ecumenical perspectives and policies. Viewed as the expert on that part of Europe, he frequently travelled to the United States, where he lectured on the European situation in American cities and at institutions like Harvard University, Princeton Theological Seminary, and Union Theological Seminary in New York. His ecumenical vision was ambitious and holistic, encompassing what he called a "Protestant Catholicism" that would unite Protestants around the world around progressive political change, including comprehensive social reforms to address poverty and the plight of the working class. He understood the issues in Europe through the lens of his concern for Protestant minorities, however, and he viewed antisemitism in that context: as the persecution of one of several religious minorities. By the early 1930s, his lectures included warnings about the growing instability across Europe, the ramifications for minorities, and the dark rise of ethnonationalism, which he described in a 1933 report as "a kind of religion – the religion of blood."[23]

Many ecumenical leaders shared his concerns. From the very beginning, ecumenism had held deep internationalist (and therefore anti-nationalist) convictions. In the early aftermath of the First World War, this was framed primarily as a broader commitment to pacifism, a critical reaction against the national loyalties that had led Christians across Europe to fight one another in the name of nationhood. As early as 1920, J.H. Oldham summoned Christians to place the bonds of international fellowship above the call of the nation: "For the Christian nationality is not the ultimate loyalty. His highest allegiance is to the Christian fellowship ... Our great need today in a world fevered and torn by national antagonisms is to be recalled to the simple and universal things."[24]

Throughout the 1920s, such attitudes inevitably pitted ecumenical figures against the emerging nationalist sensibilities across Europe. Leading figures on both sides of that debate recognized the clear distinction between ecumenical and nationalist versions of religion. In 1925, the German theologian Emanuel Hirsch (a subsequent supporter of National Socialism) attacked the ecumenical movement, "charging that the call for church unity across national boundaries was politically motivated and suggesting that the boundaries of the *Volk* and the church should ideally coincide."[25] In 1931, Hirsch and Luther scholar Paul Althaus penned an open critique of the ecumenical movement, "The Protestant Church and International Understanding," which appeared in several German church and theological publications.[26] "German theologians, when they speak responsibly to theologians of the nations who are our enemies," they wrote, "must under all circumstances and as a *conditio sine qua non* of all further understanding and cooperation, bring into the discussion a condemnation of the anti-German politics practised by these nations since 1914.'"

The resurgence of Christian nationalism across Europe in its various forms came as a shock to ecumenical leaders, who viewed these new movements as ideologically driven distortions of the gospel for political ends. Yet they also had to acknowledge that these movements represented a new, dangerous form of "Christian fellowship," albeit not the kind that Oldham had advocated in 1920. The question was how best to combat this new fellowship. Tensions grew between those who continued to view principled pacifism and internationalism as the best foundation for preventing another war and those who increasingly saw the resurgence of religious ethnonationalism as a different kind of threat that called for a theological and ecclesial response. For some, the importance of pacifism and building bridges of understanding between different churches and nations meant compromise and the search for common ground. For others, religious ethnonationalism was a perversion of Christian teachings and there could be no possible compromise. These tensions would divide the ecumenical movement throughout the 1930s and 1940s and become a particularly contentious issue in its relations with the Jewish community.

As the 1920s progressed, early optimism was replaced by the grim sense that nationalistic divisions were eroding the postwar peace. In 1932, Visser t' Hooft observed: "The great difference between 1927 and 1932 is that between the fool's paradise before the crisis and the crisis itself, between the atmosphere of calmness and expectation and the atmosphere of terror, between a world which was not facing reality and a world which simply *has* to face it."[27] Much later in his memoirs, he wrote that the early ecumenical movement "had been influenced by that far too superficial idealistic internationalism which expected a triumphant march forward of the democratic idea and the universal acceptance of a legal machinery for peacekeeping. The forces at work in the world did not work towards peace but towards war."[28]

ECUMENICAL AND INTERFAITH ORGANIZATIONS' RELATIONSHIP TO THE JEWISH COMMUNITY

For many ecumenists, the most alarming component of these new nationalistic movements was their embrace of nationalism and ethnic identity from within their respective Christian traditions, which had led to the kind of theological nationalism that Emanuel Hirsch had advocated in 1925. In political terms, ecumenists viewed this as a destabilizing development that threatened to reopen newly healed wounds between and within the nations of Europe. In theological terms, they viewed it as a distortion of the gospel, an ethnocentric and divisive interpretation of Christianity that directly contradicted the gospel's universal message.

Antisemitism and violence against Jews, however, raised very distinctive issues. The roots of antisemitism in Western culture can be traced back to early Christianity, and the self-definition of Western culture as explicitly "Christian" meant that historically Jews everywhere had been viewed not only as second-class citizens but as an inherently foreign element in society and a threat to social and cultural values. In the late nineteenth century, for example, the German historian Heinrich von Treitschke wrote: "Christian ideals inspire our arts and sciences. Christian spirit animates all healthy institutions of our state and our society. Judaism, on the other hand, is the national religion of a tribe that was originally alien to us."[29]

Such attitudes meant that Jews – even those who had converted to Christianity – were never regarded as fully assimilated. This thinking was directed against both religious and secular Jews, and it predated the twentieth century; indeed, one could argue that Luther's sixteenth-century anti-Jewish tracts targeted the Jewish community as "other."[30] As Treitschke's comment illustrates, by the late nineteenth century this racialized understanding was intersecting with ethnicized self-understandings that aligned ethnic identity with nationhood – a development that became a powerful ideology in the interwar years. Inevitably, antisemitism existed in the ecumenical movement as well. In his memoirs, Visser 't Hooft acknowledged the antisemitism in early ecumenical circles, recalling one 1923 international student meeting where Jewish students were treated "as a special Jewish delegation rather than as members of their respective national delegations."[31]

The British Anglican theologian James Parkes was one of the few to address the Christian roots of antisemitism in the 1920s. Like Visser 't Hooft, Parkes began his career in the ecumenical movement, first working for the Student Christian Movement in London and then joining the International Student Service in Geneva, where he organized workshops for students from different countries to discuss "sore spots ... conflicts of nationality, race, and political party."[32] By the end of the 1920s, however, Parkes had become convinced that antisemitism was the most dangerous challenge of that era and that it could not be addressed without confronting its theological roots in Christianity. He returned to England to pursue doctoral studies, publishing his dissertation in 1934 as *The Conflict of the Church and the Synagogue*.

Parkes was openly critical of the ecumenical movement for what he saw as its failure to address the theological roots of antisemitism. Although some early ecumenists did acknowledge the specifically Christian history of antisemitism, it is also true that, particularly in the 1920s and 1930s, they viewed antisemitism more as a form of discrimination similar to that experienced by other religious and ethnic minorities, rather than as a Christian theolog-

ical problem. The interfaith movement in the United States shared this ecumenical approach, and by the early 1930s that movement was internationally active, often working in tandem with ecumenical leaders.

The main interfaith body of that era, the National Conference of Christians and Jews, had been founded in 1928 as part of the FCC's Commission
on International Justice and Goodwill, becoming an independent organization in 1932. The founding document of the NCCJ, the "Ten Commandments of Good Will," acknowledged: "Perhaps no page of history, called
Christian, bears more blots and stains upon it than that which records the
relations of Christians and Jews during almost two thousand years."[33] The
NCCJ rejected the proselytization of Jews and stressed the need to address
anti-Judaism in interpretations of Christian texts. Like ecumenists, however,
the NCCJ leaders believed that the most effective strategy for fighting antisemitism – indeed, all forms of prejudice – was to defend democratic values
and civil liberties. According to the NCCJ's own bylaws, its purpose was "to
promote justice, amity, understanding, and cooperation among Protestants,
Catholics and Jews, and to analyze, moderate and finally eliminate inter-
group prejudices which disfigure and distort religious, business, social and
political relations, with a view to the establishment of a social order in which
the religious ideals of brotherhood and justice shall become the standards
of human relationships."[34]

The ecumenical and interfaith approach to the rise of antisemitism in
the interwar period was to treat it primarily as a cultural and socio-political
challenge, not a theological one. U.S. ecumenists in particular saw parallels
between the dynamics of antisemitism and the long-standing problem of
racism in the United States. In 1932, for example, Henry Leiper made that
connection plain, criticizing Christian antisemitism: "In a considerable
number of cases the Christians are heartily helping with no more com-
punction than some American Christians show in their unjust dealings with
the Negro."[35]

Leiper wrote this while en route to Germany, where he and several other
representatives of the FCC and the NCCJ were making a fact-finding trip to
learn more about the alarming rise in antisemitism six months before Adolf
Hitler became chancellor. Leiper travelled to Berlin with FCC general secretary Samuel Cavert, joining Everett Clinchy, the director of the NCCJ.

In Berlin they met with German Quakers, Catholics, Protestants, and Jews, including Bernhard Kahn; Protestant pastor Friedrich Siegmund-Schultze (whom the German government would expel in July 1933 for his assistance to the Jewish community); Julius Richter (a German ecumenist and head of the Protestant missions' office in Berlin); Dr Richard Horlacher, a Protestant member of the Association to Combat Antisemitism (Verein zur Abwehr des Antisemitismus); Dr Wilhelm Kleeman, head of the Jüdische Volkspartei; representatives of Jewish youth groups; and Georg Landauer, a leading German Zionist. The Jewish participants, particularly Kahn, warned of the dangers facing German Jews should the Nazis come to power and urged their visitors to highlight the issue back in the United States.[36]

Clinchy and Leiper returned to give several speeches, and both men published reports about the German situation in 1933.[37] Their reports illustrated the perspectives that shaped ecumenical and interfaith understandings of antisemitism at the time. In *The Strange Case of Herr Hitler*, Clinchy described "Hitlerism" as "an in-group and out-group psychology" that could be explained by the economic and political instability of the interwar period.[38] Despite what he had heard from Jewish representatives in Berlin, he suggested that it might still be possible for Jews and non-Jews in Nazi Germany to work out their differences, much like interfaith projects had done in the United States: "Protestants, Catholics and Jews, as fellow citizens, can share mutually the common ideals of the nation, and all work together, not for the domination of one group, but for the realization of all."[39]

Perhaps because of his already extensive interactions with European ecumenists, Leiper focused more on the problem of nationalism, which he traced back to the aftermath of the First World War, in particular to what he viewed as the unfair terms of the Versailles Treaty. Leiper had visited ten different European countries in the summer of 1932 and made a subsequent visit to Nazi Germany in the spring of 1933, so his *Personal View of the German Churches under the Revolution* drew on his impressions from both before and after the rise of the National Socialist government. Leiper believed that the growing danger throughout Europe was not simply the product of the convergence of nationalism and religion. It also reflected the ideological utilization of religion by nationalists: "Religion is part of their program just in so far as it helps glorify the nation," he wrote. "We have in Germany as in Russia a head-on collision between two religions. The difference is that in Germany, the new religion hopes to insinuate itself into the very soul of the old."[40]

He spent considerable time describing the Nazi anti-Jewish measures he had already witnessed, but was cautious: "I will not minimize the terrible injustice and inhumanity of what has happened," he wrote, before continuing that Nazi anti-Jewish violence seemed to be selective and perhaps the worst was over.[41] Yet his little book is filled with ominous references: "It seems likely that [Hitler's] campaign will be carried on in such a manner as to jeopardize many Jewish lives in the future. Hitler's language has stirred up the basest elements, and almost anything can happen to the Jews."[42]

Both accounts, of course, reflected the perspectives of 1932–33; neither man foresaw the intensifying persecution and final genocide of the Jews. But their perspectives were shared by many ecumenical and interfaith leaders. Such views antagonized Jewish activists and leaders who had worked together with the ecumenical and interfaith movement since the 1920s. Leaders of the Jewish community were immediately alarmed by the antisemitic violence in Nazi Germany and were alarmed by the gravity of the situation. In the spring of 1933, Rabbi Jonah B. Wise, chairman of the Joint Distribution Committee, visited Germany and returned "so shaken by what I have seen that I find the greatest difficulty in describing the situation lucidly ... I may say quite candidly that the leaders of German Jewry have told me point-blank that the Jews are finished in Germany."[43]

Wise had worked closely with Christian ecumenical colleagues since the 1920s, particularly on refugee issues, and in 1934 he became a board member of the American Committee for Christian Jewish Refugees.[44] When one compares Wise's description of the plight of German Jews in 1933 with the reports by Clinchy and Leiper, the dramatic difference between Jewish and Christian perceptions of Nazi anti-Jewish policies and violence becomes clear. Ecumenical and interfaith leaders were alarmed by developments in Nazi Germany, yet they continued to interpret it in a larger political context and very much in the context of their own worldviews — even, in Clinchy's case, imagining that tensions could be resolved. In contrast, Jews throughout Europe and in the United States felt directly and personally vulnerable from the beginning of the Nazi regime.

ECUMENICAL DIPLOMACY AND THE GERMAN
CHURCH STRUGGLE

The situation as just described provides the background for the international ecumenical responses to the events in Nazi Germany that unfolded after 30 January 1933. In some respects, the early ecumenical responses to Nazism, particularly in communications with German church leaders, were admirably clear. In the spring of 1933, US church leaders sent several protests to Berlin against Nazi policies, drawing angry replies from German church leaders.[45] In March 1933, Henry Leiper stated the American case succinctly: "The Jew does not always have an easy time in the United States to be sure, but as you know, there is a very deep-rooted conviction in the American mind that religious freedom is an inalienable right of man."[46] That same month, officials from the FCC wrote to Protestant church leaders in Berlin demanding a clear statement about the Nazi measures against the Jews and proposing a joint declaration from the FCC and the German Protestant Church Federation that antisemitism was un-Christian. German church leaders rejected the proposal for a joint statement as "impractical."[47]

This early clarity began to disintegrate under the pressures of two other two long-standing ecumenical priorities: to prevent another European war, and to keep ecumenical channels open to different religious communities and perspectives across Europe. In the German case, this meant maintaining ecumenical relations with all factions in the growing battle within German Protestantism that came to be known as the *Kirchenkampf*, or Church Struggle.[48]

The Church Struggle began in the early months of 1933, when a pro-Nazi faction within the German Protestant Church, the "German Christians," mobilized to appoint a Reich bishop, align the church with the Nazi regime, and pass church "Aryan" laws that would remove "non-Aryans" (i.e., Christians of Jewish descent) from the clergy and other church positions. This development raised profound theological issues (in addition to alarms about a possible state takeover of the German Protestant Church), leading to the emergence of a counter-movement that in 1934 became the Confessing Church. By the end of 1933, the German Protestant Church – to which about 60 per cent of the German population belonged – was equally and deeply divided between the "German Christians," the opposition to them, and "neutral" church leaders who wanted merely to avoid a schism and state interference.

These divisions in the German Protestant church led to equally contentious divisions within the ecumenical movement about how to respond to the situation in Nazi Germany. The fact that there were Germans with very different viewpoints about the Church Struggle who also had ties to the ecumenical movement only exacerbated the divisions. Much of the focus in the literature has been on the theologian Dietrich Bonhoeffer's ties to ecumenism, and indeed, Bonhoeffer was outspoken in advocating a clear ecumenical position on behalf of the Confessing Church.[49]

Bonhoeffer, however, was less influential than the German-born Hans Schönfeld, who arrived in Geneva in 1929 and directed the ecumenical Research Office there throughout the Nazi period.[50] From the beginning of the Third Reich, Schönfeld was instrumental in shaping the ecumenical responses in Geneva and New York to events in Nazi Germany.[51] An April 1933 report to US ecumenical officials about the German situation shows his perspective:

> Regarding the Jewish question. One must realize that it had become a real problem in Germany due to two factors. The first is that the Jews in the post-war period had gained an influence which was in fact out of proportion, not only to their numbers in the total population, but also to their significance as a cultural factor ... The second factor, and this is the more important one, is the considerable number of Jews who immigrated from Eastern Europe. They were in many cases of an undesirable type, as alien to German Jews as to the country as a whole. It cannot, I believe, be denied that their influence in numerous instances has been unfortunate and harmful. This is for an explanation – not as a justification – of the persecution of Jews in Germany.[52]

Despite Schönfeld's comment that he was not justifying the Nazi measures, his clear prejudices and his apologetic approach to anti-Jewish laws (as well as his very similar take on the "German Christians" and the Church Struggle) meant that the divisions within the Church Struggle became an ongoing consideration in ecumenical discussions. By 1934, he was the primary official in Geneva arguing that all sides in the German Church Struggle should be represented at ecumenical meetings, a stance that led to an ongoing rivalry with Bonhoeffer.

Under these pressures, ecumenical officials softened their tone, and ecumenical meetings began to focus less on the persecution of the Jews and more on the situation in the German Protestant churches; at Schönfeld's urging, there was also a move toward treating both sides in the Church Struggle equally. Throughout the latter part of 1933 and into 1934, several ecumenical figures and Western church leaders, such as Henry Leiper, British bishop George Bell, and others, made multiple trips to Nazi Germany to establish contacts with different voices from the Church Struggle. Their reports illustrate their intent to maintain channels of communication with all the factions. Reporting from an ecumenical meeting in Novi Sad, Yugoslavia, in September 1933, Leiper wrote:

> The question was how we could accept the offer of the new leadership of the German Church for continued cooperation without at the same time seeming to approve of measures which in fact we consider to be unchristian ... A way was finally found after much thought and discussion ... We felt that the last way in which we could really help our friends in the German Churches who are standing out for the freedom of the Christian conscience and brotherly treatment of the Jews would be to repudiate the United Church. We therefore found a plan finally of being both friendly and critical without compromising ourselves or the German delegates ... It means the prevention of a split in the Ecumenical movement which would have been of very serious consequences.[53]

Part of the raison d'être of the ecumenical movement had been postwar bridge-building for the sake of European peace. Now, after 1933, that approach was being used to justify maintaining a working relationship with representatives of the various church factions in Nazi Germany.

The ecumenical record after 1933 must be seen with this background in mind. Nonetheless, the ecumenical movement issued several striking statements condemning the antisemitic violence, including several that acknowledged the theological problems in Christianity and the obligation of Christians to take a clear stand. These statements include the September 1933 condemnation of Nazi racial laws in Sofia, Bulgaria, and several statements issued jointly by the World Jewish Congress and World Council of Churches in Geneva: a joint response to the November 1938 pogroms, a December 1942 condemnation of the genocide against the European Jews (this was after the Riegner telegram[54] was shared with ecumenical leaders); and a 1944 protest against the deportations of Hungarian Jews.[55] The latter came at a moment when wcc and fcc officials were renewing their efforts to mobilize Protestant support for the refugees – and also reaching out to Hungarian Protestant leaders.[56] In addition, ecumenical offices in Geneva and New York became deeply involved in refugee work, an area in which their earlier connections from the 1920s to Jewish organizations led to true cooperation.[57]

Here the personal leadership of ecumenical officials was crucial. In 1939, Visser 't Hooft pledged ecumenical solidarity with the Jewish community, noting that Christians could not "simply walk past the striking suffering of refugees in Poland … Jewish organizations are generally not in the position to undertake successful steps on behalf of their religious and communal comrades. The Jewish question touches on the heart of the Christian message; it would be a failure of the church in obeying its Lord if [the church] does not raise its voice here in protection and warning."[58]

CONCLUSION

This overview of the ecumenical responses between 1918 and 1945 illustrates how the key factors that shaped their responses to the rise of ethnonationalism and fascism during the 1920s strongly influenced their responses to National Socialism. Before and after 1933, the primary agenda driving the ecumenical approach was to build and maintain relations among the different churches while working toward preventing another European war. The challenges in both areas intensified after 1933, when their efforts to maintain relations with German Protestant leaders clashed with their desire to prevent a war and jeopardized their deepening relationship to the Jewish community. Nonetheless, ecumenical efforts, particularly wartime efforts to help refugee networks, were significant and deserve further study.

Understandably, historical understandings of the role of international Christian leaders between 1933 and 1945 have been shaped by the record of

---

Christian complicity across Europe and the widespread failure of solidarity with the Jewish community. Christian churches and theologians would begin to address both their history and their theology more critically after the Holocaust. It was in the wake of the First World War that many of the decisive issues, perspectives, and networks emerged that subsequently shaped Protestant ecumenical behaviour during the period of National Socialism and the Holocaust.

NOTES

1 The Protestant ecumenical movement was founded in the early twentieth century as a coalition of members from different Protestant denominations and national churches. A detailed overview of its history is given below in this chapter in the section on "The Early Ecumenical Movement."

2 Johan M. Snoek, *The Grey Book: A Collection of Protests against Anti-Semitism and the Persecution of Jews Issued By Non-Roman Catholic Churches and Church Leaders during Hitler's Rule*, reprint (New York: Humanities Press, 1970) is an early and fairly comprehensive compilation of these statements. See also Armin Boyens, *Kirchenkampf und Ökumene 1939–1945. Darstellung und Dokumentation unter besonderer Berucksichtigung der Quellen des Okumenischen Rates der Kirchen* (Munich: Chr. Kaiser Verlag, 1969); and Victoria Barnett, "Christian and Jewish Interfaith Efforts during the Holocaust: The Interfaith Context," in *American Religious Responses to Kristallnacht*, ed. Maria Mazzenga (New York: Palgrave Macmillan, 2009), 13–31.

3 See Victoria Barnett, "Track Two Diplomacy, 1933–1939: International Responses from Catholics, Jews, and Ecumenical Protestants to Events in Nazi Germany," *Kirchliche Zeitgeschichte* 27, no. 1 (2014): 76–86, for an overview of these networks and their roots during the interwar period.

4 See Barnett, "Track Two Diplomacy"; as well as Boyens, *Kirchenkampf und Ökumene 1939–1945*.

5 These are well-documented in Klemens von Klemperer, *German Resistance against Hitler: The Search for Allies Abroad, 1938–1945* (New York: Oxford University Press, 1992); and Uta Gerdes, *Ökumenische Solidarität mit christlichen und jüdischen Verfolgten: die CIMADE in Vichy-Frankreich 1940–1944* (Gottingen: Vandenhoeck & Ruprecht, 2005).

6 Barnett, "Track Two Diplomacy." See also Gerhart Riegner, *Never Despair: Sixty Years in the Service of the Jewish People and the Cause of Human Rights* (New York: Ivan Dee, 2006), 122–7.

7 Snoek, *The Grey Book*, i–ii.

8 David A. Hollinger, *Protestants Abroad: How Missionaries Tried to Change the World but Changed America* (Princeton: Princeton University Press, 2019), 105.

9 See Victoria Barnett, "'Fault Lines'": An Analysis of the National Conference of Christians and Jews, 1933–1948" (PhD diss., George Mason University, 2012), 42.

10 Barnett, "Track-Two Diplomacy."

11 William J. Schmidt, *Architect of Unity: A Biography of Samuel McCrea Cavert* (New York: Friendship Press, 1978), 46.

12 Willem A. Visser 't Hooft, *Memoirs* (Philadelphia: Westminster Press, 1973), 29. From the 1930s onward, Visser 't Hooft headed the ecumenical offices in Geneva. When the WCC was founded in 1948, he became its first general secretary.

13 Schmidt, *Architect of Unity*, 63ff.

14 "Mainline" Protestant churches were the churches and their offshoot denominations that can be traced back to the European Protestant Reformation or were direct offshoots of those churches: Methodist, Lutheran, Anglican or Episcopalian, Reformed, Presbyterian, Baptist, United Church of Christ, and Disciples of Christ.

15 Elesha J. Coffman, *The Christian Century and the Rise of the Protestant Mainline* (New York: Oxford University Press 2013), 12.

16 Visser 't Hooft, *Memoirs*, 29.

17 Gary Dorrien, *The Making of Liberal Theology: Idealism, Realism, and Modernity, 1900–1950* (Louisville: Westminster John Knox Press, 2003), 202.

18 Visser 't Hooft, *Memoirs*, 39–40.

19 Ibid., 77–8.

20 He was invited by Charles MacFarland, the General Secretary of the FCC at the time. See Marianne Jehle-Wildberger, *Adolf Keller: Ecumenist, World Citizen, Philanthropist* (Eugene: Wipf and Stock, 2013), 38.

21 Wildberger, *Adolf Keller*, 68–81.

22 Ibid., 77.

23 Report sent from Adolf Keller, Geneva, 19 January 1933, Presbyterian

Church, USA, Department of History and Records Management Services, Philadelphia (PHSA), Federal Council of the Churches of Christ in America (FCCCA), NCC RG18, box 9, folder 15.

24 Keith Clements, *Faith on the Frontier: A Life of J.H. Oldham* (Edinburgh: T&T Clark 1999), 168.

25 A. James Reimer, *The Emanuel Hirsch and Paul Tillich Debate: A Study in the Political Ramifications of Theology* (Lewiston: Edwin Mellen, 1989), 61.

26 Dietrich Bonhoeffer, *Dietrich Bonhoeffer Works English Edition*, vol. 11: *Ecumenical, Academic, and Pastoral Work: 1931–32* (Minneapolis: Fortress Press, 2012), 35n6.

27 Visser 't Hooft, *Memoirs*, 33.

28 Ibid., 33.

29 Sanford Ragins, *Jewish Responses to Anti-Semitism in Germany, 1870–1914* (Cincinnati: Hebrew Union College Press, 1980), 15–16.

30 See Thomas Kaufmann, *Luther's Jews: A Journey into Anti-Semitism* (New York: Oxford University Press, 2017), esp. chapter 1.

31 Visser 't Hooft, *Memoirs*, 13.

32 James Parkes, *End of an Exile: Israel, the Jews, and the Gentile World*, reprint (Bridgeville: Micah, 2005), 235.

33 Barnett, "Fault Lines," 85.

34 Ibid., 42.

35 Letter of 10 July 1932, FCAA, Leiper Family Papers.

36 Barnett, "Track Two Diplomacy," 78–9.

37 Everett R. Clinchy, *The Strange Case of Herr Hitler* (New York: John Day Company, 1933); Henry Smith Leiper, *Personal View of the German Churches under the Revolution* (New York: American Section, Universal Christian Council for Life and Work, 1933).

38 Clinchy, *The Strange Case*, 25.

39 Ibid., 30.

40 Leiper, *Personal View of the German Churches under the Revolution*, 11.

41 Ibid., 7.

42 Ibid.

43 Jonah B. Wise to Rabbi Charles M. Rubel, 18 May 1933, American Jewish Committee Archives, 1995.A.0386 – 001.

44 Minutes, 8 January 1934, Board Meeting, PHSA, NCC RG18, box 3, folder 12, "American Committee for Christian Refugees."

45 For example, see Barnett, "Christian and Jewish Interfaith Efforts," 20–3; and Wolfgang Gerlach, *And the Witnesses Were Silent* (Lincoln: University of Nebraska Press, 2000), 49–51, 62–3.

46 Letter, 15 March 1933, The Burke Library Archives, Columbia University Libraries, Union Theological Seminary Archives, Henry Smith Leiper papers.

47 Joachim Hosemann to Albert Beaven, 7 June 1933, PHSA, FCCCA, box 9, folder 15, "General Secretary Foreign Correspondence."

48 See Victoria Barnett, *For the Soul of the People: Protestant Protest against Hitler* (New York: Oxford University Press, 1992); and Doris Bergen, *Twisted Cross: The German Christian Movement in the Third Reich* (Chapel Hill: University of North Carolina Press, 1996).

49 A good summary can be found in Keith Clements, *Dietrich Bonhoeffer's Ecumenical Quest* (Geneva: World Council of Churches, 2015).

50 See Jehle-Wildberger, *Adolf Keller*, 114; Visser 't Hooft, *Memoirs*, Chapters 13 and 14.

51 Jehle-Wildberger, *Adolf Keller*, 113ff.

52 Cited in Barnett, "Christian and Jewish Interfaith Efforts," 18.

53 Letter dated 15 September 1933, PHSA, Leiper Family Papers, RG490, series 1, subseries 5, notebook 7, f. 4.

54 In the summer of 1942, Gerhart Riegner, director of the World Jewish Congress in Geneva, received detailed information from a German businessman about Nazi Germany's plans for the mass murder of European Jews. On 8 August, Riegner sent a telegram to government officials in the United States and Great Britain with these details, hoping that publicity about this would arouse a strong response from the Allied governments. See Riegner, *Never Despair*, 32-45.

55 See Visser 't Hooft, *Memoirs*, 168–9; and Riegner, *Never Despair*, 122–7. Regarding the communications between Gerhart Riegner, WCC, and FCC officials, see especially Boyens, *Kirchenkampf*, 119–25. In his memoir Riegner described the support of his ecumenical colleagues as "the light in the darkness that surrounded us." See Riegner, *Never Despair*, 127.

56 Boyens, *Kirchenkampf*, 138–42. The full text of the joint WJC-WCC statement can be found in Boyens, 138–9.

57 I explore these networks in Barnett, "Track Two Diplomacy" and "Christian and Jewish Interfaith Efforts."

58 Boyens, *Kirchenkampf*, 116.

Afterword

Doris L. Bergen

Religion, ethnonationalism, and antisemitism: this book has handled an explosive mix. The religion at the heart of the processes of denigration, exclusion, and destruction analyzed in the introductory essay and the thirteen chapters that follow is Christianity. Except in Sara Han's chapter on the Higher Institute for Jewish Studies in Berlin, Judaism and Jews feature as targets and victims, not agents, of the history recounted here. Other religions and their adherents appear only fleetingly: Hindu and Buddhist texts appropriated by the right-wing theorist Julius Evola; Muslims of Tatar heritage living alongside Jews in northeastern Poland; Jews enrolled in classes on "Islamic Studies" in 1936 Berlin; Bosnian Muslims "nationalized" as Croats under Ustaša rule. The drama of ethnonationalism in the era of two world wars, rooted in Europe and America, is presented as a Christian story, and the book directs its challenge – to identify and confront the multifarious roles of religion in ethnonationalist violence – at Christianity and Christians.

A perspective from outside Christian circles, and beyond those represented in the volume, underscores this point. Consider the account in *The Black Book of Soviet Jewry* of Emilia Kotlova, a teacher from Kiev. In January 1945, Kotlova described her experiences during the war in a letter to Ilya Ehrenburg. Kotlova was Jewish but insisted it had made little difference to anyone before the German invasion. She managed to evade the massacre at Babi Yar in September 1941 and flee with her two little girls to Zhitomir. Over the next three years, she was repeatedly denounced, arrested, interrogated, and beaten, by Germans and also Ukrainians and Russians. Again and again, she told Ehrenburg, her life and the lives of her daughters depended on her convincing people that she was not a Jew.

Eventually Kotlova, a trained kindergarten teacher, found work in a village school. Conditions were desperate: she and her children had no heat, no blankets, and nothing to eat but potatoes. Their precarious existence got even worse when Christian education became mandatory in the schools, as Kotlova explained:

> How was I supposed to know anything about religious education? ... And the priest's son (the principal) knew straight away that I was not Russian (in their way of thinking, Orthodox) ... At the village council, they asked me about my religious faith. I nearly answered Jewish instead of Orthodox. Even though it was so revolting to me that it made me cry, I had to keep silent. The priest's son, a first-class hooligan, began interrogating me. Who was I? Why didn't I recognize any holidays or even know their names? Why didn't I go to church and teach the children to pray?

Kotlova likely included the story of her failed religious test in order to demonstrate that she was a good communist and a loyal, deserving Soviet citizen. But there is no reason to doubt that the incident occurred, and the details are compelling. Many other sources confirm the picture that even in Soviet territory, whether German-occupied, liberated, or in the rear, Christianity not only survived under the Nazis but thrived.[1]

According to Kotlova, the principal reported her to the Gestapo, and she was summoned to appear at their office in Zhitomir. She continued to deny she was Jewish and, after brutal questioning, was released on the condition that she return with her papers. Having no alternative, she went back to the village, where the principal and others assumed she had been killed as a Jew. Now, she told Ehrenburg, "out of nowhere, I showed up in the village. Everyone ran out to see the 'hanged woman,' and it was only then that they became convinced that I really was a Russian."[2] In short, to the people around her, the fact that Kotlova was still alive was itself proof that, whoever and whatever she was, she could not be Jewish, because in their experience, Jews – and Judaism – were dead. Christianity, by contrast, they knew to be very much alive.

The chapters in this book pick apart the threads of societies woven out of language, politics, material conditions, national myths, shared pasts, and religious identities, practices, and beliefs. Taken together they reveal stunning continuities. Antisemitism is a constant, and its manifestations are strikingly similar from time to time and place to place. That pernicious forgery, *The Protocols of the Elders of Zion,* identified by Nina Valbousquet as the centrepiece of a transatlantic network of political Christianity, shows up in almost every chapter. The same conspiracy theories, the Judeo-Bolshevik myth, the inverted and perverted logic that blames Jews for Christian crimes, the scapegoating of Jews for economic, political, cultural, and religious woes – all of these notions emerge as habits and reflexes in widely divergent settings. Indeed, for Christians in competition and even opposition with one another, hatred of Jews provided common ground. As Charles R. Gallagher puts it in his discussion of the American Nationalist Confederation and its leader, George E. Deatherage, "pro-Christianity became a code word for antisemitism."

Yet also remarkable is the degree of specificity throughout the book, from the regional down to the local, even individual level. To a casual reader, the detailed and lavishly footnoted chapters might seem disjointed, but those details convey the force of historical context and the paths that link past and present. Paavo Ahonen and Kirsi Stjerna depict Finnish Lutherans whose religiosity and antisemitism were shaped by proximity to tsarist and revolutionary Russia and subsequently the Soviet Union. Samuel Koehne shows the distinctive strand of Pietist Protestantism in Korntal in Württemberg that produced a conservative theology skeptical of National Socialism. Danijel Matijević examines Vukovar in the Independent State of Croatia, where violence against Jews was subsumed in and often overshadowed by an anti-Serb campaign of religious conversion.

The book's insistence on historical specificity underscores a commitment to uncovering the roads not taken. Kevin Spicer frames his analysis of the wide range of German Catholic clergymen's views on how to deal with National Socialists in the late 1920s and early 1930s as a "lost opportunity to confront antisemitism" in the period we recognize in hindsight as the eve of Hitler's accession to power. Ionuț Biliuță hones in on individual Romanian Orthodox priests in Bessarabia and Transnistria, whose behaviours ranged across the spectrum from helping Jews to proselytizing, robbing, and killing them. Kateryna Budz and Andrew Kloes conclude their study of Metropolitan Andrey Sheptytsky and his efforts to combat ethnic hatred and attacks on Jews in western Ukraine with the reminder that "such violence is not inevitable." On first reading, I wondered whether a stronger statement was in order, but on reflection I realized the ethical import of their claim: history, tradition, and habit might push people in a certain direction, but they – we – are not without agency and responsibility.

Christianity is both what is shared and what is specific in this book: it is at once universal and parochial. It is also ubiquitous. That ubiquity itself generates a key insight about religion and how it functions alongside ethnonationalism, chauvinism, and violence. Religion never exists on its own but is always tangled up in other institutions and ideologies, lending strength to those partners and rivals and drawing energy from them. Such relationships can be opportunistic, parasitical, mutually reinforcing, legitimizing, and undermining, sometimes all at the same time. That they mostly occur out of sight does not reduce their significance. Indeed, as the anthropologist Michel-Rolph Trouillot trenchantly observed, "The ultimate mark of power may be its invisibility."[3] At many points in the book, the question arises: Who was using whom? Rebecca Carter-Chand's discussion of Christian minority groups and transatlantic bonds is a prime example. While Hitler's regime mobilized Adventists, the Salvation Army, Mennonites, and others for its public relations abroad, members of those groups sought to improve their own standing by demonstrating that they were loyal Germans.

Some important themes of this volume are subtle. In the one chapter that reverses the gaze to look through Jewish eyes, Sara Han presents "learning as a space of protection" for German Jews isolated and attacked from all sides. Scholarship and universities also appear in other chapters, for instance, in Ionuț Biliuță's exposition of Romanian Orthodox clergymen as sites of religious acceptance and defiance of ethnonationalism. This book itself is a testament to higher learning as an antidote to antisemitism and exclusion. But it also includes examples of the opposite, with the academy and academics fomenting division and violence. Susannah Heschel and Shannon Quigley's presentation of German Christian projects to "dejudaize" the Bible is a case in point. Likewise this book shows internationalism to have had two faces. Victoria Barnett paints a compelling picture of the ecumenical Protestant movement as a counterforce, albeit an imperfect one, to nationalism, fascism, and antisemitism. But Peter Staudenmaier's study of Julius Evola echoes Valbousquet's finding that international networks also served to disseminate and amplify hatred.

An understated issue that calls for further research is gender. Carter-Chand opens her chapter with the American Seventh-day Adventist Louise Kleuser, who was serving as interpreter for a 1936 speaking tour by the German Hulda Jost. Kleuser raised concerns that the putatively religious presentations boiled down to Nazi propaganda. It is no coincidence that both the American interpreter and the German agent of soft propaganda were women: the former in an essential but unacknowledged role, the latter chosen to put an unthreatening, feminine face on Nazism.

Women appear elsewhere in the book, but usually in passing. In his chapter, Ionuţ Biliuţă describes a Romanian Orthodox priest who stood out because he did not use Jewish men as forced labour to build churches and he did not assault Jewish women. A fascinating figure in Valbousquet's narrative is Leslie Fry, the multilingual American woman at the heart of a transnational network of antisemitism. Women are most visible in Han's analysis of the Higher Institute of Jewish Studies, where they numbered among the faculty and students and, in the person of alumna Marianna Awerbuch, among the institute's most influential historians. Present but unremarked in most chapters are the women who were consumers of Christian ministry, women as teachers, parishioners, partners, translators, mothers, sisters, and wives, and also as initiators, participants, victims, and beneficiaries of exclusion, theft, and violence. All of these women deserve more attention.

This book is ambitious in its geographic scope. Rooted in Germany, it looks outward to France, Italy, Finland, Croatia, Ukraine, and Romania, as well as to England and the United States. The issues at stake had particular salience in territories thrown into upheaval by the First World War, their states and borders seemingly up for grabs in the interwar period. That label alone – "interwar" – bears the stamp of hindsight; it allows for

no stability and is always already looking ahead to the next cataclysm. Yet
the book's attention to Western Europe and America serves as an important reminder that violence and antisemitism were not limited to the contested territories of the former Habsburg, Russian, and Ottoman empires.
From the Secret Annex in Amsterdam, in May 1944, Anne Frank recognized the contagious force of anti-Jewish violence and realized that even
the Dutch were not immune:

> To our great sorry and dismay, we've heard that many people have
> changed their attitude toward us Jews. We've been told that anti-
> Semitism has cropped up in circles where once it would have been un-
> thinkable. This fact has affected us all very, very deeply. The reason for
> the hatred is understandable, maybe even human, but that doesn't
> make it right. According to the Christians, the Jews are blabbing their
> secrets to the Germans, denouncing their helpers and causing them to
> suffer the dreadful fate and punishments that have already been meted
> out to so many.[4]

Frank appealed to her anticipated audience to "look at the matter from
both sides: would Christians act any differently if they were in our place?
Could anyone, regardless of whether they're Jews or Christians remain silent
in the face of German pressure?" Most distressing to her were rumours "in
underground circles that the German Jews who immigrated to Holland before the war and have now been sent to Poland shouldn't be allowed to return
here." She understood the excluding impulse to come from antisemitism:
"Oh it's sad, very sad that the old adage has been confirmed for the ump-
teenth time: 'What one Christian does is his own responsibility, what one
Jew does reflects on all Jews.'"[5]

The editors of this book, Kevin Spicer and Rebecca Carter-Chand, are admirably even-handed in treating their volatile subject. They and their authors avoid polemics and take care to acknowledge the individual Christians
and Christian communities that defied ethnonationalism, opposed violence,
and tried to help Jews. Budz and Kloes's appreciative account of Metropolitan Andrey Sheptytsky is the most extensive of such portraits. But that heroic
story is shot through with tragedy: as Budz and Kloes observe, "genocide on

a staggering scale nevertheless transpired in the lands over which he had so long served as a bishop." And as the historian John-Paul Himka has pointed out, to celebrate Sheptytsky is to expose his exceptionality. The same writings that articulate his courageous stance against violence and in support of aid to Jews excoriate his fellow churchmen for collaborating in the Holocaust.[6]

The interlocking forces of religion, ethnonationalism, and antisemitism remain current, although their manifestations have changed since the Holocaust, when Emilia Kotlova "proved" she was not Jewish simply by remaining alive. Still, their destructive power persists. In October 2019, on Yom Kippur, a man went to the synagogue in Halle with the intention of murdering Jews. He was not able to enter – the security system did its job, even while the camera allowed the rabbi to see him, assault weapon and all. Frustrated, the gunman, livestreaming all the way, turned back to the street, where he shot dead a woman passerby and then headed to a Turkish kebab shop where he killed a man.

Before embarking on his deadly mission, the man had posted a manifesto online, in English. It included this statement: "I think the Holocaust never happened. Feminism is the cause of declining birth rates in the West, which acts as a scapegoat for mass immigration, and the root of all these problems is the Jew."[7] In two sentences, the attacker conveyed a knot of intertwined hatreds: Holocaust denial, misogyny, xenophobia, anti-Black racism, and Islamophobia, all tied together by antisemitism. The Halle shooter did not mention religion … or did he? In the neo-Nazi imaginary, it is the "Christian West," the white supremacist Christianity of the crusades and the KKK, that needs defending from its long list of enemies. During the era of the two world wars, activists, extremists, and agitators across Europe were preoccupied with borders. In the age of globalization, climate change, and unprecedented refugee crises, the obsession is immigration. This book calls on us to reflect on the place of Christianity in the calculus of fear.

NOTES

1 See, for instance, Johannes Due Enstad, "Prayers and Patriotism in Nazi-Occupied Russia: The Pskov Orthodox Mission and Religious Revival, 1941–1944," *Slavonic and East European Review* 94, no. 3 (2016): 468–96; and

Karel C. Berkhoff, "Was There a Religious Revival in Soviet Ukraine under the Nazi Regime?," *Slavonic and East European Review* 78, no. 3 (July 2000): 536–67. On the ways churches in Germany also persisted and even flourished under National Socialism, see Olaf Blaschke and Thomas Großbölting, eds., *Was glaubten die Deutschen zwischen 1933 and 1945? Religion und Politik im Nationalsozialismus* (Frankfurt am Main: Campus, 2020).

2 "How I Was Saved from Hitler: The Recollections of the Teacher Emilia Borisovna Kotlova, from letters to Ilya Ehrenburg, 1945, Kiev, 13 January 1945," in *The Unknown Black Book: The Holocaust in the German-Occupied Territories,* trans. Christopher Morris and Joshua Rubenstein, eds. Joshua Rubenstein and Ilya Altman (Bloomington: Indiana University Press, 2010), 81–7.

3 Michel-Rolph Trouillot, *Silencing the Past: Power and the Production of History* (Boston: Beacon Press, 1997), xix.

4 Anne Frank, *The Diary of a Young Girl: The Definitive Edition*, trans. Susan Massotty, eds. Otto H. Frank and Mirjam Pressler (New York: Random House, 1996), 303, entry from 22 May 1944.

5 Frank, *Diary*, 303.

6 John-Paul Himka, "Metropolitan Andrey Sheptytsky and the Holocaust," in *Polin: Studies in Polish Jewry* 26 (2014): 337–59.

7 See Karolin Schwarz and Patrick Gensing, "Angriff in Halle: Stream voller Hass," *tageschau.de,* 9 October 2019, https://www.tagesschau.de/inland/halle-taeter-101.html.

Contributors

PAAVO AHONEN specializes in Finnish church history and Christian anti-semitism, both religious and secular. In 2017, he published *Antisemitismi Suomen evankelis-luterilaisessa kirkossa 1917–1933* (Antisemitism in the Evangelical Lutheran Church of Finland between 1917–1933). Currently, he is working on a study of Christian antisemitism in the Grand Duchy of Finland (1809–1917). Ahonen is affiliated with the University of Helsinki, Finland.

VICTORIA J. BARNETT served as director of the Programs on Ethics, Religion, and the Holocaust at the United States Holocaust Memorial Museum, Washington, DC, from 2004 to 2019. She was one of the general editors of the seventeen-volume *Dietrich Bonhoeffer Works*, the complete English edition of Bonhoeffer's writings published by Fortress Press. Barnett has lectured extensively on the history of the Protestant churches in Nazi Germany and during the Holocaust. Her books include *Bystanders: Conscience and Complicity during the Holocaust* (2000) and *For the Soul of the People: Protestant Protest against Hitler* (1992). Her most recent work is *"After Ten Years": Dietrich Bonhoeffer for Our Times* (2017).

DORIS L. BERGEN is the Chancellor Rose and Ray Wolfe Professor of Holocaust Studies at the University of Toronto. She is the author or editor of five books: *War and Genocide: A Concise History of the Holocaust* (3rd ed., 2016); *Twisted Cross: The German Christian Movement in the Third Reich* (1996);

The Sword of the Lord: Military Chaplains from the First to the Twenty-First Century (2004); *Lessons and Legacies VIII* (2008); and *Alltag im Holocaust: Jüdisches Leben im Großdeutschen Reich 1941–1945*, co-edited with Andrea Löw and Anna Hájková (2013). Bergen was a member of the design team with Daniel Libeskind for the National Holocaust Monument in Ottawa. She is a fellow of the Royal Society of Canada and a member of the Academic Committee of the United States Holocaust Memorial Museum.

IONUȚ BILIUȚĂ is a researcher at the Gh. Sincai Institute (Tg. Mures, Romania) affiliated with the Romanian Academy and specializes in the Orthodox Church's history in the twentieth century. Biliuță has held postdoctoral fellowships at the Jack, Joseph and Morton Mandel Center for Advanced Holocaust Studies, United States Holocaust Memorial Museum; the Center for Holocaust Studies, Institute for Contemporary History, in Munich, Germany; and the Institute for International Holocaust Research at Yad Vashem in Jerusalem, Israel. He has published widely, most recently "Fascism, Race, and Orthodoxy in Interwar Transylvania: Fr. Liviu Stan (1910–1973) and the 'St niloae generation,'" in *Church History* (2020).

KATERYNA BUDZ is an independent researcher who holds a doctorate in history from the National University of Kyiv-Mohyla Academy in Kyiv, Ukraine. Budz has been a Black Sea Link Fellow at the New Europe College in Bucharest, Romania (2012–13), and a DAAD Fellow at the Max Planck Institute for Social Anthropology in Halle/Saale, Germany (2015). Her research interests include the clandestine Ukrainian Greek Catholic Church in the Soviet Union and Jewish–Christian relations during the Holocaust in Galicia.

REBECCA CARTER-CHAND is the director of the Programs on Ethics, Religion, and the Holocaust at the Jack, Joseph and Morton Mandel Center for Advanced Holocaust Studies at the United States Holocaust Memorial Museum, Washington, DC. Her publications include "A Relationship of Pragmatism and Conviction: The International Salvation Army and the German Heilsarmee in the Nazi Era," in *Kirchliche Zeitgeschichte* (2020); and "The Politics of Being Apolitical: The Salvation Army and the Nazi Revolution," in *Word and Deed* (2017).

CHARLES R. GALLAGHER, SJ, is associate professor of history at Boston College. In 2017, he was the William J. Lowenberg Memorial Fellow on America, the Holocaust, and the Jews, at the Jack, Joseph and Morton Mandel Center for Advanced Holocaust Studies, United States Holocaust Memorial Museum, Washington, DC. He is the author of *Vatican Secret Diplomacy: Joseph P. Hurley and Pope Pius XII* (2008), winner of the American Catholic Historical Association's John Gilmary Shea Prize, and, most recently, author of *Nazis of Copley Square: The Forgotten History of the Christian Front* (2021).

SARA HAN is a doctoral candidate in Catholic theology and Jewish studies at the Freie Universität Berlin in Berlin, Germany. Her research focuses on theology and the history of Jewish–Christian relations and dialogue after the Holocaust.

SUSANNAH HESCHEL is the Eli M. Black Distinguished Professor and chair of the Jewish Studies Program at Dartmouth College. She is the author of *Abraham Geiger and the Jewish Jesus* (1998); *The Aryan Jesus: Christian Theologians and the Bible in Nazi Germany* (2010); and *Jüdischer Islam: Islam und jüdisch-deutsche Selbstbestimmung* (2018). She has also edited several books, including *Moral Grandeur and Spiritual Audacity: Essays of Abraham Joshua Heschel* (1997); *Insider, Outsider: American Jews and Multiculturalism* (1998); and, with Umar Ryad, *The Muslim Reception of European Orientalism* (2020). Heschel is a Guggenheim Fellow and has held research grants from the Carnegie Foundation, the Ford Foundation, the National Humanities Center, and the Wissenschaftskolleg zu Berlin. She is also the recipient of four honorary doctorates.

ANDREW KLOES is an applied researcher in the Jack, Joseph and Morton Mandel Center for Advanced Holocaust Studies at the United States Holocaust Memorial Museum in Washington, DC. He is the author of *The German Awakening: Protestant Renewal after the Enlightenment, 1815–1848* (2019) and has published in *Harvard Theological Review*. He was elected a fellow of the Royal Historical Society in 2019.

SAMUEL KOEHNE researches Nazism and religion, specializing in the National Socialists' official statements on religion and the "racist culture" that defined their world view. He has published extensively, including in *Central European History*, *Journal of Contemporary History*, and *German Studies Review*. Currently, he is researching religious concepts in the National Socialists' "recommended reading" in the 1920s.

DANIJEL MATIJEVIĆ is a doctoral candidate in history and Jewish studies at the University of Toronto. Previously, he taught at Champlain College St-Lambert and McGill University. Matijević researches the history of mass violence and genocide, modern East-Central European history, and the history of violence in contemporary Latin America.

SHANNON QUIGLEY is a doctoral candidate in Holocaust studies at the University of Haifa. Her research focuses on the Jewish people and the churches in Germany under National Socialism and Jewish-Christian relations after the Holocaust.

KEVIN P. SPICER, CSC, is the dean of the May School of Arts and Sciences and the James J. Kenneally Distinguished Professor of History at Stonehill College, North Easton, Massachusetts. He is the author of *Hitler's Priests: Catholic Clergy and National Socialism* (2008) and *Resisting the Third Reich: The Catholic Clergy in Hitler's Berlin* (2004) and editor of *Antisemitism, Christian Ambivalence, and the Holocaust* (2007). Martina Cucchiara and Spicer translated and edited *The Evil That Surrounds Us: The World War II Memoir of Erna Becker-Kohen* (2017).

PETER STAUDENMAIER is associate professor of history at Marquette University. He has published widely on Nazi Germany, Fascist Italy, esotericism, and the politics of alternative world views, including *Between Occultism and Nazism: Anthroposophy and the Politics of Race in the Fascist Era* (2014). Much of his current research focuses on antisemitic ideologies and the history of racial thought.

KIRSI STJERNA, a native of Finland, is First Lutheran, Los Angeles/South-west California Synod Professor of Lutheran History and Theology at Pacific Lutheran Theological Seminary (Berkeley) of California Lutheran University (Thousand Oaks) California. She also is on the core doctoral faculty of the Graduate Theological Union in Berkeley and a docent at the University of Helsinki. Her publications include *Lutheran Theology: A Grammar of Faith* (2021) and *Women and the Reformation* (2009). She is the co-author, with Brooks Schramm, of *Martin Luther, the Bible, and the Jewish People* (2016) and a co-general editor of *The Annotated Luther* (6 volumes, 2015–17).

NINA VALBOUSQUET is a researcher at the École Française de Rome, focusing on Vatican diplomacy and Jewish organizations. In 2020, she authored *Catholique et antisemite – Le réseau de Mgr Benigni – Rome, Europe, Etats-Unis, 1918–1934* (Bishop Benigni's Network: Rome, Europe, and the United States, 1918–1934). She has been a postdoctoral fellow at the Center for Jewish History in New York (2016–18), the United States Holocaust Memorial Museum in Washington, DC (2018), and Fordham University (2019). Her articles have appeared in *Revue d'Histoire Moderne et Contemporaine, Modern Italy, Journal of Modern Italian Studies, Archives Juives,* and *American Jewish History.*

Index

Action Française monarchist league, 54, 56, 59

Adler, Cyrus, 63

Adventist Church: attitude toward Nazism, 151–2, 166, 382; engagement in antisemitic measures, 153; international connections, 154; Jehovah's Witnesses and, 160; pacifism of, 158, 170n35; practice of worshipping, 153; restrictions on, 155, 158

Ahonen, Paavo, 13, 381

Aid Association of German Jews, 362

Alexander I, emperor of Russia, 175

Alexander I, king of Serbia, 216

Alexander II, emperor of Russia, 177

Althaus, Paul, 364

Amarant, Oded, 293

America Forward Movement for Religion and Americanism, 30, 32

American Civil Liberties Union, 360

American Committee for Christian Jewish Refugees, 369

American Jewish Joint Distribution Committee: foundation, 357, 362; staff members, 362–3

American League of Christian Women, 33

American Nationalist Confederation (ANC): adoption of swastika, 24, 25, 38, 39; formation of, 23, 25, 33; leadership of, 30; political impact of, 39; publications of, 34; requirement for membership, 24–5

Anderlić, Vilko, 220

Andrašec, Dionizije, 220, 229, 236n51

antisemitism: Christianity and, 10, 13, 48–9, 65, 139, 365–6, 381; ecumenist position on, 357, 365–6, 367, 368, 372–4; ethnonationalism and, 6, 9, 14; German Catholic Church and, 12, 65, 96, 97, 106, 112, 381–2; as political ideology, 11, 60; spread of, 15, 384

Antonescu, Ion, 311, 314

Arnet, Joseph Franz, 99, 100

Artukovi, Andrija, 218

Aryan race, 52, 75, 76, 78, 79

Asheville conference, 32–3

Association for Jewish Culture and Science, 245

Auerbach, Isaak Levin, 245

Awerbuch, Marianna, 255, 256, 383

Babii, Ivan, 287–8

Baeck, Leo, 248, 252, 256, 258, 259, 262, 263

Bailey, Brenda, 163

Baker, Kelly J., 29

Bălan, Nicolae, 311

Balfour Declaration, 55

Baličević, Marko, 239n115

Bamberger, Fritz, 258

Baptists, 153, 154, 155, 156, 162, 166

Baptist World Alliance, 161–2

Barnea, Zwi (Herbert Chameides), 292–3

Barnes, Ralph W., 122

Barnett, Victoria, 14

Barroso, Gustavo, 64

Barycka, Slavka, 293

Basso, Hamilton, 33

Bausch, Paul: on antisemitism, 341, 343; Christian politics of, 336, 337, 338; German school prayers controversy and, 344–5; on Hitler, 345–6; on "Jewish question," 342; view of Nazism, 339–42, 345, 346; *What Is the Truth?*, 339

Bavarian Episcopate, pastoral instructions of the, 111, 119n52

Bavarian People's Party (BVP), 96

Beamish, Charles, 54

Beck, Carl, 342

Beck, Tobias, 178

Bell, George, 372

Benedict XV, pope, 49, 55, 59

Benigni, Umberto, 59–61, 62, 63

Bercovitz, Carol, 318

Berney, Arnold, 253

Berning, Hermann Wilhelm, bishop of Osnabrück, 109

Bernstein, Herman, 48, 49

Bernstein, Otto, 256

Bertram, Georg, cardinal: at Krakow conference, 140; statement on National Socialism, 107–8, 109, 110, 111

Bible: Luther's translation of, 122–3, 124; Nazi interpretation of, 121, 122, 124, 125, 126–7, 128, 130

Biliuţă, Ionuţ, 14, 382, 383

Blavatsky, Helena, *The Secret Doctrine*, 80

Bleich, Yaakov Dov, 274, 275

Boggiani, Tommaso Pio, 59

Bolshevik Revolution (Bolshevism): eyewitness testimonies of, 184–5, 204n36; fears of, 11, 176; Finnish press on, 184; leaders of, 183, 193, 203n24; refugees, 184

Bolshevism and Judaism report (Brasol), 53

Bonhoeffer, Dietrich, 371, 372

Booth, Evangeline, 162–3

Bormann, Martin, 346

Bosnian Muslims, 229

Botschaft Gottes, Die (The Message of

God): antisemitism of, 140; apocalyptic ideas in, 133; changes to the New Testament, 126, 133–5, 139–40; description of the arrest and crucifixion, 135; distribution of, 129, 136; as gospel for German race, 129; Jesus's life in, 126, 130, 131–2, 133, 134; omissions in, 134–5; publication of, 126, 129–30, 135; reception of, 136–7; references to Jewish people, 131, 132–3; Sermon on the Mount in, 134–5; structure of, 131

Boulin, Paul, 60

Bourne, Francis Alphonsus, 55

Brandes, Georg, 189, 205n45

Brandt, Eugene, 61

Brasol, Boris, 53, 61

Braun, Robert, 153

Brethren, 332, 333–4

Briand, Aristide, 280

Buber, Martin, 158, 252, 260

Buchberger, Michael, bishop of Regensburg, 110–11

Buchko, Ivan, 287

Budz, Kateryna, 9, 13, 14, 382, 384

Calotescu, Corneliu, 314

Cândea, Spiridon, 311

Caro, Friedrich, 253

Carol II, king of Romania, 310, 311

Cartel Federation of German Catholic Student Associations, 109–10

Carter-Chand, Rebecca, 12, 382, 384

Cassel, David, 267n29

Catholic Center Party, 96, 106, 335

Catholic Church in Croatia: anticommunism of, 213–14; anti-Serbian campaign, 13, 211; campaign against moral decay, 213; conversions to Catholicism, 223, 224; "Friendly Advice" handbill, 221; Greater Croatianism of, 212, 213, 215–16, 232; influence of, 211; Ustaša regime and, 210–12, 215, 217, 218–19, 232, 236n47

Catholic Union, 287

Cavert, Samuel, 361, 367

Center for Jewish Adult Education, 252

Central Office for Jewish Adult Education, 259

Central Office for Jewish Economic Aid, 251

Chamberlain, Houston Stewart, 340; *Foundations of the Nineteenth Century*, 346
Chameides, Kalman, 292
Chameides, Leon, 293
Cherep-Spiridovich, Arthur, 61
Chiriţă, Varlaam, 316
Christian Constitutionalists, 33
Christianity: antisemitism and, 6, 10, 13, 48–9, 65, 139, 365–6, 379, 381; ethnonationalism and, 5–6, 379; Judaism and, 137–8, 140; nationalism and, 15, 368–9; Nazism and, 25, 127–8, 331–2, 382; politics and, 9; superiority complex, 8, 247. *See also* religious minority groups
Christian nationalism, 25, 40, 287, 364, 365
Christian Science, 154, 155, 156–7
Christian Socialists, 336, 343, 351n49
Christian Social Volk-Service (CSVD): credo of, 337; formation of, 333, 336, 343; Nazi attack on, 338–41; opposition to, 350n37; parliamentary seats, 338; political activities of, 336; popular nationalism of, 338; religious values of, 336–7
Christology, 40n7
Church Struggle (Kirchenkampf), 161–2, 357, 370, 371, 372
Chwila (Polish-language newspaper), 276
Civiltà Cattolica (journal), 52, 53
Clark, David A.R., 4
Clause, Aryan, 5
Clauss, Ludwig Ferdinand, 77
Clinchy, Everett, 367, 369; *The Strange Case of Herr Hitler*, 368
Coakley, John, 9
Cohn, Norman, 49
Colan, Nicolae, 310
Colliander, O.I., 195–6
Confessing Church, 137–8, 370
Continuation War, 175
Coughlin, Charles E., 30, 54
Council on Faith and Order, 359
Cristea, Miron, 305, 310
Criveanu, Nifon, 311
Croatia, Independent State of (NDH): "approved" religions in, 228–9; diplomatic contacts, 226; establishment of, 210, 217; ethnic groups in, 210, 233n9, 240n117; forced religious conversion in, 209–11,

222; nationalism in, 212; Roma population, 230, 239n110. *See also* Ustaša regime
Croatian Jews: conversion to Catholicism, 227–8; persecution of, 218, 220, 230, 233n10, 241n123; population of, 230, 233n10, 241n123
Croatian Orthodox Church (HPC), 226, 228, 229, 240n117, 241n122
Czeloth, Heinrich, 100

Deatherage, George: anti-Bolshevism of, 28, 38, 39; antisemitism of, 29, 35; at Asheville conference, 32–3; at the Dies hearing, 24; early years, 27; Erfurt speech, 36, 37–8; on fascism, 35; fear of global revolution, 28–9; as founder of ANC, 25, 26; Judeo-Bolshevism of, 29; Klapproth and, 34; Knights of the White Camellia and, 29–30; Leslie Fry and, 33, 34; life in India, 27–8; nationalism of, 38, 40; profession, 27, 29, 39; publications of, 34–5; publicity, 30; Rosenberg and, 38; scholarly literature on, 25–6; on swastika, 38; testimony to the House Un-American Activities Committee, 28, 30; visit to Russia, 28
Deatherage, George E., 11, 381
Defenders of Christian Civilization, 33
Der Kriegsruf (newspaper), 164
Dibelius, Otto, 342–3
Dickel, Otto, 193, 206n60
Dilling, Elizabeth, 42n34
Dinkgrefe, Bernhard, 109
Dinter, Artur, 143n16
Disraeli, Benjamin, 56
Documentation Catholique (Catholic Documentation), 53–4
Dodić, Pavao, 223
Dontsov, Dmytro, 281–2
Draganović, Krunoslav, 226
Drault, Jean, 60
Drexler, Anton, 206n60
Dühring, Eugen, 346

Eckart, Dietrich, 346
Eckhardt, Tibor d', 61
ecumenical movement: anti-Communism, 43n35; antisemitism and, 357, 365–6, 367,

368; condemnation of violence, 372–3; critique of, 364, 366–7; diplomacy of, 370, 372; emergence of, 359, 374n1; fascism and, 356, 362, 373; interfaith connections, 357–8, 359, 360, 362, 363, 367–8, 373; international ties, 356–7, 363–4; in interwar period, 356, 362–5, 373; nationalism and, 365; pacifism of, 361, 364, 365; response to Nazism, 356–8, 370, 371, 373–4; study of, 14–15; theological views of, 15

Ehrenburg, Ilya, 379, 380

Ehrlich, Ernst Ludwig, 255–6, 258, 259, 262, 263; student card of, 257, 266n5

Elbogen, Ismar, 250, 256, 259, 261

Elicker, Jakob, 240n120

Elmhurst, Ernest F., 32, 36

Eppstein, Paul, 253

ethnocentricity, 8

ethnonationalism: antisemitism and, 6, 9, 14, 199; critiques of, 14–15, 363, 365, 384–5; definition of, 6, 8; "Lutheran" theological tradition and, 199–200; vs nationalism, 7; religion and, 5–6, 12–13, 14, 379; theorists of, 11–12; transnational nature of, 12

ethnotheism, 335, 342, 347

Euler, Karl, 140

European Central Bureau for Relief, 363

Evola, Julius: antisemitism of, 11, 76, 81–2, 83; Aryan myth and, 79; background and education, 74; on Christianity, 81; on Darwinism, 78; disciples of, 78; esoteric teachings of, 80, 81; fascist rule and, 74–5; influence of, 72–3, 74, 78; Mussolini and, 74; on nationalism, 77–8; personality of, 72; photograph of, 73; publications of, 75, 78–9, 80; racial views of, 73–4, 75–6, 83; reputation of, 76; sources of, 79–80; "spiritual racism" of, 76–7; study of, 379, 383; traditionalism of, 82–3; view of modernity, 75, 82

Evrard, Joseph, 57

Fahey, Dennis, 54

fascism: antiquity and, 82; antisemitic turn, 75; ecumenical movement and, 356, 362, 373; private property and, 35; religious tradition and, 9, 50, 59, 81; strains of, 211, 231

Faulhaber, Michael von: on antisemitism, 112; pastoral instructions, 109, 119n52; photograph, 103; position on National Socialism, 102–3, 108, 109, 110, 111–12, 119n59; publications of, 54

Feder, Gottfried, 100, 344

Feinberg, Abraham L., 32

Feldman, Matthew, 9

Filderman, Wilhelm, 310

Finland: antisemitism in, 174, 176, 184, 197; capital of, 202n9; civil war, 176, 180; deportation of Jews, 202n14; economic development, 180; German alliance with, 175; historiography of, 174; independence of, 178; political development, 175, 176, 202n7; Reformation theology, 174–5, 177; Second World War and, 175; Swedish rule, 177

Finnish Jews: accusation of speculation, 180–2, 203n16; civil rights struggle, 177–8; deportation of, 180, 202n14; residence restrictions, 179–80; status of, 177–8, 179–80

Finnish Lutheran Church: antisemitism in, 13, 174, 185, 194–7, 200–1, 207n75, 381; Clergy Estate, 179; dioceses of, 178; division within, 179; evolution of, 198; head of, 178; "Helsinki group," 179; membership statistics, 201n3; political activism, 176; social role of, 178–9; theological tradition of, 178, 199; "Turku group," 179

First World War, political and economic outcome, 8–9, 50, 180

Fischer, Karl, 137

Ford, Henry, 61, 62

Fossà, Giovanni, 59

Foxman, Abraham, 274

Francis, Pope, 275

Franco, Francisco, 214

Frank, Anne, 384

Frankel, Zacharias, 245, 248

Free Churches: attitude toward Jews, 154; attitude toward Nazism, 152–3, 337; groups of, 154–5, 168n15; international ties, 154, 166n5; investigation of, 157; status in Nazi Germany, 154–6, 157; taxation of, 155; theologies of, 167n7; in Weimar Republic, 156

Free House of Jewish Studies, 252

Freemasons, 157
Freising Bishops' Conference, 113n1
French Huguenots of Le Chambon, 153
Frick, Wilhelm, 343–4
Friedländer, Hans, 253
Fromm, Erich, 130
Fry, Leslie, 33, 34, 61–2, 64, 65, 383; *Panju-daism versus Pangermanism*, 62
Fuchs, Richard, 252
Fulda Bishops' Conference, 107, 111, 113n1

Galaction, Gala: books of, 309; sympathy for Jews, 308–9, 310–11, 324n36; teaching career, 306, 308
Galicia: ethnic tensions, 280; Greek Catholic Church in, 278, 280–1; history of, 298n18; land reform, 280; massacres of Jews in, 290, 294, 382; pacification campaign in, 284; Polish regime in, 277, 278, 280, 299n28; population of, 277, 278, 294; primary schools, 280; renaming of, 280; Soviet occupation of, 289, 296n9
Gallagher, Charles R., 11, 381
Gans, Eduard, 245
Gasparri, Pietro, 48, 55, 56
Geiger, Abraham, 245, 248
Georgescu, Tudor, 9
German Catholic Church: antisemitism and, 9–10, 96, 97, 106, 112, 381–2; conflict within, 119n59; fear of communism, 96–7, 106; National Socialism and, 12, 95–6, 99–100, 102, 108–11, 112–13, 331; question of membership, 103–4, 107–8; universal human rights and, 112
German Christian movement: antisemitic policies of, 12, 140; vs Confessing Church, 137–8; convention at Berlin Sports Palace, 3–4, 5; defeat of, 141; leadership of, 125; Nazi regime and, 140, 370; treatment of baptism, 138; "Twenty-Eight Theses," 128; Volk doctrine, 127
German Communist Party (KPD), 96, 106, 114n4
"German Faith" movement, 334
German National People's Party (DNVP), 96
German Protestants: divisions within, 356, 370–1; National Socialism and, 3, 5, 331, 335–6; voting preferences, 352n59

German school prayers controversy, 344
German Students Union, 251
German universities, expulsion of Jews from, 251, 252
Gescheit, Heinrich Mikhael, 256
Gestapo, 157–8, 160, 163, 252, 254
Gheorghe, Giurescu, 315
Ginsberg, Asher, 62
Gohier, Urbain, 60, 62
Goldmann, Moses, 253
Golfberg, Rahil Froim Haim, 313
Gölis, Antun, 209, 215, 231
Götz, Hans, 107
Graetz, Heinrich, 245
Graves, Lem, Jr, 125, 143n24
Greek Catholic Church: assistance to Jews, 291–4; history of, 295n1; influence of, 274; leadership of, 274; members of, 274, 284; pastoral letter, 285–6; Polish state and, 278, 281; position on ethnonationalism, 277
Gressmann, Hugo, 251
Gross, Manfred, 256
Grumach, Ernst, 253, 256
Grundmann, Walter: career of, 128–9, 141, 145n45; Die Botschaft Gottes project and, 129, 130, 131, 133, 135, 138; German Christian movement and, 128; on Jesus of Nazareth, 139; at Krakow conference, 140; polemic with Nazi ideologues, 136; publications of, 128, 137, 139; view of Hitler, 128, 145n43
Gumă, Vasile, 312
Gummerus, Jaakko, 206n64
Gundersdorff, Leonard, 95, 98
Günkel, Heinz, 146n47
Günther, Hans F.K., 340, 341, 354n85
Gvozdanović, Pavle, 220

Haenchen, Ernst, 137
Hagemeister, Michael, 63
Halle synagogue shooting, 385
Hamburger, Wolfgang, 255, 260, 261, 262
Han, Sara, 13–14, 379, 382, 383
Hanebrink, Paul, 10, 51
Harding, Warren, 280
Harvitt, Edward, 293
Hastings, Derek, 7; *Catholicism and the Roots of Nazism*, 6

Hauer, Jakob Wilhelm, 334
Heilsarmee National Headquarters, 162, 163
Heinstadt, Heinrich Johannes, 95, 99, 100
Hep-Hep riots, 245
Herzog, Jonathan P., 32
Heschel, Abraham Joshua, 260
Heschel, Susannah, 12, 248, 383
Hidden Hand, The (weekly), 54
Higher Institute for Jewish Studies, 14
Hilmar, Josef, 245
Himka, John-Paul, 278, 285, 385
Hirnyj, Ivan, 293–4
Hirsch, Emmanuel, 126, 137, 141, 364, 365
Hirsch, Samson Raphael, 248
Hitler, Adolf, 99, 145n43, 157, 340; Mein
   Kampf, 6, 136, 281, 346
Hlinka, Andrej, 9
Hochschule für die Wissenschaft des Ju-
   dentums (Higher Institute for Jewish
   Studies): closure of, 259, 261; curriculum
   of, 253, 267n29; exams, 263; faculty of,
   250, 253, 256, 267n29; founding of, 249;
   Gestapo investigation of, 252, 254; learn-
   ing atmosphere at, 260–1, 261, 263–4;
   photograph of students of, 254; popular-
   ity of, 250–1; rabbinical diploma, 262; re-
   naming of, 266n5; reorganization of,
   252–3; as space of protection, 246, 253,
   256–7, 259, 261, 262; student enrolment,
   250, 251, 253–4, 260; women at, 383
Hofstadter, Richard, 26, 42n35
Holocaust, 15, 385
Horlacher, Richard, 368
Howard, William, 159
Hughes, Charles Evans, 278, 280
Hugo, Ludwig Maria, bishop of Mainz:
   Nazi press on, 105, 107; position on Na-
   tional Socialism, 97, 100, 104, 106, 108, 111
Hungarian Jews, deportations of, 373
Hunger, Heinz, 136
Hürten, Heinz, 103
Hutterian Brethren (Rhon-Brüderhof),
   160, 161

Ihm, Adam, 98
independent churches. See Free Churches
Indian Iron and Steel Company, 27
Institute for the Study and Eradication of

Jewish Influence on German Church
   Life: closure of, 141, 145n45; foundation
   of, 128, 129; New Testament project of,
   128–30, 135–6; pamphlet against, 137; popularity of, 129; quarterly newsletter, 136,
   148n100
International Anti-Semitic Conferences,
   45n76
International Committee of the Red Cross,
   357
International Fellowship of Reconciliation,
   359
Isopescu, Modest, 313
Italian Jews, campaign against, 75–6

Jackson, Gardner, 26
Jaeger, Samuel, 336, 350n37
Jehovah's Witnesses, 153, 154, 155, 159–60, 165
Jenkins, Philip, 26
Jewish Confederation of Ukraine, 275
Jewish Labor Bund, 203n24
Jewish literature. See rabbinic literature
"Jewish Question," 105–6, 176, 197, 339, 342,
   353n72
Jewish Theological Seminary in Breslau,
   249, 254
Jewish Youth Federations, 253
Jews: civil rights of, 202n6; great men
   among, 192; myth of world domination
   of, 188; persecution of, 9; in tsarist Russia,
   185. See also Croatian Jews; Finnish Jews;
   Hungarian Jews; Italian Jews; Romanian
   Jews
Jews in Nazi Germany: deportations of,
   256; emigration of, 256, 263; everyday life
   of, 254–5, 257–8, 259; exclusion from society and culture, 251–2, 258–9; persecution
   of, 258, 262–3, 358, 369, 371, 377n54; survival strategy, 255
Johansson, Gustaf, 178, 179, 194–5, 207n68
John, Gospel of: antisemitic content of, 121,
   123–4; composition of, 141; depiction of
   Jews, 123, 139–40; Luther's translation of,
   122–3, 124, 133–4; Nazi interpretations of,
   121–2, 124, 131, 137, 141–2, 143n16; Weidemann's version of, 123–4, 125, 126, 129, 134
Jost, Hulda, 151, 152, 383
Jost, Isaak Markus, 245

Jost, Otto Erich, 99–100, 115n14
Jouin, Ernest, Monsignor, 49, 57, 58, 62, 63, 65–6
Judaism: Kant on, 346; learning methods in, 246, 260–1; as part of European culture, 247
Judeo-Bolshevism: conspiracy theory of, 29, 183–5; spread of myth of, 10, 51–2, 54, 184–5, 188, 381; in the United States, 33–4, 63–4
Jung, Rudolf, 101

Kahana-Geyer, Ruth, 292
Kahane, David, 292, 293
Kahn, Bernhard, 362, 368
Kaila, Erkki: on Bolshevik leaders, 192–3; card index of, 193; career of, 190; ideas about Jews, 186, 190, 191–2, 193, 194; influence of, 192; media on, 194; publications of, 191, 193–4
Kant, Immanuel, 346
Kantorowicz, Ernst, 252
Kaplan, Marion, 254
Karwehl, Richard, 335
Katolički list (Catholic newspaper), 212, 214, 217–19, 221, 235n44, 241n122
Kaufmann, Fritz, 253
Keller, Adolf, 363
Kerensky, Alexander, 183
Kerrl, Hanns, 130
Kirill Vladimirovich, Grand Duke of Russia, 61
Kittel, Gerhard, 128, 140
Klapproth, Johannes, 34, 35
Kleeman, Wilhelm, 368
Klein, Daniel, 227
Klein, Leona Lili, 227
Kleuser, Louise, 151–2, 383
Kling, Hermann, 337
Kloes, Andrew, 9, 14, 382, 384
Knights of the White Camellia, 29, 30
Knox, Frank, 39
Koehne, Samuel, 14, 381
Kommende Kirche (The Future Church), 126
Konovalets, Yevhen, 281, 282
Korntal, village of, 333, 334
Korntal Brethren group: Christian Social Volk-Service and, 338, 351n49; interpreta-
tion of the Bible, 332, 348n6; political-religious division within, 332–3, 350n37; response to Nazism, 332, 334, 346–7
Kositsin, Vladimir, 28
Koskimies, J.R., 196–7
Kotimaa (Homeland) (newspaper), 179, 180, 183
Kotlova, Emilia, 380–1, 385; The Black Book of Soviet Jewry, 379
Krakow conference on antisemitism, 140–1
Krause, Reinhold, 3–5, 7
Krišto, Jure, 235n38
Kruglov, Alexander, 294
Ku Klux Klan, 29
Kulturkampf, 107
Kursell, Otto von, 187
Kvaternik, Slavko, 217

Lagarde, Paul de, 340
Lambelin, Roger, 56–7, 58, 61, 64
Landauer, Georg, 368
Lapland War, 175
Lassalle, Ferdinand, 184
Latter-day Saints, the Church of Jesus Christ of, 153–5, 165
Lavine, Harold, 26
Lazarus, Moritz, 268n29
League of Nations, 359, 361
League of Ukrainian Nationalists, 282
Lebensraum (living space) ideology, 8
Lecca, Paul Paulin, 311, 318
Lehmann, Hartmut, 334, 338
Leiper, Henry: on American Jews, 370; on Christian antisemitism, 367; ecumenical mission of, 331–2, 367–8; on leadership of the German Church, 372; on nationalism, 368–9; pamphlet of, 172n49, 368
Lenin, Vladimir, 204n26
Levene, Mark, 8
Levinson, Nathan Peter, 255
Levinson, Peter Nathan, 257, 263, 270n53
Lewin, Ezekiel, 276, 291
Lewin, Kurt, 291–2, 304n81
Lewin, Nathan, 292
Lewkowitz, Julius, 256
Lewkowitz, Selma, 256
Lewy, Israel, 267n29
Lichti, James, 154, 157

Liebesschütz, Hans, 253
Liebold, Ernest G., 62
Lietzmann, Hans, 137
Ligue Franc-Catholique, 57
Lilienthal, Arthur, 252
Lindbergh, Charles, 36, 45n80
List, Abraham, 245
Lloyd George, David, 57, 280
Lochner, Louis, 129
Lohmeyer, Ernst, 132
Lončar, Pavle, 222
Louhivuori, Verneri, 181, 182
Lucas, Dorothea, 256
Lucas, Leopold, 256, 257
Luchini, Alberto, 78
Lüdecke, Kurt, 61
Luther, Martin: anti-Jewish views, 199–200, 207–8n78, 208n79, 341, 353n68; legacy of, 4, 13; in Nazi Germany, celebrations of, 16, 127, 128; translation of the Bible, 122–3, 124

Mainz diocese, position on National Socialism, 96, 97, 104, 108, 111–12
Malin, Nils Artur, 184
Mark, Gospel of, 130
Marx, Karl, 188
Matijević, Danijel, 13, 381
Matthew, Gospel of: Nazi revision of, 124, 126–7, 130
Mattsoff, Salomon, 180
Mayer, Philipp Jakob: on Christian moral law, 104; ecclesiastical career of, 97; on hatred of Jews, 100–2, 108–9; on National Socialism, 97–9, 105–7, 112–13; photograph, 98; publications of, 104, 105
McCarthy, Joseph, 43n35
Mein Kampf (Hitler), 6, 136, 281, 346
Mekovec, Valentin, 225
Mendelssohn, Moses, 136, 137
Mennonites, 8, 153, 154–5, 157, 160, 382
Mergenthaler, Christian, 333, 334
Methodists, 153, 154, 166
Metzger, Arnold, 253
Michaelis, Georg, 350n37
Micklem, Nathaniel, 167n5
Mihălcescu, Irineu, 311
Militant Christian Patriots, 33, 63

Minerbi, Sergio, 56
Mirković, Budimir, 222, 226
Moravian Brethren, 155
Mormons. See Latter-day Saints, the Church of Jesus Christ of
Moser, Moses, 245
Mosse, Albert, 268n29
Mosse, George, 346
Müller, Ludwig, 5, 62, 162; ecclesiastical career of, 126, 144n31; on mercy, 128, 129; political activities of, 126; publications of, 126; rendition of the Sermon on the Mount, 122, 124; suicide of, 141; vision of Christianity, 127–8
Mumm, Reinhard, 343
Munteanu, Nicodim, 311
Mussolini, Benito, 74, 75, 78, 81
Mustakallio, Hannu, 197

Nansen, Fridtjof, 359
National Association for the Advancement of Colored People (NAACP), 360
National Conference of Christians and Jews (NCCJ), 360, 367
National Socialism. See Nazism
National Socialist German Student Union, 251
National Socialist German Workers' Party (NSDAP): antisemitism of, 97, 100–1, 102, 105, 343; Catholic membership controversy, 95, 101, 102, 104, 105, 107, 108, 109; events, 333; foundational ideas of, 340, 347; Reichstag elections, 3, 96, 106, 351n48; religious political parties and, 338; rise to power, 335–6; supporters of, 339–40, 352n59
National Socialist People's Welfare (NSV), 163
Nazarenes, 155
Nazi Germany: anti-Jewish policies, 251, 258–9, 358, 367, 369, 371, 377n54; compulsory military service, 170n35; educational policy, 251–2, 258; international relations, 16n9, 153; small religious groups in, 152, 153–4, 155, 157–8, 160–1, 165–6
Nazism: antisemitism of, 332; Christianity and, 331–2, 334–5, 339, 346; ethnotheism of, 335, 342, 347; German Catholic

Church and, 9–10, 95–6, 97, 99–104, 107,
335; German Protestants and, 3, 5, 331,
335–6; ideology of, 340, 342, 344, 347; militarism of, 341; as neo-paganism, 332, 334,
341; propaganda of, 383; salvational doctrine of, 334, 345; spiritual values, 342;
violence, 343
Negoiţă, Athanase, 311, 325n40
Nemirovschi (Nimirovschi), Avram, 312–13
neo-paganism, 332, 334, 335
Netchvolodow, Aleksandr Dmitrievich, 61
News Bulletin, adoption of swastika, 23–4,
28, 31
Nica, Antim, 311, 316
Nollner, Ralph, 32, 33
Nordström, Nils Johan, 161–2
Nuelsen, John L., 157

Odin, cult of, 335, 340
Oldham, J.H., 362, 364
Olympic games of 1936, 165
Omer, Atalia, 7
Oppenheimer, Franz, 253
Order of Odin's Children, 335
Organization of Ukrainian Nationalists
(OUN): acts of sabotage, 284; founding
congress, 282; influence of, 284; political
philosophy of, 282–3; press organ of, 284;
"Ten Commandments," 283–4; violence
of, 284, 286
Orsenigo, Cesare, 118n45, 289
Orthodox Rabbinical Seminary in Berlin,
249, 254
Osservatore Romano, L' (the Vatican's
daily), 54, 55–6

Pacelli, Eugenio (Pius XII), 52
pacifism, 361, 364
Pahlke, Adolph, 162
Palaghiţă, Constantin, 311
Palestine, British mandate in, 55
Parkes, James, The Conflict of the Church
and the Synagogue, 366
Pärnänen, Eevertti, 184, 185, 204n32
Pavelić, Ante, 217, 218, 220, 223, 227, 229
Pelley, William Dudley, 42n34
Perlstein, Rick, 26, 39
Petcu, Theodor, 307, 311, 314, 317

Peters, Johannes, 289, 294, 303n78
Petre-Orleşti, Gheorghe, 307, 315, 318
Philippson, Martin, 268n29
Pieracki, Bronisław, 284
Pietilä, Antti J., 181, 182
Pietism, 332, 337, 381
Piłsudski, Józef, 281
Pipiniç, Franjo, 213, 216, 224, 227, 230
Pişculescu, Grigore, 308
Pius X, pope, 59
Pius XI, pope, 58, 59, 102
Pius XII, pope, 52, 214, 275, 289, 290
Plymouth Brethren, 154, 155, 161
Pohlmann, Lilit, 293
Poincaré, Raymond, 280
Popovici, Traian, 314
Portase-Prut, David, 311
"Position of the Catholic Church Concern-
ing Radicalism and Nationalism, The,"
110
positive Christianity, 334–5, 339
Potocki, Andrzej, 286
Pottere, Georg de, 61
Preigher, Moise, 312–13
Preisker, Herbert, 129
"Protestant Catholicism": idea of, 363
Protestant ecumenical movement. See
ecumenical movement
Protestant Federal Council of Churches
(FCC), 359–60; Commission on Interna-
tional Justice and Goodwill, 367
Protestantism: in Eastern Europe, 363; international network, 361; main churches,
375n14
Protocols of the Elders of Zion, The: Brazilian version of, 64; Catholic versions of,
48, 51, 64; circulation of, 50, 51; creation
of, 50–1; dissemination of, 11, 49, 50, 52–5,
60, 64; Finnish publication of, 189;
French translations of, 49; influence of,
57–8, 65, 189, 381; Italian translations of,
58–9; Jouin's version of, 64–5; Polish version of, 57; public repudiation of, 309;
question of authenticity, 52–3; Spanish
translation of, 64; structure of, 50–1;
Vatican and, 48–9; Zionism and, 56, 62
Prus, Edward, 296n9

Quakers: international ties, 154, 163, 166; membership, 158; under the Nazis, 158–9, 163, 165, 166; persecution of, 163; political connections, 169n26; socialism and, 153

Quigley, Shannon, 12, 383

rabbinic literature, 247, 248

Rachor, Johannes, 95, 96, 104, 113n1

racial science, 76

"racial soul," notion of, 335, 342, 347

Radauš, Vladimir, 209, 215, 231

Rade, Stjepan, 223

Rathenau, Walther, 191

Redlich, Shimon, 296n9

Reich Representation of German Jews, 250

Reich Security Main Office (Reichsicher- hauptamt, or RSHA), 256

Reichstag elections, 96–7, 106, 114n4

Reichsvertretung der deutschen Juden (Reich Representation of German Jews), 252

religious minority groups: ban of, 165; in Eastern Europe, 363; military service and, 158; Nazism and, 12, 152–4, 156–8, 161, 382; persecution of, 160; public profile of, 158; studies of, 153–4; taxes on, 155. See also Free Churches; individual religious minority groups

Religious Society of Friends. See Quakers

Revue Internationale des Sociétés Secrètes (RISS), 57, 64

Richter, Julius, 368

Riegner, Gerhart, 373, 377nn54–5

Robins, Marianne Ruel, 167n11

Rockwell, George Lincoln, 40

Röder, Adam, 340

Roman Entente of Social Defense, 60, 61, 62, 63

Romania: antisemitism in, 305, 307, 310, 311; fascist government in, 310–11; Iron Guard violence, 311; National Legionary State of, 305, 311; political parties, 306, 310

Romanian Jews: baptism of, 313, 315, 316; citizenship of, 307; displacement of, 312, 314; exploitation of, 316; ghettos, 315; Or- thodox clergy and, 305–6, 307–8, 318–19, 382; persecution of, 306, 307, 312, 314; violence against, 316

Romanian Orthodox Church: antisemitic policies and, 14, 306, 307; archives of, 305– 6; early communist years, 317; ethnona- tionalism and, 382; Jews and, 307–8, 312–13, 315–16, 318–19; leadership of, 305; missionary activities, 311–12; organization of, 305; in postwar years, 317–18, 319

Romanian Orthodox Mission in Tiraspol, 308

Roma people: genocide of, 230; population statistics, 239n110; Ustaša policy against, 228

Roseman, Mark, 7

Rosenberg, Alfred, 11, 25, 36, 37, 100, 140; The Myth of the Twentieth Century, 36

Rosenthal, Franz, 253

Rosenzweig, Laura B., Hollywood's Spies, 26

Ross, Steven J., 33

Rossoliński-Liebe, Grzegorz, 281

Ruhr region strikes, 190

Russian Civil War, 28, 42n34

Russo-Finnish War of 1808–9, 175

Russu, Gheorghe, 314–15

Saint Jerome Society in Zagreb, 226

Salvation Army: attitude toward Nazism, 159, 163, 382; Der Kriegsruf newspaper of, 164; emergence of, 169n21; humanitarian efforts, 156, 163; international ties, 154, 156, 159, 162, 163, 166; in Nazi Germany, 155–6, 162, 163; political neutrality, 155; separatist movements in, 162–3, 171n40

Samuel, Herbert, 55

San Remo Conference (1920), 55

Sârbu, Ioan, 313, 318

Sasse, Hermann, 335

Schemm, Hans, 342

Schlatter, Adolf, 128

Schlund, Erhard, 335

Schönfeld, Hans, 371–2

Schottlaender, Rudolf, 259

Schöttler, Hans, 124

Schreiber, Christian, bishop of Berlin, 109–10

Schur, Israel-Jacob, 180

Second Polish Republic, 280, 284

sects. See religious minority groups

Serbian Orthodox Church, 221, 240n117

Serbs: conversion to Catholicism, 13, 210–11, 220–9, 231, 236n51, 239n115, 381; Croatization of, 227, 240n117; genocide against, 227, 228–9, 230, 231–2, 237n63, 237n70; persecution and deportations of, 220, 221, 224–5
Seventh-day Adventists. *See* Adventist Church
Sheptytsky, Andrey: advocacy of Christian ecumenical movement, 275, 276–7; archival sources about, 277, 292–3; assistance to Jews, 275, 276, 277, 291–4, 384–5; commemoration of, 274–5, 294, 296n4; condemnation of violence, 14, 276, 284, 286–7, 289, 291, 382; correspondence with Pius XII, 289, 290, 303n81; diplomatic missions of, 276, 278; ecclesiastical career of, 274; education of, 275–6; fundraising efforts of, 278; German regime and, 289; Kurt Lewin and, 291–2; leadership of, 274; letters of, 303n81; meeting with Hughes, 278, 280; pastoral letters of, 277, 285–6, 288, 289, 290–1; photograph of, 279; Polish regime and, 278, 280; political activism of, 287; publications of, 277, 285, 288; reputation of, 275, 276; Soviet regime and, 288, 296n9; travels of, 278; on Ukrainian nationalism, 281, 284–5; view of nationalism and patriotism, 285, 286, 287
Sheptytsky, Clement, 292
Sheptytsky, Leon, 287
Sheptytsky Award, 275
Shishmareff, Fedor Ivanovic, 61
Sichynsky, Myroslav, 286
Siegmund-Schultze, Friedrich, 368
Significance of the Jews in the Scope of World History, The (Wartiainen), 186, 187
Sima, Horia, 311
Simedrea, Tit, 314, 315
Simon, Ernst, 252
Simpfendörfer, Wilhelm, 333, 336, 337, 338–9, 340, 350n33
Šipuš, Vladimir, 224
Škiljan, Filip, 237n63
Slacman, Beatrice, 314
Slacman, David, 314–15
Slacman, Ida, 314

Slacman, Meir, 314
Smith, Gerald L.K., 40
Snyder, Timothy, 275
Social Democratic Party (SDP), 96
Social Gospel movement, 359
Soden, Hans von, 137
Solberg, Mary M., 7
Soviet Union: antisemitism in, 381; persecution of Catholics in, 97
Spengler, Oswald, 191
Spicer, Kevin, 12, 381, 384
Springs, Jason, 7
Srebreni, Josip, 213
Staege, Arthur, 350n33
Stahl, Heinrich, 268n29
Stanišić, Maksim, 229
Stanišić, Tomislav, 209, 215, 220, 230
Staudenmaier, Peter, 11, 383
Steiger, Alfons, 335
Steinacher, Gerald, 233n11
Steinschneider, Moritz, 245, 249
Steinthal, Heimann, 267n29
Stek, Marko, 292
Stępień, Stanisław, 284
Stepinac, Alojzije, archbishop of Zagreb: on Catholic conversions, 221–2, 223, 225, 228, 240n121; Croatian state and, 217, 218; humanitarian efforts of, 236n46; public sermon of, 219
Stern, Selma, 256
Stets'ko, Yaroslav, 289
Stjerna, Kirsi, 13, 381
Stöcker, Adolf, 179, 336, 343
Stpie, Stanisław, 284
Strauss, Herbert A., 253, 254, 255, 258
Strübind, Andrea, 156, 162
Student Christian Movement, 359, 366
Stürmer, Der (Nazi propaganda organ), 124
swastika, 23–4, 38–9, 40
Swastika or Christ's Cross, The?, 339, 343

Tabacu, Antim, 316
Tal, Uriel, 358
Task Force for General Scientific Lectures, 250
Täubler, Eugen, 253, 256
Temple-Society, 332, 346
Thompson, Dorothy, 26

Thule Society, 335
Tisserant, Eugène, 223
Toeplitz, Otto, 252
Tomasevich, Jozo, 236n47, 239n110
Treitschke, Heinrich von, 179, 366
Trilling, Lionel, 26
Trojan, Otto, 102
Trotsky, Leon: caricature of, 187
Trouillot, Michel-Rolph, 382
True, James, 46n102
Turda, Marius, 9
Turku: archbishop's seat in, 202n9

Ukrainian Catholic University in Lviv,
    296n4
Ukrainian chapter of Catholic Action, 287
Ukrainian Jewish Encounter organization,
    275
Ukrainian Jews, massacres of, 294, 382
Ukrainian Military Organization (UVO),
    281, 282, 286
Ukrainian National Democratic Alliance
    (UNDO), 284
Ukrainian nationalism, 277, 281–2, 284–5
Uniate Church. See Greek Catholic Church
Union of Evangelical Free Church Congre-
    gations, 154
Union of Ukrainian Nationalist Youth, 282
United States: far-right extremism in, 27;
    myth of Judeo-Bolshevism in, 33–4, 63–4
United States Holocaust Memorial Mu-
    seum, 277, 292, 293
United States War Refugee Board, 357
Universal Christian Council on Life and
    Work, 359
Ustaša regime: anti-Jewish policy, 218, 220,
    227, 228, 241n123; anti-Roma policy, 228;
    anti-Serbian campaign, 13, 210–11, 217–18,
    220, 221, 222, 227; Catholic clergy in, 210,
    211, 216–17, 219, 220, 231; forced religious
    conversions, 223–4, 226, 231, 239n115,
    240n121; formation of, 209, 210; national-
    ist ideology of, 216, 230; supporters of,
    215, 216, 219–20, 229; Vatican and, 210,
    223, 226, 233n11, 238n96

Valbousquet, Nina, 11, 381, 383
Vatican: international relations, 102, 118n45,
    210, 223, 226, 233n11, 238n96; position on
    forced conversions, 223, 226; Protocols of
    the Elders of Zion and, 48–9
Velehrad, Congress of, 276
Versailles, Treaty of, 338
Vinson, Carl, 39
Visser 't Hooft, Willem, 360–1, 362, 365, 366,
    373, 375n12
Voiculescu, Constantin, 312
Volk doctrine, 6, 7, 127, 341
Volksdeutsche (ethnic Germans living
    outside the Reich), 7
Volksgemeinschaft (ethnonationalist
    community), 7
Volkskirche (German people's church), 4
Vukovar district: anti-Roma policy, 228; re-
    ligious conversion campaign in, 220, 223,
    224, 225, 227–8; violence against Serbs
    and Jews in, 381

Wallace, Henry, 35
Wartiainen, Johan Wilhelm, 186–9, 194;
    The Significance of the Jews in the Scope
    of World History, 186, 187
Wassermann, Oscar, 268n29
Weber, Heinrich, 104, 117n32
Weidemann, Heinz, bishop of Bremen:
    death of, 141; education of, 125; expulsion
    from Nazi party, 126; political activities,
    125–6; postwar career, 126, 141; revision
    of Gospels, 121, 125, 126–7, 129, 140; works
    of, 143n23
Weil, Gotthold, 268n29
Weiß, Bernhard, 268n29
Werner, Friedrich, 135
West Ukrainian People's Republic, 276, 277,
    280, 294, 299n28
Whatchamacallit, 217, 234n34
White émigrés, 61, 63
Wilson, Woodrow, 57
Wiltchinsky, Thaddée de, 61, 63
Winberg, Fedor, 62
Winrod, Gerald, 32
Winter War, 175
Wirth, Herman, 80

Wise, Jonah B., 369
Wise, Stephen, 63
Wissenschaft des Judentums (Science of Judaism): concept of, 245, 246–7, 266n5; critique of, 248; institutionalization of, 249–50; Jewish theology and, 248–9; methods of, 264; promotion of, 247, 249; transformation of, 259
Wisten, Fritz, 256
Witter, Helena, 293
Wnuk, Rafał, 296n9
Wohlwill, Immanuel, 246, 247
Wojciechowski, Stanisław, 281
World Alliance for International Friendship through the Churches, 359
World Conference of Anti-Semites, 35–6
World Council of Churches, 359, 360, 373
World Jewish Congress, 357, 373

World Missionary Conference, 359
World Parliament of Religions, 362
World Service (Welt Dienst), 34, 36, 61
World Student Christian Federation, 359

YMCA/YWCA, 359
Young, C.A., 361
Yugoslavia, Kingdom of, 210, 211, 212

Zionism, 55, 56
Zubić, Ivan (Silvestar): arrest and imprisonment, 230–1; death of, 231; photograph of, 215; Serbs' conversion campaign and, 222, 224; teaching career, 209, 215; torture of, 226; Ustaša movement and, 209, 214–15, 216, 220, 226
Zunz, Leopold, 245, 246–7, 248, 249